For the Love of It

THE MAMMOTH LEGACY
OF
ROMA & DAVE McCOY

For the Love of It

THE MAMMOTH LEGACY
OF
ROMA & DAVE McCOY

ROBIN MORNING

Blue Ox Press

Photos are courtesy of Dave McCoy Collection unless otherwise noted. Burton Frasher photographs are "Courtesy of: Frashers Fotos Collection/ HJG."
Photos colorized by Steve Hylen.
Front cover photo: Roma and Dave McCoy skiing at Deadman Summit, 1938.
Back cover photo by H.F. Haemisegger.

ISBN: 978-1-7345133-0-1

LCCN: 2020905624

Initial design by Steve Hylen.
Final design and layout by Joseph Reidhead & Company.
www.reidheadpublishers.com

This book is set in Adobe Caslon, designed by Carol Twombly in 1990. It is a revival of William Caslon's Baroque typefaces of 1720-1766, whose body of work is considered the height of English Baroque typography.

Blue Ox Press
P.O. Box 1390
Mammoth Lakes, CA 93546
www.blueoxpress.com

For all the people who are this story.

Independence Ski Club, circa late 1930s.

Contents

Part Three: Love Prevails
1950–1955

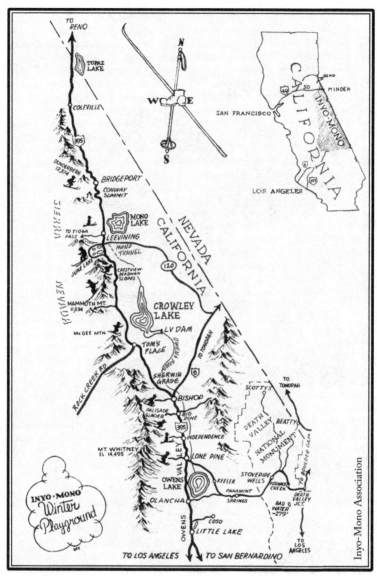

Inyo-Mono Winter Playground Map, circa 1940.

Overlay of LV Dam and Crowley Lake by Laura Patterson Design, 2019.

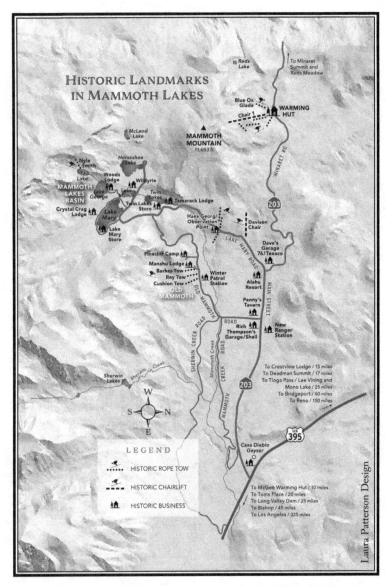

Historic landmarks in Mammoth Lakes between the 1930s and 1950s.

Preface

Dave skiing with senior racers.

I first heard about Roma and Dave McCoy in the late 1950s when my father decided skiing would be an ideal activity for his post-World War II family. As a result of our dad's love for the sport, by the 1960s, the four Morning kids had joined a posse of racers chasing Dave McCoy down Mammoth Mountain, and our skiing families had become close friends. Nurtured by Roma, coached by Dave, we got caught up in a wave of positive energy. Not only was Dave guiding numerous Mammoth racers to the U.S. Ski Team and international competitions, he was simultaneously expanding Mammoth into a thriving ski area and inspiring people along the way.

In the 1990s, I sensed that Dave's extraordinary place within California history and the world of skiing was in danger of being forgotten. Determined to keep that from happening, I felt compelled to capture his story, which also meant to recognize Roma's intrinsic role in her husband's success. With Dave and Roma's approval and my blind resolve, I began my research, little knowing how complex and demanding my task would become or how, as a historian, my relationship to the couple would gain new dimensions.

In 2008, I completed *Tracks of Passion: Eastern Sierra, Dave McCoy, &* *Mammoth Mountain*, a 365-page photo essay. Several years later, haunted by research left behind, I began writing *For the Love of It: The Mammoth Legacy of Roma and Dave McCoy*, essentially rescuing Roma and Dave's heartwarming and uplifting backstory from the editing floor. While weaving together anecdotes, photographs, interviews, and personal knowledge of the characters and subject matter, I tried to stay true to how and what each person shared with me, particularly when writing in Roma's first-person voice and when re-creating scenes and dialogue.

There have been times during my book-writing journey that the end of the tunnel seemed impossible to reach. What kept me going was Dave's confidence in me and his appreciation for what I was doing. For example, when I showed him a sample cover and pointed out that Roma's name would come first in the title, he reached for the copy I was holding and traced the photo of Roma's face with his fingertip. "Good!" he nodded, his thankfulness evident. "People don't know how important Roma was in everything I did."

Robin Morning
January 2020
Mammoth Lakes, CA

I am Roma

Roma McCoy at Mammoth. Early 1950s.

Bishop, California, 2017. That newspaper reporter was lucky he was on the other end of the telephone line instead of sitting right here in front of me. He wanted to ask a personal question. Fine. Then he says, "What was it like living in Dave McCoy's shadow, you at home taking care of little kids while your husband was outside on the mountain coaching ski racers and building chairlifts?" What gall! What a weird question. When his article came out, I couldn't even get through one paragraph before I threw the entire newspaper into the wastebasket. He made it look like all I've done with my life is change diapers.

That guy sure didn't know much about love and marriage. I'd say he could benefit from taking some ballroom dance lessons. I'm serious. He might learn not to pass judgment on who is doing what inside a relationship. You see, ballroom dancing is like a marriage. The dancers are the only ones who really understand what's going on between them. The lead guides and supports his partner to make it easier for her to do her part and that's what Dave's done for me. I've tried to be a good partner by responding to his lead while still keeping my own center of balance. Believe me, keeping balanced isn't always easy, especially living with a man like Dave who holds his feelings inside. At least the expression on his face communicates everything he doesn't say. I remember standing in the starting gate of a ski race. He'd catch my attention, nod his head a little, maybe even wink an eye, and I knew I'd just received his wholehearted approval. With that, I could do anything.

It's weird. Even now when I treasure every moment Dave and I have together, I sometimes let hurtful words slip out of my mouth. I just want to slap myself when that happens. Hurting Dave is the last thing on earth I ever want to do. I don't know where the harshness of my words comes from. Maybe I still get lonely, like the way I felt when he was so busy hunting to fill the freezer or shoveling out rope tows. Or maybe I do carry resentment for all the time he spent coaching ski racers when he could have been skiing with me. But those are feelings I try to put aside. Every couple goes through complicated twists and turns in life, and just like dancing partners, they get disconnected or give too much pressure or even blame each other for their mistakes. That's the worst. That's when everything falls apart.

I've been lucky though. When Dave sees me losing balance, he brings me back to center just by doing something simple, like reaching across the dinner table and taking my hand, reminding me what we have together. Then he looks at me with those twinkling eyes and I start laughing. Laughter. Dave loves to make people laugh. The more laughter he gets, the more he carries on. The other night, he made up a little song, singing phrases that didn't make much sense, and then he'd come back to, "Every day is what ya make it. Every day is what ya make it." Well, that's Dave for you, spreading his life philosophy in the chorus of a funny song.

Oh Lordy, here come the tears. Just thinking about how Dave makes people laugh makes me cry. I don't mean to be tearful. The truth is, I'm scared. There are nights when I wake up panicked and I can't calm down until I reach over and touch his back and find he's still by me, warm and breathing softly. You know, I can't do this dance without him.

Oh, the stories I can tell you about the life Dave and I shared. But before I get lost in my memories, I want you to promise me you'll let the world know that I never lived in Dave McCoy's shadow, no matter how many diapers I changed. I have lived in his light, his strength, his generosity, his laughter, and his love. I still do.

Long Valley Dam shaft house at Crowley Lake.

The view from the backyard of the Department of Water and Power (DWP) house where Dave and Roma lived while he was working as a hydrographer. From upper left: McGee Mountain with snow chutes, Mammoth Mountain covered in snow, the Minarets, Mt. Ritter, and Banner Peak. Center: Crowley Lake. Out of the frame to the lower right: Long Valley Dam.

This is Dave

Dave at Mammoth Mountain, 1955.

C rowley Lake, 1953. Dave McCoy kept the screen door from slamming as he slipped outside into the Long Valley dawn. He took a moment to welcome the November chill that penetrated his white short-sleeved T-shirt and breezed through his wavy brown hair. Sitting on the barren cement doorsteps with the cold pressing against his faded Levis, he concentrated on pulling each lace of his weathered work boots to the tension he preferred. Satisfied, he strode briskly across the frozen lawn. Just as he approached the stone steps that led to the Long Valley Dam shaft house, two deer bounded across his path and disappeared into the sagebrush hills. Behind him, daybreak peeked over the White Mountains.

Dave flipped on the exterior light switches of the building, unlocked the door, and lowered himself down the 170-foot ladder that was attached to the shaft's cement wall. At the bottom, he made sure the communication tube was free of sediment and inspected the sump pump to see that it was working properly. He then scrambled back up the ladder and walked over to the hillside weather station where he recorded an air temperature of 18 degrees Fahrenheit, a northwest wind of five miles per hour, and zero inches of precipitation. Dave would phone these measurements into the Los Angeles Department of Water and Power (DWP) before 7 a.m., a daily routine he had completed thousands of times. Yet today felt different.

Back on the lawn, one of the few places in Long Valley where a person can see both McGee Mountain and Mammoth Mountain in one view, Dave gazed across Crowley Lake to the panorama of the High Sierra. In the growing daylight, he could see that the previous night's storm hadn't dropped enough snow for him to run his McGee rope tows. He turned his eyes to Mammoth Mountain and the distant Minaret peaks still etched in darkness against the blues and grays of the changing sky. With a base elevation 2,000 feet higher than McGee, Mammoth could have received over a foot of fresh powder. Skiing would be great. Dave looked forward to his skis accelerating through the light fluff, his racers chasing behind. Thinking of the racers, he smiled. How he loved their enthusiasm, their laughter, their dedication.

The drone of a distant car engine interrupted Dave's thoughts. Though he couldn't see Highway 395, he imagined the headlights of a station wagon traveling north, skis and poles strapped on top, and sleepy-eyed skiers crammed inside. Fatigued after driving all night from Los Angeles, the skiers would be motoring toward Mammoth Tavern, the only restaurant within 20 miles. There they were sure to find a fresh pot of coffee percolating and a bowl of pancake batter resting by the hot grill.

Thoughts of arriving skiers woke Dave from his reverie. He'd better get going. What a relief that he could clear Minaret Road with the Sno-Go he had recently purchased to facilitate skiers being able to drive to the base of his Mammoth tows. With the racers helping him shovel snow, carry fuel, and ski pack the towline, he should be able to get his rope tows running within a few hours.

Dave turned toward the house that had been his home for the past 12 years and gazed at the chips of white paint falling among the dormant leaves of iris he had planted. He envisioned those still asleep inside: Roma, with her long hair curling across the pillow, her slender arm resting near their week old son Randy; their five older children tucked in tiny bunks in one small bedroom; and junior racers from Bishop sprawled in sleeping bags across the living room floor. To think of leaving the security of this dwelling behind, the home they all affectionately called the Crowley house, filled Dave with both nostalgia and excitement.

For the past several months, without sharing his thoughts with anyone, Dave had deliberated the pros and cons of a career change, analyzed various lines of logic, and listened attentively to his heart. If he gave up his job as a DWP hydrographer, he could devote all his energy to developing a ski area rather than splitting his time between responsibilities. However, resigning from his steady DWP job meant relinquishing a guaranteed monthly paycheck of $185, the privilege of living rent-free in the DWP house at Crowley, and income from the lucrative fishing-guide and boat-rental businesses he'd built up on Crowley Lake.

Yes, a career change would be a financial gamble, but money wasn't the only question at hand. Dave longed to immerse himself in the sport of skiing. As it was, working double-time to complete his DWP duties and operate his Mammoth and McGee rope tows left him little time for family. The more he acknowledged the downsides of dividing his time, the more he realized his feelings were undivided.

The prior evening, as soon as Dave arrived home from his DWP rounds, he had gone straight to Roma. Using his favorite term of endearment, he said, "Toots, I need to tell you something."

"Just a second," she responded, "I've got to nurse Randy." Roma settled into a chair and placed their infant son on her breast.

Dave's words came slowly. "You know, there aren't enough hours in a day for me to be a hydrographer and run our ski business." His eyes didn't leave Roma's face. He was confident she would support him, just as she always did, but he wanted to be sure she wouldn't harbor resentment or fear. "So," he said slowly, "I applied for a leave of absence from the DWP."

Roma brushed her fingertips across her infant's face and continued to nurse. After a short silence, she looked up and asked, "Well, Honey, where're we gonna live?"

Now, standing outside in the coolness of morning, thinking of Roma still asleep in their warm bed, Dave longed to tell her how much he appreciated the way she believed in him. He ran up the cement steps, quietly passed back through the screen door, and tiptoed over the Bishop ski racers and into the bedroom. There he stopped, suddenly hesitant to disturb Roma's slumber. He glanced through the window just as the first rays of morning sunlight hit the summit of Mammoth and awakened the mountain in a golden hue. As if sensing his presence, Roma opened her eyes and sat up abruptly. "I must have slept in. Oh Honey, why didn't you wake me?" She stood up and slipped into her bathrobe, tying it around her waist. Dave reached for his wife, turned her to him, and said, "Roma, we're going to build the best ski area in the world and have a lot of fun doing it!"

"I don't doubt that!" Roma laughed. "Now, there's no need to fuss over me. You've got enough to think about!" She placed Randy in the crib and kissed her infant's forehead. "I've got to start breakfast and make lunches. I know you're in a hurry. Looks like a sunny day! Did it snow last night? I can't believe I slept in."

Just then, a pillow fight erupted in the living room. Roma's eyes sparkled. She knew what was coming next. Dave grabbed two pillows off their double bed. Like a lion on the hunt, he crept toward the doorway. The telephone jingled with the long-long-short-short of the McCoys' party line. Bare feet sounded across the floor. A young boy's voice answered, "Hello," then called out, "Dad, it's for you."

With a playful holler, Dave pounced into the living room and hurled pillows at young Bobby Kinmont, Rhubarb Marcelin, and Kenny Lloyd. He tickled Bobby's older sister, Jill, jumped over two sleeping bags, and landed on the couch by the hand-cranked magneto telephone. Kicking away an onslaught of pillows, he picked up the earpiece, leaned into the box, and greeted the caller with a self-assured lilt, "Good morning, this is Dave."

Roma and Dave in Virginia City, August 1938.

PART ONE

Falling in Love

1915-1941

CHAPTER ONE

A Meandering Youth

Dave in Washington on his first day of skiing.

L ate Monday afternoon of the 1935 Labor Day weekend, 20-year-old Dave McCoy stood on Main Street in Bishop, California, hitchhiking south. Since the annual rodeo crowds had already thinned out, few cars drove by. In time, a pipeline worker driving a Department of Water and Power truck pulled over and inquired, "Where're you headed, son?"

"Independence," Dave replied, beaming with enthusiasm. An hour later, the driver double-parked in front of a restaurant called Jim's Place and waited for the young passenger to grab his fishing gear and rucksack. Dave thanked the man for the ride, then jogged up the doorsteps and walked through the front door, past the candy jars, the ice cream counter, the dining tables, and into the kitchen.

Amid steaming pots and pans, Dave saw Edna McCoy assembling

dinner plates. He tiptoed up from behind, threw his arms around his mother's ample waist, and called out, "Hi Mom!" Hoisting the broad-shouldered woman into the air, Dave twirled her around as if she were a tiny thing. Big in size and bold in temperament, Edna laughed with glee. "Sonny, can't you see I've got work to do? Now you stop this nonsense and make yourself useful!" Dave's heart warmed at the sound of his mother's voice. He gave her a quick kiss on the cheek, donned an apron, filled the sink with soapy water, and started washing a stack of dinner dishes.

After seven years of envisioning that he would one day make Independence his home, Dave's dream was coming true. Having earned a high school diploma from the state of Washington, he felt capable and ready to begin this new phase of life. If he needed to start as a dishwasher, that was fine. Laughing to himself, he said, "There probably isn't anyone in this world who can wash dishes as fast as I can or scrub them half as clean."

DAVE's desire to live in the Eastern Sierra had been kindled in July 1928, just before his 13th birthday, when he and his mother were visiting their longtime friends, the Frank Cooper family. The Coopers had relocated from Southern California to Independence, a high-desert town in the Eastern Sierra, where they purchased Jim's Place. For months, Gladys Cooper had been corresponding with Edna, inviting the McCoys to visit. In one letter, Gladys wrote:

> *Edna, you'll love it here. The men can go into the high*
> *country and fish, the kids can play, and you and I can*
> *catch up. I'm sure you'll have ideas for the menu, you're*
> *such a good cook. We're feeding at least 50 local workers*
> *daily, and I tell you this because I want you to know*
> *there's a lot of work around here. The county courthouse*
> *is down the street, state road-building contractors have*
> *projects on the highway, and DWP's main Owens*
> *Valley office is just a few blocks away. Wouldn't it be*
> *something if Mac fell in love with the area and you*
> *moved here?[1]*

Edna longed to visit the Coopers, but her husband, Bill "Mac" McCoy declined. Sonny couldn't figure out why his father didn't want to go. The McCoy family did everything together. But Sonny didn't question Mac. That was something he simply would *not* do. A kid's position was to respect adults. *Period.*

Still, questions flooded the boy's inquisitive mind. Couldn't Mac's employees handle the road job for a few days without their boss? And, why did Mac buy a Model A Ford for the trip? Dave laughed to himself thinking about Edna at the wheel of one of the company trucks. She could drive them as well as any of the guys, out swearing any one of the men in the process. But, most of all, Sonny wondered, why would his father say no to a fishing trip with Frank Cooper? During all the years Mac and Frank had worked together at the Standard Oil Refinery, Mac had never missed an opportunity to go fishing with his friend. No, something didn't make sense, but being just a kid, Sonny kept his thoughts to himself.

Just after sunrise on the day of their departure, Mac jostled young Sonny's hair saying, "You go fishing with Frank and catch a few for me, ya hear? You and your mother will have a real nice time." The boy climbed into the passenger seat of the Model A. He watched his parents exchange their parting words and noticed with surprise that they didn't share their usual embrace. Edna double-checked the picnic box tucked behind her seat, settled into the driver's seat, straightened her skirt, and started the engine. With forced cheerfulness, she said, "OK, Sonny. Off we go." The boy turned to wave goodbye to his father, but Mac was already walking away.

Down the road, Sonny opened the window and looked out. In youthful exuberance, he called out, "Whoopee! We're on vacation!" Any confusion he felt about his parents drifted into the open sky.

Several hours later, driving through the heat of the Mojave Desert, the travelers stopped at Little Lake Hotel, originally a station for the Owens River Stage Line. An attendant washed the windshield and checked the tires, oil, and water while Sonny pushed and pulled the big handle on the Gilmore pump, filling the tank with 13-cents-per-gallon gasoline.

Back on the road, Sonny floated his hand in the hot air outside his window and looked around at the barren landscape. He was curious to know what the Coopers liked about the sweltering desert heat, cactus, lava flows, and cinder cones, and he wondered what his childhood friend, Owen Cooper, did for fun.

Approaching Lone Pine, Edna and Sonny drove past the nearly dry Owens Lake where chalky white dust stretched toward the eastern horizon. This region marked the beginning of the Sierra Nevada's east side. North of Lone Pine, Highway 395 extended through the Owens Valley like a hundred-mile aisle, bordered on the left by 14,000-foot, snow-capped peaks and on the right by the equally high but drier Inyo Mountains. Awestruck, he exclaimed, "Mom, look! There's snow up there on the mountains in the middle of July." Edna laughed and told him one of those peaks was Mt. Whitney, the highest mountain in the United States.[2]

Near twilight, Edna and Sonny pulled up to Jim's Place on the main drag of the two-block town of Independence. The Coopers welcomed their friends with warm embraces and then showed them around the restaurant. Frank told Sonny to order anything on the menu and promised to take him fishing the next day. Eleven-year-old Owen whispered, "I'm glad you're the one going fishing and not me. I don't much like to hike." Later that evening, after the dinner crowd departed Jim's Place and the adults sat down to visit, the two boys went behind the soda fountain and made the fanciest hot fudge sundaes Sonny had ever seen.

Interior of Jim's Place, late-1920s.

THE next morning, Frank and Sonny drove up Onion Valley Road, a pre-cipitous winding dirt road that led to the Kearsarge Pass trailhead. At this popular gateway to the High Sierra, they shouldered their rucksacks, then hiked up wildflower-lined switchbacks. About three and a half miles up the trail, Frank led Sonny cross-country to the far side of Heart Lake.

While Frank rested, Sonny hiked up to a snowfield, fired off a few red-tinted snowballs, and then slid down the slope on his feet, his slick-soled tennis shoes gliding over ripples of summer snow and his arms waving in the air for balance. Frank explained that the red tint in the snow was algae, the ripples were called sun cups, and the way Sonny descended the snowfield was known as glissading. He then helped the boy bait his line and tutored him on casting. As the twosome fished their way around the high-alpine lake, Sonny couldn't help but wish his father was with them.

BACK in Independence, Sonny learned that Jim's Place was the social cen-ter of the small town, a place where friends gathered over a cup of coffee or a chocolate malt and shared the latest news. Helping Owen bus tables, he overheard heated debates about violent water wars between the City of Los Angeles Department of Water and Power and Eastern Sierra res-idents. Ever since the aqueduct was built in the early 1900s, people had been enraged about DWP's deceptive acquisition of water rights. Still, some ranchers and farmers felt fortunate they had sold their land for a good price and now had stable DWP jobs that eased the financial insta-bility they had previously known.

Sonny especially liked to listen to DWP hydrographers discuss snow surveys, snow depths, and river gauges. He admired their physical strength and knowledge of the mountains.[3] They, in turn, took note of the boy's interest in their conversations and invited Sonny to sit with them. The men took time to explain how the measurements they recorded—water levels, water trends, and stream flows—affected California's efforts to ensure water for the land and the people. They seemed proud that their method of taking snow surveys was the same method pioneered in 1906 on Nevada's Mt. Rose by Dr. James E. Church, the "father of hydrography."

The hydrographers teased Sonny, telling him he was just about old enough to strap on a pair of skis and accompany them on a snow survey.

With a curious look on his face, Sonny asked, "What are skis?" After their laughter subsided, the men explained that early California skiers, mostly of Scandinavian descent, used wooden boards—sometimes called skis or Norwegian snowshoes—as a means of winter transportation.[4]

SKI TRACKS
Roots of California Skiing
1850s to 1890s

Between 1856 and 1876, Snowshoe Thompson used skis to deliver mail across the Sierra Nevada.[5] In the 1870s, gold and silver miners from Plumas and Sierra Counties organized high-stakes, head-to-head, elimination-format contests that might have been the first down mountain ski races held in the U.S. Competitors crafted their 10-to-15-foot, single-grooved skis from vertical-grained Douglas fir. They waxed the bases with "dope"—secret concoctions of whatever they thought might travel fast on snow—made of beeswax, tallow, bear grease, pine tar, whale oil, or bacon fat. Good dope could determine the winner.[6]

The hydrographers told Sonny that a group of 1880s miners—who lived about 100 miles north of Independence in Mammoth City—skied on 11-foot-long pine planks.[7] Thirty miles farther north, Louis DeChambeau made skis at his Mono Lake ranch. In 1889, he was selling a pair of skis with an accompanying single pole for the reasonable price of eight dollars. Unfortunately, his children didn't have dope to wax their skis. As a result, sometimes when they were skiing to school, several inches of snow stuck to the bases, making it impossible to get any glide.[8] All Sonny could think was, "What a fun way to be tardy!"

DRIVING back to the Central Valley after their week in Independence, Edna seemed preoccupied. Sonny was glad she was quiet. That meant he didn't have to talk. Listening to the hum of the car engine, he stared out the window lost in thought. Never before had he questioned the way his family moved from town to town following Mac's road jobs. To him, change was the norm. He was used to making friends one day and then never seeing them again. But now he wondered what it would be like to live in a real house instead of a tent and to attend the same school with the same friends, year after year. He vowed that one day he would return to the Eastern Sierra. Maybe he'd even make Independence his home.

Sonny looked over at his mother and recalled the previous night when he had accidentally interrupted a conversation she was having with Gladys. To his surprise, Edna had been crying. Embarrassed, he'd hurried away and tried to assure himself that nothing was wrong. Edna wasn't the crying type. No, she was a happy woman with a strong will and a laugh so big it could fill a room, and it usually did.

But the reality was, Edna was brokenhearted. Her husband's heart had strayed, and she was struggling to find a way to prevent her marriage of almost 13 years from falling apart. Gladys had advised her to be patient, that men sometimes needed space to work emotional things out, and eventually, they would come back home. Edna wasn't convinced. She wistfully recalled her wedding day: a sunny California afternoon in December 1914 when Mac, a free-spirited 21-year-old wanderer, and Edna, a naïve 19-year-old girl, had vowed to love and cherish each other forever.

Mac McCoy originally came to Southern California in search of a life far from his parents' farm in the rainy state of Washington. Chasing visions of orange blossoms and sunshine, he made his way to the "City of Angels." On the historic Wednesday of November 5, 1913, shortly after his arrival in Los Angeles, Mac mingled with 30,000 Angelenos gathered in the San Fernando Valley.[9] People had traveled by trains, automobiles, wagons, buggies, and horseback to witness the formal gate-opening of the Los Angeles Aqueduct. This ingenious and controversial engineering project promised to deliver Eastern Sierra water to Los Angeles, a feat designed to ensure a bright future for the growing city.

While waiting for the first trickle of water to appear after its long journey from the High Sierra, Mac struck up a conversation with some friendly folks, Chris and Adelaide Metcalf, and their attractive daughters, Edna and Millie, who were standing nearby. As the first surge of Owens

Valley water tumbled through the aqueduct gates, the voice of William Mulholland, chief engineer for the DWP, thundered through the loudspeaker, "There it is, take it."[10] Watching the water tumble down an artificial cascade into the San Fernando Valley, Mac and Edna joined the crowd in a raucous cheer.

Captivated by Edna's contagious laughter and easy conversation, Mac made arrangements to meet her again. Within a year, he proposed marriage. After the wedding, the couple settled into a rented house in the coastal town of El Segundo. Nine months later, on August 24, 1915, they celebrated the birth of their 12-pound infant, David Robert McCoy. Though they named their newborn after Mac's younger brother, David, and Mac's father, Robert, the name was mere paperwork. Mac and Edna would call their boy Sonny.

The McCoys enjoyed life in Southern California. Edna took pride in being an immaculate housekeeper, diligent gardener, exceptional cook, and dedicated parent. A muscular woman who wasn't afraid of hard work, she kept Sonny close by as she cleaned house, washed clothes in a barrel of heated water, hung them on a line to dry, and tended long rows of squash, beans, carrots, tomatoes, watermelons, and head-high corn. Beyond the garden fence, Edna raised a cow, rabbits, pigs, and chickens.

Each weekday morning, Mac walked from the house to catch the nearby Red Car, an electric cable car serving Los Angeles. He rode one stop to the El Segundo Standard Oil Refinery, where Edna's father, the Gate 21 watchman, had helped him secure employment. The dirty and tedious manual labor of monitoring oil tanks was ill-suited to Mac's freewheeling nature, but it provided the McCoys a steady income. What kept Mac's restlessness at bay was playing on Standard Oil's prestigious baseball and horseshoe teams. Several evenings each week, Edna packed a picnic basket and with Sonny by her side, rode the Red Car to the company field. There, mother and son cheered on the team's star player.

For fun, the McCoys often walked to the nearby beach. Mac fished the shore break with a big casting pole and heavy lead sinkers, while Sonny pulled a trap through the water, strained out soft-shelled crabs, and tossed them into the bait bucket. On warm days, Mac scooted Sonny into the shallow waves. With wet curly blond hair glued to his forehead, the little boy would squeal with joy and then beg for another ride.

Mac and Edna kept their front door unlocked, an open invitation for guests to drop by, particularly Edna's longtime friends, the Coopers, Haines, and Lippets. Like an extended family, these friends spent many evenings together, sitting on the front porches of their beach homes, talking, dining, and drinking homebrew while they watched their children play.[11] But of all the people who visited, Sonny's favorite was Edna's sister, lighthearted Aunt Millie. Millie adored her nephew and made a point of spoiling him.

In April 1917, when the United States entered World War I, Mac's role in oil production prevented him from being called to duty. Sonny was too young to remember this "war to end all wars" except for people singing, "Over There," a patriotic fight song. Neither did he understand the postwar recovery years and how the social upheaval of prohibition, influenza, women's suffrage, and the Roaring Twenties affected the population. By then, one out of every three people in Southern California owned an automobile.[12] Joining this revolutionary transportation trend, Mac purchased a Model T Ford.

The McCoys had only owned their vehicle a short time when the car door slammed on Sonny's finger and ripped off his fingernail. Though pain shot through his body, he held his breath and fought back his tears. Crying would have made Mac furious and making his father angry was something the boy avoided. Nothing was more important to him than Mac's approval, and Sonny had learned at a young age that to gain this approval, he needed to follow four basic rules: listen carefully, do what you're told, tell the truth, and don't be a sissy. As a result, Mac only needed to ask Sonny to do something once. If Sonny didn't move instantly, his father pulled off his leather belt, snapped it hard, and warned, "Hey! Next time, do it!" With respect for the belt and for his father, Sonny behaved.

By the early 1920s, Mac McCoy had heard about Central California's road-building frenzy.[13] Intent on pursuing a job more to his liking than working at the refinery, he applied for a position with a central-valley road-building company out of Visalia, California. Valley Paving needed men who could handle heavy equipment on rugged road jobs. They looked through Mac's application, noted the qualifications he listed, and hired him immediately. The McCoys packed what belongings they could carry in their Model T. Riding in the back seat, looking forward to adventure, six-year-old Sonny waved goodbye to the Southern California beach life.

Mac soon recognized that self-employment offered opportunity for a hard-working man with initiative. He sold the family's Model T, used the money as down-payment on a dump truck, and began working as a subcontractor hauling materials for road-building companies. Gradually, Mac built his fleet to include four Sterling trucks, two Mack trucks, a Fresno Scraper—an earthmoving machine pulled by horses—and a Fordson tractor. Sonny swelled with pride each morning as he watched his dad's trucks line up for a day of work.

California's original paved highways were too narrow, paved too thin, and composed of too weak a mixture of concrete or asphalt. In some places, the weight of trucks hauling material to improve the roads wrecked the very routes contractors were trying to extend.[14] A new generation of road builders—men like Mac McCoy who weren't afraid of getting their hands dirty fixing their own machines—unceremoniously replaced roads with an expertise in highway technology matched only by the state of New York. These capable men followed jobs as they progressed, sometimes renting houses, but mostly living in tent camps near contract locations. Visalia, San Luis Obispo, Lost Hills, Shandon, Wasco, Williams, Salida, Rio Vista, Sacramento, Yuba City, North Hollywood, Gilroy, Hilmar, Merced, Fresno, Turlock, Irwin, Santa Cruz, and Modesto were among the places the McCoys temporarily called home.

During Sonny's fourth grade year alone, the McCoys moved at least six times. As the 10-year-old transferred from school to school, he fell behind in academic fundamentals other kids took for granted. His spelling suffered most. In September, when Edna enrolled him in yet another school in yet another town, the teachers decided to hold him back. Sonny was glad. Maybe he could learn basic spelling rules.

EDNA didn't complain about moving from town to town. She cared for her tent camp households just as if she were living in an elegant home. Upon arriving in each new location, Edna placed two beds against the 4-foot-high heavy canvas sidewalls and organized the family's belongings inside the 10- by 12-foot floor space. For a kitchen, she set up their Coleman gas stove on a table outside the tent.

Sonny changed mantles on the Coleman lanterns, hauled water to fill a galvanized tub, and built fires underneath to heat the water for washing dishes, taking baths, and scrubbing clothes. His favorite job was helping Edna bottle the root beer and hard cider she home-brewed.

One evening while Edna and Mac were at a Christmas party in a co-worker's tent, Sonny decided to find out what his parents liked about hard cider. He opened a bottle and took a sip. Even though the taste was strange and bitter, he guzzled as much as he could get down and ended up sicker than he'd ever been in his life. From that moment on, just the thought of liquor made him queasy.

Despite often being the only young person in the tent camps, Sonny was never bored. After completing his schoolwork and chores, he shot marbles, roller-skated, or filled cigar boxes with rattles from snakes he killed. Sonny used whatever he could find around the camps—snuff cans, cigar boxes, and old bike chains—to build toy trucks, train tracks, and roads. He made model airplanes from balsa wood, rice paper, and rubber bands and built a scooter by taking apart a pair of roller skates, nailing the wheels to the bottom of an orange crate, and attaching a stick for a handle.

When other kids were around, Sonny joined in rowdy games of football and stick hockey. The rougher the game, the more he liked it. During the hot Central Valley summers, he and his friends cooled off by jumping in irrigation canals or, when near a town, playing with garden hoses. One of his favorite games was to scare mud hens out from under the embankments of shallow reservoirs and splash after the fowl that darted through the water just out of reach. If there was a community swimming pool, Sonny found it. He prided himself on being able to swim four or five laps underwater without taking a breath.

What Sonny liked best was spending time with his father. After work and on weekends, they played catch, pitched horseshoes, and trained whatever dog they had recently adopted. Teddy, a full-chested German shepherd, was the family's pride and joy. Mac purchased a punching bag and two pairs of 16-ounce gloves and gave Sonny boxing lessons. He taught his son how to drive the company trucks and loaders, and how to tear an engine down, overhaul it, and put it back together, creatively using whatever tools and parts were at hand. Mac bought Sonny a .22 rifle, taught him how to be responsible with a gun, and supplied him with all the ammunition he wanted. From then on, Sonny spent most afternoons roaming the hills with Teddy, often shooting over 500 rounds in one session of target practice.

When Mac listened to football games on the radio, Sonny would lie on the floor with pencil and paper, and by the light of the Coleman lantern, diagram each play as he understood it. Other times, father and son drove to an open field, parked the truck, and left the lights on to illuminate any wild rabbits that might run by. At the time, there was no stigma against practicing marksmanship on these animals.[15] As far as Mac and Sonny's rabbit hunts, their goal was to take home a few youngsters for Edna to make a pot of rabbit stew.

One Sunday morning, when the McCoys were living in Wasco and the Haines family from El Segundo was visiting, Mac suggested, "Let's take a picnic lunch and go rabbit hunting." Only then did he notice Sonny's downcast face. The McCoys didn't practice any religion, but as a curious pre-teen, Sonny had recently made a personal commitment to attend church. Acknowledging his son's conflict of interest, Mac said, "Well then, Sonny, just come on out when you finish what you have to do."

Knowing the rabbit hunting was a fair distance away, Sonny asked, "How should I get there?"

Mac teased, "Drive the truck," chuckling at his joke.

At church, Sonny had difficulty paying attention to the sermon. He kept thinking about what his dad had said. Even though Mac had been joking, he *did* say, "Drive the truck." Mac had taught him to manuever the big trucks around the yard, but they'd never ventured out on the highway. Sonny dreaded being punished for defiance, especially in front of others, but driving the truck would be obeying his dad's words. By the end of the service, he had made up his mind. Sometimes a boy has to take a chance.

Sonny sprinted home from church, grabbed his rifle, and climbed up into the driver's seat of the dump truck. Standing so his legs could reach the gas and brake pedals, he held on to the oversized steering wheel, set his square jaw, and, with youthful determination, started the engine. When Mac heard the rumble of a truck approaching, he looked up and saw his Sterling bouncing toward them in a cloud of dust, the driver's face barely visible over the dashboard. Mac's mouth dropped open in surprise. Then he burst out laughing. That afternoon, Mac and Sonny rode home together with a bucketful of rabbits in the back and a grin on both their faces.

At 14, Sonny qualified for an underage driving permit issued by the State of California to enable youth from rural areas—such as the tent camp just east of the Pacific Coast Range where the McCoys were then living—to drive to school. On days when neither Mac nor Edna needed the car, Sonny drove himself to the school in the small town of Shandon, his senses heightened by the freedom and responsibility of driving. One morning, he saw a bird of prey sweep down into a flock of sheep, grab a newborn lamb in its talons, and fly away. The fearful scream of the bleating lamb sent shivers down his back. Another time he hit a section of road so greasy the car went into a slide. Barely managing to regain control, he pulled to a stop, walked back, and saw hundreds of tarantulas crossing the road in a mass migration.

Sonny's rural driving career ended when Mac secured a long-term trucking contract to work on Highway 101 near Gilroy. The McCoys packed their belongings, drove 200 miles north, and moved into an actual house. For the first time since kindergarten, eighth-grader Sonny McCoy attended the same school for almost the entire academic year. With this stability, his academics improved, even though he still tried to avoid the written word. To compensate for his poor spelling, he learned to listen carefully, memorize what he heard, and synthesize information into articulate and perceptive oral responses. Teachers praised his verbal skills and credited the many hours Edna had spent reading to him.

Living in a real house in a town, doing well in school, feeling capable and independent, Sonny decided to splurge. He used money he had saved from helping his parents to purchase a sheepskin-lined coat, an electric train, and a bicycle. Life was looking good.

On October 24, 1929, a day that came to be known as Black Thursday,

15

the American stock market crashed. Almost overnight, ten percent of American workers lost their jobs and government benefits, thousands of personal bank accounts were wiped out, and billions of dollars disappeared. At first, the McCoy family was spared financial disaster. Mac retained his Highway 101 contract, his family stayed in the house with a real kitchen, and Sonny continued to attend the same school.

In June, Sonny graduated at the head of his eighth-grade class and received the American Legion Award for honor, courage, and leadership. His classmates chose him to deliver a speech they had written as a group. Standing at the podium, Sonny spoke slowly and with confidence, never missing a beat in his presentation, never once looking at his notes.

Aunt Millie had driven from Tucson, Arizona, to attend the graduation. As a gift, she invited Sonny to spend a week with her. He gladly accepted, thrilled by the idea of having time with his adventurous aunt. Riding in the rumble seat of her Ford as they crossed the Southwest, hearing Millie's joyful laugh, Sonny couldn't have been happier. To his dismay, within a year, she would die of cancer.

SUMMER 1930. The economic stress of the depression altered people's values.[16] Smoking became the norm, an inexpensive pleasure in hard economic times. Even Edna, who had complained about Mac's smoking, took up the habit. She told Sonny she was trying to please her husband.

In the face of the failed economy, Mac found a short-term job near Irwin, a small community about 70 miles northeast of Gilroy, and rented a ramshackle house where the family could live. Sonny didn't mind, but he could tell his mother wasn't happy. Edna, the jubilant woman known for creating delicious tent-camp meals, seemed to have lost interest in cooking, conversation, and laughter. To escape her depression, Mac and Sonny passed the warm summer evenings walking down the road to Arthur Fletcher's store where they shared Mac's favorite double dessert—a pineapple milkshake and an apple turnover—and listened to the lilt of Fletcher's singsong British accent. Sonny made friends with Mr. Fletcher's 15-year-old son, also called Sonny, and the boys became inseparable.

By early September, Mac secured a short job north of Sacramento on Highway 99. The family moved to Williams, a town later depicted by

Dave as "so small, people would miss it if they blinked their eyes while driving down the highway." Sonny missed his friend Sonny Fletcher, but Williams High School suited him just fine. The school recruited him to play on the varsity football team as a freshman.

On days without football practice, Mac took Sonny duck hunting in the irrigated rice fields between Williams and Mt. Shasta. Both excellent shots, they would easily bag their limit and then spend the evenings plucking feathers. One afternoon, Mac intentionally sighted and killed a swan. Sonny couldn't believe his eyes. Killing a swan was not only a bad omen, it was illegal, and breaking the law was against Mac's principles. Yet, Mac had done it. Why? Driving home, neither Sonny nor Mac spoke a word.

The McCoys stayed in Williams just long enough for Sonny to finish fall football season and earn his first varsity letter, a proud accomplishment for a rookie freshman. The family drove south to Modesto and rented a motel room. Mac asked Sonny to run an errand while he and Edna unloaded the car. When Sonny returned, he noticed the curtains weren't yet drawn open. He opened the door and hesitated before stepping inside. The thick smell of stale cigarettes clogged his senses. As his eyes adjusted to the dimness of the musty room, lit only by a yellow bulb glowing through a faded lampshade, he saw his father standing, suitcase in hand. Edna was sitting on the edge of the bed, a forlorn expression on her face. Sonny froze. He dared not speak but looked to his father for an explanation.

Mac turned to his son and said, "Sonny, I'm leaving." Confused, Sonny reached out to shake his father's free hand just as he always did when saying goodbye. "No," Mac interrupted. "We're not saying goodbye. I'm just not going to be around anymore." Mac turned and walked out of the room. He closed the door behind him with a finality that resonated in Sonny's head like the sound of his whole world crashing down.

AFTER Mac left, Edna spoke in a voice that allowed no room for questioning. "Sonny, we'll be leaving tomorrow. We're catching a Greyhound bus to Washington. That's where your grandparents live, and that's where you'll stay for a while." Sonny's mind spun with questions. What did his mother mean, "going to his grandparents?" The only grandparents he'd ever known were her parents, the Metcalfs in El Segundo, and they had passed away.

Out of character, Sonny blurted out, "Please don't send me away. Let me stay here with you. We can run the trucking business together." Edna didn't reply. She looked at her son with a far-away yet determined expression, her eyes red from crying. The details had already been worked out. Sonny's parents were going their separate ways, and he was being sent to live with strangers. He felt helpless, hollow, and completely alone.

The next day on the long and drowsy Greyhound bus ride bound for Tacoma, Washington, Edna talked openly with her son. "Your father loves another woman. Her name is Grace, and she's married to one of the drivers who worked for us in Shandon. Their romance has been going on for a few years. There was nothing either one of us could have done to stop him from leaving." Edna turned Sonny to her and looked him straight in the eye. "Sonny, you didn't do anything wrong. Love's a powerful thing." Edna released his shoulders and reached for her handkerchief.

As if a lightning bolt of memory shot through the air, Sonny realized why his mother had been crying with Gladys Cooper in Independence. He closed his eyes and tried not to think, but Edna continued, her firm voice ringing with resolve. The bank was repossessing Mac's trucks. Edna already had a job cooking and cleaning for a family in Sacramento. No, Sonny couldn't go with her. His grandparents, Bob and Katie Cox, who were Mac's mother and father, would be taking him in. This was just the way things were. Worrying or arguing wasn't going to change anything.

After a pause, Edna said, "There's one more thing you should know. Your dad's name isn't Mac. It's Bill. Bill Cox. His parents called him "Willie" when he was young. He left home as a teenager and changed his name; not legally, he just did it. I don't know why. I guess he didn't want his parents to find him. He didn't even tell *me* the truth. When we got married, he wrote on our marriage certificate that his father's name was Robert McCoy. But that was a lie. His father, your grandfather, is Robert Cox."

Edna finally fell asleep, leaving Sonny to his thoughts, unable to grasp why his father wanted to leave the family. He thought his parents were content. A kaleidoscope of memories ran through his mind and then narrowed to a single vision. Several times while walking to the store during school lunch break in Shandon, he had noticed the family car parked at a house where one of his dad's drivers lived with his wife, Grace, and their two sons. The sight had given Sonny a sick feeling in his stomach. Surely Grace's husband was on the job working. Sonny had shoved the image out of his mind. But now, riding on the bus to Washington, his mother asleep in the seat beside him, the vision rose like an ugly monster.

Sonny stared through the window into the wet grayness. A rainy mist blurred the passing pines, Douglas firs, and hemlocks. He didn't want to be sitting on this bus on his way to live with strangers, yet neither did he want to be a burden to his mother. She had enough to worry about. He decided to accept his new life without complaining. This was just another change, another move.

KATIE Cox was waiting for Edna and Sonny at the Tacoma bus station. As unhappy as Sonny felt, he couldn't help but take a liking to this small kind woman. Riding in the back seat of her Studebaker as she drove the winding roads lined by evergreens, he could barely see her fluffy gray hair. Under a sandstone arch, she slowed the car almost to a stop, proudly announced, "Here we are in Wilkeson," and then drove over a bridge that spanned a tumbling creek, through the business and residential sections, and out of town. Every direction the boy looked, moss climbed up tall tree trunks and moisture hung in the air.

"Granny," as Sonny would call his grandmother, pointed out a series of beehive-shaped ovens that paralleled the railroad tracks. She explained that more than 150 of these ovens were used to heat coal into coke, a high-quality concentrated fuel derived from distilled coal, the pride of Wilkeson. Sonny listened politely, feigning interest. If only he could drift off to sleep and wake up to find he'd only had a bad dream.

About a mile past the ovens, Granny turned into the mining camp of Wilkeson Coal and Coke Company.[17] The camp was practically a town of its own. Besides the mining complexes, there was a commissary, a multi-purpose room, a beautifully furnished office, homes for the married men, and a company hotel for those who were single.[18]

Granny Cox pulled into the driveway of a large house with a well-kept lawn. Inside the open garage, a man stood at a workbench rewiring an electric motor. "Bob," said Katie, "meet our grandson, Sonny." The lean but muscular 60-year-old looked up through wire-rimmed glasses that exaggerated small sharp facial features. With a welcoming smile, he reached out to shake Sonny's hand. "Hello, son," he said, "Pleased to meet you." Though his voice was friendly, his body language made it clear he was on the job and needed to get back to work.

Sonny thought to himself, "My grandpa is just like my dad."

Robinson "Bob" Cox was born in Caledonia, Nova Scotia, Canada, in 1870 to a pioneer family of Irish and Scottish origin. As young men, Bob and his brother John emigrated to Washington state. Rugged individuals and talented handymen, they bought a farm outside the town of South Prairie, and secured jobs in the coal mine. In 1892, Bob married Ellen Rees, a Welsh woman who was living down the street from him. Within the next few years, Ellen gave birth to two children: Willie Cox, who was Sonny's father but had changed his name to Mac McCoy, and Dave, the uncle whom Sonny was named for. In 1896, when the Cox children weren't yet of school age, Ellen passed away.

Bob remarried during the spring of 1899. With his new wife Katie caring for Willie and Dave, Bob worked long shifts in the coal mine and farmed his land. In the strict pioneer tradition, he expected his two sons to follow his footsteps and work the land until they were old enough to go down in the mine. But by their late teens, Willie and Dave both left home in search of a lifestyle far away from farming and mining.

Holding a different view of Bob's occupation than her sons shared, Granny Cox's pride in her husband was evident. After dinner on Sonny's first night in Wilkeson, she explained that Bob had performed every job at the mine, from electrical maintenance to working underground in the excavated rooms. By 1923, this well-respected man had become foreman of Wilkeson Coal and Coke Company. By the time Sonny arrived in the fall of 1930, Bob Cox was in charge of the mine's 200 employees.

Before departing for her new job in Sacramento, Edna surprised Sonny with a gift, the family's Brownie camera. "I think you'll get more use out of this than I will," she said softly, then added, "Sonny, when we visit each other, you can share your adventures by showing me the photos you take."

The tenderness in her voice revealed her sadness.

Sonny enrolled as a freshman at the high school in the nearby town of Buckley. With each introduction at Buckley High, he held out his hand and said decisively, "Hi, I'm Dave McCoy." Determined to let go of his past, he deliberately left the name "Sonny" behind.

Right away, Dave made friends with three schoolmates who lived at the mining camp: Joe Logan, George Bartoy, and Americo "Bosty" Bostenero. Each morning the four boys walked a mile down the railroad track from the complex to the town of Wilkeson, talking sports along the way. There, they caught the school bus to Buckley. In the afternoons, when they weren't working out with a school sports team or playing catch, they'd be inside the multipurpose room at the mining camp, shooting hoops or boxing.

As a guest in his grandparents' home, Dave carried his weight by mowing the lawn, helping in the garden, chopping kindling, and filling the shed with wood. He felt particularly responsible to ease Granny's burdens. Many years prior, due to an infection, one of her legs had been amputated. Though Granny didn't complain, Dave could see from her limp that she suffered chronic pain. He didn't inquire about her leg. Neither did he ask why as teenagers his father and his Uncle Dave had run away from home and disowned the Coxes as parents. Dave accepted what little he was told. About his uncle, he knew little more than that he'd lost his leg while trying to jump a train.

Even with new friends, sports teams, and the love of his grandparents, Dave longed for his family and for the sunny blue sky of California. The wet grayness of Washington oppressed him. When he mentioned the incessant rain to his friends, they just chuckled in reply, "Rain? Oh, that's just Oregon mist. Missed Oregon, hit Washington!" Dave laughed along with them, but it wasn't until his grandpa introduced him to the basics of fly-fishing that he found reason to ignore the wet climate.

Grandpa Cox gave Dave an old steel telescopic Bristol fishing pole, not designed for fly-fishing, but usable. On the days his grandfather couldn't join him, Dave scrambled up a steep hill near the mine and made his way through the trees and undergrowth to Snell Lake. Here, he'd stashed a raft he'd made of cedar logs on which he could fish every corner of the lake.

Only oncoming darkness would remind him to grab his string of fish and head home for dinner.

WHEN Christmas break drew near, Dave decided to return to California and find his parents. The Coxes understood. They let Dave know he was welcome back anytime. He packed his small rucksack, put the little money he had saved into his pocket, and walked the train tracks to Wilkeson.

Through the winter chill, in the heart of the Great Depression, 15-year-old Dave McCoy hitchhiked south toward Sacramento, joining folks of all ages and walks of life who had taken to the road and rail. Dave's natural tendency to listen instead of talk and to quietly withhold his own opinion served him well. He learned to toughen up, avoid rough encounters, ignore cold, thirst, and hunger, and accept kindness, as when a stranger showed him that a particular mark on a fence indicated the owners of this house would exchange a meal for a half-day's work. On the road, Dave found that most of the apparently downtrodden hobos and tramps were generous, kind, honest, and intelligent individuals who had lost their money in the stock market crash the preceding year. Many of these people, whose character Dave came to admire, had interesting stories to share.

On Christmas Eve morning 1930, after hitchhiking 750 miles in five days, Dave strode through the streets of Sacramento asking strangers for directions to the home where Edna worked as a cook. For days, he had imagined his mother's hefty arms pulling him into the kitchen where the familiar aroma of her cooking would fill his senses. Just as he had expected, when Edna answered the door and found her son standing on the doorstep, she welcomed him with her big laugh and an even bigger hug, then fussed over the hot stove preparing a midday meal that warmed his soul as much as it filled his empty belly.

After lunch, Edna and Dave walked downtown to see the Christmas decorations. Through one storefront window, he noticed a man sitting at a table tying flies. Dave walked into the store, admired the flies, and asked a couple of questions. The stranger gave him a few tips, a piece of beeswax, and a catalog from which he could order everything he needed to tie his own. The man advised Dave, "Make sure you get to know your trout and what food they like. Each spot is different, even in the same lake. Mind you, your fuzzy dry flies need to match the personality of the fish you want to catch, and the seasons too. You can use bits of deer hide, scraps of silk or bird feathers, snippets of wool, string, strands of hair, anything … just observe carefully, that's the key. Then you can be creative and use your imagination."

Dave relished every moment of Christmas Eve dinner with his mother. But as the evening wore on, disappointment shattered his feeling of good-will. Edna drank and smoked more than he remembered. He dutifully obeyed when she asked him to light her cigarette, but he felt disgusted. Her cigarettes reminded him of the Modesto motel room where Mac had walked away from the family.

Edna told Dave that Mac was living with Grace and her kids in Cedarville, California. Christmas morning, she walked her son to the bus station. "Now Sonny," she said, "Don't forget to eat the sandwich I packed. You've got a six-hour bus ride ahead, and I don't want you to be hungry." She refused to betray any misgivings or sorrow.

Alone on the bus, the hours dragged by. Midday, Dave ate the sandwich Edna had prepared, but as the afternoon stretched on, hunger gnawed at him. Convinced he'd soon be enjoying Christmas dinner at his father's table, he reminded himself that having an appetite was good.

Mac's house was easy to find, and Dave recognized Grace's children playing in the front yard. To his surprise, the reality of their easy laugh-ter shook his confidence. Here lived a family of which he was no part. Dave decided against surprising his father. He approached the boys, explained that he was Mac's son, and asked them to tell Mac he'd come for a Christmas visit and would be back in about an hour.

Near twilight, Dave returned. Through a lighted window, he saw figures sitting at a dinner table. He knocked on the door. Nothing. He knocked again, then smiled at the sound of footsteps approaching. But instead of the door opening, whoever had walked toward him stopped, pulled down the window shade, and retreated into a cruel nothingness.

Dave stared at the closed door, numb, unable to move. He couldn't think. His chest throbbed. Silence thundered through his head. He fought off an onslaught of tears, turned, and walked away into the darkness. Down the road, he saw a barn and headed toward it. He eased the door

23

open and crept inside. No one noticed. Not even a dog barked. Cold and hungry, the young teenager burrowed under a pile of hay and shivered through the night.

STIRRED by hunger and by daylight streaming through the barn windows, Dave awoke from a restless sleep. He brushed the straw off his clothes, stepped outside, walked toward the highway, and caught a ride. When the driver asked where he was going, Dave started to say Sacramento but stopped himself. He was in no mood to see his mother. Sonny Fletcher's house. That's where he would go. "I'm on my way to Irwin," he replied.

The Fletchers welcomed Dave without question. They treated him as if his visit was no surprise, fed him a hot meal, and invited him to stay the night. By the end of the next day, Dave asked if he could stay on, live with them, go to school with Sonny, and work on their farm. Without hesitation, the Fletchers took him in.

Monday after Christmas break, Dave enrolled in freshman classes at Hilmar High, just as he had already done twice that year, first at Williams and later at Buckley. Far behind his classmates academically, and afraid of drawing attention to himself, Dave kept quiet in class. But as soon as the last bell rang, he hurried outside into the warm California sunshine, full of energy and ready to spend the afternoon with Sonny Fletcher, the closest friend he'd ever known.

Sonny was a year older than Dave, bigger and stronger, but the boys were well-matched in personality. Renewing their friendship right where they'd left off, they jumped into canals, swam in aqueducts, boxed, played fierce games of handball, and battled through impromptu wrestling matches. All the while, they challenged each other's strength, courage, and athleticism, *and* attacked each other's weaknesses. At the end of every battle, they walked away laughing as best friends do.

One evening, Mr. Fletcher gave the boys a lecture about the importance of trust. That night, Dave tossed and turned, unable to sleep. He'd had his lesson in trust. Alone in the barn on Christmas night, he had learned the only person he could depend upon was himself. Now, living at the Fletchers' in Irwin, thinking of his parents, Dave fought off loneliness. Wasn't there *someone* in this world he trusted? Visions of Bob and Katie

Cox came to his mind. The next morning, he thanked the Fletchers for their hospitality, said goodbye to Sonny, packed his fly-tying gear into his rucksack, and began the long hitchhike north to his grandparents in Washington.

Back in Wilkeson, Dave settled into his day-to-day life with renewed enthusiasm. He took on the responsibility of cleaning and polishing the Studebaker. In return, his grandparents designated him as their official driver. With Dave at the wheel, Katie and Bob Cox sat in the back seat holding hands, while their beloved oversized Airedale stuck his head out the front passenger window, as if to show off he was riding shotgun to his partner, Dave McCoy.

Once Dave was back in the rhythm of school, Bob Cox hired him at the mine for the part-timers' pay rate of $4 per week. Grandpa Cox planned to rotate Dave through all aspects of the operation so the young man could eventually learn the entire line of work. Not wanting to show preferential treatment, he sent his grandson into the heart of the mine. Shortly thereafter, a big rock crashed down onto the railroad tram and killed the man sitting directly behind Dave.

Late that night, after taking care of the heart-rending details concerning the death of his employee, Bob quietly slipped into Dave's bedroom. He sat in the dark on a wooden chair near the bed and listened to his grandson's quiet breathing. Cox's mind drifted back to a dark day in 1908 when a section of the mine had collapsed and killed his brother John. Twenty-two years had passed, but the memory still hurt. Before leaving Dave's room, Bob Cox whispered, "Son, that will be your last trip down in the mine."

THE next day, Grandpa Cox taught Dave how to monitor boiler room gauges. He added, "There are idle periods inherent to this job, and I give you permission to study or tie flies during those times." Quiet hours in the boiler room provided Dave the perfect setting to follow the advice of the fly-tying master in Sacramento and tie flies that simulated what he saw in natural hatches and local ecosystems. Dave took photos of stringers of fish he'd caught in specific settings and placed an advertisement in the local paper.

Fish?
Use a fly made to order?
Rods rewrapped and refinished
Dave McCoy, Wilkeson, Phone 32

Local fishermen saw the photos and recognized the locations. Before long, Dave had so many orders for his hand-tied flies that he spent all his spare time trying to keep up with demand.

Grandpa Cox invited Dave to join him on overnight fishing excursions with friends Carl Sandell, a foreman at the mine, and Milt Allen, Carl's nephew. The four multigenerational fishing fanatics hiked into remote lakes with their fishing gear in hand and their rucksacks stuffed with a cooking pot, an iron skillet, and boiled potatoes, bacon, and onions Granny had packed into used coffee cans. They tied blankets wrapped in waterproof tarps to the back of their packs. Dave took notice of how big, kind, and gentle Carl Sandell inevitably found a way to carry the heaviest load without hurting the pride of his much older friend, Bob Cox.

Milt, who attended high school in the nearby town of Enumclaw, looked up to Dave, a few years his senior. He struggled to keep up with Dave's powerful strides as the two boys ran ahead of the older men, collected pine needles to make sleeping pads, and gathered logs to build fishing rafts. Talkative Milt was awed by how easily Dave caught fish and amused by Dave's indifference to cold and rain. Milt got a few laughs sitting around the campfire, watching Dave gobble up fried fish and potatoes without noticing the rain dripping off his head onto his food.

Envious of Dave's fly-tying skills, Milt prodded him to share his secrets. Dave stubbornly refused to divulge the subtleties of his art. Then one fall day, Milt piqued Dave's interest with an unexpected proposition: "Dave, if you teach me how to tie flies, I'll teach you how to ski." Milt had learned the basics of skiing from his Scandinavian brother-in-law. He urged Dave on, "Skiing is the most fun sport ever! And soaring off a ski jump is a good way to impress the girls!" Dave couldn't resist this opportunity to attempt the sport that had intrigued him ever since his conversations with the hydrographers in Independence. That same afternoon, he gave Milt fly-tying lesson number one.

With guidance from his woodshop teacher, Dave built a form in the shape and dimensions of Milt's skis. Then he shaped a piece of ash—a strong, yet elastic, hardwood—clamped it to the form, and molded the ski at the mine's steam plant by placing it inside a pipe and steaming the wood until it held the proper curve. Dave repeated the process to make a matched set, and then, according to Milt's instructions, finished the tops with linseed oil, applied pine tar to the bases to seal and harden them, and attached straps of inner tubes as bindings. As soon as the ski poles he had ordered from the Montgomery Ward catalog arrived, Dave was ready to hit the slopes.

When the first snow fell, Milt and his older brother Houstie drove Dave to a slope called Parkway. The three boys carried their skis up the hill and slipped their hiking boots into their rubber bindings. Milt shouted out his two-word lesson. "Follow us!" Dave observed as Milt and Houstie headed straight down the slope, crouching forward with bent knees, holding their arms out to the side for balance. As their speed increased, they dropped one knee toward the snow in the Nordic-based telemark position in which the heels are "free" as opposed to being attached to the ski. Where the hill flattened out, they advanced one ski forward and semi-gracefully turned to a stop.

Dave thought, "Okay, that doesn't look too difficult." He pointed his skis downhill, imitating Milt and Houstie's body positions. As he gained speed, he deepened the bend in his knees. Near the bottom, he dropped one knee low and threw his skis to the side as his friends had done. Laughing like crazy, Dave completed his very first ski run without falling down. Invigorated, the boys placed their skis over one shoulder and climbed higher up the slope for a longer and faster descent.

After a few runs, Milt told Dave the time had come to ski off a jump. The boys hiked over to three jumps some other skiers had shoveled. Milt and Houstie skied off the smallest and caught a little air. Dave followed. No problem. They then skied off the middle-sized jump, caught good air, and landed without a mishap. Naturally, Dave wanted to try the biggest jump. Milt said, "Forget it, not for me." Dave shrugged. He climbed to the take-off, pointed his skis straight down, let them run, launched high into the air, and lost his balance. Flapping his arms in vain to gain stability,

Dave landed with a crash and then cartwheeled down the slope. After sliding to a stop, he stood up, happy to still be in one piece. Dave brushed the snow off his pants and noticed he'd ripped them. Granny was not going to be pleased. These weren't just any pants. They were Tin Pants—expensive, heavy-duty work pants made of stiff, waterproofed canvas. Except for one pair of Levis, these were the only pants Dave owned. But the damage was done. He might as well take another jump, and then another, and another, striving for more distance with each attempt.

As soon as the school year was over, Dave hitched to Irwin to spend the summer working with Sonny Fletcher on his family's farm. The two friends harvested apricots, peaches, cherries, plums, and grapes, cutting the ripest specimens in half before laying them on trays to dry, eating their fill of succulent fruit as they moved along. They pooled their money to buy a used Model T Ford for $7.50.[19] On their way to the orchards one morning, the car broke down. Dave looked beneath the chassis and saw a broken rod. He told Sonny, "Don't worry, we won't be late." With the "can do" attitude his father had modeled while fixing mechanical problems, Dave used his belt buckle to rig the rod together. As the car bounced down the narrow farm road getting the boys to work on time, Dave envisioned how proud his dad would be of this innovative repair.

Continuing his habit of hitchhiking between Washington and California, Dave was back at Buckley High for football season. As a sophomore, he ran, tackled, and slid across the muddy fields of Washington state on his way to a second football letter. By winter, Dave was back in California living with the Fletchers going for a basketball letter at Hilmar High. The opening day of fishing season lured him north to Wilkeson where he earned letters at Buckley in the spring sports of boxing and track. By the following autumn, Dave was again with the Fletchers and enrolled at Hilmar High, playing as a junior for his third football letter.

While helping care for the animals on Fletcher's farm, Dave became curious if a pig or chicken could get drunk. In a "science experiment" based on memories of his mom making hard cider at the tent camps, he poured water over grape pulp left in Mr. Fletcher's wine vats and let the mixture ferment. On the morning of the test, before going to school he stirred the fermented mash into the feed and distributed it to the barnyard animals. A few hours later, the school secretary received an angry call from Arthur Fletcher. With his British accent flared up well beyond its usual lilt, Fletcher requested the secretary be so kind as to send Dave McCoy home "forthwith" to gather the pigs that were running through the vineyards and the chickens that were strutting around one moment and falling over the next.

That spring, with a Hilmar football letter in his rucksack, Dave hitchhiked back to Washington to finish his junior year at Buckley. He went out for winter basketball, but his season ended the day he came home from a practice overcome with chills, a sore throat, and a headache. By evening, he began to vomit. His fever soared to 104 degrees, and his skin turned red from a rash. Diagnosis: scarlet fever, a potentially fatal disease. The doctor prescribed a two-month quarantine. Grandpa Cox moved into the company hotel while Granny stayed home with Dave. Due to her exposure to the illness, she was forbidden to mingle with others.

While the disease ran its course, Dave didn't have strength enough to get out of bed. He wasn't allowed to read because light hurt his eyes. Unable to swallow solid food, he lived on liquid nourishment that Granny prepared. Each day, she sponged Dave down with warm solutions of soda water, rubbed him with olive oil, gave him liquids to gargle, disinfected his clothes and linens, and aired out his room while shielding him from the draft. Eventually, his red skin started to peel, sometimes in flakes, sometimes in strips, and the natural color of his skin returned. He began to regain his strength, and with it, a new appreciation for the love of his grandparents and all they had been willing to sacrifice for him.

By spring of his junior year, Dave was back in school, training on the track team under the careful guidance of Coach Mullen. As the annual conference track meet neared, Mullen spoke of Dave as a threat to place in the hurdles. But due to tragic news from Irwin, Dave never made it to the competition. Sonny Fletcher had been diving off a car into the canal, just as the two of them had so often done together. But this time, Sonny miscalculated the depth and broke his neck. Dave's closest friend was dead.

Overcome with sadness, Dave hitchhiked south to help the grieving

Fletchers with their farm. Without Sonny, Dave had no desire to attend school. Mr. Fletcher understood and hired Dave to work full-time as his orchard field boss. Still, everything Dave did in Irwin, everywhere he looked, reminded him that Sonny was gone. By spring 1934, the Fletchers encouraged him to return to Wilkeson and finish high school the next year. With a heavy heart, Dave bid farewell and put his thumb out to hitchhike, just as he had done so many times before.

When Joe Logan heard that his high school buddy had returned, he dropped by the Cox's house. "Hey, Dave," he suggested with his typical enthusiasm. "Let's take a summer road trip, you and me. I just made the final payment on my Model A, and I want to give that 1929 buggy a run for its money. You're the seasoned traveler. You can decide where we go."

Dave didn't think twice about the itinerary. They would travel down the coast of California to visit his mother in Santa Cruz where she was now working. Next, they'd drive south to Hermosa Beach to visit the Lippets, and then north on Highway 395 up the east side of the Sierra Nevada to see the Coopers. They would stay in Independence for a month hiking, fishing, and working whatever jobs they could find to finance their way back to Washington in time for football practice. Joe boxed up $40 worth of canned food from the mine commissary store where he worked. Dave folded his life savings of $46 into his wallet to pay for gasoline, and the two young men took off.

The boys spent three days in Santa Cruz camping on the beach at night. Each morning Dave swam out and around a buoy, renewing his love for the ocean. Visits with his mother were limited to the time she could take off from her job. Sadly, rather than enjoying the reunion he had envisioned, his discomfort with Edna's use of alcohol and cigarettes worsened.

Joe and Dave drove down the California coast from Santa Cruz to Hermosa Beach, where they savored a few days of warm Southern California surf and Marie-Jean Lippet's home cooking. When they left for Independence, Marie-Jean sent one of her chocolate cakes with them. Just as dusk settled in, having struggled through three flat tires, road-weary, hungry, and out of canned food, they made camp on a hill north of Olancha. Just then, a cottontail made the unfortunate decision of darting past. As Joe described, "That night, we sat by the campfire eating roasted rabbit and chocolate cake."

Dave and Joe arrived in Independence on July 8, 1934, almost six years to the day since Dave had first seen the Eastern Sierra. The region was exactly the paradise he remembered. Joe wiped his forehead with a handkerchief and wondered how he could handle the heat.

Frank Cooper helped the boys find jobs working on the highway where they labored under the sweltering desert sun, each earning $5 a day. A never-ending parade of biting red ants toiled beside them, working for free.

One day after work, Dave and Joe drove up Onion Valley to the Kearsarge Pass trailhead and hiked to Heart Lake, where Frank Cooper had taken Dave when he was just 12 years old. Now, using Dave's hand-tied flies, the friends caught their limit in no time. Back at Jim's Place, Dave decided to quit the road work, display his fish on a bed of ice near the front window at the Specialty Shoppe, and open a fly-tying business. Within days, a group of fishermen from Los Angeles hired him to guide a backcountry trip over Kearsarge Pass, past the crystal waters of Charlotte Lake, up the dry, rocky trail over Glen Pass, and into the remote Sixty Lakes Basin. Three days later, Dave led the group back to the Owens Valley via the steep Sawmill Pass, stopping to fish Sawmill Lake on their return. Meanwhile, Joe Logan continued to get sunbaked with the red ants on the highway job.

Frank Cooper invited Dave on a day trip to Grant Lake, one of Mono County's prime fishing spots, and for the first time, Dave saw the countryside north of Independence.[20] Traveling up Highway 395, they passed miles of wide-open space, high desert landscape, and rugged mountains. Just north of Bishop, Round Valley's rambling cottonwood trees and hedges of wild roses framed bucolic meadows where peaceful cattle and horses grazed.

Continuing north, the Sherwin Grade climbed 2,400-feet in elevation as the road wound up to the meadowlands of the Long Valley caldera. On the surrounding hillsides, green leaves of thirsty aspen, birch, and willows outlined ice-cold creeks that tumbled down from the high country. Across the flatlands, under the protective eye of their herder, hundreds of sheep grazed near Crooked Creek as it meandered toward the Owens River. In the distance, a range of jagged peaks resembling the European Alps came into view. Frank told Dave that this was the Minaret Range, Mt. Ritter, and Banner Peak, and in the foreground, Mt. Mammoth.[21] Frank promised Dave, "I'll take you there one day. There's great fishing up past Mammoth Camp in the Lakes Basin."

IN early August, Dave and Joe left Independence and headed home. Just before Lee Vining, they turned west onto the dirt road that climbed over Tioga Pass toward Yosemite. While Joe drove, Dave reflected on advice he'd received about becoming a DWP hydrographer. As an out-of-state candidate, he needed to establish a one-year California residency, be a high school graduate, and pass a civil service exam. The idea of being a hydrographer filled Dave with purpose and gave him reason to graduate from Buckley High. With his diploma in hand, he would return to Independence and establish residency. Once settled in Independence, he would order a series of correspondence courses and prepare for the exam.

Looking over at Joe, Dave spontaneously punched him on the shoulder. Joe glanced at him in surprise. Dave grinned, "Just making sure you're tough enough for next week." With a quick laugh, Joe faked a punch back at Dave. "Hell week" for the 1934 Buckley High football team had begun.

DAVE's senior year at Buckley High turned out to be a time of stabilization during which he wove together the threads of who he had been and designed the tapestry of who he would become. With quiet confidence, he let go of what he didn't like in life, archived his yearnings for a reunited family as relics of the past, and focused on the present. The strength of his identity flourished. He emerged as a natural-born leader—as were his father and his grandfather—whose greatest desire was to make the most out of each day.

Playing both sides of the ball on the 1934 Buckley High football team, Dave gained a reputation as a tough but fair competitor. Due to a shoulder injury incurred by accepting a bet to throw a football over the gymnasium, when playing offense he was only able to receive and run. As a defensive linebacker, his aggressiveness made up for what he lacked in size. One opponent suffered a broken leg from Dave's flying tackle. The accident was unfortunate, but the referee ruled fair play.

During the times Dave monitored gauges in the warmth of the boiler room, he studied. His grades improved, and he gained confidence in his academic ability, except, as always, in spelling. He kept his feelings of inadequacy to himself until the day one of his teachers insulted and embarrassed him by using his work as an example of careless spelling errors.

When this teacher assigned the students to write an essay and stand in front of the class delivering it to the other students, Dave's oral presentation began with, "It is insensitive, hurtful, and ineffective to teach by pointing out the weaknesses in others." Suddenly, the teacher realized Dave was referring to her. She called his essay inappropriate and demanded he stop reading. Dave ignored her, read his entire essay, and then walked down the hall to Catherine Monk's classroom.

A favorite teacher among the student body, Miss Monk was known for her devotion to students. She listened to Dave's explanation of what had happened, and then went directly to the principal, Mr. Phillips, to prevent disciplinary action. For the rest of the semester, Miss Monk tutored Dave in the basic rules of spelling. However, this short tutelage wasn't enough to make up for all he had missed. For the rest of his life, Dave suffered from embarrassment about his poor spelling.

WHEN snow came to Washington that winter, Dave and his school buddies began a Sunday morning ritual. They packed their ski gear into Joe Logan's Model A, drove to Milt Allen's house in Enumclaw, and threw pea gravel at his bedroom window to roust him. After loading Milt and his equipment, they headed off to ski. The boys parked the car by accessible snow-covered slopes and attached sealskins to the bases of their skis, which provided traction so they could climb straight up hills.

One Sunday morning, Milt jumped in the car filled with unusual enthusiasm. "Guys, there's a ski competition today at Snoqualmie Summit. We've got to go." At Snoqualmie, the Wilkeson boys watched ski jumpers zip down the steep in-run, soar in the air for over a hundred feet, and land with one knee bent in the telemark position. On the slalom course, marked by 3-foot poles with triangular flags attached, racers connected tight turns, most of them skiing the Arlberg style, a technique introduced to America by German and Austrian instructors.

The following weekend, Dave and his friends drove to Mt. Rainier, a 14,000-foot volcanic cone in Washington's Cascade Mountains. While tightening their bootlaces inside Rainier's Paradise Lodge, they overheard skiers talking about the Silver Skis, an annual ski race on Rainier sponsored by the *Seattle Post-Intelligencer*. In the inaugural competition held the prior winter, 64 competitors had climbed to the start at the 10,000-foot Camp Muir. At the sound of a pistol, they took off *en masse*. The racers fought the rough terrain and varied snow conditions trying to get ahead of each other. As the newspaper reported, "... the smooth snow surface suddenly changed to shingled windrows and waves, bringing about a fearsome explosion of cart-wheeling humanity."[22]

In just a few weeks, the boys heard, the elite of American skiing was expected to compete in the second annual Silver Skis. The race would determine the 1935 U.S. National Champions in slalom, downhill, and combined, and would serve as a qualifier for the first-ever U.S. Olympic *Alpine* Ski Team.

SKI TRACKS
Alpine Skiing to be in the Winter Olympics
1935

The first three Winter Olympics—1924 in Chamonix, France; 1928 in St. Moritz, Switzerland; and 1932 in Lake Placid, New York—had included only the Nordic events of cross-country skiing and ski jumping. At long last, the international governing body for skiing, *Fédération Internationale de Ski (FIS)*, had convinced the Scandinavian contingent of the International Olympic Committee (IOC) that an alpine event was worthy of Olympic status.[23]

On Saturday, April 14, the Wilkeson boys joined 7,000 other spectators on the slopes of Mt. Rainier. Because of dense clouds shrouding more than half of the two-mile-long downhill course, competitors could barely find their way to the start, much less see the flags that marked the course, or find their line racing down. Some lost their way completely. Others hit unseen frozen tracks and slammed to the ground. Officials agonized over the mess that was unfolding. However, with so much riding on the results, they judged the race would go on.

Most spectators stood near the final schuss, where visibility was better. The highlight of the day was when Austrian Hannes Schroll came flying out of the fog. He let out a joyful yodel mid-air, landed, pushed for more speed, and still yodeling, passed the finish line in 1st place, a full minute faster than America's favorite, Dick Durrance. The cheering crowd went wild. Their consensus was the Americans had a long way to go to catch up to this Austrian, who the *Seattle Times* described as "a tornado on skis, a whooping, yodeling, hat-throwing, rip-snorting fool who doesn't respect ice, precipices, avalanches, or traditions."[24]

Hannes also won the slalom with ease. Using skis and poles that were longer than those of his competitors, he constantly shifted his weight to eliminate friction and pick up speed. He also took a wider line around the gates to avoid the wet triangular slalom flags that tended to wrap around the boots of racers who clipped in close. The Wilkeson boys laughed about whether Hannes' skiing or his yodeling had impressed them more.

As the Washington winter drew to a close and opening day of fishing season approached, Dave became preoccupied with angling. He scouted creeks and lakes taking note of each habitat, and he worked double-time filling orders for his handmade flies. In Wilkeson Creek, Dave discovered some roe—orange-reddish salmon eggs—and concocted a salmon spawning experiment, transplanting the eggs to an 18-inch ditch that ran right near his grandparents' house and placing them on gravel where just enough water flowed to oxygenate the eggs without washing them away. Several weeks later, Dave saw tiny salmon swimming about, preparing to navigate downstream toward the confluence of the ditch and Wilkeson Creek. Success! Now he would just have to wait until the following year to see if the salmon made their way up the backyard ditch to spawn.

During the week before the opening day of fishing season, the high school principal, Mr. Phillips, made several announcements reiterating that any student who ditched school to go fishing would receive double detention. Despite the warnings, opening day attendance sheets reported 30 students absent. The following morning, Mr. Phillips called those who had been truant into his office and quizzed each one individually about where they had been. Their answers ran the gamut. When Phillips interrogated Dave, the teenager answered without hesitation, "I went fishing, sir."

With a stern expression, Mr. Phillips assigned him six hours of detention.

"Yes sir," Dave responded, "I know. When do I start?"

Surprised by Dave's honesty and his willingness to accept punishment, Mr. Phillips challenged, "Well, it might have been worthwhile if you'd caught anything."

"I caught my limit, sir."

Phillips raised the stakes, "Too bad they weren't big enough to count for anything."

Dave smiled. "They were all between 12 and 14 inches."

Not willing to give in, Phillips shook his head, "Why son, that's a little hard to believe."

"I guess I might just have to prove it to you, Mr. Phillips." Dave excused himself to begin working off his detention. That evening, he had Granny Cox take a photo of him holding his string of fish. On the back of the photo, he wrote, "These are the fish that caused me six hours of detention."

The next day, when Mr. Phillips returned home from running errands in town, his wife handed him three 14-inch trout, saying, "Honey, a young man dropped these off for you."[25]

In June, Dave walked as a member of the 1935 graduating class of Buckley High. He had made the honor roll, served as vice-president of his senior class, helped decorate the gym for dances, built sets for the vaudeville productions, and served on the yearbook staff. He also officiated as president of the "B" Club, organized by the school lettermen to promote better and cleaner athletics. On stage, diploma in hand, Dave saw that his grandparents were sitting next to Carl Sandell and his wife, four people whose friendship, guidance, and love he cherished. He hurried down to thank them. Carl congratulated Dave and handed him a graduation present. "It's time you had a tackle box of your own." Dave could barely restrain the emotion he felt.

Alone in his bedroom that night, Dave read the handwritten notes that filled his yearbook, the well-wishes for his fly-tying business, jokes about his plans to take dancing lessons, and praises of his athleticism. He studied Coach Mullen's inscription, "Certainly will miss your 150 pounds of fight and fine spirit on the athletic teams," and he reminisced over the 1934 football season.

Dave glanced at his football sweater—given to team members by the Kiwanis Club—lying across the back of a chair. The stripes sewn on each sleeve represented football letters earned. Dave's sweater was unique among his teammates'. Along with two red stripes from Buckley, he also had a yellow stripe from Hilmar and a green one from Williams.

Looking at his senior portrait, Dave pondered the description his classmates had chosen for him, "a ready smile and an unsung power." Funny, he thought, how people see each other. This boy who doesn't drink, swear, or smoke, and is too shy around girls to ask one on a date no matter how much he wants to, might not be as calm and happy on the inside as he appears on the outside.

Just that night, while eating cookies and drinking lemonade with a few of his classmates, some drunk college boys had pounded on the door looking for a fight. Enraged, Dave had stood up, ready to take on the attackers. His friends had to restrain him from opening the door.

Thumbing through the final pages of his yearbook, Dave came across Miss Monk's inscription about the importance of friends. "Friends," Dave thought. This word should elicit joy, but to Dave, it evoked sadness. He questioned the value of becoming attached to anyone, just to lose them. Sonny Fletcher, Aunt Millie, his parents. Dave's mind wandered to nights in the boiler room when he would carefully sharpen a pencil until it had one long side and one short side, just as he remembered his father doing. Then he would practice his signature, trying to write "McCoy" exactly as Mac had written it.

Through the darkness of the night, Dave pondered his future. He recalled the hydraulic engineering class he'd audited at the University of Washington, and how he'd understood every point the professor had made. Wanting to learn more, he was considering accepting one of the athletic scholarships offered him by Washington State, University of Washington, Pullman College, and College of the Pacific in California. But how would college help him become a hydrographer in the Eastern Sierra?

The next morning Dave awoke sleep-deprived but full of energy. At breakfast, his grandmother spoke of a job picking apples in Wenatchee, but Dave stopped her mid-sentence. In a soft voice, he said, "Granny, thank you. Thank you for everything, but I won't be needing that work. I've decided to go to Independence, and I'll be leaving today." With his Kiwanis football sweater and a few other clothes already folded in his rucksack, Dave embraced his grandmother and assured her she didn't need to worry about him. He threw his pack over one shoulder, grabbed his fishing pole and tackle box, stepped out the screen door, and turned around to wave goodbye just in time to hear her say, "We're sure gonna miss you around here."

Dave found his Grandpa working at the mine. Hearing his grandson's plans, Bob Cox nodded without surprise. He extended his hand to Dave and said, "Good luck to you, son." Their handshake lingered longer than was the custom; their eyes communicated everything they needed to say.

Making the rounds to bid farewell to his friends, Dave wished them well and invited them to visit him in California. With a lively stride, he walked out of the mining camp, past the coke ovens, through Wilkeson, under the sandstone arch, and down the road. An image of his father walking this same path heading to California 20 years prior flashed through Dave's mind. He imagined they looked exactly alike.

The summer air was warm, already filled with the scent of fertile soil and new growth. On such a clear day, were it not for the tall trees, Dave could have seen Mt. Rainier standing alone against the sky. He inhaled deeply, as if to breathe in everything he had grown to love about Washington. Hearing the sound of an approaching car engine, he raised his thumb to hitchhike. Independence was on his mind.

THAT the country was still suffering from the Great Depression, relentless dust storms were currently ravaging the Midwest, and political storms were brewing in Europe did not stifle Dave's enthusiasm as he made his way south. He looked forward to the future with youthful ambition and optimism.[26]

In Sierraville, California, where his mother was now working as a hotel cook, an experienced gold panner taught him how to scrape ore from the bottom of the river and offered him a 50 percent partnership in a gold panning business. Dave accepted, purchased lumber, and built a sluice box. With gold valued at $16 an ounce, by his 20th birthday on August 24, 1935, he had saved enough money from his share of gold to feel he was making a decent living.

Then, without consulting him, Dave's partner brought his son in on the deal, changing the arrangement to a three-way split. Dave felt betrayed. The so-called "partnership" was a farce. To make matters worse, literally adding injury to insult, the boy accidentally dropped a heavy rock that smashed Dave's finger. A local doctor had to use pliers to remove the damaged nail.

Dave questioned what he was thinking. His mother had left for Independence, and was temporarily cooking at Jim's Place. The Coopers needed help because Frank had fallen ill and was in a hospital in Los Angeles. The end of August had drawn near, and here was Dave, hundreds of miles away, distracted by the sparkle of gold. Leaving his sluice box behind, he headed for the highway, vowing never to enter a partnership again.

LABOR Day, 1935, Dave had the feeling Lady Luck was traveling on his shoulder. The weather was pleasant. Rides came easily. In Reno, Nevada, he put a quarter in a slot machine and won 14 dollars. Farther south in Bridgeport, California, a man in a Ford coupe offered to take him to Bishop, that was if Dave didn't mind waiting while he dropped off some packages at towns along the way.

The driver turned off Highway 395 near Casa Diablo Hot Springs and headed up a winding dirt road toward Mammoth Camp, the summer town Frank Cooper had once told Dave about. Ten minutes up the dirt road, the driver dropped Dave off near Mammoth Creek and told him to wait by the side of the road while he made his deliveries, just in case another ride came along.

Dave looked down the short street of the rustic town. A sign for

Mammoth Creek, Penney's Bakery, and Mammoth Mountain.

Penney's Bakery stirred his hunger. He sat on the bank, leaned his head against his pack, and gazed across a meadow to a rock outcropping that jutted out beneath the ridgeline.[27] The warmth of the afternoon sun, the gentle breeze, and the singsong of the creek made him smile. Thirty minutes passed without a single car passing. Dave didn't care. He'd never been here before, yet he was in no rush to leave. He loved this place. Everything about it. He felt as if he had come home.

BACK in the car descending from Mammoth Camp's 8,000-foot elevation to Bishop's 4,000-foot valley floor, taking in the panorama of the Eastern Sierra, Dave was well aware that a new and exciting era of his life was beginning. Once in Independence, Ben Boyd, a DWP employee who lived across the alley from Jim's Place with his wife and two children, offered Dave free lodging in his dirt-floored, single-car garage. Together, the men plumbed water, hooked into the sewer line, installed a washbasin, shower, and toilet, and built a wood floor six inches off the ground, creating Dave's own home sweet home. When college football scouts from Washington located him and renewed their scholarship offer, he wasn't even tempted to leave the Eastern Sierra. He already had too much going on in his new hometown.

With roller skates ordered from the Montgomery Ward catalog, Dave skated the cement sidewalk that looped in front of the Inyo County Courthouse. On Thanksgiving Day, he attended a Bishop High School football game. Hydrographer Vic Taylor invited him to join the Independence baseball team, but at the first practice, his high school shoulder injury flared up, ending his short-lived baseball career. Dave attended dances at the American Legion Hall and earned the name "twinkle toes," not because he knew the dances, but for the quickness of his feet when he jumped around to the music.

At Black Rock Springs, a fishing hole about eight miles north of town, Dave would wade through the shallow water and observe the fish darting among the weeds and watercress. With his delicate touch, he would cast his line, and easily catch his limit, which in the Sierra was "a weight of ten pounds and then one more fish." On a solo backpack trip over Kearsarge Pass, a mountain lion followed him for four days, never disturbing him, just watching from a distance, as if they were traveling companions.

To top off his new life in Independence, one of Dave's new friends, Bob Vinsant, a co-worker at Jim's Place, took him for a ride on his Harley Davidson. After one ride, Dave started saving money to purchase his own.

Settled in his garage home, Dave contacted his mother, who was then cooking for a wealthy family in Reno, and retrieved his .22 rifle that she had been storing since the family broke up. Word spread quickly that Dave McCoy could shoot ducks on the fly with his .22. The game warden claimed nobody could shoot that well and challenged Dave to prove it. At a pond outside of town, the two men scared a flock of ducks into the sky. When the fowl were out of shotgun range, the warden told Dave to shoot the lead bird. Dave raised his rifle, sighted, pulled the trigger, and the duck fell. Impressed, the game warden pursued the challenge. "Rumor has it you can shoot jackrabbits on the run." Dave smiled. They drove out toward the airport and stirred the sagebrush until one ran out. Dave sighted, pulled the trigger, and with a single shot, dropped the rabbit.

ONE Saturday afternoon, while Dave was working as a soda jerk at Jim's Place, a group of cheerleaders from Bishop Union High School stopped in. The girls moved through the room as if they owned the place, giggling and laughing on their way to a table just beyond the ice cream counter. Dave felt awkward and bashful around these girls, particularly the one with the long curly brown hair and the lively smile whom the others called Roma. Something about her captivated him. He served the girls their ice cream sundaes and then acted busy behind the counter, averting his eyes while listening to their chatter. Too soon, in the same flurry they had entered, the girls waved goodbye and bounced down the steps. Dave watched them drive away, letting the image of the brown-haired girl named Roma linger in his mind. He wondered if he would ever see her again.

CHAPTER TWO

Roma: A Bishop Girl

Roma, the little dancer.

I don't understand why people are afraid to dance. It couldn't be a question of shyness. Look at me. When I was little, I was so shy that sometimes I was afraid to talk. But dancing? When I was dancing, talking didn't matter.

I'll never forget seeing Judy Garland sing and dance on the stage at the Bishop Theater. She lived in Lancaster, about three hours south of Bishop, and her mother drove her here to perform. Since my father was the piano player at the theater, I got to go backstage and talk to her. I couldn't believe it. All she wanted was to be a normal girl who stayed home and walked to school every day like I did instead of having to travel from town to town as she was doing. All *I* wanted was to be like her, on stage, and dancing. But as a young girl from Bishop, I wasn't going to be traveling anywhere, at least not yet, so I took to creating my own stages.

I started in the orchards across from our house on Academy Street. I'd leap and twirl and jump over fallen apples and pears, waving my arms as if I were covered in long flowing scarves. Then there were the rock pillars in front of Elm Street School that Jeanne Crow and I used to climb so we could dance on top, confident we were charming our imaginary audience with our antics. Or I would skip down to Main Street and swing on the rope between the hitching posts in front of Black's Grocery Store, pointing my toes, kicking my legs, and singing my heart out into a stick, my pretend microphone. That was until I saw Grandma running down the sidewalk toward me. When I didn't arrive home with the milk and butter she'd sent me to pick up, she knew exactly where I was. She'd try to knock a little sense into me by waving a switch at my legs while we walked home. Talk about quick dancing feet. I called my steps, "Dodging the Switch." But really, I wasn't afraid. I knew Grandma wouldn't hit hard. She loved me too much. And she had good reasons for wanting me to behave.

My grandmother, Frances Marie Folk, was born in Texas, raised twelve children, and outlived three husbands! I'd say she was as strong as a Texas-born woman in the 1800s had to be. I mean, she sure didn't have anything handed down to her but hard work. To think that at one time, she moved her whole batch to Fort Smith, Arkansas. How she must have sweated and worried, pregnant all the time, trying to make ends meet, working the land to keep her family clothed and fed.

Grandma's youngest child was my mother, Lorena Folk, born in 1888. Somehow Lorena ended up in Bakersfield, California, and that's where my father, Marshall Carriere, courted her. Father was an artist and a musician. He'd migrated from Washington D.C. to Bakersfield, where he directed the Conservatory of Music and Fine Arts and started the Carriere School of Music. He taught everything from voice to piano and everyone called him Professor Carriere. I bet he loved that. As I was told, he raised $2,000 to purchase an organ for St. Paul's Episcopal Church in Bakersfield, and that organ is still played today.

Mother and Father married in Los Angeles in 1913. It wasn't Father's nature to lie, but he sure didn't tell my mother the whole truth about himself. Not until sometime after their wedding did Lorena learn that her husband was actually 22 years her senior. A 47-year-old man marrying a

25-year-old woman was crazy. I don't think Mother would have married Father if she'd known their age difference, much less that he'd been married before and had a previous family in Hamilton, Montana. But maybe the way he played that church organ would have charmed her even if she knew the whole story. Anyway, Mother wasn't truthful either. She didn't tell Father that her heart had been damaged by rheumatic fever. Secrets. They never do anyone any good.

REGARDLESS of their age difference, my parents made a lovely couple. Mother was tall, about 5-feet 10-inches. She had coal-black hair that curled around her fair-skinned face and framed her bright blue eyes. Father's hair was light brown, just like mine, and he stood as handsome as the sound of his name. On October 23, about a year after their wedding, Mother gave birth to my sister and named her Frances Marie after Grandma. By then, Father had grown restless in Bakersfield. He had a longing to live in the country where he could paint natural landscapes, so he up and moved the family, Grandma and all, to the little town of Bishop at the foot of the Eastern Sierra.

In Bishop, Father struggled to make ends meet. In the evenings, he played piano for the silent films at Bishop Theater. Everyone in town loved how his improvisations made the screen actors come alive. He also tuned pianos, gave music lessons on piano, guitar, and woodwinds, and composed music. Some of his compositions are still kept in the Laws Railroad Museum just outside of Bishop.[1] I don't know how he accomplished all he did, especially considering that he was half deaf.

One time when I was a little girl, Father had to tune a piano at somebody's house in the little village of June Lake, some 60 miles north of Bishop, and we all went with him. On a hillside just above the road on the far side of town, Mother spread a tablecloth. Just as she was setting out the picnic lunch, we heard the sound of galloping horses. We looked up to see wild Indians with war paint on their faces whooping and hollering and headed right for us. Mother yelled to my sister, "Frances, grab Roma. Run and hide!" Come to find out the gang was just a bunch of boys fooling around. I bet they had a good laugh watching my mother screaming and Frances dragging me down the hill.

Not long after our family moved to Bishop, the United States entered World War I. Father was too old to enlist, but Grandma told me we contributed to the war effort by planting a victory garden to grow food for the community. She said that President Woodrow Wilson promised this would be the last we would see of wars, but she didn't have much faith in that statement. Grandma never hesitated to say how things really were or to remind me that no matter what a person does to keep life good, bad things happen. Like in 1918, when the Spanish flu spread to Bishop.[2] Grandma told me that this was the most devastating disease in recorded history, even worse than the Black Plague. It killed millions of people all over the world. Even in Bishop, theaters, churches, and schools closed their doors, and people wore masks. Bishop High was converted into a makeshift hospital where Father, kind and generous man that he was, volunteered to care for the ill. Then he came down with that dreaded fever. I'm sure Mother was beside herself with fear of losing him. But he was one of the lucky ones. He lived.

The horrible flu pandemic lasted about a year. Then, about the time it ended, on the lovely day of May 12, 1919, my brother, Marshall Bence Carriere, was born. Marshall was a strong, healthy boy, but oh, my poor mother. She got pregnant again right away, lost that baby, and then got pregnant with me. When I arrived, on August 12, 1920, Mother had little strength left. Due to complications from her rheumatic heart condition, she almost lost her life delivering me. Afterward, she was so weak she could hardly get out of bed. What a nightmare for my father, having to work to put food on the table, worrying about Mother's health, and taking care of three children. So, my parents gave me to my grandmother, Frances Folk.

A 62-year-old woman taking in a wiggly infant was really something, but from the moment Grandma took me in her arms and carried me into her house, we were inseparable, even though my constant moving around drove her crazy. She'd say, "Child, could you please just sit still for a few minutes?" I would try to obey. I didn't want to be troublesome, but really, "Mischief" should have been my middle name.

One night when I was about three or four, Grandma arranged for a babysitter so she could go to a dance with a friend. Well, I had a cat fit. I was furious that she could even think of leaving me behind, so I decided I'd show her. I waited for the babysitter to go to sleep, then I tiptoed outside to the porch, climbed inside a trunk where we kept extra blankets, closed my eyes, and fell fast asleep.

When the babysitter awoke and couldn't find me, she panicked and ran downtown to find Grandma. Grandma called the police and then proceeded to get all of Bishop searching for me. By the time she came back to the house, I'd woken up, but I still didn't show myself. I listened to the ruckus being made about my whereabouts, and only when I felt sure Grandma had learned her lesson, did I peek out of the trunk. Was Grandma ever relieved. She picked me up and gave me the biggest hug ever. Then she turned me over and gave me an even bigger spanking. The trouble I must have caused her. But you know, Grandma never hired a babysitter again. Looking back, I feel so selfish. Grandma, on the other hand, was never selfish. Not ever. In a way, she gave her life to me.

Having two households didn't bother me at all. We only lived a block away from each other, so I could visit my family whenever I wanted, except for when Mother was resting. What with her weak heart, it was hard for her to be up and about for long, but then again, she was full of surprises. On the days she felt energetic, she'd fish the creek at Five Bridges Road near Chalk Bluff just north of Bishop. She loved to fish, and she was good at it. And, she loved to hold me on her lap and read stories to me, sort of like she was making up for lost moments. I think my brother and sister were jealous of me when I got so much of Mother's attention, but that's the way it was. They had her the rest of the time.

One of the benefits of having two households was that I could leave either one whenever I wanted, like the times Mother and Father argued about money. When they started in, I'd put my hands over my ears and run home. You know, Grandma and I didn't have much money either, but we didn't fight about it. We were happy with what we had. Our dirt yard might have made us look like we were poor, but we weren't.

Back to Father. Even though he had trouble making ends meet, I was always proud to be his daughter. He did have a temper, but fathers can be that way, really strict and still loving at the same time. I think musicians are probably the worst. They love everything about music, and they want

47

their children to follow in their footsteps and be musicians too. Father had so much hope for me. He tried to teach me piano, and he insisted I learn to read music. How boring. Why should I read music if I could play by ear? When he was explaining notes on the staff, I'd just look out the window. We'd struggle through a lesson, and then he'd rant and rave about how music was a grand art that required sacrifice. I couldn't sit still through his lecture. He'd finally get exasperated and tell me to go outside and waste my natural talent. I'd think, oh good. I couldn't wait to get away from that piano, out the front door, and into the fresh air.

Being outside was where I belonged. I helped Grandma tend our vegetable garden, and on summer days before the temperature got too hot, I'd follow her down the rows of vegetables, and she'd teach me how to nurture each plant. And then there was taking care of our cackling chickens. I enjoyed collecting eggs, and I didn't mind plucking feathers, but I wasn't going to be any part of the awful slaughter. Thank heavens Grandma didn't need my help. Coming from farm life in Texas and Arkansas, she knew precisely what to do.

I swear, my grandmother could do just about anything. She took in sewing and ironing to make money, *and* she sewed all our family's clothes. My classmates envied my outfits. On top of all that work, Grandma cooked dinner *every* night for about 15 miners. They lived in boarding houses in town but paid for a spot at our table.

I thought I was someone important to be the server, handing out the plates. I called my favorite miners our "star-boarders." Sometimes they gave me a dollar bill, and with that kind of money in my pocket, I could go horseback riding. I loved being around horses. I'd walk to the stables on Dixon Lane and then ride to Otey's Corner, the little market that used to be where West Line Street starts heading up Bishop Creek. In those days, there weren't many houses or cars, just cattle ranches, alfalfa fields, and fruit orchards. Usually I rode alone, but if anyone did ride with me, it was most often a boy. Boys were more fun than girls, mostly because they liked to play outside. Anyway, at Otey's, I'd buy my favorite soft drink, a Delaware Punch, and then ride home.

When I was about 12, one of our star-boarders gave me a horse, a palomino named Misty. My own horse! I rode bareback at first, but then another star-boarder gave me a saddle he wasn't using anymore. I'd throw that saddle over my shoulder and carry it out to a field off East Line Street where I pastured Misty. Then I'd ride her back to our house. If Grandma wasn't there, I'd lead her inside and feed her sugar cubes, just for fun—or maybe, just to do what I wasn't supposed to. Talk about being a brat.

I have to say, my life in Bishop was terrific. I had the run of the town with two houses, a dog, a horse, and a family that loved me. There was nothing to be sad about. Not until December 1933, a day I will always remember. I was 13 years old, sitting at my classroom desk when the principal walked in and called my name. At first, I wondered what I was in trouble for. Then he took me outside and told me my mother had passed away. Just like that.

I remember standing there on the sidewalk staring at his feet, refusing to believe his words. My mother couldn't be dead. She was only 45 years old. She'd gone to Bakersfield to visit a friend, I was sure. So why was I being swept away into this bad dream? My stomach hurt and I felt like I might get sick. If I could just hold on, *not* cry one tear, and *not* look up at the principal's eyes, I would wake up sitting on Mother's lap and she would be combing my hair.

I told the principal I had to get home to Grandma, but he told me she was helping Father take care of things, and that my sister Frances was on her way to get me. Then he said softly, "Roma, I'm sorry." That's when the principal's words hit me. Mother was gone, forever. All I would ever have of Lorena Carriere were a few photographs, my memories, and a deep, sad, empty space where she used to be. I started crying. No, I was sobbing.

I didn't know how the rest of my family was doing. Back then, I didn't think about their feelings, only mine and Grandma's, and I knew Grandma would be hurting straight through like a knife was cutting into her heart. I'd already seen her lose her son, Uncle Bence. He was a favorite relative of mine. He used to bring me candy, and we'd hide it quick so Grandma wouldn't know. She would have put a stop to such shenanigans right then and there, just like she did when she found out about Bence's whiskey still.

Whiskey. I hated to even think about that horrible stuff. Drinking had destroyed one of my older cousins, or so I heard. People said she ran around with men she didn't even know, and that she lied and stole from the family.

But Uncle Bence wasn't that way. He sold the whiskey; he didn't drink it. Anyway, one day Uncle Bence was sitting on our porch when he suddenly had a terrible asthma attack. Grandma started screaming, "Roma, help me get him inside. Pat his chest! Keep rubbing! Roma, don't stop!" Grandma and I both patted and rubbed, trying to get the life back in him, both of us weeping the entire time. But we couldn't save Uncle Bence. He died right there in front of us.

I don't think Grandma ever completely regained her happiness after losing a son and then her youngest daughter. As for me, I still had her, my closest friend, my foundation, my security. If she had been the one to die, my tears would have flooded the entire Owens Valley. I missed my mother, but without Grandma, I would have felt alone in this world.

Gradually, the memory of Mother's physical struggles faded, and I pictured her strong and full of energy, standing on the edge of Silver Lake, catching more trout than anyone around her, so happy to be there.

Then I have this other memory that still tears at my heart. We were taking a family drive out past the alfalfa fields north of Bishop, and Mother begged my father to stop the car so she could pick a bouquet of wild iris for me. Her heart was so weak she could barely get out the door. I thought she would give up, but no, not Mother. Father separated the barbed wire fence so she could crawl through, and then she made her way toward the meadow of blue, picked a few flowers, and started back toward the car. On the way, she stumbled into a small creek. Father ran to help. Me, I sat in the car, helpless. To this day, I can see her, my mother, lovely, determined Lorena Carriere, wet, tired, and muddy, carrying that bouquet of wild iris to me.

All the heartache that I stuffed down inside me when I lost Mother and Uncle Bence came flooding out when my horse, Misty, died. She was pregnant, due to deliver any time, and a lady who lived near the pasture noticed she had started to give birth but was having trouble. She called the vet and found me, but we were all too late. The foal had died inside Misty's belly. The vet tried to save Misty by cutting the dead foal in pieces until he got the entire body out, but Misty couldn't hold on. She lay on the ground and I leaned my head against her body, tears running down my cheeks as I felt the life go out of her. It took four men to pull me off and take me home. As far as I was concerned, nothing in the world was fair. I didn't ride for a long time after that.

I don't know why I'm thinking about all those sad times. I prefer to talk about the good things in my life, like going to our Christian Science church on Sundays with Grandma and spending time with my sister and brother. Frances was six years older than me. She reminded everyone of Mother, real tall with tumbling curls, and she sold tickets at the Bishop Theater just like Mother had done. Frances would let me sit in the booth with her and tear the tickets off. There I was, acting grown-up talking to the customers, sitting with the most glamorous girl in town. That's right. People called Frances the "Belle of Bishop."

Oh, I wanted to have curls like Frances did. We couldn't afford curlers, so I'd wet my hair and scrunch it with my fingers. I didn't dare use a brush or comb, because that would have straightened the curls out. Grandma got so frustrated with my tangled mess that she decided to help. Before going to bed, she'd tie strips of rags into my hair. I'd go to sleep so happy to know that in the morning, I would wake up with curls, just like Frances.

Now, my brother Marshall, he had the biggest, warmest personality you've ever met. Everybody loved him, especially me. I worked and worked to skip second grade so I could be in his class. One time I was staying in Reno with one of my aunts, and I heard Marshall was coming to see us. I got so excited that I ran down and sat in my uncle's car, waiting impatiently for Marshall to arrive. I couldn't keep still. Without thinking, I used the cigarette lighter to burn the end of each one of my toes, not much, just lightly. It didn't hurt but did my aunt ever raise a ruckus. She said that when Grandma heard about what I'd been up to, she'd never let me visit her again. I felt bad. I hadn't wanted to cause trouble. I just wanted to see my brother.

OF course, this is no surprise, but by the time I was a teenager, what I loved more than anything was to go to dances at Keough's Hot Springs just south of Bishop, or at the American Legion Hall in town. I don't mean to brag, but my dance card was always full, from the first dance to the last. Whether the band played a waltz or a foxtrot or a swing tune, as soon as I heard the music, my feet knew what to do. And if I got interested in a boy, well, my teenage romances hinged on only two things: the young man's dancing ability and Grandma's approval.

I insisted Grandma go with me to the dances. I couldn't bear the thought of her sitting at home alone while I was out having fun. She didn't care that there weren't other grandmothers for her to talk to because she liked to listen to the big bands and watch the dancers. And I'd watch her. If I caught her yawning, I knew it was time to go home.

Besides dancing, the other best part of high school was cheerleading. I loved to wear my blue long-sleeved letterman sweater with a big "B" on the back for Bishop Broncos and matching blue skirt that came down to my knees. I don't know how we jumped around in those uniforms when the weather was hot.

One day, on our way to cheer a football game in Lone Pine, a group of us stopped at a little restaurant in Independence to have an ice cream sundae. I had just turned 15, so it must have been the fall of 1935. We walked by the candy counter, sat at a table, and when I looked up to give my order, I kind of lost my breath. There, standing right in front of me, was the *most handsome* boy I'd ever seen. I guess I should say "*man.*" He was definitely older than me, probably about 20, and he looked like a movie star, all muscular and tanned with wavy brown hair.

My girlfriends flirted with him but didn't get much response. I thought he must be a quiet person, shy like me. Back in the car, I didn't say much to the other girls. I was preoccupied. That's when they started teasing me, "Roma's got a crush on the soda jerk."

I didn't reply. I was wondering if that boy knew how to dance.

CHAPTER THREE

Independence

Dave's Harley loaded with skis and poles, and a dragon painted on the front.

C hilly mornings, hot afternoons, and diminishing daylight defined
Dave McCoy's first autumn in Independence. When not working at Jim's Place, the 20-year-old could most often be found
speeding up and down Highway 395 on the back seat of Bob Vinsant's
motorcycle or hitchhiking to trailheads that led to the pristine lakes of the
High Sierra.

Dave enjoyed hiking by himself, uninterrupted by idle conversation or
careless footsteps. Alone, he could cover as much territory as he pleased
and spend as much time as he wanted tracking wildlife or tempting local
trout to bite his custom flies. He roamed through late-blooming rabbit-
brush that covered the high desert with the pungent scent of its yellow
flowers, climbed up canyons past the rushing water of cold alpine streams,
and crossed fields of gigantic boulders just to view the other side of a

ridge. Always scouting for deer migrating down from the high country to warmer winter grounds, Dave kept alert for rare sightings of bighorn sheep. He delighted in seeing the green leaves of willows, aspens, and cottonwoods transform to vibrant shades of yellow, orange, and red, and then twirl to the ground, stripping the trees to their naked bark, mulching the forest floor with a musty carpet of faded fall color. Occasional thundershowers darkened the Sierra skies, and Dave watched the sheets of gray precipitation move swiftly from one place to another as the squalls drifted over the Owens Valley. And, on each outing, he scanned the local topography looking for slopes to ski come winter.

Like the squirrels he'd seen scurrying up and down evergreen tree trunks stashing their winter food supply, Dave readied for the first snowfall by making a pair of skis. Starting with a block of ash, he applied what he'd learned in high school woodshop to shape the skis, finishing the tops with linseed oil and the bases with pine tar. He ordered bindings and bamboo poles from Montgomery Ward, and once all had arrived, he assembled his ski gear against the wall of his apartment and took a snapshot.

Vic Taylor and Sammy Griggs, two of Dave's hydrographer friends, followed his ski-making project with curiosity.[1] These experienced mountain men had never considered making their own skis even though DWP snow survey protocol mandated they strap a pair to their packs as an alternative to snowshoes. From the hydrographers' perspective, skiing was a form of transportation, not a recreational activity. By contrast, Dave was interested in skiing just because it was so much fun.

Dave felt sure that recreational skiers, like those he'd seen in the state of Washington, had discovered the Sierra Nevada. His intuition was correct. During the 1920s, European immigrants had skied slopes from Southern California to Donner Summit, from Yosemite's Ahwahnee Hotel to the Tahoe Tavern on the north side of Lake Tahoe. Wherever they found snow on an accessible slope, they built jumps, formed clubs, and organized competitions.[2] In 1929, California had even sent representatives to Lausanne, Switzerland, to submit a bid to host the 1932 Winter Olympics.

Ski Tracks
California and the Winter Olympics
1929

When the California delegation made its case in Lausanne, neither the International Olympic Committee (IOC) nor the National Ski Association (NSA) believed claims of California's heavy snowfall and high mountains.[3] In their minds, California was a land of semitropical fruits, year-round flowers, and sunny beaches. Therefore, they denied the bid. In response, on October 7, 1930, the California Winter Sports Committee held a meeting at San Francisco's Palace Hotel and formed the California Ski Association (CSA) to organize and promote California skiing.

AFTER a January 1936 storm covered the foothills of Independence in a blanket of snow, Dave asked Owen Cooper to drive him up Onion Valley Road to a slope near Grays Meadow so he could test his handmade skis.[4] Not much interested in skiing, but always ready to be amused, Owen agreed. With his girlfriend, Thelma, sitting by his side, Owen motored his car up the unplowed road. Dave sat in the back, looking out the window at the freshly fallen snow, filled with excitement about his first day of skiing in the Eastern Sierra.

In the warmth of the midday sun, Dave arranged his skis and poles on the snow and took a snapshot. He then attempted a few turns, but his skis refused to glide. To change direction, he had to make 180-degree jump turns. Puzzled, Dave took off a ski and found three inches of snow stuck to the base. He couldn't figure out why the snow was so sticky. He looked back to where Owen and Thelma sat perched on the fender of the car, giggling. Throwing his arms in the air, Dave let out a laugh, collected his gear, and rejoined his friends. They spent the afternoon throwing snowballs, taking pictures, and maneuvering Owen's car back to town, without getting stuck in the softening snow.

That evening, Dave grilled his friends, DWP employees Ben Boyd and Sammy Griggs, with questions about snow. The two explained that heat from the sun transforms fine crystals of cold powder snow into a wet mush that adheres to wood. Not even the mixture of pine tar and resin—which skiers had been applying to their wooden skis since the 1600s—could prevent snow with rounded molecules from sticking. It was no wonder, the friends agreed with a laugh, that early California miners had rubbed bear grease and bacon fat on their bases.

Dave, Ben, and Sammy brainstormed about ways to mechanically pull a skier uphill. Before long, the three friends were spending their after-work hours in the DWP machine shop, scheming over engines, pulleys, and ropes, working on what they called their "midnight project."[5] Applying mechanics similar to those used by skiers who in 1934 had built a rope tow on a hill in Woodstock, Vermont, the threesome created their version of an up-ski. They harnessed a differential from a discarded pickup truck, cut out an axle, capped it, turned it vertically, attached the driveshaft to the truck bed, and connected it to a rear wheel.

The trio drove the contraption to Grays Meadow and parked on the side of the road. From there, they carried a 600-foot rope to a spare car wheel they hung on a tree about 150 yards up-slope, looped the line back to the bottom, and spliced it. Next, they jacked up the frame of the truck, which caused a spring to push down and tighten a belt they had attached to two different-sized pulleys. The men set the throttle speed, started the engine, and the rope moved.

Elated, Dave stepped into his bindings, grabbed the rope as it sped by, and held on tight. In less than a minute, after having expended minimal effort, Dave was standing at the top of the tow. In pure delight, the three friends let out a spontaneous cheer. Their up-ski, believed to be the first ever used in the Eastern Sierra, was a success.

Dave pointed his skis downhill and made about six turns before reaching the bottom. His bases slid easily across the snow, partially due to the paraffin wax he had applied, but also, because a series of hot days and freezing nights had transformed the previously mushy snow into rough granules, creating a firm yet buttery surface known as "corn snow."

Grinning, Dave called out to Ben and Sammy to join him as he grabbed onto the rope and headed up for another run. Within a few hours, they skied more vertical feet and made more turns than Dave had made during the entire time he had skied in Washington. He joked with his friends, "At this rate, we might even learn how to do this sport."

By trial and error, using common sense and sheer muscle strength, Dave improved his skiing skills. He found if he kept his knees bent, he had an easier time pushing his long wooden skis through free-heel telemark turns, and if he held his ski poles forward—like the racers on Mt. Rainier had done—he felt stable no matter how fast his skis ran.

Residents of Independence soon heard about the fun skiers were having on their local slopes, and curious onlookers arrived to watch. The more ambitious borrowed equipment and gave the sport a try. Those hesitant to ski helped with potluck meals and the drying out of wet wool and denim. The mechanically minded, such as Dave, tinkered with their makeshift tows, experimented with various diameters of sisal ropes, and developed techniques to coil, carry, and uncoil ropes for efficient set-up and teardown. To prevent the ropes from twisting, the men weighted the pulleys with snow-filled burlap bags.

Before long, about 30 locals formed the Independence Ski Club, and ski outings became the highlight of their week. Eventually, they built a permanent tow in Grays Meadow, using telephone relays for safety switches, dry cell batteries for power, and a speed control unit to slow the rope down so that skiers could more easily grab hold. On February 14, 1936, the *Inyo Independent* reported that:

> *Doc Wolfe and several other Independence residents enjoyed snow sports Sunday at the saddle above Seven Pines [near Grays Meadow]. Ralph Bell and Bill Poole took several pictures of Dave McCoy ski jumping. McCoy has been making several jumps lately on courses above Seven Pines and also at Crestview [north of Mammoth]. At the latter place, he made a 65-foot jump.*

DAVE and his friends were unaware that their passion for skiing reflected a much larger movement in America. From skiing backyard rope tows to riding up-skis financed by wealthy businessmen, the sport was taking

Dave on McGee Mountain, ski jumping in his school sweater.

off nationwide. Outside Ketchum, Idaho, a sleepy sheep-ranching town in central Idaho, railroad magnate Averell Harriman of Union Pacific Railroad purchased 3,888 acres for $39,000 with the intent of building a destination ski resort he would call Sun Valley.[6] In the Northeast, thousands of skiers were packing into "snow trains" that carried them to the slopes.[7] In Tahoe City, a few hundred miles north of Independence, Bill Bechdolt built a 1,300-foot-long rope tow.[8] On the west side of the Sierra Nevada, Don Tresidder proclaimed Yosemite's Badger Pass "The Snow Capital of California," built his $32,000 Tyrolean Ski Lodge, and installed a tow in which skiers rode uphill sitting in a sled, rather than clinging to a wet rope. With these improvements, skier visits at Badger Pass tripled.[9]

Simultaneous to this surge in American ski area development, U.S. athletes were preparing to compete in the 1936 Winter Olympics, the first Olympics to include alpine skiing events, to be held in Garmisch-Partenkirchen, Germany. As Olympian Clarita Heath recalled:

> *My mother and I were living in Kitzbühel, Austria,*
> *that winter. This was unique in that not many people*
> *were traveling to Europe because of Hitler. Alice Wolfe,*

the U.S. women's team manager, invited me to try out for the team, and I made it. At the Olympics, to keep the sport from favoring the rich, officials required us to use the same pair of skis in both downhill and slalom. At the top of the downhill course, they stamped our skis to identify them. It was unnerving that during the glory of the Olympics, Hitler's chilling presence could be felt. In town, people were supposed to "Heil Hitler" when they walked by a shrine for unknown soldiers. Mother and I refused to Heil.[10]

Meanwhile, almost 6,000 miles and an ocean away from the Olympics, snowstorms hit the Eastern Sierra with a vengeance. Rain washed out the truck route south of Independence and caused the Los Angeles Aqueduct to overflow.[11] Up Big Pine Canyon, north of Independence, an avalanche crushed the historic Glacier Lodge cabins into kindling.[12] The state road department had trouble keeping Highway 395 open past Toms Place, just 25 miles north of Bishop. As a result, the few winter residents of Mammoth Camp, the tiny summer community nestled at the base of 11,053-foot Mt. Mammoth, and those of June Lake, a similar-sized village 20 miles farther north, depended on skis, snowshoes, and dog teams for transportation. When the storm systems at long last cleared, a panorama of brilliant skies and sparkling snow broke through. Skiers returned to the slopes as fast as they could dig out their cars.

By late March of that snowy winter, Dave had worked at Jim's Place for over six months and saved $300, enough money to purchase a motorcycle of his own. He folded the cash into his wallet, jumped on the back of Bob Vinsant's bike, and the two set off on a five-hour ride south to Riverside.[13] When they returned home, they were each riding their own Harley, sitting tall with their backs held straight, and their heads held high. They pulled in front of Jim's Place and revved their engines until everyone inside the restaurant came out to applaud.

Dave treasured the freedom of owning a motorcycle. He painted a fire-breathing dragon on the front windshield, rigged a side-rack that could carry two pairs of skis, poles, and fishing gear, and then offered to give any willing passenger a ride. When a waitress at Jim's Place returned from her lunch break with her hair a tangled mess and her cheeks flushed, there was no doubt she'd been riding on the back of Dave's Harley.[14]

Mostly, Dave and Bob rode together. They covered hundreds of miles, sometimes riding to Reno and back, and then continuing south to Bakersfield before returning home again. According to Vinsant:

> *Dave and I sealed our friendship riding side-by-side*
> *as often and as fast as we could. I considered him a*
> *true friend. He was quiet, didn't pay much attention to*
> *girls, didn't cuss, and never touched any liquor or cig-*
> *arettes. He was easy to be around, and the only thing*
> *that seemed to bother him was my drinking. He never*
> *said anything to me about it. I could just tell.*[15]

IN April, DWP hydrographers Vic Taylor and Ed Parker invited Dave to join them on their three-day Mammoth Lakes snow survey. Dave jumped at the opportunity to gain firsthand experience taking snow samples. The three men left Independence in the City truck—the "City" was a local reference to DWP—and drove north to Mammoth Camp. Just past an open meadow known as Windy Flats, Vic pulled the truck to a stop at Tex and Ruth Cushions' Winter Patrol Station, where the men would stay during their snow survey. This two-room cabin—one room for sleeping quarters, the other for cooking and dining—was called "Mammoth Dog Team, Freight and Passenger Service" and also served as the Cushions' home.[16]

As the barks and howls of the official welcoming committee settled down, the men heard a car engine running behind the Cushion's cabin. There they found Tex and several other skiers riding an automobile-powered rope tow up a snow-covered slope.[17] Just as Dave had thought, not only were recreational skiers enjoying the Eastern Sierra, but this group was even using an innovative up-ski.

The up-ski was a creation of Tex's friend, Jack Northrop, an accomplished aeronautical engineer from Southern California. The preceding weekend on this very slope, Northrop had gotten frustrated that he spent more time walking uphill than skiing down. He'd gone home to Santa Monica, crafted a way to transform his automobile into an up-ski, assembled the necessary components, and the next weekend drove back to Tex's.

Shortly before Dave and his buddies arrived, Northrop had backed his car up to the bottom of a slope behind Tex's cabin.[18] By fate, by chance, or just by the blessing of a patron saint of skiers—Ullr, Skadi, or perhaps St. Bernard of Montjoux—Dave McCoy and his friends witnessed the "grand opening" of Jack Northrop's automobile rope tow, the first up-ski ever used in the Mammoth Lakes region.

AMONG those skiing at the Winter Patrol Station that day were Dr. H.F. Rey and his family, who had learned to ski in their native Switzerland before emigrating to Ventura, California. Since 1927, the Reys had been spending their Easter week vacations taking ski trips to Mammoth Lakes. Using their long wooden skis, they sometimes toured the Windy Flats meadow and other times followed the snow-covered road up to the Lakes Basin. On Easter Sunday, their tradition was to climb the mountain they called Mt. Mammoth, purely for the fun of skiing back down. "Gold mine!" thought Dave. "The Reys were genuine Eastern Sierra recreational skiers!"

Dr. Rey told Dave that only once in his ten years of skiing Mammoth had he encountered other skiers. Tex confirmed that he, too, had only seen a few skiers in the region. Among them were Will Vaughn, president of Southern California's Big Pines Ski Club, and his son, who in 1934 were skiing Mt. Mammoth. Having already skied most of the organized ski runs in the Western United States, Vaughn told Tex that the slopes of Mt. Mammoth could not be excelled. He then met with the Bishop Rotary and suggested they start a ski club. Skiing was becoming so popular, Vaughn told the Rotarians, that in only a few years, his Big Pines Ski Club had grown from a handful of members to a thousand.[19]

During the snow surveyors' three-day-stay at the Winter Patrol Station, Tex and Ruth Cushion amused Dave with their rough-yet-irresistible charm. While Ruth towered over Tex's stout, muscular build, his dashingly handsome features, flirtatious smile, and free-spirited personality more than compensated for his height. Part of Ruth's charm was her reputation for waving her cast iron skillet in the air to let female guests know that *she* ruled the roost, the Winter Patrol Station was *her* household, and Tex was *her* man.

Tex and Ruth had come to the region as winter caretakers of the Mammoth Camp Hotel, where they initially hosted the Reys on their spring ski trips. When a movie-making crew wanted to leave its dog team in Mammoth Camp, Dr. Rey financed Tex's purchase of the canines. In this way, Tex and his dog teams became the region's primary source of winter transportation and communication. After the hotel burned down in the late 1920s, Dr. Rey purchased a summer cabin with six lots, and Tex constructed the Winter Patrol Station on a nearby piece of land. Dr. Rey also gifted Tex a set of ski equipment and instructed him on the basics of skiing. Thus, Tex became the local ski expert.[20]

Anxious to try out Northrop's tow, Dave, Vic, and Ed fetched their ski gear from the City truck and joined the others. They each took turns sitting in the driver's seat as designated rope-tow operators, invariably trying to jerk the other skiers off the tow by stepping on the gas and then slamming on the brake. Northrop didn't seem to mind potential damage to his differential. As long as he could ski down without having to climb up, he was happy. However, on the way home that afternoon, his active engineer's mind was already building an even better up-ski.

The next morning, Dave and his friends rose early, devoured stacks of Ruth's sourdough pancakes, packed sandwiches for lunch, and attached seal skins to the bottoms of their skis for uphill travel. Tex and his favorite dog, Como, accompanied the group. The men took turns breaking trail to the snow course near Mammoth Pass while Como romped and frolicked in the snow, running back and forth among them. For the first time, Dave saw the still-frozen lakes—Mary, Mamie, Horseshoe, and McLeod—the rock outcrop of Crystal Crag, and the open slopes on the south side of Mt. Mammoth, and he made note of these landmarks.

The snow courses were permanent sites that represented snowpack conditions at a given elevation in a given area. Years before, Vic Taylor had identified the 1,000-foot intervals used as courses in the Mammoth area.[21] Every 50 feet along each course, the surveyors used the Mt. Rose snow sampler to extract and weigh snow samples before calculating water content.[22]

Tex's Winter Patrol Station.

The following day, the men drove the City truck up the unpaved Minaret Road—which in the summer wound past the north side of Mt. Mammoth down to Reds Meadow and Devils Postpile—toward the second Mammoth course.[23] Vic parked the truck at the snowline, and the men broke trail uphill. When the ridgeline of the Minarets, Mt. Ritter, and Banner Peak came into view, they paused to admire the grandeur. Dave commented that these mountains resembled photographs he'd seen of the European Alps. He listened as Ed and Vic pointed out peaks and ridgetops that had been scaled by climbers, but his gaze kept returning to the view of Mt. Mammoth's north side. To Dave, the wide-open spaces of skiable terrain held more intrigue than mountaineering feats.

On day three of their snow survey, Vic, Ed, and Dave took snow samples on an easy-to-reach course just below the Lakes Basin. This course was near an 1880s mining site and stamp mill that had once been used for crushing ore. By midafternoon, the men were in the City truck bouncing down Highway 395 to Independence. Dave listened while Vic and Ed discussed their plans for stockpiling food, firewood, and whiskey in the high-elevation cabins used on overnight surveys. He noticed they mentioned three courses in Rock Creek Canyon above Toms Place, three in

Big Pine Canyon just north of Independence, and three in Cottonwood Canyon, just south of Mt. Whitney.

South of Bishop, the conversation lulled, and Dave reflected on how much he had enjoyed the trip. He felt peaceful after having been in the winter wilderness, yet invigorated by the exertion, inspired by potential slopes to ski, and pleased over his blossoming friendships. Taking snow samples hadn't been difficult, although Dave recognized that beyond the mechanics of the work, a snow surveyor needed to be sensible, cautious, and always use good judgment concerning the weather, terrain, and snow conditions. Dave trusted his intuition, yet he knew he had a lot to learn about the mountains, both in winter and summer. But that wasn't a problem. There was nothing else he would rather be doing than putting his time and energy into gaining the necessary education.

Dave rested his head against the seat. His mind drifted back to Tex Cushion's farewell words, "See you in a week!" Tex and the Reys had invited him to join their upcoming Easter Sunday ski ascent of Mt. Mammoth.

APRIL 11, the Saturday before Easter, Dave pulled on his leather boots, strapped his skis, poles, and rucksack to his motorcycle rack, and rode from Independence to Mammoth Camp. Nearing the Winter Patrol Station, his Harley engine echoed through the silence of Windy Flats and aroused the sleeping dogs.

Over dinner that evening, Tex dominated the conversation with stories about recent adventures of Dr. Walter Mosauer and Robert Brinton, two men who played leading roles in the Ski Mountaineers—a branch of the Sierra Club.[24] After conquering Mt. Dunderberg above Conway Summit, Mosauer and Brinton had hired Tex and his dog team to pack them into a cabin in the Lakes Basin. From there, they attempted a ski ascent of Mt. Mammoth. Just 300 feet beneath the summit, high winds and stormy weather forced them to abort the trip. Undaunted, they awoke the next morning to bright blue skies and prepared to try again. This time, the pair summited, celebrating their conquest with an exhilarating descent on wind-packed snow. Tex wrapped up his storytelling by shooting a grin over at Dave and saying, "Believe me, young man, if the slopes are still wind-packed tomorrow, you're in for a thrill! That kind of snow makes you feel like a ski champion."

EASTER Sunday, just as daylight peeked through the evergreens, the Rey family and friends followed a summer trail up the south side of Mt. Mammoth. Besides Dave, among the group was Norwegian ski-jumper John Elvrum, an early promoter of Southern California skiing who would eventually build a ski area called Snow Valley in Running Springs near Big Bear Lake. Under brilliant skies, with only a slight breeze blowing and the air temperature neither too hot nor too cold, they carried their skis on their shoulders as they climbed, breathing in rhythm to the crunch of snow beneath their boots. Sweat glistened on their foreheads, then quickly evaporated in the dry air. Once on top of the mountain, they each signed the worn Sierra Club booklet they found tucked away in a rock cairn.[25] Dave took a snapshot of his skis and poles leaning against the rocks, and then joined the others basking in the sun, eating sack lunches, and enjoying a 360-degree view of the Eastern Sierra and the Long Valley caldera.

When the time came to descend, Dave strapped on his skis and poled near the edge of the cornice. He gazed across Long Valley to the White and the Glass Mountain ranges. Turning his focus inward, he breathed deeply, trying to let go of anxiety about the drop-off below him. Only one way down, he told himself, and this was it. He leaned into his poles and launched his body over the edge and into the rush of weightlessness. Seconds later, he bent his knees to absorb the landing, checked his speed with a sweeping turn on the wind-packed snow, and then continued down the thousand-foot-long-slope. Just as Tex had foretold, Dave felt like a champion. At the tree line, he stopped, breathless, looked back up at his tracks, the blue sky, and his friends, and let out his rendition of a joyful yodel.

From that day on, as often as possible, Dave would ski the slopes of Mt. Mammoth—which would come to be known as "Mammoth Mountain."

As the Owens Valley awakened from winter dormancy, a scattering of rainstorms welcomed Dave to his first spring in the Eastern Sierra. Blades of grass and swollen buds reached up to the sun. Leaves sprouted from the slumbering branches of deciduous trees, and the pinkish flowers of desert peach, a wild shrub in the rose family, blossomed amidst the sagebrush.

The land vibrated with the joy of rebirth. Mule deer and their fawns crossed the highway on their journey from the valley floor to the high-country meadows. Heifers, mares, and ewes grazed in the valley's verdant pastures, knowingly tracking which newborn calf, foal, or lamb was their offspring. Amid weathered barns, nanny goats romped playfully with their curious four-legged kids, and sows rested against the fences of their pens, nursing the hungry little piglets that nuzzled up to them.

In the valley towns, purple lilacs saturated the air with their fragrance while softly scented wisteria blooms hung from vines that tangled across rickety wooden porches. Friends greeted one another on evening strolls and admired the pastel blossoms of fruit trees, sharing their hope that the last freeze had come and gone, and they would realize a plentiful crop of apricots and cherries.

At the higher elevations, snowfields clung to the Sierra peaks even as the snowline receded. Ice cold snowmelt trickled, then rumbled, under snow bridges, gaining in volume as it joined the spring runoff that would ensure water for wildlife, summer crops, orchards, wells, and of course, Los Angeles. Dave McCoy discovered that spring in the Eastern Sierra allowed him to do everything he most loved—ride his Harley, ski, and fish—all in one day.

Wanting to take a trip to visit his relatives in early summer, Dave gave fair notice to the owners of Jim's Place, packed his rucksack, tied his fishing gear to his motorcycle, and headed north, planning to seek new employment when he returned home. First stop, Reno. Dave took Edna for a spin on his motorcycle, and she squealed with joy the entire ride. How great to hear his mother's laughter! He savored a few of her home-cooked meals and showed her the scrapbook of photos he had taken. Then, ever restless, he bade farewell and rode on to South Prairie, Washington, where his grandparents had relocated when the Wilkeson Coal Mine shut down.

Relieved to find Granny and Grandpa Cox content and happy, longing for them to understand his love for the Eastern Sierra, a region they had never seen, Dave described his adventures in detail as he shared his photo album. After a few days of helping them with odds and ends around the house, he revved his Harley, waved goodbye, and set off for Enumclaw to visit his high school fishing and skiing buddy, Milt Allen.

That same weekend the famous ski pioneer, Otto Lang, was giving a skiing demonstration at White Pass.[26] Dave invited Milt to ride with him to watch. Milt jumped on the back of Dave's bike with gusto, but soon was clinging to his friend's leather jacket, hanging on for dear life:

> *We were flying down those winding roads, leaning through the turns. Dave couldn't stop talking about how Otto Lang had jammed his poles into the snow, did a complete flip, and without missing a beat continued down the hill. I hardly noticed the skiing because I was too busy dreading the ride home.*[27]

After delivering Milt safely back to Enumclaw, Dave rode on to Canada, just to cross the northern border of the United States, then turned around and headed south. By instinct and mood, he mapped his way through Washington, Oregon, and California, sometimes choosing to speed through the flatlands and fertile valleys, other times winding along the coastal cliffs, breathing in the Pacific Ocean salt air. In San Diego, he picked up Joe Logan—his friend from Buckley High, who had just completed U.S. military boot camp—and together, they rode to Tijuana, Mexico, just to cross the southern border.

BACK in the Eastern Sierra, with only three months left to fulfill the one-year California residency required to become a Department of Water and Power hydrographer, Dave submitted a job application to DWP so that his name would be on the list of candidates for employment. Meanwhile, he scanned the help-wanted ads of the *Inyo Independent* and saw that Lone Pine High School was looking for someone to sand the new gymnasium floor. Dave bid the job, won the contract, purchased a sander, strapped it to his motorcycle, and went to work. After finishing the gym floor, he completed a sanding job for a new restaurant in Olancha, and then one for a rest home in Lone Pine, all the while keeping his eyes open for other opportunities. Although Dave liked working as an independent contractor, sanding floors didn't hold long-term appeal.

On July 3, 1936, the *Inyo Independent* headlined that President Franklin D. Roosevelt's Works Progress Administration had designated $324,000 for DWP to spend on Owens Valley jobs. Work would start immediately for more than two hundred men. Dave applied. Within a week, DWP assigned him to a crew resurfacing two miles of the Los Angeles Aqueduct between Olancha and the Haiwee Reservoir Power Plant, east of Highway 395, south of Independence and Lone Pine.

On the first day of the job, Dave's foreman asked if anyone could assemble a pontoon raft using the construction materials laid out on the ground before them. Dave took one look at the supplies and raised his hand. This raft would be much easier to build than those he had put together on fishing excursions in Washington. Despite being the youngest guy on the job, Dave found himself in a leadership position. His boss—who called him "that crazy kid on a motorcycle"—took to leaving gasoline cans at the job site with the casual mention that the fuel would work fine in a Harley. In return, Dave would arrive at the job site Friday mornings with fresh trout for his supervisors to take home to their families.

The job assignment for Dave's crew was to remove cement that was peeling off the aqueduct walls, then build forms, and pour fresh cement. The men divided the task into three sections. First, working off the pontoon rafts, they restored the upper-level cement. Next, DWP diverted the water while Dave's crew refurbished the lower level. The final leg of the job, chipping out the abutment that rose above the aqueduct, turned out to be the most difficult. Working in pairs while standing on the aqueduct's edge, one man would swing a sledgehammer against a piece of steel held by the other, trying to knock the old cement off the aqueduct walls.

Dave's partner was hesitant, afraid of accidently hitting Dave with the sledgehammer. After a few weak and inaccurate swings, he failed to dent the cement. Dave asked him to wait a minute while he strapped on his leather motorcycle helmet—the kind that airplane pilots then wore, with a circle of sheepskin covering the ears—and told him, "I'm protected now, so you can swing harder." His partner took a deep breath and let loose with full force, landing his swing on the side of Dave's head. Dave fell to the ground, unconscious. A few minutes later, he slowly stood up and looked around in a haze. Once he figured out where he was and what had happened, he calmed his partner down with the promise that he was still alive, picked up the sledgehammer, and said, "Okay, let's switch positions and get back to work."

THROUGH the summer of 1936, while Dave was swinging sledgehammers in the desert heat, American teenagers were swing dancing to Count Basie, Duke Ellington, and Benny Goodman. National polls indicated that President Roosevelt—who would eventually serve four terms as president, the longest tenure in American history—had a chance to be reelected for his second term. Overseas, the Spanish Civil War had broken out just as American athletes were making their mark at the 1936 Summer Olympics in Berlin, Germany. Jesse Owens "single-handedly crushed Hitler's myth of Aryan supremacy" by winning four gold medals in track and field.[28] And the eight-man American crew team stroked to victory in the rowing regatta, leaving the German crew in their wake and Hitler outraged.[29]

That same summer, Averell Harriman installed the world's first chairlift—an innovative up-ski with wooden chairs hanging from an overhead cable—at Sun Valley. More tourism and automobile traffic inundated California's Eastern Sierra than the region had ever before experienced. Pack stations ran out of horses and mules to supply the record number of deer hunters heading to the high country. Visitors to the Mammoth region complained about the noise from steam shovels, drills, and dynamite blasts resounding from the grading of a more direct route between Highway 395 and the Mammoth Lakes Basin.[30] The new 30-foot-wide road completely bypassed the existing community of Mammoth Camp, which from then on would be known as "Old Mammoth."

As "new" Mammoth's first entrepreneurs, Frank and Norah-Bob "Ma" Penney closed Penney's Bakery in Old Mammoth and built Penney's Tavern, a hostelry, restaurant, and bar, at the intersection of the new asphalt highway and the dirt road to Old Mammoth.[31] The state made only minimal provisions to keep Main Street open in the winter, and no arrangements to keep the Lake Mary Road open. Why should they? There were no winter services in the Lakes Basin, and the road passed under a dangerous avalanche path off the south side of Mammoth Mountain.

THE first item on the agenda for Independence Ski Club's fall 1936 meeting was a presentation by pharmacist George Deibert, owner of Bishop Drug Store. Known as "Mr. Bishop" for his leadership of the Rotary Club and American Legion, Deibert got straight to the point. "The Eastern Sierra has been napping in regard to the potential of winter tourism. The state estimates that over one million people will experience snow sports in California this winter, so the time to wake up is now!"[32] To that end, Deibert had organized the Eastern Sierra Ski Club (ESSC). Headquartered in Bishop, officers would represent the entire Eastern Sierra ski community, from Lone Pine to Bridgeport.[33] Deibert asked, "Would the Independence Ski Club like to join?" Club members applauded Deibert's forward-thinking and elected a representative to attend ESSC's first meeting.

Deibert waited for the room to quiet before delivering his most exciting news. A permanent ski tow, the first in the Eastern Sierra, would be built on Long Valley's 10,886-foot-high McGee Mountain, across Highway 395 from Peter Steffen's fox farm.[34] This site had excellent ski terrain, wide-open treeless slopes, held snow for most of the winter, and was easily accessible by automobile. Designed by engineer Jack Northrop, Tex Cushion would manage the up-ski and Cortlandt "Corty" T. Hill, another of Northrop's friends, would finance the project.

Minnesota-born Corty Hill *loved* to ski. As a grandson to James J. Hill, the famed Canadian-American founder of the Great Northern Railroad, Corty and his siblings had learned the sport in the early 1930s under the tutorship of Hannes Schneider and his legendary Arlberg Ski School in St. Anton, Austria. Now living in Southern California, Corty longed to be involved in the ski world. As an heir to the Hill family fortune, he had discretionary income to invest. Financing a ski area in his adopted state where the mountains reminded him of the Austrian Alps offered the ideal business opportunity.

UNDER the guidance and support of Corty Hill, George Deibert and the ESSC planned on holding a grand opening for the up-ski as soon as snow arrived. In December, without a trace of snow on McGee Mountain, the *Inyo Register* reported:

*One ski course has been laid out in Long Valley, and the
highway has been widened, providing parking for 200
to 300 cars. Material is ordered for the funicular.[35] It
is going to extend 2,500 feet up the hill with plans for
a toboggan course as well as one for slalom and downhill skiing. A work party will be held next Saturday,
December 6, at Long Valley. All are welcome and urged
to bring a pick, shovel, or mattock, and lunch. There
will be some extra tools and plenty of work.*

DUE to the lack of snow, Dave invited Bob Vinsant to ride to Reno and
spend Christmas with him at his mother's house. Bob accepted the invitation. On a warm spring-like day, the young men raced their motorcycles
north on Highway 395, stopping briefly at McGee to view progress on the
up-ski. Dave and Bob parked their bikes, walked up the slope to where the
towers had been set, and tried to imagine the lift in operation.[36]

Walking back down through the dry sagebrush to their motorcycles,
Dave commented on Jack Northrop's ingenuity. "An overhead cable with
slings around the waist," he said. "What a great idea!" The friends hopped
on their bikes and resumed their journey north. In Reno, Edna welcomed
them with a hug and a holiday presentation of her delicious food.

When Old Man Winter finally arrived on Christmas Eve, massive
storms blasted across the Western United States. Cars skidded into each
other, slid off highways, and got stuck in a mess. In Reno, Dave and Bob
watched the snow pile up on their motorcycle seats while they waited
for the storm to subside and the roads to reopen. Fortunately, they had
brought along their leather jackets, pants, and gloves. They purchased tire
chains and hoped their Harley windshields would shelter them from the
cold. On the way home, they found the road through Walker Canyon
too slick and treacherous to continue. Agreeing their lives were more
important than their pocketbooks, they drove back to the first motel with
a vacancy sign, pooled their last bit of cash, and took a room for the night.

The next day, Dave and Bob waited for the sun to soften the ice and
warm the roadway before they headed south. Curious about how the new
sling-lift had survived the storm, they again stopped at McGee. With

head high snowbanks now lining the road, they had to stand on the seats of their motorcycles to look over. All they could see was a carpet of snow with the tops of several towers peeking through.

THE Grand Opening of the McGee up-ski took place on Saturday, January 16, 1937. Automobiles crammed the parking area. Some people came to ski, others just to join the fun. The Cushions invited their friends, Nan and Max Zischank, to assist them as opening day hosts. While Tex and Max operated the lift, Ruth and Nan sold hot dogs. Hazel Steffen walked over from her fox farm with sandwiches and drinks to sell to the crowd. Having driven from Los Angeles, Corty Hill and his wife Blanche coached beginners in the intricacies of the snowplow and stem turns.[37]

Down the road about a half-mile south, Dorrance Keough welcomed skiers to her McGee Creek Lodge, the only nearby foodservice and lodging. Initially built in 1929 for summer guests, the lodge had not been winterized, yet Dorrance created an inviting après-ski ambiance with a full-service bar, restaurant, eight upstairs rooms for rent, and a hot fire crackling away in the rock fireplace.

Though the McGee sling-lift proved to be temperamental, working together, Tex, Max, Corty, and Dave trouble-shot the problems and kept it operating. According to Corty:

> *This was the beginning of my lifelong friendship with Dave. He showed up at the original tow on his motorcycle to ski, but whenever the tow broke down, he was there right away to help. It would be storming, and while everyone else would go have a cup of coffee, a few of us would stay out and get the lift running. Dave just wouldn't quit. He was indefatigable.*[38]

FORTY skiers from Lone Pine to Bridgeport, including Dave McCoy and Bob Vinsant—who, naturally, arrived by motorcycle—drove to Bishop to attend ESSC's February 1937 meeting. The camaraderie and enthusiasm of attendees reflected how ski club activities had become the social gathering for locals, even those who didn't have the remotest interest in skiing.

Fun-loving Bill Whorff hosted the meeting at his Kittie Lee Inn.[39] From the club's inception, he had taken a leading role in ESSC activities. Besides dedicating an entire area of his Inn as a club wax room, complete with tar-papered walls and wooden waxing tables, Whorff loved ski adventures. When the snowbanks at McGee were high enough, he and his friends, ESSC members Chet Janes and Dr. "Scotty" Scott, would climb to the two pine trees high up on the slope, schuss straight down, and jump over Highway 395.[40]

At the meeting, Corty proposed that ESSC sponsor a springtime ski race. With a smile, he added, "What better way to celebrate the first winter of our sling-lift than to organize the first ski races ever held in the Eastern Sierra? We could call the event the Inyo-Mono Championships!" Club members voted unanimously in favor of Corty's idea. They set a date for April 11 and formed committees to organize volunteer referees, starters, timekeepers, scorers, and flag-keepers. During the ensuing weeks, members located a sound system and gathered stopwatches, clipboards, paper, and tables. They collected willows to use as slalom poles, sewed triangular flags of red, yellow, and blue to tie to the poles, painted start and finish banners, and ordered trophies for various classes of the competition. Event patrons Corty Hill, George Deibert, and Mono Inn's Venita McPherson donated perpetual trophies.[41]

EARLY February, another monster storm hammered the Eastern Sierra. All roads north of Bishop closed. Nine feet of snow buried Carson City, Nevada. Reno endured winds of over 60 miles per hour.[42] In the lower elevations of Owens Valley, torrential rain turned streets into rivers and vacant lots into lakes.[43] And then a cold spell hit. Pipes froze. Three inches of ice covered the sidewalks, and City crews had to dynamite the iced-over Los Angeles Aqueduct to keep the water flowing.[44]

Once the skies cleared, Tex mushed his dog team from Old Mammoth to McGee. There he found avalanche debris spread across the slope and one tower of the sling-lift knocked out of place. It would take him until the middle of March to have the lift running again. Meanwhile, he encouraged club members to climb the slopes and enjoy the fresh powder.[45]

Due to the storms, DWP's snow surveys took longer than usual.

Hydrographer Vic Taylor suggested to his supervisor, George Lewis, that the City hire someone with better skiing skills, and Vic added, he knew the right man for the job: Dave McCoy. Still working on the WPA project at that time, on weekdays, Dave was building settling basins for streams that flowed into the L.A. Aqueduct between Shepherd Creek and Independence Creek. On weekends, he skied. Vic encouraged George to drive to Seven Pines, a popular ski hill just above Grays Meadow, to judge Dave's skiing skills for himself. He assured George that Dave wouldn't be hard to recognize. He would be the tanned one, skiing without a shirt, wearing a bandana tied around his head, and more than likely soaring off the jumps he'd built.[46]

That Sunday evening, George was at the drugstore when Dave stopped in to pick up some pictures he'd had developed. Known for a lack of formality, George approached Dave and said, "Young man, when you show up for work tomorrow morning, you better be wearing a shirt." Dave stood in shock as George walked out of the drug store without saying another word. Just like that, Dave's dream of working for the DWP came true.

Early the next morning, Dave walked into DWP headquarters in Independence dressed in a clean shirt and jeans. He greeted his new boss with enthusiasm, "Good morning, sir!" George slid three sheets of unmarked graph paper across the table, each with the name of a different creek written across the top:

> Go to the clock stations at these streams, replace the completed sheets of graph paper with these. Then bring me the papers you retrieve. They're our record of last week's water flow fluctuation. This might be more than a full day's work, but we need to get the job done. You know where these creeks are, son?

Dave nodded, and the conversation ended without any small talk. Around one o'clock that afternoon, Dave returned to the office. George asked, "What's the matter, couldn't you find the clock stations?"

Dave pushed three pieces of recorded graph paper across the desk, just as George had done that morning with the blank sheets. "No, sir. I found them just fine. Here are last week's sheets."

George tried to hide his smile before looking up. "Well, you might as well go home for the rest of the day," he muttered with as much gruffness as he could muster. "Just be sure to arrive on time tomorrow." As Dave walked out of the office, he couldn't stop grinning. He liked his job, and he liked George Lewis. Little did he know that this man would become his chief supervisor and, in a sense, his father figure, for the next 16 years.

ALTHOUGH DWP assigned Dave the duties of a hydrographer, they hired him as a laborer at the wage of $135 per month. Dave didn't mind the discrepancy in his pay. He knew the figures would be reconciled once he became officially classified as a DWP hydrographer. Therefore, he ordered a hydraulic engineering course from International Correspondence Schools (ICS) and began to study for the civil service exam.

Dave felt fortunate that he was getting paid to spend his time in the places he loved to be. Doing everything from repairing broken skis to shoveling snow, monitoring clock stations at Bairs, Shepherd, Oak, and Independence creeks, and traveling into the mountains on snow surveys, he saw that a hydrographer's work demanded creative thinking and the ability to handle unforeseen situations. As he learned to read terrain, snow conditions, avalanche indicators, creek crossings, snow bridges, and wind and weather patterns, he became keenly aware of the ever-changing dangers of snow and ice—some universal, others unique to time and place.

Meeting the challenges of his new job head-on, Dave heeded his intuitive voice of caution and safety. He respected how his boss took precautions to protect his employees. For instance, George Lewis considered metal edges an unsafe novelty and mandated that snow survey skis could not have them. He forbade solo overnight surveys, insisting that two or three hydrographers back each other up in their decision-making about which route to travel and when to lie low in the surveyor cabins waiting for a storm to pass or a snowfield to settle.

APRIL 11, 1937, dawned with blue skies and a gentle breeze, ideal weather for the inaugural Inyo-Mono Championships. By 9 a.m., 400 automobiles had filled the parking area at the bottom of McGee Mountain. Spectators, volunteers, and 75 competitors—including Hollywood celebrities Claudette Colbert and her husband, Joel Pressman—swarmed the staging area. Hazel Steffen set out her assortment of sandwiches to sell, and Dorrance Keough once again opened her McGee Creek Lodge for après-ski gatherings. Earlier that morning, Corty Hill had set a three-quarters of a mile-long slalom course. Now, the bright red, yellow, and blue flags sewn by ESSC club members were tied to each gate, waving in the sun, adding color to an already festive scene.

Riding his motorcycle from Independence, Dave felt strong, limber, and primed with the competitive spirit. The Inyo-Mono Championships would be his first ski race. Inspired by his memories of America's star skier Dick Durrance and Austrian ski champion Hannes Schroll racing down Mt. Rainier, Dave was ready to give his best. But unexpectedly, as soon as the race course came into view, doubt sabotaged his confidence. Dave caught himself. He recalled Hannes Schroll yodeling to the finish as he won the Silver Skis, and he laughed out loud. Yes, Hannes had it right. Today, every day, should be about having fun.

Dave pulled into the McGee parking area, awestruck by the number of automobiles, the splendor of the course, and the enthusiasm of the crowd. He filled out his entry form and wrote with pride that he was representing DWP. Dave admired the trophies displayed on the registration table, covered his face with white zinc oxide for sun protection, tied his racing bib around his waist, and rode up the sling-lift to inspect the course. He took a few runs to warm up, then made his way to the start.

As Dave watched the racers ahead of him, his senses sharpened, and his heartbeat quickened. He pulled his bib over his head, tied the side strings, and took a series of long, deep breaths to calm the butterflies in his stomach. Once again, apprehension caught him off guard. How would he perform? Intuitively, he coached himself: *Just do the best you can. Have fun.* At last, Dave heard his bib number called. His mind grew quiet as he focused on the first gate. He would go for the win.

The start assistant made circles in the air with a red-flagged slalom pole, a signal that the racer was ready. At the finish, the chief timer called out to his crew, "Clear your watches!"

As the starter rested his hand on Dave's back, the start assistant lowered the red flag to the snow. "Ready," prompted the starter.

The assistant raised the flag to the sky. With gloveless hands, Dave clicked his ski poles. "Set," said the starter.

Dave bent his knees deeper, tightened his grip on his poles and pushed them into the snow. The timers at the finish stood alert. In unison, the start assistant whipped the red flag to the ground, the timers clicked their stopwatches, and the starter commanded: "GO!" Dave poled out of the starting gate with all his might.

Cutting around the first slalom pole with his weight on his downhill ski, Dave kept his knees supple and his arms out in front. He concentrated on the next turn, and then the next. Gate by gate, he attacked the course, his muscles firing in quick succession, now accelerating with ease, now skidding through a rut and fighting to regain his balance.

When the last gate came in view, Dave skated for extra speed. He passed under the finish banner, and turned to a stop, gasping for air, yet exhilarated. Waiting for his breath to return and his heart rate to slow, he leaned on his ski poles, watched the next racer come down, and wondered how his time would stack up in this local championship. With the Class B event still ahead, Dave had one more chance to ski faster and cut each gate tighter. He could hardly wait to be in the course again.

Race day passed quickly, almost like a dream. In the Class B event, Dave felt a confidence he'd lacked in the championship race. While still skiing aggressively, his movements were more relaxed, and his turns more precise. He thought he'd had an excellent run, but he would have to wait for the awards to find out the results. Meanwhile, he helped the other racers tear down the course, gather the flagged willow poles, stack them at the bottom of the up-ski, and then joined the crowd cheering for Como as he pulled a toboggan loaded with cases of Coca-Cola into the finish area.

As Master of Ceremonies, Corty Hill called everyone together for the awards. Without mentioning he had skied the fastest time in the first heat but had withdrawn to give others a chance to win, Corty thanked the volunteers, spectators, and racers. He invited the crowd to cheer "Ski Heil!" three times as he announced the name and time of each competitor who received an award. In the Alps, he explained, "Ski Heil" was a winter greeting meaning, "Long live health, happiness, and skiing." To offer this message to victors was a European tradition. The crowd heartedly joined in cheering for all.

When Corty called Dave's name for 2nd place in the local championships, the crowd cheered three "Ski Heils" in his honor, and Dave walked forward to accept his trophy with a feeling of self-satisfaction and accomplishment. Waiting for the Class B announcements, he warned himself not to get his hopes up too high. He looked at the 3rd place trophy almost with dread. He thought, *Please, don't call my name...*

Then came the 2nd place award. *Do I dare wish I don't win this trophy?*

"Now, for first place," Corty announced. Dave swallowed hard. "Three cheers for Dave McCoy!" How Dave's grin grew even bigger than it had been was a phenomenon of pure joy!

Before leaving for Independence, Dave strapped his trophies to his motorcycle alongside his skis and poles, triple-checking that his new treasures were secure. On the ride home, he relived the races over and over again in his mind, imagining the thrill of cutting into the turns and accelerating out. Yes, Dave had admired ski racers from afar, even envied them, but never had he envisioned that being on a course, alone, giving all of himself to get through the gates as fast as possible, would be so meaningful. In high school, he had loved playing team sports, but none had given him such exhilaration as this first ski race had.

THE first ski competition in the Eastern Sierra proved to be a success.[47] Local excitement about the Inyo-Mono Championships mirrored the growing popularity of skiing across America. Renowned broadcaster Lowell Thomas lauded the sport on his radio program to an audience of 20 million. At "The Battle of Fifth Avenue," a winter sports show held in New York's Madison Square Garden, thousands of spectators watched ski jumpers soar off a scaffolding covered with ice and snow.[48] In the mountain regions, skiers besieged winter highway crews with pleas to open unplowed roads. In Colorado, ski trains ran 55 miles from Denver to Berthoud Pass to alleviate the weekend congestion of several hundred cars parking along the highway. In Sun Valley, Averell Harriman held a star-studded Grand Opening of his exclusive resort, which featured the world's first chairlift. He announced that later in the season, he would

Courtesy Frashers Fotos.

Finish gate at the Inyo-Mono Championships, April 11, 1937.

host the inaugural Harriman Cup, an invitational ski race for elite racers.[49]

In Southern California, skiers packed the slopes in ever-growing numbers. Up Highway 395, Eastern Sierra residents operated up-skis at Whitney Portal, Onion Valley, Big Pine's Glacier Lodge, Bishop Creek Canyon, McGee Mountain, Mammoth Mountain, Crestview, Deadman Summit, the June Lake Loop, Lee Vining, and Bridgeport. Farther north, Southern Pacific Railway scouted for a place to build a ski area, while Soda Springs installed the first up-ski on Donner Summit.

LATE spring 1937, DWP assigned hydrographer Ed Parker to head a new division in Big Pine and relocated Dave to Bishop to fill Parker's previous position. After moving his belongings into a Bishop bunkhouse, Dave checked into the DWP office on Main Street. Several surprises awaited him. He had a desk right next to his new boss, District Manager Pat Coons. On his desk sat a Monroe calculator ideal for making stream gauge calculations, and a set of keys, one of which belonged to a City truck designated for his exclusive use.

Dave's new job included monitoring clock stations north of Bishop—the Owens River at Pleasant Valley, plus its tributaries Rock Creek, Pine Creek, Horton Creek, and Mammoth Creek.[50] He would also assist Pat Coons tracking underground water from the wells between Bishop and Chalfant Valley, 15 miles to the northeast. Finally, he would help coordinate a "water-spreading" project. Due to the heavy snows of the previous winter, the aqueduct flow had doubled from 400 to 800 cubic feet per second. DWP usually funneled surplus water into the Owens River, but to handle the load of that year's volume, the department chose to spread the overflow across the valley floor.

Pat and Dave soon developed a close friendship. In a sense, Pat mentored Dave, encouraging the young man to carry insurance and to open a bank account, and he included Dave in his family's activities.

ONE afternoon not long after settling into Bishop, Dave stopped by The Toggery—a clothing store known for western wear. In search of a new pair of Levis, he struck up a friendship with the cheerful, down-to-earth salesperson, Marshall Carriere. A senior at Bishop High School, Marshall loved to ski and fish, just as Dave did. He told Dave about the time a friend had driven him up Sherwin Grade and let him loose on a pair of "not-so-easy-to-turn 14-foot boards." He then described how he had made a pair of shorter, more maneuverable skis. When the conversation turned to fishing, Marshall talked about the abundance of brookies, rainbow, brown, and cutthroat trout in the region. Dave's voice sparkled in reply, "Let's go catch some of those rascals. In fact, let's go skiing too. How about this weekend? I'll pick you up on my motorcycle. We can strap our skis *and* our fishing gear to my bike."

Sunday morning, Dave drove Marshall to Mammoth Mountain, where they skied snowfields all morning. In the afternoon, they headed down a dirt road near Toms Place and hiked into the Owens River Gorge for an afternoon of fishing. Marshall got a good laugh about trying to keep up with his new friend. He recalled, "I don't think Dave realized how strong he was. He ran back up out of the Gorge with me trailing behind, huffing and puffing, and the rocks and pumice slipping under my feet."

Another time, Dave came by The Toggery and showed me the most beautiful golden trout I'd ever seen. He'd caught them at Wallace Lake out of Lone Pine. He drew me a map of how to get there and the next Sunday, Vernon Holland, Dean Kiner, and myself drove to Whitney Portal, found where Dave told us to leave the trail, and started hiking straight up. This was the hardest hike I've ever attempted, mostly off-trail, up six or seven steep miles with a 7,000-foot elevation gain before dropping down to the lake to fish. True to Dave's word, the goldens were there. But then I had to retrace my steps to get home. Well, I made it. I felt pretty good that Dave considered me strong enough to follow his footsteps. I always looked up to him, not only for his skiing prowess but because everything he did seemed to be just a little beyond average. [51]

One day, when Dave stopped by The Toggery for a visit, Marshall skipped his usual small talk. "Come on," he urged, "I want to introduce you to someone." Marshall led Dave down the street to Jack Black's grocery store. There, he put his arm around a pretty girl who was carrying a half-filled shopping bag. "Dave," he said with a grin, "Meet my sister, Roma."[52]

Dave lost his breath. Here was the cheerleader who had caught his eye two years prior when he was working at Jim's Place. He knew that any guy in his right mind would jump at a chance to talk to a girl like her. But all he could think about was getting out of that grocery store as fast as he could. Blushing, he shook Roma's hand, made an awkward excuse about having to be somewhere, and left.

Speeding north through Round Valley, Dave tried to clear his mind. Blast it! If he weren't so shy around girls, he would have said something, asked Roma a question, anything. But no, he had to do his disappearing act. Dave recalled a time in high school when he'd been interested in a smart and talented girl who was clearly attracted to him, but did he ever show her a hint of what he felt? No.

On Sherwin Grade, Dave leaned into each turn, cut the corners tight, and then accelerated for traction. Once he got to Long Valley, he focused on the wind against his face. He looked up to the mountains. The rugged peaks and swirling colors of uplifted rock brought him solace. He started to relax. A few miles past McGee Mountain, he turned left, rode to the Convict Canyon trailhead, and parked his bike. Fishing gear in hand, he jogged the familiar trail that ran alongside the deep waters of Convict Lake, and at the far end, turned up the canyon. At the creek crossing, rushing waters forced him to leap from rock to rock to get across. From there, he made his way up a sidehill of unstable scree. When he reached Lake Dorothy, Dave walked directly to an area of calm water where he knew the brookies would bite. After about an hour of casting, he stashed his catch in his creel, and in the soft glow of twilight, jogged back down the trail to his motorcycle.

Chasing his headlights down Highway 395, Dave thought about his life. He was too busy to worry about dating. Plenty of girls had flirted with him, and he'd been interested in some, but never made an effort to develop a relationship. Dave wasn't about to give up his sports—motorcycles, fishing, hiking, and, skiing—just to hang around with a girl. And Roma Carriere? She was still a teenager, too young for him. So, why did he shy away from meeting her? What was he so afraid of?

CHAPTER FOUR

Roma: Still Dancing

Frances and Roma playing.

Dancing. It's odd I was confident about my dancing when I was so shy in other areas of my life. But dancing came easy to me. I'd be the girl twirling across the wooden floor, moving in rhythm to the big band music, feeling like I was on top of the world. Those poor girls sitting on the sidelines. They must have felt awful, just waiting and hoping someone would invite them to dance.

I tell you, if ever there was a happy and contented, born-and-raised Bishop girl, that would be me. As a teenager, well, I flitted around as if I owned the place. In those days, my friends and I didn't have cars, none of us, and we didn't care. We had fun walking from place to place, chatting away. Bishop was so small, it was easy to get where we wanted to go, especially for me because the high school was just a few blocks from my house. Anyway, Bishop was the perfect place to be while I prepared to go off chasing my dancing dreams.

Boy, did I keep busy. I took up the violin—mostly to make my father happy—and I joined the school orchestra. Between attending classes, going home to check in with Grandma, and then walking back to school for music lessons or dress rehearsals or cheerleading practice, I didn't have much spare time. Still, I wouldn't let a day pass without visiting my older sister Frances. I'd scurry over to the Automobile Club before she finished work so we could share the latest gossip.

I could talk to Frances about anything from the most trivial matters to my deepest questions about life. The older I got, the more important our conversations became, especially with me trying to figure out how I was going to be a professional dancer. I was sure that someday I would get myself to a city where things were happening. Yes, I had my eyes on the big time, maybe even the silver screen. What I didn't think about was how scary it would be to actually go out on my own.

Oh, a girl's dreams can be so confusing. The closer I got to the age where I thought I would be leaving home to pursue my dreams, the more afraid I became. Where in the world would I find the courage to step out in the world? Frances would listen to my worries and then quiet me down in her calm voice. "Roma," she'd say. "You don't need to make any decisions today. You're going to have a wonderful life. For now, you just dance your heart away." So that's what I did.

As far as boys went, the only ones that interested me were those who loved to dance. One summer, I got infatuated with a guy who was visiting from Bakersfield. I'd never seen such a good dancer. The problem was, once the dance was over, we didn't have much to say. That was a pattern for me.

But then, there was dancing with my brother Marshall. Now, he made everything fun. He even let me teach him to tap dance. Since I'd learned by imitating others, I was sure he could learn from me, and I was right. We worked out a routine, and then I got the bright idea that we could perform on the high school stage. Can you imagine a teenager willing to tap dance with his younger sister in front of all his friends? Well, that was Marshall. We were a great pair because we didn't care if we did everything perfectly. If either one of us missed a step, I'd start giggling, and then Marshall would join in with his big laugh.

It seems as if we just blinked our eyes, and high school was over. There we were, June 1937, walking on stage with 18 classmates, the girls wearing formal gowns and the boys in dark suits. Father, Grandma, and Frances were in the audience, so proud of us. Poor Grandma, she was all teary-eyed. I think she feared I would run off somewhere like I always talked about. I put my arms around her and told her not to worry. No matter what I'd said about leaving Bishop, I wasn't ready. Even I knew that. I was only 16, a young graduate, and too immature to go out on my own. Nope. Bishop was the place I needed to be. So, I got a job as a secretary at the Bank of America, right on Main Street.

I must admit, another reason I wanted to stay in Bishop was that I had the biggest crush on this guy I hadn't even met! My secret stranger. I didn't even know his name. I'd first noticed him a few years before in Independence, and now here he was in Bishop. What a sight for a young girl's eyes.

Everything about this guy fascinated me. He looked kind of wild, wearing bellbottom pants, little round goggles over his eyes, and a red bandana tied around his head. He hardly ever wore a shirt, just showed off his tanned skin and big muscles. I don't know where he got his ideas about fashion, but I'm surprised all the other boys in town didn't imitate him.

Almost every day I'd see him riding his motorcycle past the front window of the bank, and I'd wonder where he was going. I'd hear him rev his engine, and imagine he was trying to get my attention, but he didn't even know I existed. How could he?

Well, what do you know? One day, Marshall told me about his new friend who rode a motorcycle, and who was just as wild about skiing and fishing as he was. Just like that, my secret stranger had a name: Dave McCoy.

After I got the crush on Dave, almost all my conversations with Frances were about how I could get a date with him. But Frances had met Dave. She would shake her head and warn me: "Roma, you'll never get a date with Dave McCoy. Even if he wants to ask you out, he won't. He's just too shy." I refused to believe her.

The craziest thing was, my interest in Dave was illogical. He didn't fit into my life plans. I'd never seen him at a dance, and I could just imagine what Grandma would say if I told her I had a date with an older guy on a motorcycle. To tell you the truth, I thought it was odd that Marshall and Dave were even friends. They seemed so different from each other. Marshall was kind and funny and safe. Then there was Dave, the dashing stranger, older, more experienced, kind of scary. Oh, why, I wondered. Why does this mysterious Dave McCoy occupy my thoughts? I tell you, when it comes to romance, logic disappears.

Frances must have told Marshall I wanted to meet Dave because *I* hadn't spilled the beans to my brother. No way. Are you kidding? I'm smarter than that. I loved Marshall to pieces, but he was always joking around, even when things were serious. And I was serious about meeting Dave McCoy. But of all the introductions I'd imagined, having Marshall drag him into Jack Black's grocery store, without giving me any warning whatsoever, wasn't among them.

I could've strangled Marshall for catching me off guard. But he just grinned from ear to ear, as if he'd pulled off a good one. While I stood there, blushing a thousand colors of red, Dave seemed just as embarrassed as I felt. It was obvious he couldn't wait to get out of the store. He reached out to shake my hand, and said something I couldn't understand, then walked outside, revved his motorcycle, and zoomed off. Just like that, he was gone.

I made up my mind right then and there that my crush on Dave McCoy was a silly thing. I had a big life in front of me, and this guy wasn't part of it. He probably didn't even like to dance, and me, well, I planned on going to every single dance in Bishop. In fact, that very Saturday night, a six-piece orchestra was going to play in the outside pavilion at Keough's Hot Springs. I intended to be there, flying across the dance floor, not sitting home, hoping a motorcycle-riding, fish-loving skier might call me. Still, I couldn't help but scold Marshall. In my angriest voice, I told him, "Now you've gone and wrecked everything!"

I waved my finger in the air, ready to read Marshall the riot act, but he interrupted me with his big laugh and said, "Don't you worry, Roma. You and Dave are a good match."

CHAPTER FIVE

Getting To Know Roma

Roma and Dave at the Easter Egg Hunt.

When DWP District Manager Pat Coons and his family returned from their 1937 spring vacation, Dave rode to their house to welcome them home. At the sound of Dave's currently favorite motorcycle, a dark maroon Indian, Pat's young sons, Don and Dale, ran outside to greet him. As usual, Dave gave them each a ride on the back of his motorcycle. After a few laps, he parked his bike, grabbed the bundle of fish he'd caught that morning, and walked to the front door, the youngsters scurrying behind.

Inside the house, Pat introduced Dave to a dark-haired stranger named Joan. The Coons had seen this attractive girl hitchhiking, offered her a ride, and invited her to stay with them. Straight off, Joan expressed a keen interest in both Dave and his motorcycle. When he offered to give her a ride around the Owens Valley, she happily accepted, and this initial sightseeing excursion evolved into other extended tours of the Eastern Sierra.

On a ride to Lake Tahoe, Dave began to feel uneasy about Joan's grow-ing affection. He enjoyed her company, but romance wasn't on his agenda. That evening before he left the Coons' house, she reached for his hand as casually as if they were a couple, and said, "Dave, there's a carnival coming to Bishop this weekend. We should go." The warmth in her voice made Dave's gut tighten with resistance. Disconcerted, he shook his head and muttered, "I'm sorry, Joan. I already have a date."

Filled with regret for having told a boldfaced lie, Dave tossed and turned in his bed that night. In one thoughtless sentence, he had betrayed his principles, compromised his integrity, and displayed poor character. Weak behavior irritated him, and yet, here he was, acting as weak as a man could be. Why hadn't he just accepted Joan's invitation?

The truth was, Dave had been thinking about inviting Roma Carriere to the carnival. He'd procrastinated, partly because of her age—Roma was five years younger—and partly because of his shyness. Now, in the midst of his turmoil, he questioned the real reason for his hesitation. Perhaps he was afraid of developing feelings for someone only to lose that person in the end, as had been the pattern in his life.

By morning, Dave had resolved to face his fears and to follow his heart. He motorcycled to the Bank of America, walked straight to Roma's desk, and invited her to the carnival. Roma's surprised look and spontaneous smile brought a lightness to him, as did the heartfelt way she flustered through her answer, "Why yes... of course... I'd love to go with you..."

No one was more excited than Marshall Carriere to hear the news that Roma and Dave were going to the carnival together. He coached Dave: "Grandma's *not* going to like the idea of my sister riding on a motorcycle. You've got to have her approval, or Roma won't pay any attention to you. Don't worry about the dancing. You can learn to dance. And don't get intimidated by how pretty Roma is. She's just as shy as you are. Remember, talk. You can't forget to talk! Ask her questions. Anything." Dave listened to Marshall's good-hearted advice and started to laugh. He wasn't con-cerned about impressing Roma with idle conversation. He just wanted to spend time with her.

Marshall's worries were for naught. The evening of the carnival, everything went smoothly. Dave acted his natural self, and Grandma Folk didn't even seem concerned about the motorcycle. At the fairgrounds, the magic of romance filled the air as Dave and Roma walked among a bustle of smiling people. The couple worked their way toward the bright lights of the amusement park rides, past the carnies calling out their games, and the vendors selling cotton candy and caramel corn. And then, just as Dave had anticipated, Joan approached them. He introduced the two girls, they had a short conversation, and, to his relief, Joan moved on.

Having vowed to himself to be truthful about matters of the heart, Dave told Roma he had lied to Joan. Roma seemed to appreciate his honesty. She *did* get quiet, but quiet was a familiar and comfortable place for Dave. Most important, every time he looked at Roma, she smiled back as if there was no where in the world she would rather be.

A few weeks after the carnival, Dave called Roma's house to invite her on a day hike to Paiute Pass. At first, Roma sounded hesitant, but the enthusiasm in Dave's voice must have won her over. Saturday morning, they rode up Bishop Canyon to the North Lake trailhead. From there, they hiked past creeks, rock ledges, and waterfalls. At Paiute Lake, they stopped to skip rocks and eat a snack. Dave strung his rod, tied on a fly, pointed to a fish, cast his line, and boom, the fish was on the hook. He let Roma reel in the catch and showed her how to slice the belly, remove the guts, and cover the fish with wet grass in his creel. Roma didn't mind cleaning the fish, especially when Dave told her she could take the fresh trout home to her grandmother.

Back on the trail again, Dave and Roma climbed through high alpine meadows, across a red-tinted summer snowfield, and then, there they were, standing on top of Paiute Pass. Roma threw her arms wide open with joy. She had hiked four miles, gained 2,000 vertical feet, and she wasn't even feeling tired. To the contrary, she was invigorated. She looked to the east where the familiar White Mountains framed the Owens Valley and then to the west where, for the first time in her life, she saw a view of the interior of the Sierra Nevada. The raw beauty of Humphreys Basin and Golden Trout Lake awed her.

For the remainder of summer and fall, each Saturday morning Dave picked Roma up early, and off they would go on another high-country adventure. They hiked a new trail every weekend, at first averaging 8 to 10 miles roundtrip, but gradually increasing the mileage as they explored trails as far south as Cottonwood Lakes out of Lone Pine and north to Virginia Lakes above Conway Summit. They shared light conversation as they moved along, keeping a lookout for wildlife, sometimes sighting a deer grazing in aspen trees, a bighorn sheep scampering across a rocky ledge, or a playful marmot sunning on a granite rock. Now and then, they heard a quail rustle through the underbrush or watched an eagle soar overhead before reaching out his talons to land on the highest branch of a barren pine.

Finding so much pleasure hiking with Roma, Dave's thoughts raced ahead. Maybe, come winter, he would teach her to ski. Slow down, he cautioned himself. One step at a time.

At the December 1937 meeting of the Eastern Sierra Ski Club, George Deibert reported good news to the 80 members in attendance. The California Department of Transportation—commonly known as Caltrans—had appropriated $108,000 to house a Sno-Go at Crestview Road Maintenance Station. Caltrans hired Nan and Max Zischank as on-site caretakers for the complex and designated Max as the Sno-Go operator to clear snow off Highway 395 between Mammoth and Lee Vining. The state also committed to building a similar maintenance station at the north end of Long Valley.

According to Deibert, the California Chamber of Commerce was advertising the "... glories and temptations of winter..." on highway billboards and city streetcar banners. They also distributed two winter sports movies—*Better Skiing* and *Jack Frost Entertains*—to sports-related agencies and mailed 250,000 copies of a Winter Guide to organizations across California.

The bad news was that the Winter Guide didn't mention Inyo or Mono County. In response, ESSC members pledged to make their presence known. They formed committees to furnish California newspapers and radio stations with biweekly reports about Inyo and Mono ski news, snow depths, and road conditions. They also voted to adopt an insignia, apply for California Ski Association (CSA) membership, and submit a bid to host next year's 1939 State Championships on McGee Mountain.

Dave McCoy, newly elected to ESSC's Board of Directors, volunteered to take responsibility for a portable rope tow the club had recently purchased.[1] Tex Cushion announced he had rebuilt Corty Hill's sling-lift and planned to have the up-ski operating as soon as snow arrived. Snow! Already December, and not a snowflake had fallen. Until a storm blew in, the sling-lift stood idle on McGee's sagebrush slopes. Weekend skiers took one look at the dry conditions and continued north about 20 miles to the higher elevation of Deadman Summit.[2] At Deadman, they found a gentle slope with plenty of snow, ESSC's portable tow that Dave had set up, and off to one side, a ski jump he had shoveled for all to use.

As president of his own company, Pacific Railway Equipment, Corty Hill spent his weekdays in Southern California. Rather than idly complaining about the drought, on Friday afternoons he drove his glamorous, then-revolutionary, front-wheel-drive Cord to Bishop, and on Saturday and Sunday mornings, chauffeured Dave and his ski gear to Deadman. There, the two men spent the day critiquing each other on the Arlberg technique. In the Arlberg, boot heels were secured to the skis, a distinctly different method of skiing than the free-heel, dropped-knee telemark style Dave had learned in Washington.

Using a pocket-sized edition of Otto Lang's technical reference book, *Downhill Skiing*, Corty and Dave practiced the schuss, snowplow, snowplow turn, stem turn, stem christiania, and eventually, the expert parallel christiania. Regardless of the disparity in their upbringing or their age difference—Corty was eleven years older than Dave—these two men bonded as close friends who shared a passion for skiing and mutual respect. As Dave recalled:

> *Corty was so much fun, not competitive. He encouraged me to replace my Bass boots with a $50 pair of Pete Limmer boots, which made a tremendous advancement in my skills. Corty was interested in everything about skiing and was generous in all he did.*

Crest View Lodge.

After skiing all day at Deadman, Corty and Dave would drive a few miles down the road to Crest View Lodge, across from the Caltrans maintenance yard, to join their friends for some après-ski camaraderie.[3] Clarence Wilson, who had built the lodge in 1927, had recently installed a rope tow across Highway 395 on the slope behind the Caltrans yard, put up lights, and was now advertising night skiing.

DAVE loved his ski outings, but he missed spending time with Roma, so he offered to teach her to ski. Roma agreed to learn, on the condition that Dave let *her* teach *him* to *dance*. Why not? Dave had gone to dances when he was living in Wilkeson and Independence. Even without knowing the steps, he'd had fun jumping up and down to the music.

On a Saturday morning in late January, Roma and Frances arrived at Deadman wearing borrowed ski gear. Dave guided the sisters through the basic skills, and within hours, they were snowplowing the lower slopes, smiling all the way down. Before heading home that afternoon, Roma skied up to Dave and cajoled, "It's time you shine your dancin' shoes!"

Dave couldn't start his dancing lessons right away because he had already booked his calendar. The next weekend, he traveled with Corty and Tex to a February ski race at Donner Summit, north of Lake Tahoe. This meet, hosted by Auburn Ski Club, was their first race away from McGee. The men performed well enough in the slalom, but the downhill turned out to be a waxing disaster.

All morning, while the competitors hiked up the south-facing course, the sun had glared down on the snow. By the time the race started, those who "hit the wax" skied aggressively with their skis sliding easily over variations in the snow. Those who "missed the wax," like Corty and his protégés, had to ski cautiously and stay on guard of the dangerous stop-and-go effects of wet snow. Without warning, especially when passing from shade to sun, their skis would suddenly slow down while the momentum of their body continued forward, thrusting them off balance. The threesome from McGee made it down the course without falling, but their times were slow. Upbeat as ever, Corty encouraged Dave and Tex not to be disappointed. Skillful waxing was part of the learning curve.

The following weekend, George Deibert, Bob Vinsant, and Dave McCoy traveled to the tiny town of Mineral on Mt. Lassen, to attend the annual CSA meeting that was being held in conjunction with the 1938 California State Championships. At the meeting, Deibert submitted a formal proposal for ESSC to host the 1939 State Championships on McGee. CSA accepted the bid. The men spent the rest of their weekend making mental notes of how to stage an elite competition.

Roma and Frances skiing.

Back in Bishop, Vic Taylor, Pat Coons, and Dave loaded the City truck with their hydrographic gear and drove to Mammoth, where they would stay at the Cushions' Winter Patrol Station while they completed the three-day Mammoth snow survey. At the intersection of State Route 203 and U.S. 395, the group parked the City truck and walked over to a frozen geyser. They wanted to get a closer look at the geological phenomena currently landmarking the turnoff to Mammoth Lakes.

SKI TRACKS
Frozen Geyser at Casa Diablo Hot Springs
1937

On Tuesday, December 21, 1937, about 4:00 in the afternoon, a clogged underground pipe gave out near Casa Diablo. The naturally existing superheated water, mixed with fine material and steam, burst through the surface to a height of at least 150 feet in the air. This spontaneous geyser then subsided to its current 90-foot height and froze in place.

The geyser at Casa Diablo.

With their curiosity satisfied, the men drove on to Penney's Tavern, loaded their gear onto Tex's dogsled—the only means of carrying a load to Old Mammoth—and went inside to have a drink before heading to the Winter Patrol Station. Tex tossed down a whiskey, Pat and Vic savored cold beers, and Dave, who still found alcohol unappealing, drank a Coca-Cola. While sitting at the Tavern bar, a radio broadcaster interrupted the men's banter with his report that a sizeable snowstorm was heading toward the Eastern Sierra.

Tex suggested they move the DWP vehicle down to the lower elevation of the Casa Diablo bar where the men decided to have another drink. There they heard that the oncoming storm appeared to be more extensive and threatening than previously described. The men caravanned farther south, parked the DWP vehicle at the Whitmore Tubs turnoff, and rode back to Penney's Tavern in Tex's truck.

During the dogsled ride to Old Mammoth, nimbostratus clouds darkened the sky, the air temperature plummeted, and wind gusts intensified. At the Winter Patrol Station, the men leashed and fed the dogs, then moved inside to the warmth of the woodstove and revived their conversation while Ruth prepared a hearty dinner and set the table. Outside, the growing gale swirled through the trees, rattled the building, and blew a massive snowstorm over the Eastern Sierra.

For the next twelve days, snow fell nonstop. The only choice for man and dog was to hunker down until the blizzard passed. Every few hours, day and night, the men pulled on their boots and shoveled snow out of a tunnel they maintained between the front door and the top of the snowpack, trying to prevent the Winter Patrol Station from being completely buried. They then climbed outside wearing snowshoes, lifted each dog chain above the deepening snow, stomped the powder down around the stakes, gave the dogs a quick pet, and retreated inside.

As supplies ran low, Ruth rationed the canned food she had stockpiled for winter. Tex had no way to resupply horsemeat and roadkill for the dogs, so the men fed the team strips of meat cut off the side of beef the Cushions kept hanging frozen in the mudroom. Tex voiced concern about the welfare of Mammoth's other four winter residents. He stayed in contact with the Penneys on his crank phone, but the only way to check on

The entrance to Tex's in 1938.

the Phillipses, who were living in another small cabin in Old Mammoth, would have been to ski through the blinding blizzard. Such a venture was too dangerous.

As soon as the storm let up, Dave skied to the Philips' cabin. To his surprise, a flat white landscape covered the spot where he expected to see a building. Dave thought he'd skied to the wrong place. Then he noticed a trickle of smoke curling up through the snow and heard muffled voices. He took off one of his skis and probed it toward the sound. Hollering as loud as he could, Dave got the Phillips' attention, yelled that help was on the way, then skied back for Tex, Pat, Vic, and four shovels.

Buried under at least 10 feet of powder, the Phillipses had become afraid of running out of food, fuel, and perhaps even oxygen. The only way they could escape *out* of the snow cave was to shovel snow *into* the cabin, passing the one shovel in their possession between them. When Dave made contact with the couple, they were packing snow into the living room. They had already filled the kitchen sink and bathtub.

The men spent the rest of the day rescuing the frightened couple. Progress was slow because they had to handle each shovelful of snow multiple times as they worked their way down. In the end, all was well. Ruth welcomed everyone to the Winter Patrol Station with a crackling fire, a hot meal, and several shots of whiskey.

In the cold that followed the epic storm, bright blue skies invited the men to take their time as they broke trail to the snow survey course on Mammoth Pass. Why not breathe in the splendor as they passed through pristine winter wilderness where snowflakes sparkled like diamonds in the sun? They wouldn't be leaving Mammoth until Max Zischank cleared U.S. 395 with the Sno-Go, and *that* was going to take a while.

Tex eventually transported Vic, Pat, and Dave to the City truck, helped shovel it out, and then mushed farther south to the McGee sling-lift. Two weeks later, he had the up-ski ready for a belated opening day, delayed first by no snow and later, by too much snow. Tex offered half-price tickets to ESSC members and free instruction for all. In response, busloads from Southern California's Jonathon Club, Sierra Club, and Auto Club arrived at McGee.[4] George Deibert and Corty Hill joined Tex in giving free lessons while Ruth Cushion sold hotdogs and soda pop from a small food shack Tex had built the previous summer.

On March 12, less than one month after Switzerland hosted the 1938 World Ski Championships, Hitler and his Nazi troops crossed the border into Austria and, in a political aggression called the *Anschluss*, seized the Austrian government. Though some Austrians welcomed the Germans, the famous ski instructor, Hannes Schneider, made no secret of his hatred for the Nazi reign of terror. For this "crime," he was arrested that same day.

SKI TRACKS
Hannes Schneider Arrested by Hitler's Troops
1938

At 3 a.m. on March 12, 1938, in St. Anton, Austria, the Nazis arrested Arlberg Ski School's Hannes Schneider— one of the most famous, widely respected, and well-loved sportsmen in the world—and locked him in an empty coal bin in the cellar of an overcrowded jail.[5] As ski racer, Clarita Heath, recalled, troops were marching all around, and planes were flying low.

Hearing about Hitler's hostilities in Europe and the horrendous bat-
tles between Japan and China, American skiers appreciated that the U.S.
was still isolated from war. Free from worry about personal safety, they
planned their ski vacations. Those with thick wallets purchased the latest
ski fashions, while people on slimmer budgets saved pennies to buy warm
gloves and goggles. That winter, ski media advertised an aerial tramway
on Cannon Mountain in Franconia, New Hampshire; Janet and Brad
Mead imported a T-bar from Europe to install on Pico Peak in Rutland,
Vermont; and Ted Ryan and Billy Fiske made plans for a ski resort in
Aspen, Colorado.[6] Skiers crowded the slopes in Loveland Basin, Colorado,
and Mt. Hood, Oregon.[7] In California, Soda Springs and Rainbow Tavern
operated J-bar lifts, Donner Peak ran several rope tows, and Yosemite had
an application pending for an aerial tramway.[8]

On January 22, 1938, Jerome Hill's movie, *Ski Flight*—a ski instruction film starring Otto Lang—opened on the same bill as Walt Disney's
first feature-length animated film, *Snow White and the Seven Dwarfs*. That
same winter, Charles "Minnie" Doyle organized the National Ski Patrol
System whereby volunteer members could ski for free at participating
slopes, provided they were skilled in first aid and willing to help injured
skiers. America's most successful ski racer, 1936 Olympian Dick Durrance,
won Sun Valley's prestigious Harriman Cup for the second consecutive
year, and Averell Harriman offered free room, board, skiing, and coaching
for talented ski racers.

In California, the Eastern Sierra Ski Club staged the second annual
Inyo-Mono Championships. Three hundred cars crowded the McGee
parking area, one carrying a group of German skiers from the University
of Munich. Unbeknownst to the Americans, these "students" were actually Olympic-caliber ski racers handpicked by the Hitler regime to make
a public relations tour and impress Americans with their superior talents. Indeed, these highly skilled European skiers were a highlight of the
weekend.[9]

Despite the stiff competition from overseas, Reno Ski Club's Wayne
Poulsen—a key figure in the development of Squaw Valley—won the
downhill.[10] German racer Xavier Kraisy won the slalom and the cross
country. During this demanding race, the German competitors zigzagged

gracefully up the slope in energy-saving switchbacks while Dave, who knew nothing about cross-country techniques, used strength, determination, and unorthodox skills to herringbone straight uphill. Still, Xavier was the only racer who could stay ahead of Dave. After the race, he congratulated Dave on his 2nd-place finish, adding in his heavy German accent, "If you vud learn to use your ski poles to stride across ze flats and up ze hills, you vud be an excellent Nordic racer."[11]

DUE to the massive February snowstorm, McGee Mountain still had skiable snow in April. Therefore, rather than join the Rey family on their traditional outing to the top of Mammoth, Tex hosted Easter Sunday festivities at the McGee sling-lift. About 11 a.m., he announced over the loudspeaker that contestants should prepare for the costume parade. With his typical enthusiasm and friendly offbeat comments, Tex acknowledged each entrant as they skied by the judges. When Dave McCoy and Roma Carriere approached in their matching hula skirts, Tex remarked that the couple might be wearing interesting sunburns by the end of the day.

After the parade, Tex asked all costumed skiers to stand side by side in a horizontal line halfway up the slope. He explained that near each of the flagged willow branches below them, dozens of brightly colored Easter eggs had been buried early that morning. The red flags were for women, the blue for men, no exceptions! At high noon, Tex shot his pistol into the sky, and the egg hunt began. Contestants skied in a mad dash, racing toward the flagged poles, clawing in the snow for eggs. They then tried to avoid hitting each other as they carried their loot to the bottom, adding their personal flair to what would become a favorite annual event for local skiers.

BY the time summer approached, Dave had been dating Roma for nearly a year. He felt content and secure in their relationship. The five-year age difference had lost importance. Affection had replaced shyness. To Dave, Roma was the perfect partner. Rather than detracting him from his favorite activities, as he had once feared a girlfriend would do, Roma enhanced them. Dave didn't talk about his feelings or use the word love. That term didn't exist in his emotional vocabulary. But he spent most of his free time with Roma, that is, when he wasn't skiing or fishing with Marshall.

At least once a week, Dave picked Marshall up early, strapped their skis, poles, and fishing gear to his motorcycle, and headed north. Riding through the growing village of Mammoth Lakes, the men commented on how, just a few years before, nothing but tall pine trees had lined the road. Now, as they motored along Main Street, they passed Penney's Tavern, Reed's Mammoth Garage, the Lutz store, the new Forest Service ranger station, an ice house, the post office, and a Standard service station.[12] Climbing to the snowfields on Mammoth, they explored various routes and became familiar with different aspects of the mountain. On their way back to Bishop, they extended their adventure by seeking out new fishing spots to cast their lines.

Roma envied the fun Dave and Marshall were having together, but when she asked Dave to take her to the top of Mammoth, he responded with decisive protectiveness. She could come once he was sure she was able to ski off the cornice of the headwall. Until then, the answer was no. Dave didn't want to risk Roma taking a fall that could turn into a dangerous, even disastrous, 1,000-foot slide. But not to worry, he had a better idea.

Dave suggested the couple make a standing date to ski each month of the year. Roma loved this plan. They had already skied Deadman in January and February, and McGee Mountain in March and April. During May, June, and July, they could ski the middle elevation slopes of Mammoth and Carson Peak off the June Lake Loop. From August through October, they could hike into the backcountry where they would surely find more snowfields. Then hopefully, new snow would be falling in November and December.

In August, just before Roma's 18th birthday, an unusually cold midsummer storm dumped snow down to 8,000 feet, the elevation of Minaret Road. As a result, on August 15, 1938, Dave drove Roma to the snowline and the couple climbed a hundred yards up the slope, Roma chattering with excitement as they walked. After strapping on their skis, Dave made an exaggerated bow, gestured downhill, and said, "For you, my lady, on your birthday." Roma took off carving turns in the soft snow. Once she stopped, Dave let out his makeshift yodel and made figure eights in her tracks.

The following weekend, Dave invited Roma to escape Bishop's

sweltering August heat by taking a motorcycle ride to Virginia City, a historic mining town in the hills of Nevada about 200 miles north of Bishop. After a wonderful day together, the couple started home later than they had planned. Still, with the midnight sky illuminated by starlight, Roma's arms wrapped around Dave's waist, her head resting on his shoulder, the world felt like a perfect place.

About a half-hour from home, Dave rounded a corner into an area known as Skunk Hollow, hit an oil slick, and lost control of the bike. Instinctively, he yelled, "Push!" and shoved as hard as he could against the handlebars, sending both he and Roma flying away from the machine. The motorcycle skidded ahead and crashed to a stop. The horn blasted through the otherwise silent darkness.

Desperate to find Roma, Dave sprinted back and forth across the road, shouting her name. Was she hurt? Where was she? At last, he saw her walking toward him. Alone on the highway in the middle of the night with the motorcycle horn still sounding, they held each other in gratitude that they were both alive and free of serious injury. Roma had suffered a few scrapes, not much damage considering she'd been wearing only lightweight summer clothes and Dave's soft crash helmet. Dave's body was unharmed, protected by his leather jacket. Not so, his emotions. He was outraged with himself for having endangered Roma's life.

Dave unplugged the horn and yanked the motorcycle upright. Roma walked by his side as he pushed the bike up Highway 395 and down the Benton Crossing road to Whitmore Hot Tubs, where her half-brother Leonard was the caretaker.[13] Leonard let them use his telephone to call Grandma. When daylight broke, he drove the couple to Bishop. Rumors about what had happened were already flying around town.

Distraught over the motorcycle accident, Dave understood the family's concern for Roma's welfare. He remained in the background when Frances encouraged Roma to enroll in a Southern California business school. Not wanting to complicate matters, Dave didn't voice what he was feeling. But, after Roma left Bishop, his life changed. The Eastern Sierra turned lonely. His DWP job seemed mundane.

Unable to imagine waiting a year for Roma to return, Dave thought of his past, and wanderlust crept into his mind. How easy it would be to take to the road. But standing alone near a clock station on Pine Creek, scanning the ridgeline of the Sierra Nevada, appreciation overcame his self-pity. Smiling to himself, he knew that this land was where he belonged. He made a promise to himself. No matter how lonely he felt, this time, he would *not* run away.

Around noon, Dave returned to the DWP office to complete his streamflow calculations. On his desk, he saw a yellow telegram imprinted with the Western Union logo. He opened the folded paper and read the message slowly. "Coming home. Meet me. Today. Bishop bus station. 3:15. Roma." He reread the telegram several times to make sure he wasn't misunderstanding the message. Yes, Roma was coming home that afternoon. Dave put the telegram in his back pocket, left the office, went to the bank, and withdrew $700 cash from his savings account. He had an errand to run before she arrived.

AT the bus station, Dave leaned against a pole, appearing calm as he waited. Only the intensity of his eyes focusing on the approaching vehicles betrayed his anticipation. Finally, the northbound Greyhound pulled into the parking area. Dave stepped forward to see the disembarking passengers. There was Roma, as lovely as ever, but with an anxious expression on her face. He shuddered. Were his expectations incorrect about this moment?

As soon as Roma saw Dave, she broke into a smile, ran to him, and just about jumped into his arms. Tears flowed down her cheeks as her words tumbled out... how she had missed him... how unhappy she'd been in the city. Dave held tight to Roma's hand and guided her to a shiny black 1938 Chevrolet coupe with red flames painted on the hood.[14] Bewildered, Roma looked around and asked, "Where's your motorcycle?"

Dave's eyes twinkled. "I thought we'd look real good sitting side by side on the front seat of this fine car, with our skis and poles sticking out the trunk!"

CHAPTER SIX

Roma: Young Romantic

Roma ready to ride to Virginia City on Dave's latest Harley, August 1938.

After Marshall's disastrous attempt to introduce me to Dave McCoy, I pretty much gave up hope of ever dating him. I went on my merry way working at the bank, going to dances, flirting with the boys, spending my free time with my sister Frances, watching out for Grandma, and trying my best to push Dave and his motorcycle out of my mind. Then one morning, completely out of the blue, here he came, striding into the bank, walking directly to my desk, and asking me on a date to the Bishop Carnival. I was so surprised I couldn't speak. I barely got the word "yes" out of my mouth.

On the day of the carnival, I hardly ate a thing. I couldn't. My nerves had ruined my appetite. Poor Grandma. She tried to get me to nibble on some snacks, but all her efforts only made me more nervous. She scolded me for fussing over my clothes, saying things like, "Why, child, you looked just fine in the first outfit you tried on." And, "Bless my soul, I don't know why you want to wear those capris instead of the pretty flowered sundress I sewed for you." Her questions made me cringe. You see, I hadn't told Grandma I would be riding to the carnival on the back of a motorcycle.

Finally, I was ready to go. Grandma told me I looked pretty, and we sat down on the couch together. There we waited, barely saying a word. She must have been hoping this guy was worth all the anxiety he'd brought into our household. Me? I was a wreck, trying to stay calm. To this day, I don't know what worried me most, riding on a motorcycle or just being on a date with Dave. What if Grandma had a cat fit over the motorcycle, or if she thought he was too old for me? Or, worse yet, what if he didn't like me? Well, at long last, we heard the rumble of a Harley engine coming to a stop in front of our house. Grandma looked out the window, and her face turned pale. Oh no, I thought.

Little did I realize I didn't need to worry. Dave could have charmed a rock with that smile of his, so warm and genuine. He was all cleaned up, wearing nice blue jeans and a white T-shirt, looking so handsome he just about made me crazy. And he was so polite to Grandma, right away showing interest in her as if he considered Frances Folk to be someone important. And she was. Bless her heart. Grandma didn't say one word about the motorcycle, just told us to have fun and be home by such and such a time. I've often wondered if she knew about Dave and his motor-cycle all along, Bishop being such a small town, and Dave and Marshall being such good friends.

I hugged Grandma goodbye, and Dave and I stepped outside, me pre-tending to be confident as we walked toward his bike. He swung his leg over the seat, and then, in the most encouraging voice, told me to hop on behind him and put my arms around his waist for safety. So, I did. He started the engine, and the sudden roar made me jump. Without even thinking, I grabbed on tighter. I can tell you there wasn't an ounce of fat around Dave's stomach. All muscle. Then the weirdest thing happened. Riding down Main Street, all my fears disappeared. Something about how strong and steady Dave handled the bike made me feel like I didn't need to be afraid of anything, and neither did Grandma.

Frances and Marshall had told me that Dave was just as shy as I was, so I wasn't surprised that we didn't talk much when we got to the carnival. But still, I started feeling uncomfortable. I was so worried about saying the wrong thing I could barely get a single word out. I thought maybe Dave had lost interest in me when I told him I didn't like to hike, or perhaps he thought I was boring and couldn't carry a conversation. To make matters worse, a dark-haired girl approached us, acting all haughty like she knew something I didn't. Dave introduced us, and we talked a little, but was I ever glad when she walked away. I don't know why, but I got this feeling she and Dave were more than just friends. Then he told me about how he had lied to her.

I could have been happy that Dave chose me over that other girl, but I didn't see things that way. I felt like a deflated tire. My heart broke. Completely broke. I was merely a fill-in meant to cover up Dave's lie. Tears welled up inside me, and I got the urge to run home, leaving him at the carnival to wonder where I'd gone. The only thing was, I knew I'd be crying all the way, and I wasn't about to let tears drip down my cheeks in a public place. Nope. I decided to stand my ground and have a good time for the rest of the evening. I put a big smile on my face and pretended Dave's words didn't bother me one bit. Believe me, once I make up my mind, I know how to be stubborn.

As the evening wore on, my feelings softened. Every time I looked over at Dave, he was smiling at me. And he was so thoughtful that I kept forgetting how furious I was. At the food vendors, he asked if I'd like something to eat. I thanked him and said I wasn't hungry. The truth was, I was starving. I felt like ordering a hotdog, popcorn, *and* cotton candy. But Marshall had lectured me not to be a burden. He said Dave worked hard for what little money he had, so I shouldn't go and cause him reckless spending. Well, he bought us root beer floats anyway. I'm not sure how to explain this, but I don't think a root beer float ever tasted as good as the one Dave McCoy handed me that night at the Bishop Carnival.

Back home, after the sound of Dave's motorcycle faded away, I thought about how I had loved being with Dave, yet I was still upset about that other girl. I figured she must be a wild one, and I decided that whatever relationship she had with Dave, well, what did I care? I just hoped that whoever she was, she would leave Bishop and never return.

One thing for sure, I was determined if Dave McCoy ever asked me on a date again, he was going to have to beg. The only trouble was I already longed to see him, to ride on the back of his bike leaning close to him, my arms wrapped around his waist. My crush was bigger than ever, and that was completely crazy. I wasn't about to stop going to dances, but I was also yearning for—I don't know, I guess more motorcycle rides with Dave.

Well, one week passed, then another, and I didn't hear a word from Dave. Marshall kept hinting that he wasn't dating anyone else. Still, no word. I decided that Dave just didn't like me, which made me angry with myself because I was thinking so much about him. Finally, he called, acting as if nothing was out of the ordinary, like no time had passed since our carnival date. He invited me to ride with him up Bishop Canyon and then hike from North Lake to Paiute Pass. Wouldn't you know? All my scheming flew straight out the window. I accepted before I remembered how much I hated hiking. Well, I didn't really hate hiking. I just never imagined that climbing up dusty, rocky trails could be fun. Boy, was I mistaken.

On the hike, I kept right up with Dave without a problem. I was strong from my dancing, but also, I think he deliberately set a comfortable pace for me. Anyway, in what seemed like no time, we were standing on Paiute Pass and looking out over the Sierra Nevada as if we owned the world. That moment changed me forever. When I lay my head on my pillow that night, I couldn't sleep. Every detail of the day spun around in my mind like a record player repeating a love song over and over again.

For the rest of the summer and fall, Dave took me hiking almost every weekend. How odd that I was the one who'd grown up in Bishop, but he was the one introducing me to our mountains. We usually started on a trail but ended up bushwhacking cross-country. Dave kept track of our whereabouts, so I didn't ever worry about getting lost.

I'd never seen such wildflowers. In the foothills, we walked by purple lupine and clusters of bright red Indian paintbrush intertwined among yellow mule's ears and white mariposa lilies. Farther up the canyons, especially by the creeks, we'd see wild roses, monkey flowers, pastel-tinted columbine, bright orange tiger lilies, and violet fireweed. The blue delphiniums and monkshood were so similar that I could hardly tell them apart.

One day, near the top of Bishop Pass, I decided it would be romantic to reach the summit in Dave's arms, so I pretended I was too tired to climb the whole way. I begged Dave to carry me the last few steps. Did he hold me in his arms over the top? Oh yes. Was he aware that I was only fooling around? I don't know. But he was so playful my silliness wouldn't have mattered. Dave loved to make me laugh. I swear, he was filling my heart with so much joy, there was no room left for my earlier misgivings.

Grandma was funny about Dave, always trying to hide how fond she was of him, like on the day he decided to train me for crossing creeks. On our hikes, we had to walk over logs that might be wet and slippery, so, for practice, Dave lifted me onto a six-foot fence near my house and had me walk along the top, teetering away, my arms stretched out for balance. Of course, he walked alongside, ready to catch me if I fell. But when Grandma looked out the window and saw what we were up to, she had one of her cat fits. She scolded Dave, telling him he was going to kill me one day. Five minutes later, she had him in the kitchen, eating her fresh-baked cookies and drinking lemonade.

Our weekend hikes came to an end in December when snow fell on Deadman Summit. Dave started spending his weekends skiing with his friends, people I didn't know. Just as I was feeling left out, he offered to teach me to ski. You can imagine how happy I was. Then I got this idea about making a deal. I told Dave that he could show me how to ski *if* he let *me* teach *him* to dance. Ha! He said yes. I couldn't believe it!

I expected Dave to pamper me on the ski slopes, but boy, was I in for a surprise. On my first run, I fell straight into a tree well.[1] I reached up for him to pull me out, but, he said, "Roma, you've got to learn how to take care of yourself. What if someday I'm not here to help you?"

At first, I was furious. Then I decided that if I wanted to hang around with Dave McCoy, I better toughen up. I took off my skis and poles, hefted them out of the tree well, and clawed my way out. Dave stood there, watching with a big grin on his face. He wasn't making fun, though. No, not at all. He was proud of me.

Skiing came easily to me, just like dancing had, and going on ski outings with Dave soon became part of my life. Everything to do with skiing was fun, from sliding down the snow on a pair of wooden boards to meeting new friends, sharing picnic lunches, and just being outside in snowy landscapes and winter air.

Dave kept his word about the dance lessons and did we ever have fun. We practiced square dancing over at the Coons' house, entertaining those kids as we spun across their wood floor. Dave was such a natural athlete that he caught onto the basics right away. I was sure he would be a terrific dancer. But as time went on, I realized his heart wasn't into dancing like mine was. I mean, at the ski club dances and at Keough's, he would get out there on the floor, but I could tell he was only trying to make me happy.

OF all the activities Dave and I did together, riding on the back of his motorcycle was my favorite. There were times he picked me up after work, and we rode north to Reno, or south to Bakersfield, just for dinner. He'd go about 70 miles per hour, except when he slowed down to 50 or 60 so he could weave around road stakes as if they were a slalom course. I wasn't afraid, not one bit. When he invited me to go swimming at Whitmore Tubs, I told him I'd only go if he touched the fenders to the ground on the corners of the Sherwin Grade, like he'd done before.

I asked Dave to teach me to drive his motorcycle, and under his coaching, I got pretty good. We'd go down to a big flat dirt area near the Owens River, and I'd sit on the back while he spun donuts, putting his foot down for balance, teaching me to lean correctly through the turns. Then we'd switch positions. Pretty soon, we'd be riding down the highway and I'd ask him if I could take a turn at the handlebars. Without slowing down, Dave would lift one leg in the air, and I'd crawl under. As soon as I was settled in front, he would give me control. I'd even run slalom through the road stakes as long his hands were on top of mine.

People might say Dave and I were crazy doing what we did. But to us, everything seemed perfectly normal and safe and right. Of course, Grandma didn't like it that I was riding a motorcycle, but she knew that Dave had no other means of transportation, and she liked him. If she had known exactly what we were doing, she would have put her foot down.

As the summer went along, I realized I was trying to live two lifestyles at once. I'd come home from an adventure with Dave and be too tired to go to a dance. If I did go to a dance and Dave arrived at my doorstep the next morning, all smiles and ready to go, I'd be so tired I'd have to pry my eyes open. I didn't dare tell him how much I longed to sleep in. Something had to give. So, I started skipping dances. The thing was, I didn't feel like I was making a sacrifice. My priorities had changed. I was in love.

Yes, love. That's what I was feeling. I loved Dave's maturity and kindness, his judgment and his strength. I knew he would take care of me no matter what we were doing. He wasn't wild like I had initially thought, just adventurous, and he was more fun than anyone I'd ever met.

I told Grandma my feelings, praying she would approve. She encouraged me to take my time. Dave was a fine young man, she said, but the relationship would only work if I got along with his mother. Grandma's advice made me shiver. You see, on one of our motorcycle rides to Reno, I'd met Edna McCoy, and from the moment she'd opened the front door, I felt uneasy and out of place.

Edna was intimidating, not warm and welcoming like Dave. The home where she worked as a housekeeper was immaculate with shiny silver pitchers and serving platters on display through the glass doors of fancy cupboards. Edna hardly acknowledged my presence, didn't ask one question about me but did she ever dote on her "Sonny." Then, as if I wasn't even there, she invited Dave to stay for dinner so he could meet her rich employer, doctor so and so, and his lovely daughter who was graduating *with honors* from the University of Nevada. How uncalled-for was that? Obviously, I wasn't pretty enough, or smart enough, or rich enough for Edna McCoy. I thought then and there, if Dave's mother was going to insult me, then I wasn't going to have anything to do with her. After all, I was in love with her son, not her. Thank heavens, he told Edna we couldn't stay. He took my hand and we walked down the sidewalk, both of us knowing that his mother was watching. I held my head high as if to say, Dave might be your son, but *I* am the woman in his life.

My dream summer of 1938 came to a sudden end in late August when Dave and I were riding home from a motorcycle trip to Virginia City. I had my arms wrapped around his waist, my head resting on his back, and my eyes closed. When he felt the bike going down, he pushed us off. I must have flown to the side of the road and down the bank, but I don't remember. The next thing I knew, I was in the dirt and the sagebrush. It took the terror in Dave's voice to bring me to my senses. I scrambled up the bank and walked through the darkness toward him.[2]

You know what's funny? Most people would have been upset about being in an accident like that, but I wasn't, not at all. I was delighted to be walking by Dave's side while he pushed the wrecked bike through the darkness. As far as I was concerned, my boyfriend was a hero who had just saved my life, and the thousands of twinkling stars lighting our way would bless us forever.

I had no premonition of the reception that was waiting for us in Bishop. Oh, was Grandma mad. She barely talked to me. And then my sister Frances started in, preaching about how I should go to a secretarial school. My boss at the bank threw in his two cents, too. He was furious, all riled up and carrying on about how I was getting a bad reputation riding on the back of a motorcycle with an older man. If I didn't quit going around with this careless, irresponsible guy who couldn't even afford a car and had almost killed me, then I should look elsewhere for a job.

Why wouldn't people just leave me alone instead of telling me what to do, or think, or feel? Didn't they realize I was in love with Dave, and that he was the finest man in the universe? Couldn't they see how much fun we were having?

If I had been more rebellious, I would have asked Dave to run away with me, right then and there. But I had been raised to respect my elders, so I listened to what they said. I started to wonder if I *did* need to make more of my life. After all, going to a professional school didn't mean Dave and I had to break up. Maybe we wouldn't see each other as much, but we would still be in love. I would learn to be a really good secretary, and Dave and I would have a bright future together.

Frances was determined that I would attend Westwood Business School. She found me work as a maid, housecleaning for a wealthy family in Beverly Hills in exchange for room and board. I could ride a bus to school, and I would be right near UCLA, where there would be lots of opportunities to meet nice young people and take dance classes. Grandma encouraged me to go. She assured me she would be fine on her own.

In the middle of my confusion, Aim Morhardt, a new teacher at Bishop

Aim Morhardt, 1938.

Roma by the Owens River.

High, offered to help me. Aim was a skilled photographer—he used to travel with Zane Grey, the cowboy author, taking pictures—and a genius. I mean, literally. A government study had identified him by IQ tests and was tracking his life. Well, with Grandma's blessing, Aim took portfolio photos of me and mailed them to his friend in New York City, the center of the world for a dancer. Aim's friend wrote back and suggested I move to the city and work as a photographer's model while studying dance.

Back and forth my mind swayed. New York, Southern California, Bishop, being a dancer, making money as a model. Why, maybe I could earn enough money to buy Grandma the new dining room set she'd wanted for so long, and... and... I swear, right in the middle of trying to fill my head with positive thoughts, I threw myself on my bed and wept. I didn't want to go to New York City. I wanted to keep spending my time with Dave, where I was happy. Working to be a professional dancer sounded like a lonely struggle, and worst of all, my family was angry with the man I loved. What a mess.

Dave didn't say a thing to stop me from leaving. He just told me he would support whatever decision I made. I wasn't surprised. He felt so terrible about the accident that he couldn't even think straight. I told him I would write once I got settled. That's how we left everything. Vague.

As soon as I boarded the Greyhound heading south, my heart felt like a heavy stone. In Los Angeles, my life felt like a living nightmare. First off, the business school was a waste of time. I already knew everything they were teaching me. I called a boy I used to dance with who was living down there, but talking to him only made me miss Dave. I couldn't stand the way the family I was working for talked down to me. The daughters, who were my age and attending UCLA, ordered me around as if I was less of a person because I was making their beds and washing their dishes.

I'd been in L.A. less than a week when I knew I didn't belong there. I got this feeling I needed to get right back to Bishop, or I would regret it for the rest of my life. I packed my suitcase, took a city bus to the Greyhound station where I knew there was a Western Union office, and sent Dave a telegram.

On the six-hour bus ride home, I thought about how much I longed to tell Dave that I wanted to spend the rest of my life with him. Then, typical me, as the bus motored up the highway, stupid doubts crept into my head. What if he hadn't received my telegram? What if he'd left for the Navy to become a pilot like he'd once mentioned? What if his mother had influenced him to date that girl in Reno, or maybe, just maybe, something else bad had happened, who knew what? By the time the bus passed through Lone Pine, I'd worked myself into a complete dither.

An hour later, we reached Bishop. I stepped off the bus wearing all my worries on my face, looking around for Dave. And there he was, walking toward me, looking as handsome as ever, grinning away with a big "welcome home" smile. All my fears disappeared.

Without saying a word, Dave pulled me in real close with those strong arms of his, and tears of relief rolled down my cheeks. We walked through the parking area directly toward a shiny black Chevy with red flames on the hood. Before I could ask about his motorcycle, he opened the passenger door for me, then bowed like a gentleman and said that a lady deserves to ride in the style her grandmother would approve.

CHAPTER SEVEN

A Leader in Local Skiing

Dave racing at McGee.

S eeing Roma at the Bishop bus station, tearful and vulnerable, Dave wanted to keep her by his side, to take care of her, to love her. They should marry. Today, tomorrow, next week. Why wait? They could drive three hours to Reno, marry that day, and be home by evening. Confident she felt the same, Dave loaded her suitcase into the trunk, offered his hand as she stepped into the car, and walked around to the driver's side. Roma slid to the middle of the bench seat and looked up. Her eyes glowed with happiness. Dave returned her gaze—and then he faltered. What was he thinking? Roma was only 18 years old. She would never marry without her grandmother's approval, and that was something he'd lost with the motorcycle accident. He felt sure he could regain Grandma Folk's trust, given time. But for now, he needed to be patient.

Dave put his arm around Roma's shoulder and pulled her close. He kissed her slowly, hoping she would feel how much he cared for her. Then, to distract from the intensity of the moment, he asked, "How does this hot rod compare to my old motorcycle?" They both started laughing as if enjoying a truth they alone knew. No matter how terrific Dave's new car, *nothing* could compare with the fun they'd had riding his motorcycle.

By the fall of 1938, most of the towns between Lone Pine and Bridgeport had formed ski clubs, each with its own Forest Service permits, bylaws, up-skis, and unique challenges. The biggest concern for the Bishop-based Eastern Sierra Ski Club (ESSC) was that there was no longer an up-ski on McGee Mountain. To avoid a lawsuit with fox-farm owner Peter Steffen—who had filed a complaint that noise from skiers was causing his foxes to eat their young—Corty Hill had dismantled his sling-lift and relocated the materials to a Little Round Valley slope just north of Toms Place, across the road from Happy Jacks.[1] There he constructed two up-skis in tandem and named his new ski operation "The Hill."

Envisioning an upscale ski resort that catered to their affluent Los Angeles social set, Corty and his wife Blanche organized a private ski club called "Wooden Wings." Among the founding members were Hollywood celebrities Hank and Frances Fonda, Tyrone Power and his fiancée Anabelle, and others. For their clubhouse, the Hills leased Toms Place from the owner Ma Yerby, remodeled the building to resemble a Bavarian lodge, and hired Austrian ski instructor Sepp Benedikter to teach the Arlberg technique.[2]

In response to Corty's relocation, ESSC obtained a permit for a permanent tow on McGee's south-facing slope, about a mile from the fox farm. Dave and two other club members converted a discarded truck engine into a heavy-duty 1,200-foot rope tow and installed it parallel to an access road they had graded straight up the slope.[3] Skiers would have to park their cars on McGee Canyon Road and hike about a hundred yards to the tow, but at least they wouldn't be bothering the foxes.

Meanwhile, ESSC president George Deibert organized work parties to construct a small warming shelter and initiated a search for a European ski instructor. By the time the snow fell, Deibert had lured Hans Georg away from Soda Springs, where he had taught skiing the previous winter, by offering him the opportunity to run his own ski school on McGee.

SKI TRACKS
Hans Georg Comes to the Eastern Sierra
1938

Born in Würzburg, Germany, in 1911, Hans Georg was known as an international ski stylist. He held the highest certification from Switzerland's St. Moritz Ski School and claimed to be the first Swiss ski instructor in America. The California Chamber of Commerce named him an honorary member and printed his ski conditioning exercises in its California bulletin on skiing. Hans' instructional book, *Simplified Skiing*, sold 1,500 copies in Pacific Coast bookstores during the winter of 1938-39 alone.[4]

Life had not been easy for Hans. Ever since the mid-1930s when his family's Jewish heritage had caused them to abruptly leave their comfortable home in Germany and move to Switzerland, Hans had faced emotional challenges. He had to fight to keep himself from sinking into depression when he learned that relatives who had remained in Germany were killed by their own countrymen. Looking for a new start, he shipped his BMW and his skis to the United States and followed close behind. Unfortunately, all was not roses in America. There were people who Hans felt were prejudiced against him not only because he was Jewish but also because he was German. Again looking for a new identity, he changed his name, drove to California, and introduced himself as a Swiss ski instructor.

As soon as Hans saw the potential of Eastern Sierra skiing, he began a campaign directed toward Southern California skiers. He submitted articles and photos to magazines, solicited radio interviews, courted Hollywood skiers, and secured a position as ski writer for the *Los Angeles Examiner*. Hans also designed brochures that advertised skiing on Mt. Whitney, as well as branches of the Hans Georg Ski School at Bishop Creek, Rock Creek, McGee Creek, and Crestview.[5] Local skiers wondered how this energetic man was going to be able to instruct in so many different places at the same time!

Once snow covered McGee Mountain, skiers from Santa Monica, Ventura, Pomona, and Los Angeles came to ski ESSC's new tow. Gladly paying one dollar per day to cover the cost of fuel, these guests skied an average of 500 runs on Saturday, and then again on Sunday. ESSC members sold tickets and refreshments, while Claude James and Dave smoothed the ski tracks, monitored the tow, fueled the engine, trouble-shot mechanical breakdowns, and spliced the rope when it frayed.[6] Hans Georg taught beginners and intermediates, guiding his students into a parallel turn by having them place their outside hand on their stomach. Amused by this unfamiliar technique, Dave joked that Hans was teaching the "Appendicitis Turn."

Filled with the afterglow that comes from spending a day on the mountain, skiers stopped by McGee Creek Lodge for après-ski gatherings. Dorrance Keough welcomed them to her recently winterized hostelry, where they enjoyed her new wine and tearoom and small dance floor. Her guests could fuel up at her service station, use her telephone and telegraph, ice-skate on a frozen pond across the road, and soak in the geothermal waters of Whitmore Hot Tubs, only a 25-minute cross-country ski away.

Late afternoons after visiting skiers departed, Dave restarted the rope tow so club members could practice for the upcoming Ski Mountaineer's

Lift lines at Eastern Sierra Ski Club's McGee Rope Tow.

Proficiency Exam.[7] Skiing down, he made wide-sweeping arcs and then short-radius turns, while Roma followed right behind him, striving to match his tracks. Only when the sun dipped behind McGee Mountain causing daylight to fade did Dave shut down the rope tow.

By the winter of 1938-39, the U.S. skiing population was estimated to be in the millions. Many of these skiers considered ski vacations a way to quell nervous anxiety about war, a threat never long out of the public consciousness. Downhill skiing had already become so popular that across the nation, skiers and non-skiers alike were noticing advertisements and articles about ski fashion, equipment, romance, adventures, and up-skis.[8]

SKI TRACKS
More Up-skis for More Skiers
1939

Word is out that the ski world is booming. Mont-Tremblant, the highest mountain in Canada's Laurentians, recently opened for skiing. Easterners claim that Stowe, Vermont, has the longest and coldest chairlift in the country. In the northwest, die-hard skiers boast of a three-mile ski run on Mt. Rainier, Washington, even if the up-skis are inadequate and there are no nearby accommodations. Austrian Hannes Schroll and Walt Disney are working together to find financing to develop Sugar Bowl, near California's Donner Summit. Elite U.S. ski racers are training at Sun Valley, while the area's Ski School weeks are so popular that entire classes are making advance bookings for reunion lessons. In February 1939, Hannes Schneider became ski school director at Cranmore Mountain, New Hampshire. Due to negotiations between infamous Nazi leader, Heinrich Himmler, and Hannes Schneider's powerful friends—one a renowned lawyer and the other an international financier—Schneider had been released from prison and allowed an exit visa to America.[9]

In Southern California, "weekend warriors" so enjoyed their sport they were willing to drive hundreds of miles for just a few days of skiing. They valued the long drive as an opportunity to spend time with family and friends. Once they arrived, they didn't mind paying for rope tow services, food, and lodging, and they accepted inconveniences such as stormy weather, icy roads, and long up-ski lines as part of the ski experience.

At times, Dave wondered if there was a future for him in the ski business. His willingness to transport, set up, and tear down rope tows, along with his passion for skiing and ski racing, had inadvertently positioned him in a significant role as part of this young, yet expanding, industry. His belief that the success of a ski operation depended on the camaraderie of people having fun together intrigued him, but a quick reality check made him discard the idea with a laugh.

Sure, people loved to ski. And yes, Dave had mechanical ability, physical stamina, common sense, and a growing knowledge of Eastern Sierra snow. But those qualifications couldn't overcome blizzards, avalanches, mechanical breakdowns, road closures, economic ups and downs, and too little or too much snow. The only certainty for a ski area operator was that business would be unpredictable and erratic. Even having an abundance of money didn't guarantee success. Look at Corty Hill.

Corty's railroad inheritance couldn't generate a snowstorm, prevent the winds from blowing snow away, or protect his up-ski from breaking down. As it was, the lifts on The Hill endured so many mechanical breakdowns that Corty asked Orrin Broberg, a skier-friend who worked for him as an engineer, to troubleshoot the problems. On a weekend trip, Orrin managed to get the up-skis operating temporarily. However, skiers still had to risk breaking through a thin layer of crusty, wind-affected snow while trying to maneuver around sagebrush and rocks. According to Orrin's wife, Alice, the most memorable part of their ski trip was visiting with celebrities such as the Fondas, Letitia Fairbanks, Phoebe Hearst, and Tyrone Power.

By January 1939, lack of snow forced both Corty and the ESSC to close their respective Long Valley up-skis. Once again, skiers migrated north to Deadman Summit. Under blue skies and high-altitude sunshine, the ladies skied the gentle terrain in halter tops while the men skied shirtless or in short-sleeved T-shirts. Dave and Roma sported embroidered leather suspenders that Corty and Blanche had brought them from Europe. With Hans Georg instructing beginners in the Swiss St. Moritz method and only steps away, Sepp Benedikter teaching the Austrian Arlberg technique, the scene resembled a celebration of snow, skiing, and friendship.

Early in March, there was enough snow on the south side of Mammoth Mountain for the Eastern Sierra Ski Club to hold the third annual Inyo-Mono Championships. Dave swept the field, winning the downhill, slalom, and cross-country events. At the awards ceremony, the American Legion awarded him a two-foot-high perpetual trophy. Hans Georg amused the crowd by donating a copy of his *Skiing Simplified* to "the lucky winner of last place in combined."[10]

The following weekend, Corty drove Dave to Badger Pass to compete in the inaugural Far West Kandahar. During the ten-hour drive north to Reno, over the Sierra Nevada to the west side, and south to Yosemite Valley, Corty shared his well-thought-out ideas about ski instruction, ski safety, and ski racing.

In the morning, Dave and Corty inspected Yosemite's Rail Creek downhill. Sideslipping from gate to gate, they learned why this course had

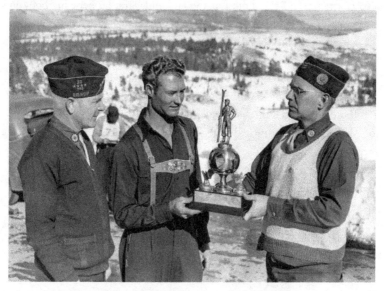

Dave receiving a trophy from members of the American Legion.

a reputation for testing a racer's ability to handle distance, speed, and air. The two men discussed the line they would take, paying extra attention to the final challenge, a threatening bump at the summer railroad crossing. Here, they needed to "pre-jump." If timed right, the racer could avoid the natural kicker by making a small jump just before the highest rise, skimming over the lip, and landing softly on the downhill side. Miscalculating the timing of a pre-jump would launch a skier high into the air. If a racer fell here, there was no way to regain speed across the flat to the finish.

After inspection, racers ran the course in sections, gradually increasing their speed. In the mandatory nonstop training run, Dave and Corty felt confident. Their wax ran fast, and their lines were good. They prepped and waxed their skis, then enjoyed dinner in the luxury of the Ahwahnee, where they lounged around the grand rock fireplace before retiring to a good night's sleep. The next morning, Dave awoke in high spirits, ready to make a mark in California ski racing.

Dave skied the upper course aggressively, adjusting his knees and ankles to the irregular terrain. In the turns, he initiated directional changes early and passed by the gates with his skis running straight and smooth. No chattering, no skidding. On the straightaways, he kept his body in an aerodynamic position and approached the railroad crossing faster than he had in the nonstop. Misjudging his speed, he initiated his pre-jump an instant too late—the very mistake he'd hoped to avoid. The lip of the bump launched him upward and forward. He catapulted through the air, out of control and off-balance, and then he crashed. Hard.

Protocol dictated that racers complete the race even if they had trouble on the course. Dave picked himself up and poled across the flat to the finish gate. Hiding his disappointment, he chalked the race up as another learning experience and set his sights on the 1939 California State Ski Championships, only a week away, to be held on his home ground.

WITH McGee still snowless, ESSC staged the championships on the south side of Mammoth. This competition would be the first CSA-sanctioned race ever held in the Eastern Sierra, and the first time Mammoth's long winter season and dependable snow conditions received widespread publicity. Determined to make the event a success, club members spent weeks planning every detail of the competition.

George Deibert arranged for racers to be housed in Bishop and made provisions for water and sack lunches. Chief timer Tex Cushion and race secretary Claude James organized entries and start orders. Using their sparse equipment, Caltrans worked tirelessly to clear Lake Mary Road to the staging area. Chief starter, Forest Ranger Fred Meckel, tested the telephones he had borrowed from the ranger station and set up a loud-speaker system on loan from the local Standard Oil station. Hans Georg set control gates and nailed directional markers on pine trees to delineate the downhill course. Dave strung telephone wire from bottom to top, and then set up the club's two portable tows in tandem to transport racers and officials as far as possible up the downhill course.[11] From there, athletes and officials would have to climb the rest of the way to the start.

Finally, race weekend arrived. Never before had the Eastern Sierra hosted so many high-ranking ski racers, celebrities, and well-known ski personalities. Among the guests was Dr. Joel Hildebrand, one of America's leading authorities on skiing. A renowned chemistry professor at the University of California and a former Sierra Club president, Hildebrand had also managed the 1936 U.S. Olympic Alpine Ski Team.

The first day of the meet was the cross-country competition. Members of Wooden Wings Ski Club stood near the finish, cheering racers on by shaking cowbells Corty had brought back from Europe for just that purpose. Amidst cheers and bells, Dave fought to a 3rd place finish, an excellent start to what he hoped would be a great weekend.

The next morning, under a bright blue sky, racers sidestepped up the slalom course, memorizing the gates as they packed the snow. At 10 a.m., ski icon Otto Steiner and ski instructor Sepp Benedikter foreran. They reported to officials that the course was in good condition. The chief timer radioed to the top and instructed Fred Meckel to start the race.

Dave had felt out of sorts all morning. Sidestepping to the start, he tried to ignore his discomfort, but to no avail. By the time his turn in the starting gate came, the flu had the best of him. He attempted to race but skied so poorly he wished he'd dropped out. Dave told himself to forget his slalom results and focus on the downhill, scheduled for the next day. He should feel better by then.

Sunday morning, 40-mile-per-hour winds blasted across the downhill course. The race committee debated canceling but decided to go forward as planned. Racers, officials, and volunteers bundled in their warmest clothes and worked their way to the start. As ski writer Ethel Severson described, "… the Sunday course was like glass, with icy particles on the faces, icicles forming on eyelashes and beards, and racers wearing overcoats. The most stubborn of spectators huddled around a smoky fire, and the snow which melted on the clothes promptly froze when they turned away."

Dave felt sicker for the downhill than he had in the slalom. Partway up the course, he stopped climbing. Too ill to continue, he skied down to the finish line. To his surprise, Corty's attitude was as upbeat as ever. Sure, it was bad luck to get sick. But that's all there was to it. Athletes have ups and downs that need to be taken in stride. "You'll see," Corty said.

After the race, a crowd gathered in the warmth of Penney's Tavern. As Ethel VanDegrift reported, "When the results were posted, a throng of skiers six feet deep stormed the bulletin board, anxious to see their times."[12] During the awards presentation, the CSA president declared that despite the storm conditions, the race was one of the outstanding meets in the history of California skiing. Dr. Hildebrand proclaimed in his speech, "The Eastern Sierra is the finest region I've seen in California for all types of skiing."[13] ESSC members were jubilant. They had met their objectives in holding the state championships. The Eastern Sierra had earned a place on the map of California skiing.

A few days after the championships, Corty contacted Dave and asked, "Why don't you go to the U.S. Nationals with me? I'll sponsor you." Corty's words stunned Dave. He knew that the 1939 National Downhill and Slalom Championships, scheduled to be held at Mt. Hood, Oregon, on April 1 and 2, were also the official tryouts for the 1940 Olympic Alpine Ski Team. The top ten men and eight women finishers would be invited to train at Sun Valley, Idaho, where their coaches would be Friedl Pfeifer and Peter Radacher, two renowned European racers. To be able to support themselves but still maintain their amateur status, athletes were to be offered jobs unrelated to skiing. Dick Durrance, the reigning collegiate and national ski champion, was already gainfully employed by Sun Valley as a public relations representative. During the pre-Olympic summer, he planned to stay fit by cutting ski trails on Bald Mountain.

Corty's invitation offered Dave a chance to race against the best in the country, to try out for the 1940 Olympic Team, and to compete on a downhill course that met the F.I.S. international requirements. According to the official program for the race, the course would have two schusses: one where racers reached speeds of 60 to 70 miles per hour, the other, not so steep but bumpy. Some sections were to be so difficult and fast that they couldn't be taken straight but would require long sweeping turns. Nowhere would the course be so slow as to "turn the downhill into a giant slalom and ruin a fine sport."

Trying to ground himself, Dave wondered if he could afford to spend a year focused solely on ski racing. What if he missed an opportunity to get into the ski business? What about his steady DWP job and his dreams of becoming a hydrographer? How would Roma feel if he suddenly left the Eastern Sierra to train in Idaho and then, if he made the Olympic team, headed overseas to race in Europe? She was already unhappy about being left behind when he traveled to California races. And beneath all these concerns loomed the biggest question of all. What chance did he have to qualify for the team?

There was no doubt that Dave longed to excel at ski racing. But so far, his results had been inconsistent. He recalled his joy when he'd won the Inyo-Mono Championships, his disappointment when he'd crashed in Yosemite, and his frustration about being sick at the state championships. Clearly, success in athletics was fleeting. Dave thanked Corty for his generous offer and graciously declined, explaining why.

Corty listened attentively. After a pause, he broke into a smile and teased, "Well then, if you aren't going to try out for the Olympics, how about being a movie star? Yes, I can definitely get you into the film business. You've got the good looks and I've got the connections." The two friends laughed. They both knew Corty was right. They also knew Dave McCoy wasn't about to leave the mountains for Hollywood.

SKI TRACKS
The Games That Never Were
1940

The 1940 Winter Olympic Games were politically charged
from the beginning. Originally awarded to Tokyo, the
Japanese forfeited after the second Sino-Japanese War
broke out, and the Games were assigned to St. Moritz,
Switzerland. That's when the International Olympic
Committee (I.O.C.) ruled that ski instructors were ineligible to compete as amateurs because they had received
money for their sport. As a result, the I.O.C. designated
alpine skiing as an exhibition sport. Switzerland refused
to host the Olympics unless skiing was restored as a competitive event. Rather than bend to the will of Switzerland,
the I.O.C. transferred the competition to Garmisch-
Partenkirchen, Germany. This assignment was short-lived.
According to I.O.C. bylaws, a "belligerent" country could
not hold the Olympic Games. Therefore, when Hitler
attacked Czechoslovakia in March 1939 and invaded
Poland that September, Germany disqualified itself as an
Olympic host country.

The 1940 Winter Olympics turned out to be the "Olympics that never
were." Two days after Hitler's invasion of Poland, France and Britain
declared war on Germany, and World War II began. In Europe, terror and
fighting for survival now eclipsed the simple pleasures of life. Ski racing
existed only as a treasured memory, a dream disappeared.

CAUGHT between the threat of war and recovery from the Great
Depression, Americans held their collective breath and prayed the fighting
would end before their country joined in. With the strengthening economy, individuals earned more money and, in turn, spent more money, even
purchasing luxury items such as nylon stockings, invented the previous
year and now the rage. To escape their worries, Americans danced to the

jazz rhythms of Benny Goodman and Count Basie, packed theaters to watch movies such as Gone with the Wind, and some skied.

Indulging in their favorite pastime, American skiers crowded local ski tows, conscious that each trip could well be their last. Affluent Americans who normally would have been skiing the Alps joined the local crowds. In California alone, at least 65 permanent up-skis plus numerous portables and privately-owned tows pulled skiers up the slopes. Northern California's Southern Pacific Railroad transported skiers to the ski hut at Donner Summit's Norden Station. In Southern California, plans to build a million-dollar aerial tramway at Mt. San Jacinto were underway. Big Bear had a new chairlift in the works, and skiers were campaigning to develop San Gorgonio, the highest peak in the region.[14]

In the Eastern Sierra, winter travel increased by 50 percent, and employment doubled as business owners winterized their buildings to welcome visiting skiers. One group of individuals envisioned a J-bar on the lower slopes of Carson Peak near June Lake, and another designed a series of three portable tows in tandem extending from the western shore of Mono Lake to the geologic bench above.[15] A Mr. Robert Routh submitted a proposal to build a 7,000-foot aerial tramway on the east side of Mammoth Mountain. Nothing came of any of these plans.

Still, the media continued to promote skiing as a relief from America's worry over war. Documentary filmmaker and radio host Lowell Thomas broadcast his radio show from ski resorts, and at least 20 million listeners—one-sixth of the U.S. population at the time—heard him declare that joy could be found skiing in the mountains.[16] Ford and Buick released full-page newspaper ads featuring skiers in fashionable skiwear leaning against shiny cars parked near McGee Mountain. Bishop's Bob Brown, executive director of the Inyo-Mono Association, mailed a weekly press release to 200 out-of-town businesses, wrote articles for the popular magazine *Ski Heil*, and created Eastern Sierra skiing exhibits for display in department stores and at the state Capitol building in Sacramento. The *Los Angeles Times* hired Ethel Severson to write a biweekly column called "Ski Slants." Every Tuesday and Thursday, readers now had a source to find out snow conditions, lodging rates, upcoming events, race results, ski travel, ski instruction, and general ski trivia.

Ski Tracks
Excerpts from "Ski Slants"
1939

... one hundred miles between Bishop and Bridgeport is the answer to the skier's prayer written in sun and snow. Man has added punctuation marks in the way of lodges, lifts, and snowplows, but nature has been preparing this country for the skier for eons now, and it is ready for you.

... your first day on skis will be one of the most exciting experiences of your life. And the fun won't wear off. The most harried adult becomes something of a child again the minute he puts a pair of these zany boards on his feet...

Throughout the December 1939 holidays, skiers packed the Eastern Sierra. To accommodate this regional overload, rope tow operators from Lone Pine to Bridgeport acted as clearing agents, sending skiers to other tows when theirs got too crowded. Some skiers outright avoided the busy rope tows and climbed virgin slopes with sealskins on their ski bases in search of untouched powder. Hans Georg offered to guide skiers over Mammoth's expansive terrain.

Newly elected ESSC president Dave McCoy operated one of the club's portable tows on the north side of Mammoth. He was more than happy to spend his energy meeting the demands of a record number of skiers, partly because he had an unusual amount of free time on his hands. During the preceding few months, his relationship with Roma had spiraled downward. In late November, the couple had broken up.

Not even Dave and Roma's closest friends knew what had come between them. Perhaps fear of war had caused tension and confusion. Maybe Grandma Folk was still harboring resentment about the motorcycle accident. Possibly, one of them wanted to marry, but the other didn't. Whatever the cause, neither Dave nor Roma had the communication skills to work through emotional problems. They simply avoided discussing what had come between them and agreed to go their separate ways.

After all, being in love was supposed to be fun.

Now, when Dave and Roma saw each other in public, they acted as if they were casual acquaintances who'd never been in love with each other. They proceeded forward in life as attractive, vibrant, and eligible individuals. Dave opened his heart to other women. Roma double-dated with her sister, Frances, and attended every dance that came to town.

WHEN a January blizzard shut down Minaret Road, Claude James and Dave revved up ESSC's permanent tow on McGee. That autumn, the two men had installed an engine at the top of the tow, and they were anxious to see if pulling from above, rather than pushing from below, would provide power enough to accommodate more skiers. Success!

The only problem with the tow was that the high number of skiers it could now carry made the slopes crowded and unsafe. On two separate occasions, out-of-control skiers hit Dave while he was standing in the rope tow line. One collision lacerated his shoulder; the other left a deep gash in the back of his thigh. Both times, Dr. Scott accessed his ever-ready medical kit to clean and stitch Dave's wounds. Angered by the rising danger on the slopes, Scotty began to document and analyze skiing accidents at club-sponsored activities.[17]

On March 2, 1940, club president Dave hosted ESSC's fourth annual Inyo-Mono Championships at McGee. On race day, he issued volunteers their assignments and then joined his fellow competitors for the cross-country race. Waiting for the mass start, the racers worked their skis back and forth against the snow to keep their wax from sticking. At the sound of the gun, they took off, winding up the hill toward McGee Creek and then looping back to the start/finish. As later reported, "Dave McCoy with his good condition and racing skis won in the excellent time of 27.22 minutes, followed by 'leather-lunged' Fred Meckel in 28.59 minutes, and Lee Vining's Augie Hess—a last-minute entry racing on downhill skis—in 30.15."[18]

That afternoon, Dave won the men's slalom. The next morning, wearing bib number one, he left the starting gate for the downhill as the first skier on the course. One minute and 38 seconds later, he crossed the finish and turned to a stop, out of breath. Satisfied with his run, he looked back up the course to watch the others.

Racer number two, Michigan-raised Carl Grebe was already on course. Carl, who barely knew how to ski, was racing on a whim. Two months earlier, he had taken a job caretaking the Cushions' Winter Patrol Station. Tex had given him a pair of skis, taught him how to snowplow, and then left for Bishop, leaving Carl in charge of the dogs and the snow shoveling. Tex returned to Mammoth just before the championships and invited Carl to join him mushing the dog team down to the race. At McGee, Carl got caught up in the excitement and filled out an entry form.

Carl had watched Dave attack the course. Having no other strategy, he tried to mimic Dave and headed straight downhill. But unlike Dave, Carl was immediately out of control. He skidded into a snowplow, crashed, cartwheeled head over heels, somehow landed on his feet, and continued onward, eventually making it to the finish line in one piece. Dave skied over to this crazy stranger covered in snow and introduced himself. As Carl recalled that day, "We hit it off right away, and that was the beginning of a lifelong friendship."[19]

AT the time of the championships, Roma and Dave were both involved with other people and barely on speaking terms with each other. Still, throughout the weekend, Dave watched Roma from a distance. Seeing her so happy, confident, and carefree, laughing and talking with the women racers, he felt a tug on his heart. The decision for them to go in different directions was *not* what Dave wanted. He watched Roma speed into 2nd place in the slalom feeling as if she were *his* protégé. He stood frozen in place as she raced the downhill, breathed a sigh of relief when she passed the finish line, and swelled with pride when he heard she'd won.

Roma had no idea Dave had paid such close attention to her skiing. What she *did* know was that when he congratulated her after the race, her heartbeat quickened. Then, just as Dave was walking away, he said, "Roma, you've got the skills to ski Mammoth. I mean, off the top, this spring. That is, if you're still interested." The familiar sound of Dave's voice stirred a feeling in Roma she hadn't even realized she'd been missing.

ALSO competing in the 1940 Inyo-Mono Championships was the Bishop

High Race Team, sponsored by Aim Morhardt. A newcomer to town working as a long-term substitute teacher for the high school orchestra, Aim had learned to ski in Europe in 1926.[20] Still attracted to the sport, he volunteered to help the ESSC with whatever the club needed, and he organized the Bishop High School Ski Club.[21] Outings included trips to ESSC's McGee rope tow, ski lessons, classification tests, an interclass meet, and a ski tour on Mammoth Mountain.[22] Once the Bishop High School Ski Club was established, Aim organized the best male skiers into a race team and recruited Dave McCoy to coach the athletes on Wednesday afternoons.

The first training session was down by the Owens River, where the boys helped Dave cut and trim willow branches for slalom poles. On Wednesdays after that, Aim transported the boys to wherever Dave was operating ESSC's tow. Dave set courses and occasionally offered advice, usually just saying, "Have fun!" Believing that the best way to improve ski ability was to ski, Dave encouraged the group to join him on the weekends. In turn for free rope tow tickets, they could smooth out the ski tracks that built up under the rope tow line.

When the boys expressed an interest in racing against other schools, Aim petitioned the California Interscholastic Federation (CIF) to approve skiing as a school-sanctioned sport. Next, he created the Interscholastic Ski Federation (ISF) to coordinate California and Nevada high school ski racers. Finally, he organized the first interscholastic ski meet in California. The success of this meet would determine whether CIF would sanction skiing as a school sport. Cosponsored by Bishop High School and the ESSC, visiting teams slept in sleeping bags on the Bishop High gym floor.

After a hard-fought battle on a rhythmic slalom course, which Dave had set on the north side of Mammoth, the race concluded with a Saturday night awards dance in the gymnasium. Portola High School, located in Plumas County, about 250 miles north of Bishop near Truckee, took home the first place Keough Cup, a perpetual team trophy donated by Dorrance Keough of McGee Creek Lodge.[23] Bishop placed a respectable 3rd. Soon after the meet, Aim received two letters, one from CSA's president complimenting him on the race, and the other from the CIF sanctioning ski racing as an official competitive high school sport.

For two winters, Corty Hill had struggled with minimal snow and low skier numbers at The Hill. One problem was that since Wooden Wings was a private club, skiers assumed The Hill must be private as well. To correct this misconception, Corty advertised moonlight skiing and lessons with Sepp Benedikter. But the promotional push came too late. Sepp no longer held the distinction of being the only European instructor in the region. Besides Hans Georg, Austrian Hans Kolb was now teaching at Crestview and German-born, Swiss-trained J. Gottfried Schmidt-Ehrenberg replaced Austrian Sigi Engl at Conway Summit.

In the spring of 1940, Corty disbanded The Hill and ended his Toms Place lease with Ma Yerby. Disappointed but upbeat, he now had time to focus on standardized ski instruction. Due to Corty's foresight, energy, and financial backing, Yosemite hosted CSA's first ski instructor certification.[24] Sepp Benedikter attended as the sole Eastern Sierra representative. Knowing the certification would be based on the Arlberg technique, and not wanting other instructors to mock his St. Moritz methods, Hans Georg declined to attend. So did Dave.

Dave had no desire to engage in debates over ski methodology. In fact, discussions about technique irritated him. Not that he was opposed to standardized ski instruction, he just wasn't interested. What attracted Dave to skiing was the pure joy of the sport, the challenge of operating ski tows, and the excitement of ski racing. His approach to helping the Bishop kids with their skiing was to respect them as individuals with unique personalities and athletic abilities, and to make sure that no matter how easy or how hard they were working, they were still having fun.

Late April, a cycle of freezing nights and warm days created corn snow, perfect conditions for Dave to take Roma skiing on Mammoth. But he hesitated. He knew that Grandma Folk had recently died, and Roma would be grieving her loss. Then again, he thought, what better way to lift Roma's spirits than to take her on a spring ski outing? Dave and his new friend, Carl Grebe, had already planned a Sunday trip up the mountain, so why not bring Roma along? Carl could make the saddest person laugh, and Dave believed laughter could help heal anything.

The quiet tone in Roma's voice when she answered Dave's phone call disclosed her sadness. Dave offered his condolences and then invited her to ski Mammoth. Roma's voice perked up. Yes! She would love to join him. She could make sandwiches. Was there anything else she should bring?

Before hanging up, Roma said she wanted to share something important with Dave. "I realize things were difficult between you and Grandma ever since the motorcycle accident, but I want you to know that all she ever wanted for me was happiness. I'll bet you she's smiling right now because I'm so happy about getting to ski Mammoth. And, because you called me."

Early Sunday, on the drive north from Bishop to Mammoth, Roma and Dave acted as awkward and shy as they had on their first date, years prior. But this time, Dave made an effort to converse. He told Roma she might remember Carl Grebe and how he'd tumbled down the course at the Inyo Mono Championships. They both laughed. By the time they reached the Winter Patrol Station to pick Carl up, they once again felt at ease with each other.

Dave paced a comfortable tempo as the threesome hiked up the mountain, resting their skis on their shoulders and holding their poles in one hand as they climbed. At the steep section below the summit, Dave paused to take Roma's skis and then continued upward, kicking the toe of his leather boots into the snow to make steps. Staying close behind, Roma punched the toe of her boot into each hole. As she neared the top, Dave reached for her hand, helped her up and over the edge, and then breathed a sigh of relief. Now he just needed to get her down safely.

Once on top, Dave, Carl, and Roma each signed the Sierra Club register, then sat down to eat lunch. Carl kidded Roma about the calamity she would have caused if she'd missed a step and fallen, knocking him over on her way down. Roma shook her head at Carl's teasing and then joined in his laughter. How long had it been since she'd laughed like this?

Preparing for the descent, Dave saw that Roma was frightened of jumping off the steep section. He understood her fear. The drop-off was scary for even the best of skiers. But, this was the only way down. With Dave prompting, Roma leaped off the edge, landed gracefully, and continued down, linking turns in the velvety corn snow.

After the Mammoth outing, Roma and Dave once again started spending most of their spare time together. They didn't talk about what had happened, whom they had dated, or how they had felt when they were apart. Instead, at least on the surface, they acted as if their relationship had never been interrupted or threatened by outside forces.

There was no question in Dave's mind that he wanted to marry Roma. Not only did she love to do the same things he did, but even more import-ant, her lifelong dedication to her grandmother exemplified the devotion she had for the people she loved. If Roma were to marry him, *their* chil-dren would never suffer the pain of a family breakup. Still, Dave didn't formally propose to Roma. He just started making casual statements like, "When we're married, we'll do such and such," and teasing her with ques-tions like, "How big a car do you think we'll need to carry around all the kids we're going to have?"

At ESSC's fall meeting, club members elected Claude James as president for the winter of 1940-41. Dave volunteered to operate the club's portable tows on weekends, holidays, and Wednesday afternoons, to store them at his Bishop bunkhouse when not in use, and to chair a committee that would organize competitions, draw up race rules, and gather the equip-ment needed to host races. Scotty offered to train a few club members to handle medical emergencies, thus forming the first organized ski patrol in the Eastern Sierra. Roma volunteered to be club treasurer and joined a committee that sold club patches and memberships and priced lift tickets. Non-members could choose to pay 10 cents a ride or 12 rides for $1.00, while club members paid 5 cents a ride or 30 rides for $1.25. Members could also earn 10 free rides for an hour's worth of work.[25]

Bob Brown continued to be in charge of public relations. He wrote arti-cles for *Ski Illustrated, Ski Heil,* and the *Western Ski Annual,* boasting miles of timber-free ski terrain a mere hundred yards from the recently improved Highway 395. He also doubled the number of weekly press releases mailed to department stores, oil companies, travel agencies, newspapers, radio stations, automobile clubs, the U.S. Forest Service, the Weather Bureau (now the National Weather Service), and the Department of Agriculture. Besides updates on skiing, Brown reported there was ice-skating on Ellery Lake, June Lake, Horseshoe Lake, North Lake, and Fish Slough. He announced that folks were skating on 15 acres of ice at Benton Station, north of Bishop, and that Bridgeport Reservoir boasted five square miles of glistening ice, the largest natural rink in the region. One of Brown's press releases about an Eastern Sierra snowstorm made national news.[26]

After the now-famous October storm subsided, skiers flocked to McGee Mountain. There they found clear roads, snow-covered slopes, parking space for two hundred cars, first aid, ski instruction, a small warming shelter with food service, and a temperamental 1,400-foot-long rope tow. The operator sat on a small board near the engine house and pulled a length of fishing line to start the engine. If the engine started, it required constant attention. One time, the exhaust pipe set fire to the engine house. Another time, the fuel line froze. But the worst incident was when carbon monoxide inhalation almost killed Claude James and Roma's brother Marshall. The two men had been inside the engine house working on the motor. They both started to feel groggy, so they stepped outside for fresh air. Claude, who had been working closest to the engine, collapsed unconscious onto the snow. Dave just happened to be nearby. He saw what happened, grabbed the toboggan stored at the top of the tow, quickly loaded a nonresponsive Claude, and schussed straight down to the road. Already alerted by Marshall, Dr. Scott was waiting at the bottom. Fortunately, Scotty was able to revive Claude with artificial respiration.

Midwinter, Howard More, a visiting skier who had previously built a rope tow for the Seven Springs ski hill in Pennsylvania, heard about ESSC's up-ski struggles. He proposed that for $725, he could fabricate a rope tow capable of hauling 40 skiers at a time. If the club poured the foundation and set the wooden towers, he said he could have the new tow delivered, installed, and operational for Easter week.

True to his word, Howard trailered the new rope tow to McGee right on schedule. According to plan, club members and racers were ready to help with the installation. The group used a friend's tractor to haul the engine to the top of the tow. As promised, Howard's powerful new 40-person tow moved crowds of happy Easter week skiers quickly through the lift line.[27]

WITH the growing number of skiers frequenting ESSC's McGee tows, Long Valley became a place to establish viable winter businesses.[28] In that regard, Nan and Max Zischank set out to purchase an acre of land from

Harold Eaton—not far from the McGee tows in an area called Skunk Hollow—and asked Tex to accompany them to the bargaining table. Wise in the ways of liquor, Tex suggested Nan and Max bring along a bottle of whiskey to loosen Eaton up. They did, and the meeting went well. The Zischanks not only purchased their desired lot, but also they secured water rights to a hillside spring.[29] Now all they needed was a building.

SKI TRACKS
Nan and Max's Long Valley Lodge
1940

When DWP announced it was auctioning off a 50-foot-by-125-foot bunkhouse that had housed men building the Mono Craters Tunnels, Nan and Max wanted to make a bid but didn't know how much the building was worth. Nan asked her friend, Ruth Cushion, who, in turn, asked her friend William Mulholland. Mulholland, then head of the LADWP and the man responsible for building the Los Angeles Aqueduct, suggested the Zischanks bid $165. DWP accepted.

Max hand-sawed the building into three parts. He sold a section to the Cushions for their Winter Patrol Station and paid $500 to have the other two sections moved to his Long Valley lot. He patched the building back together, built a water box at the mountainside spring, dug a trench, and laid a pipeline to connect to an existing culvert that ran under the highway. Nan hauled wheelbarrows of cow manure to insulate the pipes and sanded cigarette burns off the interior windowsills.

On New Year's Day 1941, the Zischanks celebrated the grand opening of their new Long Valley Resort, commonly known as Nan and Max's.[30] Guests could sleep on a cot using their own sleeping bags, borrow one towel for a shower, and eat a family-style breakfast, lunch, and dinner, all for seven dollars a day. Unlimited skiing using a 300-foot-long tow that Max installed across the road from the resort was complimentary. The restaurant soon became known for Nan's vivacious congeniality, her fresh-baked pies and one pound steaks.

MID-JANUARY 1941, Mammoth's winter residents met at Penney's Tavern and formed the Mammoth Mountain Ski Club and Winter Sports Organization with the intent of creating interest in winter recreation. At that time, winter business at Mammoth was nil, the roads were rarely cleared of snow, and Tex's dog teams were sometimes the only means of communicating with the outside world.[31]

The Mammoth Ski Club, as the organization came to be known, functioned as a social group and an unofficial town management team. Members obtained permission to use an abandoned Civilian Conservation Corps building as a community hall from where they distributed winter bulletins and organized box socials, dances, and the annual Easter Egg Hunt. They circulated a petition requesting the mail drop at Penney's Tavern be increased from three days per week to daily delivery and lobbied to keep Lake Mary Road open during the winter to provide access to a rope tow at Observation Point. Initially built by Lloyd Nicoll, then taken over by Nyle Smith, this was the first permanent rope tow in the Mammoth region.[32]

In the spring, Nan and Tex represented the Mammoth Ski Club at the CSA convention in Yosemite. Club members rented three connecting booths in the central courtyard of the Los Angeles Auto Club Outing Show to display a 40-foot-by-70-foot hand-painted mural depicting a cabin in the scenic Sierra, and Tex spread a thick bed of ice where he tethered seven of his dogs to his sled. To capitalize on nearby snowfields that often lasted into August, the club formed a Summer Entertainment Committee. As chairman of summer skiing, Nyle Smith advertised his home on the backside of Lake George as a ski and fishing camp.[33]

FOR Dave and Roma, the winter of 1941 was all about skiing. An ESSC newsletter teased, "Members will be happy to hear that *even* Dave McCoy got enough skiing last weekend." The article also praised Roma's skiing, saying she "had them all sweating in a follow-the-leader. Her form is something to hang an eye on."

Dave continued to help the Bishop High racers on Wednesday afternoons and weekends. As a result, their skiing kept improving. At the second annual CIF meet, Bishop placed second against 14 other California and Nevada schools. Whenever Dave received compliments about the team's results, he laughed and said something like, "We had so much darn fun out there, working hard and skiing hard."

Pursuing his personal race schedule, Dave took Roma to June Lake for the Snow Festival, a gala event organized by Tuffy Conn, the proprietor of June Lake Lodge. To make the slalom engaging for spectators, ski instructor Slim Mabery set two parallel courses and started racers simultaneously in what may have been the original dual slalom.[34] Peter Lindstrom opened the race by forerunning while his wife, international screen star Ingrid Bergman, worked on a photoshoot for *Life Magazine*. Two brothers from Lee Vining, Stan and Augie Hess, placed first and second, with Dave McCoy coming in right behind them in third.

Local crowd-pleasers Dave and Augie continued their friendly rivalry at the 1941 Inyo-Mono Championships on McGee Mountain. As reported by the *Inyo Register*:

> *Lee Vining's Augie Hess won the downhill, beating defending champion Dave McCoy by just 3/5 of a second. After a timeout for lunch, the contestants took their turns on a difficult two-run slalom. This was Augie's day, and he was not to be denied. Augie walked away with a clean sweep of men's downhill, slalom, and combined.*

Early in April, Dave and Augie went at it again in the Class A California State Championships at Sugar Bowl, northwest of Lake Tahoe. This time, competing against a stiff field of California's best racers, they both placed just outside the top ten.

At Big Bear Lake's Winter Sports Carnival, Dave came in second behind California's rising ski racing star, Chris Schwarzenbach.[35] Next on the calendar was the President's Ball at Crestview.[36] This night-skiing show, organized by Mono Ski Club, benefited the Infantile Paralysis Fund, a nonprofit organization that President Franklin Roosevelt had founded in 1938 to combat polio.[37]

SKI TRACKS
The President's Ball At Crestview
1941

At the President's Ball, Slim Mabery and his troupe of entertainers from June Lake sang cowboy songs over the loudspeaker while Hans Georg amused the crowd with his antics skiing down the illuminated slopes dressed as a woman in a long, billowing skirt. Next came the feature act, a skiing exhibition choreographed around the theme of a night air raid. Using fireworks, red and green lights, sparklers, colored flares, Roman candles, and a motor and propeller, the show depicted scenes of a campfire, the sound of an alarm, the trail of a burning plane, the dropping of incendiary bombs, the crash of a dive bomber, and the escape of a pilot in a parachute, creating an illusion the air raid was real.

The final ski race of the 1941 season was the inaugural, much-anticipated "Flying Skis," a CSA-sanctioned competition just off the June Lake Loop. Racers were to ski some four miles of the most precipitous terrain in the Sierra, dropping from Carson Peak at 11,000 feet to the finish at 7,200 feet. Only the most experienced skiers would participate. Experts predicted the race would be tougher than Italy's famous Marmolada and as challenging as the renowned "Silver Skis" on Mt. Rainier, the "Inferno" on Mt. Lassen, and New Hampshire's Tuckerman Ravine.

On race morning, competitors started their ascent in the early hours to reach the top by the 10:30 start time. Hiking on firm spring snow, carrying their skis over their shoulders, they zigzagged upward. Some sections were so steep their inside elbows touched the snow as they climbed. From the finish line below, the racers looked like a parade of ants.

Standing on top, the starter sent racers off at one-minute intervals. Without control gates to define where they went, competitors chose their own lines. Some checked their speed by making a few quick turns out of the start. Others headed straight down and then controlled their speed with big sweeping turns, letting their skis run as the course opened up to the final descent.

SKI TRACKS
The First Flying Skis
1941

> Only two women attempted the race, Olympian Clarita Heath and local Nan Zischank. A third woman trudged to the top, but when she realized how steep the course was, she decided to walk back down. Clarita raced in good form until the lower section, where she hit a soft patch of snow heated by the sun, then smacked to the ground and dislocated her shoulder. Holding on to her arm, she got back on her feet and finished the race with the winning female time. Chris Schwarzenbach won the men's division with a time of five minutes and fifty seconds. Sportswriter Chappy Wentworth placed second, and Augie Hess came in fourth, also recovering from a fall in the soft snow.

The morning of the race, Dave started climbing Carson Peak in good spirits, but about a mile up the course, he was overcome with stomach pain. He decided to drop out. For the second time, sickness interfered with his racing. But Dave didn't dwell on this misfortune. He had something more important on his mind. Saturday, May 10, 1941, the date he and Roma had decided to marry, was only one week away.

CHAPTER EIGHT

Roma:
Ups and Downs of Love

Roma Carriere and Grandma Folk.

I doubt there's ever been anyone in the world happier than I was the day I got off the Greyhound bus in Bishop and saw Dave McCoy standing there waiting for me. Everything about Dave—the light in his eyes, the words he spoke, the way he took my hand in his—made me confident that our feelings were mutual. To think that less than 24 hours before, I'd been forlorn and out of place in Los Angeles. Now I was back home and feeling like a princess.

I got a job as a bookkeeper and cashier at Jack Black's grocery store and settled back into my life in Bishop living with Grandma. The sad thing was, she had no intention of opening her heart to Dave, but I figured it was only a matter of time before he gained back her approval. And the first step was to let her know I'd be riding around in his Chevy coupe instead of on the back of a motorcycle.

Almost every weekend that autumn, Dave and I went hiking. After the snow came, we skied. His philosophy was, the more fun you have skiing, the better you'll get, and that's what happened. ESSC even asked us to guide club members through the Ski Mountaineer proficiency exams. I knew they respected Dave's skiing, but to think they also admired mine! I even went to a race in Big Bear with some ESSC members, the "Original Bishop Race Team." We had so much fun skiing new places, ordering meals in roadside cafes, and of course, bringing home trophies. Dave took second in the Invitational Class A division, right behind Chris Schwarzenbach who was a contender for the 1940 U.S. Olympic Ski Team. Dave really liked Chris. He said Chris was the first person who'd ever hiked to the top of McGee Mountain just for the fun of skiing down.

Looking back on those prewar days, I feel guilty about all we took for granted trying to make the most of every moment we had. While we were outside hiking and skiing, people in other parts of the world were being stripped of their personal rights by people like Adolf Hitler. Our country didn't want to go to war, but somehow we had to protect the right to feel safe and carefree, the right to feel happy. But how fast life changes. One moment, the world makes sense. The next minute, everything falls apart. That's what happened to me in 1940, and I wasn't even at war. I was simply learning about the ups and downs of love.

Maybe the problem started with Grandma's resistance to Dave and her worry about my poor relationship with his mother. I didn't see Edna much, but when I did, she had this way of letting me know that, in her opinion, I certainly wasn't good enough for her Sonny. I think she looked down on me because I'd grown up in the little town of Bishop instead of a fancy city like Reno. Or maybe she considered me a wild girl because I liked riding motorcycles. I don't know. But I vowed that I wouldn't let one bad word come out of my mouth about Dave's mother. I didn't tell him how Edna hurt me. I just put up a wall to protect myself. Maybe that was the problem. Well, the gist of it was Dave and I grew apart, and broke up.

I could tell Grandma was relieved, but boy, did I feel confused. Dave and I had been so in love, and then, there we were going our separate ways. How could that be? I mostly blame my age. I was too young and too immature to handle what I was feeling. I wanted to marry Dave, but the things that attracted me to him also scared me. His good looks, his independence, his lust for life, his high standards. What if I didn't meet his expectations? What if his self-confidence made him not need me? Girls were always flirting with him. What if he became attracted to one of them? What if... oh, I could think of "what ifs" forever.

But, stubborn as ever, no matter how awful I felt about breaking up with Dave, I wasn't going to sit around feeling sorry for myself. Nope. I decided that if Dave got interested in another girl, someone prettier and more experienced than me, well, that was his business. All I had to do was go to one dance in Bishop, and there would be plenty of guys wanting to swing me across the wooden floor. So that's what I did, and boy, did I have a good time dancing again. But still, I did miss skiing and spending time with our ski club friends. So, when the Inyo-Mono Championships came around, I thought, why not enter? What a perfect way to have some fun.

On race day, standing at the top of the course waiting for my bib number to be called, I started to feel really nervous. I thought about what Dave would say, probably something like, "Just ski naturally," or "Go have fun," and those thoughts calmed me down. And guess what? I won the downhill, got second in the slalom, and brought home the Deibert Cup for best female skier in combined. It's funny how those three shiny trophies made me feel powerful, independent, and in control of my life again.

After the awards, Dave came over to where I was standing and offered his congratulations. Did that ever surprise me. Then he told me I was skiing well enough to handle the top of Mammoth Mountain. What? Where was he going with this? I laughed, you know, like people do when they're nervous. There was no way Dave and I were going to start seeing each other again. He was involved with someone else, and I was enjoying the dances. But before he left, he said that he would let me know when the snow transformed to corn. I tell you, with everything that had happened that day at the championships, I went home floating on air.

Then, Grandma died.

TEARS still sting when I think about my last moments with Grandma. I had the feeling something wasn't right when she went to bed early that night. Just before she fell asleep, she called me to her, and I lay down by her side like I often did. She said ever so softly, "Oh, there you are, dear Roma. I knew you would be here." She touched my hand, and with the gentlest smile, she whispered, "You'll be fine, my child. Just follow your heart." Sometime during the night, her lifetime of hard work caught up with her and she passed on peacefully. I like to think she went to sleep comforted by her belief that when she opened her eyes, she'd be in heaven, the place she'd cherished throughout all her earthly days.

What a sad day I had moving over to Father's house, but at least I had somewhere to go, a sanctuary where I could cry my eyes out. The fact that Grandma was 83 years old when she died didn't make losing her any easier. She was my backbone, my safety net. With her, I never felt lonely. Now that both she and my mother were gone, there was no one left in this world who would ever love me like they had, the way a mother loves her child. You see, the love you have for the person who brought you up starts right at the beginning of life and grows from there. That's different from the love you have for the person you want to marry. Marriage. Oh, why did I even think about that word? Dave and I weren't together, and there wasn't anyone else I could even consider marrying.

A few days before Memorial Day weekend, Dave called and asked if I would like to join him skiing Mammoth on Sunday. Hearing his voice on the other end of the line made my heart speed up. I tried to relax. I was *not* going to get excited about seeing him again. I had to remind myself he was just taking me on a ski outing. That was all.

Dave picked me up early so we could get to the Winter Patrol Station by 7 a.m. to pick up Carl Grebe. But, when Carl saw me sitting by Dave, I swear his smile faded. He probably thought I was going to slow them down. Well, I'd show him. After Dave parked the car on Minaret Road, I laced my boots, put my skis over my shoulder, and started walking so close behind him that Carl had no choice but to pick up the rear.

Oh, how lovely the morning was. We hiked up a gully by a meandering creek and tiny wildflowers peeking out from behind the rocks. I was so happy to be on the mountain, and to be with Dave again. And I was happy that I stayed ahead of Carl though I've got to admit, he was pretty funny, bantering away, amusing us with his stories. He talked about the time when he and Dave skied so fast coming off the top they both crashed and broke the tips off their skis. They sent them back to the Groswold Ski Company in Colorado. Groswold honored the warranty and mailed them each a new pair. But then, Dave broke a second pair. The factory replaced those skis with a third pair but attached a note that read, "No more warranty. No more skis."

Above the tree line, we hiked up a snowfield. That wasn't hard until the slope got steeper. I finally understood why Dave had been hesitant to take me there. The last 20 feet of the headwall were almost vertical. Every time I took a step, my knees nearly hit my chin. I knew that if I lost my balance, I would slide all the way down the mountain and probably take Carl out with me, so I moved slowly, making sure my foot was secure in each toe-hole Dave had kicked before putting my weight on it.

Dave must have felt how afraid I was. Each time he turned back to see how I was managing, he encouraged me saying, "Roma, you're doing great. Just think about one step at a time." I did exactly what he said, my heart pounding the whole time. When he reached the summit, he kneeled on the snow, put his hand out for me, and pulled me over the top. Then Carl climbed over the edge, and there we were, the three of us standing on top of Mammoth Mountain, more than 11,000 feet above sea level.

After all that exertion climbing Mammoth, we were more than ready to eat, so I passed around the sandwiches I'd packed for lunch. We relaxed in the sunshine, Carl and I laughing at Dave trying to stab the end of his ski pole through the caps of the Coca-Colas he'd brought along. All three of us were in such a good mood I almost forgot about what was ahead.

How was I was *ever* going to leap off the headwall, which was precisely what I had to do. If I had been alone, I might have stayed up there forever. But Dave and Carl were waiting, so I inched forward just enough to glance over the edge That was a mistake. I lost my breath and backed up. Three times I did that: inching forward on my skis, peeking over the drop-off, then backing away. My nerves had gotten the best of me. Dave said in his calm voice, "Keep your knees bent and your arms forward, and you'll do fine." I was still scared to death, but I told myself, "You've got to do this."

As I pulled forward again, I felt the lightest pressure of Dave's hand on my back. Without saying a word, he nudged me off the cornice, and away I went. I didn't even have time to be angry with him.

For a few seconds, I was suspended in space, and then, all of a sudden, I landed, and I was making long sweeping turns down the wide-open slope, gliding over the corn snow. When I finally stopped, I looked up to the summit. Dave and Carl were both cheering. I wanted to be right back on top so I could ski down again, in spite of the headwall. Then one after the other, the guys jumped off the top and skied down to me.

At the bottom of the snowfield, the three of us stood together admiring the tracks we'd made and talking about how great the snow was. I couldn't stop grinning. I don't think I've ever been so happy. I looked over at Dave, my hero, and Carl, whom only hours before I had considered my archrival. Both said how proud they were of me, Dave, with a nod of his head and a big smile, Carl recounting every detail with a humorous twist.

How my life had changed *again*. I could have still been asleep in my bed in Bishop, but instead, I was spending my Sunday morning outside in the open air, skiing Mammoth Mountain with two of the most dashing men in the world. I looked up at the sky and felt sure Grandma was smiling down in approval.

SKIING reunited Dave and me. The months whizzed by, and before we knew it, April had arrived, and we were once again wearing our hula costumes at the annual Easter Egg Hunt. Mammoth Ski Club members had buried 30 dozen boiled and decorated eggs on the slope of Nyle Smith's Observation Point rope tow. Tex gave the opening speech, rambling on about how we were going to receive thousands of dollars in free publicity from Los Angeles newspapers, and how *Life Magazine* was going to want to cover the event the following year, and so on.[1]

There was only one thing about Easter Sunday that made me sad. My sister Frances wasn't there. Just a few weeks earlier, she had married Zach Martin, a DWP employee, and the newlyweds had moved to Los Angeles. I was glad for Frances, but I missed her terribly. Actually, her happiness was a wake-up call for me. I got the feeling that if I didn't pay attention to what was right in front of me, love might pass me by. After all, almost every day Dave had been telling me, "Roma, I don't care how long it takes you to decide. You're going to be my wife."

The truth was, Dave's confidence made me feel confident. His joy made me joyful. And his thoughtfulness convinced me I had nothing to fear. Edna McCoy would grow to like me. And Grandma? I already told you. She had given me her blessing.

You should have seen the smile on Dave's face the next time he brought up marriage. Yes, I said, I would marry him. I would be *happy* to marry him. I would *love* to marry him.

On May 10, 1941, well before the crack of dawn, Dave and I left Bishop for Zach and Frances' house in North Hollywood. The four of us drove to Yuma, Arizona, a town where we could purchase our marriage license and be married the same day. It was weird. The trip through the scorching heat of the desert seemed to take forever and to go by really fast at the same time. Zach hung wet towels in the windows to cool us down, and Frances divvied out the picnic lunch she had packed for us.

We were having a ball, singing along with the radio, everything from Glen Miller's "Chattanooga Choo Choo" to Billie Holiday's "God Bless the Child" when an emergency newscast interrupted the music. I couldn't stand hearing this news, so I put my hands over my ears, but the sound came through. German air raids had set London on fire. Over a thousand people were killed. Landmark buildings and homes were destroyed. Only a month before, Hitler had invaded Yugoslavia, which was horrible enough. But this attack brought the fear and terror even closer to home. I had to push the visions of war out of my mind. This was my wedding day, and I wasn't going to let anything spoil it.

We arrived in Yuma in the late afternoon and found a justice of the peace to marry us. Dave paid the man $4.50, we signed the marriage certificate, and the five-minute ceremony began. With Zach and Francis as our witnesses, Dave and I promised "till death do us part," and I became Mrs. Dave McCoy.

Punkin, Roma, Poncho, and Dave on Crowley Lake.

PART TWO

Passion Grows

1941–1950

CHAPTER NINE

A Rope Tow of His Own

Dave and Roma at the Crowley house.

With the harsh realities overseas worsening and Hitler ordering his Nazi troops into Russia, newlyweds Roma and Dave knew that chances of the United States remaining isolated from World War II were getting slimmer. They rented a room in a Bishop boarding house, grateful for their time alone together insulated from world troubles. In the quiet conversations that belong to the wee hours of morning, the couple shared their innermost dreams and gained a deeper understanding of one another. They agreed there would be children, lots of them, and they imagined the merriment of a large family filling their household with a resonance neither had known in their youth.

The most pressing problem Dave faced at that time was bickering that had surfaced within the Eastern Sierra Ski Club. He breathed a sigh of relief when Inyo National Forest Supervisor Roy Boothe offered to mediate a club gathering at McGee Creek Lodge. Dave trusted Boothe as a kind and gentle man who went out of his way to support the advancement of winter sports while taking care of public lands.

Boothe reminded the group that everyone had benefitted from the previous two years of growth in winter sports, and now they should let petty jealousies and competition give way to a broader cooperative spirit. There was no need for clubs to threaten disbanding, to fight over the Arlberg versus the St. Moritz method, or to argue about the name of their ski operation and how much money to charge skiers. Boothe advocated that business owners blend their interests and work in harmony finding solutions to the bigger problems, such as road access to the slopes.

Dave supported Boothe's plea for teamwork, but before the meeting was over, voices grew loud and angry as arguments flared, a telltale sign this group was not going to work as a unit. Seeing no reason for controversy, Dave kept his distance. To him, skiing was about having fun. Period. The time had come for him to forge his own path. He dropped his club membership and set out to build an up-ski of his own.

Using a design similar to Jack Northrop's 1936 makeshift auto-powered rope tow, Dave converted his '38 Chevy into a roadside up-ski. He then sought out Mammoth District Ranger, Doug Robinson, to obtain a permit. Robinson had long supported the local ski community, occasionally ferrying skiers up Minaret Road in his small Forest Service bulldozer, clearing snow as he went. He assured Dave he didn't need a permit because his tow wasn't a commercial venture.

After the first snowstorm of the season, Dave and Roma loaded their Chevy with fixings for a barbecue, tools, pulleys, ropes, and a plywood wheel Dave had made and drove up Minaret Road to the snowline on Mammoth's north side. Dave backed the car against a hillside, jacked up the rear end, replaced the tire with the plywood wheel, and wound the end of a long rope around the rim. He then hauled the rope and a deadman pulley up the slope, attached the pulley to a tree, looped the rope around it, walked the remaining rope to the bottom, and spliced it together. Next, he disconnected the emergency brake from one side of his car so the differential could run twice as fast as the car registered. There it was. Dave had a roadside tow. No fussing over group decisions, no arguments, no grumbling. Just a beautiful day on Mammoth Mountain, fresh snow, and Roma by his side.

After a few runs, Dave dug a pit, built a fire, and barbecued hamburgers. Driving back to Bishop that afternoon, he reflected on the day. Despite tired arms, wet gloves, and the limiting features of his rudimentary tow, Roma and he had enjoyed their ski outing, and that's what counted. Now he just needed to find a portable tow that was more functional.

Dave negotiated to buy one of ESSC's Sweden tows for $135 and secured an $85 loan from the Bank of America for a down payment. He tuned the engine, refurbished the ropes and pulleys, and purchased liability insurance. For the annual fee of one dollar, he obtained a year-to-year roving permit from the Forest Service that allowed him to operate his tow on any slope from the top of Sherwin Grade north to Deadman Pass. Essentially, Dave could follow the snowline. He showed the paperwork to Roma and said, "Hey Toots, we're gonna ski ourselves silly this winter!"

Early the next Saturday morning, driving with their ski gear and portable tow sticking out of the trunk, Roma and Dave parked at the Minaret Road snowline and dragged the tow over the snow to a hillside with an open glade.[1] By the time Dave had his tow rigged and operating, several skiers had joined them. That evening while dining at a restaurant down the street from the boarding house, he took Roma's hand in his and chuckled, "Isn't it amazing how skiers find us wherever we put up a tow?" Roma delighted in his enthusiasm. There seemed to be nothing her husband enjoyed more than spending weekends creating a bustle of activity around skiing.

A few days later, Dave learned that his DWP paycheck was delayed until the following Monday. Knowing they had enough money to buy either food *or* rope-tow fuel, Roma asked in distress, "Honey, what're we gonna do?" Without any trace of concern, Dave reminded her their roving permit allowed them to charge people to use their tow. How about asking each skier to contribute 50 cents a day to help pay for fuel? Roma thought this was a terrible idea. Dave's eyes twinkled. "Don't worry, Toots," he said. "People will be happy to pay for the fun they're having skiing."

Dave was right. Just like that, as a matter of necessity rather than intention, Dave and Roma McCoy crossed an invisible line of destiny and became professional ski tow operators.

AFTER DWP completed building Long Valley Dam in 1941, the Owens River and its tributaries began to transform the Long Valley caldera into a man-made reservoir.[2] This stored water was designated to be used in the Owens Valley and Southern California. Emotions still ran high about water rights, but few denied the beauty of how the growing body of water reflected the blue sky of the Eastern Sierra.

On a mid-October Sunday afternoon, a thousand people gathered for the dedication of the reservoir. These precious waters would be called Crowley Lake in honor of local icon Father John J. Crowley, who had died in an automobile accident in 1940.[3]

SKI TRACKS
Father Crowley Will Be Remembered
1941

> Skiers take notice! When you drive north of DWP's new Long Valley Dam on the way to your favorite Eastern Sierra ski tow, you will now pass by Crowley Lake. At the viewpoint, you will find a granite monument with a bronze tablet that bears Father Crowley's name and explains why people loved this man. Known as the Desert Padre, Father Crowley united the region in the belief that tourism could save the local economy. A master at bringing people together to have fun, he organized carnivals and plays and once held Mass on top of Mt. Whitney. Each year on opening day of fishing season, he held a 3 a.m. Fisherman's Mass in Bishop.

After the dedication, Dave drove Roma to a plateau directly above the dam. There, DWP workers were converting old buildings from the Mono Basin Tunnel Project—where the Zischanks had obtained the building for their Long Valley Resort—into a small complex. Here would be a galvanized four-car garage, a storage shed, a bunkhouse for summer workers, and three small buildings that would house an office, the dam caretaker, and a hydrographer.

Father Crowley.

Harboring hopes of becoming the Crowley Lake hydrographer, Dave spent his evenings at the Bishop boarding house studying for the upcoming civil service exam. As his study partner, Roma quizzed him on sample hydraulic engineering tests that accompanied his correspondence courses. Dave borrowed books from Pat Coons to learn the history of California water issues and to memorize definitions of water terms. As the exam date approached, he felt confident he had done his best to prepare. In his own words, he had tried to learn "anything and everything that pertained to water."

George Lewis drove his protégé to the courthouse in downtown Los Angeles to take the exam. Lewis reached over from behind the wheel and rested his hand on Dave's shoulder. "Hey, my boy, you'll be out of there in record time. It's not a matter of luck," Lewis said. "It's a matter of knowledge and common sense, and you've got both." Dave followed the signs to the exam room, reached for the sharpened No. 2 pencils he had tucked in his shirt pocket, and sat down in a roomful of people seeking various state jobs.

Dave not only passed the exam, but he also earned the highest score of all his fellow examinees, as he had set out to do. His name advanced to the top of DWP's list of hydrographer candidates. Next, he passed through three interviews with DWP officials, and then he waited.

One autumn afternoon, Dave arrived at his office and found George Lewis beaming like a proud father. Lewis handed him a DWP document designating him as the Long Valley Dam hydrographer, effective immediately. Due to a lag in paperwork, Lewis explained, Dave would receive only a laborer's wage even though he would take on all the official hydrographer duties. Could he live with that? Dave grinned. No problem! Lewis then shifted into his fatherly role and offered to help Dave and Roma move their belongings, including a cookstove, to their new residence in the complex at the dam.

Heated by an oil stove, the Crowley house had a small living room, two small bedrooms, one bathroom, and a kitchen so tiny Roma could hardly turn around when cooking. However, as if to compensate for the small dimensions of their dwelling, their back door opened to a panoramic view of Long Valley.

At dusk on the day Roma and Dave moved into the Crowley house, they stood together in the backyard waiting for the sun to go down beyond the mountains. Roma rested her head on her husband's shoulder and watched the lake waters ripple. Dave looked across the valley to the sagebrush slopes of McGee, then to the top of Mammoth. They both were well aware that one of their dreams was coming true.

While Roma organized the house, Dave made plans to cultivate a lawn to keep dust down, construct a white picket fence around the yard, and add a latticework trellis arching over the front gate. There, Roma could plant a climbing rose. But first, Dave needed to fill an oversized shed across the driveway with a winter's worth of food staples and a deep freezer filled with wild game.

When visitors from Southern California heard about Dave's fishing and hunting skills, they put in orders for trout, venison, and geese. Some clients paid in cash. Others bartered. One couple traded bundles of iris bulbs for their yard, a luxury for the McCoys.

Dave loved his new DWP job. Whether working in the field, completing math calculations at his desk, or hiking into the backcountry to stock the winter snow survey cabins with food, firewood, and whiskey, he was happy. Some of his co-workers complained to their superiors that Dave was being treated like their fair-haired child because he had time to hunt, fish, and operate his ski tow during working hours. But, the DWP defended him. Their policy was clear. Once employees completed their official responsibilities, extra time in the day was their own.

Year-round, Dave tended the clock houses on Mammoth Creek, Hot Creek, Convict Creek, McGee Creek, and Rock Creek. At each station, a tall tin shed with a corrugated steel roof housed a float and a seven-day clock recording water flow. These stations documented every cubic foot of surface water that flowed from the Long Valley Basin into the Los Angeles Aqueduct.

In addition, Dave monitored numerous DWP flumes (channels that convey water) and weirs (small dams that control water levels). Once a week, he inspected a DWP evaporation pan floating on Crowley Lake. The square pan, about the size of a card table, was attached to a barge made from telephone poles and held together by chains. Buoys kept the barge afloat. Dave's job was to measure the water level in the pan and correlate that figure to the area of the reservoir. DWP could then estimate how much water had evaporated from Crowley Lake that week.

Along with routine duties, DWP assigned random tasks such as inspecting waters around the outflow of the Mono Basin Project—an 11.3-mile, 9-foot diameter tunnel constructed under the Mono Craters—to see if live fish were making it through. The tunnel, which transported Mono Basin waters into the L.A. Aqueduct, was a controversial project adversely affecting local ecosystems.

Once DWP directed Dave and a coworker to maneuver a small boat through the tunnel to check for cracks, stalactites, cave-ins, or any other indications of weakening in the walls. For several days prior to allowing anyone to enter the tunnel, DWP blew powerful fans to evacuate the deadly levels of accumulated carbon dioxide. Once the outflow of air at the East Portal exit-point tested safe, DWP lowered the water level to about 18 inches and adjusted the flow to approximately 10 to 15 cubic feet per second. They then issued Dave and his coworker portable lighting for visibility and sawed-off paddles to push the small boat along in case it scraped the bottom. About four hours after taking off, the men emerged from the dark and dank underground, breathed in the fresh air, and celebrated the light of day as if greeting their long-lost best friend.

In October 1941, members of 30 ski clubs attended the California Ski Association's annual convention in Yosemite. Attendees agreed that California skiers needed more ski lifts, ski huts, ski schools, and parking places to accommodate the people who had taken up the sport the prior winter.[4] Contributing to skiing's surge in popularity was the classic ski film *Sun Valley Serenade*, created by Hollywood producer and avid skier Darryl Zanuck. The film glamorized skiing for millions of movie fans. The title song, "It Happened in Sun Valley," became a radio hit. Assuming that skiing and romance went hand in hand, movie fans flocked to any ski area they could get to in search of their own love stories.

Trying to reach aspiring skiers, the California State Chamber of Commerce distributed its *Winter Sports Guide*, this time featuring a cover photo of McGee Mountain. ESSC's public relations chairman, Bob Brown, calculated that each visiting skier spent a minimum of five dollars per day with local merchants. This income prompted Brown to mail a slick brochure and short film to California retailers, including May Company, Bullocks, Saks Fifth Avenue, the Army & Navy store, the Broadway, and the Automobile Club. June Lake's Almour family mailed out a brochure advertising skiing at their Fern Creek Camp. George Conn, the owner of June Lake Lodge, titled his brochure *Skiing in the High Sierra at June Lake Lodge*. He also submitted an article to *Ski Illustrated* describing the parallel slalom and second annual Flying Skis competition on nearby Carson Peak.

Just before Thanksgiving, Old Man Winter dropped ten inches of powder on Mammoth's hardpack base. Mammoth Ski Club sent a pre-holiday press release stating that Dave would operate his portable tow on the north slope Thursday through Sunday, adding, "All vacationers should carry chains to get up Minaret Road... and don't forget your long johns!"[5]

Southern Californians loaded their automobiles with friends, family, frozen turkeys, and ski gear, and headed north in search of powder snow, winter sunshine, and skiing romance. Resorts from Toms Place to Crestview overflowed with guests. Dave ran his tow overtime to service the crowds, making sure the visiting college ski teams—Pasadena Junior College, UCLA, and USC—had plenty of hill space to hold their ski team tryouts for the upcoming season.[6]

At the end of the bustling holiday weekend, Dave and Roma spread their rope tow money across their bedspread. They couldn't help but laugh at all the cash. Roma set aside $85 to pay off their bank loan for the portable tow, then scooped up another $50 for the balance due to ESSC. Dave tossed the remaining bills and coins into a dresser drawer without bothering to count the money. Why should he? He knew the numbers. Roma had collected 50 cents from each skier who rode the tow, which was at least 100 people per day of the four-day holiday. This meant the couple had grossed over $200, far more than his monthly DWP income. Dave closed the drawer. Grinning, he said, "At this rate, it won't be long before we can buy another portable tow with a more powerful engine that can carry more people."

Dave's offhand comment reflected his feelings about the "ski business." Any money made from skiing would go toward expanding and improving ski operations. This approach to finances established a precedent that continued throughout his career.

MEANWHILE, across the Atlantic, the 1941 Alpine World Ski Championships held at Cortina d'Ampezzo, Italy, turned out to be a farce. Only Nazi-friendly or neutral countries during World War II were allowed to participate. Therefore, Germany and Italy won all 18 medals. To regain the credibility of international ski racing, the National Ski Association took a stand against Nazi involvement. NSA invited the Canadian and Chilean ski associations to a late November meeting in Milwaukee, Wisconsin. There they formed the Ski Union of the Americas and made plans to host their own international championships. Despite the good intentions, world events intervened, and the races never took place.[7]

ON Sunday morning, December 7, 1941, Japanese forces bombed the U.S. Naval Base in Pearl Harbor, Hawaii. The assault lasted less than two hours yet claimed the lives of nearly 2,500 people, wounded more than 1,000, and damaged or destroyed 18 American ships and nearly 300 airplanes.[8]

In shock, Americans spent that night glued to their radios, listening for updates on the attack, horrified by the devastating reports. The next morning, at 9 a.m. Pacific Standard Time, President Franklin D. Roosevelt addressed the U.S. Congress wearing a black armband in mourning for the lives lost at Pearl Harbor. In a ten-minute speech, he called for war on Japan. To thunderous applause and the stamping of feet, he closed with the oath, "So help us, God." Within an hour, he had received approval from Congress for a declaration of war against the Empire of Japan. There was only one dissenting vote, from a pacifist in the House. At 1:10 p.m. PST, Roosevelt signed the war documents.[9]

Three days later, Japan's allies, Italy and Germany, declared war on the United States. That same day, December 11, 1941, the United States government responded with a declaration of war on Italy and Germany. Thus, the U.S. entered World War II on both fronts.

CHAPTER TEN

Roma: Newlyweds

Roma collecting money from skiers.

I f I had my life to live over again, I'd have married Dave McCoy the moment he asked me, and I'm sure Grandma would have understood. I must have been nuts to wait so long.

As we drove to Yuma for our wedding and then back to North Hollywood that night, Dave pulled me in so close by his side that you couldn't have dropped a hairpin between us. I rested my head on his shoulder and watched our headlights break through the darkness, content to know he was at the wheel guiding us into our new life. I thought about how our wedding vows, for richer or poorer, in sickness and in health, weren't about a white wedding dress or a diamond ring. They were about a lifelong promise to be each other's best friend.

We arrived back at Frances and Zach's house sometime after midnight, planning to stay two nights with them and then drive to San Francisco for our honeymoon. But while we were at the movie theater, somebody broke into our car and stole my purse and our suitcases. I was so mad, but Dave didn't get upset at all. He calmed me down and told me I didn't have anything to worry about because all our money was safe in his pocket. Next thing I knew, we were both laughing about how disappointed the thieves must be to find nothing but old clothes in our suitcases. But, after being robbed, I could hardly wait to get out of the big city and back to Bishop, where we didn't need to lock our cars or our houses.

By the time we arrived home, Dave had dreamed up a new plan for our honeymoon. He would ask George Lewis if we could stay in the DWP cabin near Rock Creek Lake. I didn't have the foggiest idea what to expect, but Dave had enough enthusiasm for both of us. DWP was good with our plan, so we packed our rucksacks with fishing gear, sleeping bags, and food, and parked our car at Toms Place. We attached sealskins to our skis and started up Rock Creek Road with our packs on our backs. Dave broke trail and I followed right behind, climbing 3,000 vertical feet in nine miles, arriving at our destination late in the afternoon. What a fairytale setting! A log cabin in the snowy woods. Just steps away, Rock Creek bouncing along, welcoming us with the bubbling voice of spring runoff.

Inside the cabin, there was a wood-burning stove, a stack of dry firewood, a table and chairs, two cots, and food leftover from the snow surveyors' winter supplies. We opened the windows and doors to freshen the air of its musty smell and arranged the furniture to our liking. Dave started a fire in the wood cookstove to warm the cabin and to provide hot coals for cooking. Then he skied another quarter mile to Rock Creek Lake, cut through the ice with his ax, and fished for our trout dinner. I stayed in the cabin to make strawberry shortcake. Oh, yes, I'd even brought along whipping cream, fresh berries, and eggs. That's when I realized how unprepared I was to be a wife.

All I knew about cooking was what I'd learned while watching Grandma prepare dinners for our boarders. I just assumed I could cook too. But standing alone in the Rock Creek cabin, listening to the crackling and spitting of the fire, faced with preparing food that would please my new husband, I felt intimidated and helpless. Knowing what an excellent cook Dave's mother was didn't help me one bit. I had a lot to live up to, and I wasn't sure if I could.

Well, I do believe a guardian angel must have flown into the room just then, landed on my shoulder, and woke me from my fear by whispering into my ear: *Roma, mix the batter!* So, that's what I did, and as I creamed the butter and sugar, my confidence came back. I shifted the wood coals to even out the oven temperature, placed my cake on a rack in the center, then sliced the strawberries and whipped the cream. The dessert was delicious. I should have known I didn't need to be afraid. Dave would have been pleased with whatever I cooked.

Being in the Sierra alone with Dave for a week was the most romantic honeymoon ever. Each morning we woke to the melody of the water rushing downstream and the birds chirping their hearts away. When the sun hit the porch, we'd sit outside, hoping to see wildlife. Sure enough, little gray and white mountain chickadees landed on our hands to peck for food, and a big, blue and black Steller's jay tried to claim the porch as his own, scolding us with his harsh call when we didn't toss him morsels of our syrupy pancakes.

Each day after breakfast, I packed our lunch, and we skied up past Mosquito Flat and through Little Lakes Valley. Sometimes we climbed a side chute for a steeper run. Once the snow had softened into corn, we skied down, then found a big rock where we could relax in the sun while taking in the magic of springtime in the mountains. At night, we gazed at the sky, identifying the planets and constellations. By the time we snuffed out our lantern, millions of brilliant stars were dancing overhead as if they, too, were celebrating our night together.

BACK in Bishop, Dave rented us a room in a boarding house on East Line Street. Without kitchen facilities, we ate our meals out, usually at Marie's Diner or the Rainbow Café. Those were the days when a Coca-Cola cost five cents, a quart of milk twelve cents, and a new dress about three dollars.

A few weeks after our marriage, Dave asked me to quit my job. Actually, he didn't ask. He told me to quit. I got so confused. I was perfectly capable of working, and I liked having a job. Between our two paychecks, we could bring in close to $300 a month. I worried that without my income, we wouldn't have enough money. But Dave insisted, "I'll not have a wife of mine working." I didn't think of him as being a bossy person, but the commanding sound of his voice about knocked the breath out of me. I tell you, when Dave makes up his mind, his jaw gets square, and there's no doubt how things are going to be. There was no use in arguing. Besides, he wasn't the only man in those days who believed his wife shouldn't work outside the home. That's just the way things were back then.

The problem was, without a job, a place to cook, or money to go shopping, all I did was wait around for Dave to get home. I asked him what he thought I should do to fill my time, and he told me to just have fun exploring Bishop. Did that ever make me laugh. As if I wasn't already familiar with every nook and cranny of my hometown.

Next thing I knew, Dave came home wheeling a bright red, single-gear bicycle with a wicker basket on the front and a little bell on the handlebars, just for me. Having a bike of my own, I rode through town, out of town, anywhere I could, as long as I didn't go too far from help, I mean, in case I got a flat tire. I thought I knew Bishop but on my red bicycle, I learned to appreciate my town as I never had before: the brilliant roses blooming in yards, the scent of olive-colored sagebrush, the peacefulness of horses and cows grazing on green ranchlands with snow-capped Mt. Tom in the background.

I especially liked to ride on the dirt roads down by the irrigation canals that channeled Owens River water. On scorching 100-degree summer days, I'd stay cool sitting in the shade of an old cottonwood, daydreaming about having a garden of my own with a white picket fence, and little pink roses climbing up a trellis. Sometimes, I'd play tag with the blue herons. They'd stand by the canal watching me ride toward them. As soon as I got close, they'd flap their enormous wings and fly off just a few feet above the water as if they were teasing me.

One day, I watched a mama duck swimming with her ducklings darting in and out of her wake. She let them play for a while, then used her wings to guide her family to the bank, doing just what a mother should do, nurturing and protecting her offspring. I pedaled down the canal looking for the male and what do you know, I came across three drakes having a grand old time, their bright feathers shimmering in the sunlight as they paddled along, showing no apparent interest in what the female or her babies were doing.

Those male mallards made me think of men in a smoky barroom drinking whiskey. I'd seen enough of that type when I walked past the open doors of the bars on Bishop's Main Street, and Grandma had told me plenty of stories about the evils of alcohol. Just the thought of liquor upset me, but I didn't need to worry. My husband wasn't the kind of man who would leave his wife home taking care of the kids while he went out drinking.

WITH my red bike, springtime passed quickly. Summer too. Before I knew it, nights had cooled down, and green leaves had turned to gold. Sometimes, Dave would say, "C'mon, Toots. Let's drive up to Long Valley to see the fall colors and check out progress at the dam." I'd smile with pride every time we drove past the granite monument honoring Father Crowley. The way this beloved priest liked to make people happy reminded me of Dave.

On one of those autumn days, we were hiking up McGee Canyon when Dave mentioned we should have a rope tow of our own. "Why would we want that?" I asked.

"So, you and I can ski whenever and wherever we want," Dave grinned. He had a point. We were the kind of people who liked to get up and go without waiting for group decisions.

The Eastern Sierra Ski Club was happy to sell us one of their tows. We just needed a down payment, so I encouraged Dave to use one of his motorcycles as collateral for a loan at the Bank of America. Boy, did that idea ever stir up a scene! When I heard that the banker said Dave wasn't a good candidate for a loan, I stomped right over to his office and told him there was no one in this world more reliable than Dave McCoy. Then I listed all the ways Dave was a responsible person, speaking my mind so loud and clear the banker was forced to listen. I reminded him I had been a valued employee of his bank, and that he had once respected my opinion. Then, in my sternest voice, I said, "Sometimes people just need to trust the character of a person and make decisions on good faith." Well, that did it. The next day, Dave signed the papers for an $85 loan!

Everything about owning our rope tow was great until the day Dave told me we needed to start charging skiers so that we could make ends meet. I was a nervous wreck, carrying his fishing creel as a cash box, apologizing, and asking for money. To my surprise, the skiers were all happy to contribute. Some of them even paid extra. At one point, I hid behind a tree and counted the money. Fifteen dollars! When Dave skied down, I waved my arm, called him over to me, then whispered, "Look at this! We eat!" Dave just laughed. I began to think that the idea of making money from skiing had been on his mind for a long time.

WATCHING Dave study so hard for the Civil Service exam, I was sure he would ace it, so I started saving money to buy a cookstove for the house at Crowley. Then one night when Dave and I were walking home from a movie, I realized I'd left my purse—where I kept the stove money—in the Bishop Theater. It took a few minutes to build up the courage to tell Dave. But mishaps about money didn't bother him. He said, "Roma, don't worry. The theater's closed, and your purse is safe. It'll still be there in the morning." Sure enough, he was right again.

After the Civil Service exam, our life changed really fast. Before I knew it, Dave was the hydrographer at Long Valley Dam, and we were living in the DWP complex, making our first home together! I couldn't have been happier. Life seemed perfect. Of course, I was still so young I had no idea about the kinds of challenges that lay ahead.

Dave's new job required him to be in the field the better part of each day, which meant I spent most of my time home alone without too much to do. One day I decided to paint our kitchen ceiling red, my favorite color. I couldn't wait for Dave to see my work of art. But when he got home, his only remark was, "Does red mean you're angry?" His tone of voice caught me off guard as if I'd done something wrong. I was so surprised I couldn't say a word.

The last thing I wanted was to fight over the color of the kitchen ceiling, so the next day, I applied three coats of white paint to cover the red. When Dave came home that night, we both acted as if the incident had never happened. Neither of us ever mentioned the ceiling again. Thinking back, I can see we'd just had our first lesson in avoiding confrontation: silence. I can't say this was good, but it's what happened. Anyway, I ended up liking the white ceiling. It brought light into our kitchen.

The hardest times for me at Crowley were when Dave went on his over-night snow surveys. I wasn't worried about him out there in the mountains. He could take care of himself. No, the problem was me. I dreaded being by myself in the darkness. You know, growing up with Grandma, I'd never spent a single night alone. So, when the sun went down at Crowley, I'd pull the shades, put on my pajamas, and climb into bed shivering and afraid.

One evening, Dave came home early, about 5:30 p.m., and there I was under the covers in a darkened room. I started crying and blurted out my fears. From then on, he came home every night, no matter how late. To this day, he still says he didn't mind the hardship I must have caused him.

GETTING ready for our first winter at Crowley, Dave made arrangements with Ma Yerby to park our Chevy at Toms Place so we wouldn't get stuck in the snow on the rough road that led to our house. So, when Dave heard news of a snowstorm coming our way, he drove to Toms Place, put the tire chains on, stored the battery inside the lodge, and walked the three miles back home.[1] What a smart move that was. The next morning, we woke to a foot of snow on our doorstep.

Dave and I were young and strong and didn't mind skiing to our car. When the weather was good, I'd ski out to Toms Place to meet him on his way home from work. Of course, when we needed the car, he had to shovel it out, reinstall the battery, crawl under the engine, ignite a tin can full of gasoline with a blowtorch, and let it burn to heat the fuel line.

Every two weeks, we'd celebrate Dave's DWP paycheck by making a special trip to Bishop to buy groceries, have dinner, and see a movie. Afterward, we'd park at Toms Place, stuff our rucksacks with the food and supplies we'd just purchased, and ski home under the stars. One full-moon night, the sky was so bright that we let our skis run straight and fast down the final hill to our house. Dave's ski got caught in the sagebrush, and he spread-eagled to the ground. A carton of fresh eggs, which we'd carefully packed on top, splattered across the snow. We both started laughing like crazy. Dave got untangled, we raced home, grabbed a mixing bowl and spoons, and by the light of the moon, scraped the broken eggs off the snow.

Back home, I unloaded the groceries as quickly as I could, and then cuddled up to Dave on the couch. I'd been thinking all afternoon how to tell him the news, and I decided to act serious as if something was wrong. I said, "Honey, you know I saw the doctor today and well…" Dave looked at me with concern. I continued slowly, "The doctor said… I… should teach you to fold a diaper because come next July, you're going to need to know how." Dave looked at me with so much joy in his eyes that my entire being lit up.

I didn't want to be left behind on weekends when Dave set up our tow, so I told him I planned on skiing right through my pregnancy, but my good intention got interrupted on December 7. The day started out like a typical Sunday morning skiing with friends in Dave's favorite spot at Mammoth, a slope in an open glade that was safe from avalanche danger.[2] Around noon, we skied back to the car for lunch. Dave grabbed our bag of sandwiches and switched the car radio on expecting to hear the happy sounds of a popular tune. But instead of music, we heard a tense-voiced newscaster repeating the same message over and over again. The Japanese had attacked Pearl Harbor.

CHAPTER ELEVEN

A Personal Battle

Dave, Roma, Gary and Edna.

As Americans learned more about the devastation at Pearl Harbor, initial fears escalated into raging anger. Patriotism soared to an all-time high, and a rush of men volunteered for the military. Others waited until their conscription number was called, determined to squeeze every bit of joy out of their lives before having to fight a battle from which they might not return.

Dave instinctively wanted to help protect his country. He considered enlisting to become a fighter pilot in the U.S Navy, but his DWP job was deemed "essential," prohibiting him from joining the military. His official conscription classification—IIIB: men with dependents engaged in work essential to national defense—placed him on the 16th of 25 conscription tiers. Required to stay at his post, Dave would serve his country as a DWP employee protecting California's water supply.

After Pearl Harbor, the U.S. government feared that foreigners living in the United States were involved in subversive activities. Japanese Americans ordered into internment camps weren't the only ones to suffer. The U.S. government accused Austrian ski instructors in Sun Valley, Idaho, of being enemy aliens and possibly Nazi informants.

SKI TRACKS
Sun Valley Ski Instructor Arrested
1941

On the second morning after the attack on Pearl Harbor, Friedl Pfeifer awoke to a loud pounding on his front door. Two men in overcoats, definitely not Sun Valley guests, stood on his porch with a warrant for his arrest. They hustled him away in handcuffs and shame, first to a prison in Salt Lake City and later, along with 200 other detainees, to an old, unused Army camp at Fort Lincoln, North Dakota. Friedl would spend a few months there before the FBI released him.[1]

Trying to maintain a degree of normalcy, Mammoth Ski Club members held their long-planned Box Lunch, a fundraiser for the annual Easter Egg Hunt. They played card games and auctioned homemade lunches, with the highest bidder winning one of Helen Eaton's luscious cakes.

In late December, the California Ski Association hosted its annual Skiers' Ball at the Fairmont Hotel in San Francisco. CSA president Jimmy Connell presented ski mountaineer and racer awards, showed Walt Disney's new cartoon movie, *The Art of Skiing*, and updated the guests on how the war was affecting skiing. The U.S. Forest Service didn't expect to close any ski areas except where essential utilities were in danger, so Connell encouraged ski clubs to provide facilities for servicemen.[2] The state had agreed to make a tremendous effort to keep Highway 40 over Donner Pass cleared to support possible military movements across the Sierra Nevada, so, at least for the meantime, Sugar Bowl Ski Resort, located along that strategic line of transportation, would remain open.[3]

THE U.S. military was unprepared for war, particularly one with tanks and aircraft as the weapons of choice. Therefore, President Roosevelt immediately made money available to train 50,000 pilots and to build planes to support them. Many of those contracts went to Southern California manufacturing plants.

SKI TRACKS
Southern California Defense Plants
1942

> The pioneering firms of Douglas, Lockheed, Consolidated Vultee, and Ryan transformed from struggling backyard enterprises into enormous complexes. New firms such as North American, Hughes, and Northrop (founded by the same Jack Northrop who ran the first tow at Mammoth and designed the first up-ski at McGee) emerged. These manufacturing plants soon covered thousands of acres in Los Angeles, Long Beach, Santa Monica, San Diego, and El Segundo, all of them painted over or covered with patterned, olive-drab netting that passed for camouflage.

Attracted by the high wages of government contracts, skilled and unskilled workers migrated to Southern California to work in the aircraft industry. From 1936 to 1943, the number of Southern California defense industry employees grew from 20,000 to 243,000. For many of these workers, company ski clubs served as the social center of their lives, winter and summer. Members pooled rations—food, fuel, rubber (for tires)—to participate in their club's potluck dinners, beach parties, folk dances, and ski trips. As a result, during the war and afterward, defense industry ski clubs were the heartbeat of Eastern Sierra skiing.

One diehard skier, Stanley Voorhees, a top designer at Douglas Aircraft, outfitted his 1940 Ford with two carburetors and three fuel tanks (one for rationed gas to start the engine, two more for butane, cleaning fluid, kerosene, and the like). Stanley drove to the ski hill using different pedals for each tank, making the drive a bit like playing an organ.

ON New Year's Day 1942, a monster snowstorm hit the Eastern Sierra and didn't let up for the next 36 hours. ESSC members talked excitedly about another 10-foot snow year on McGee, not realizing that during the storm, an avalanche had destroyed their tow and ski hut. Unable to ski on McGee, visiting skiers continued north. Some went to tows in the June Lake Loop.[4] Others tried to reach Nyle Smith's Mammoth Ski Lift at Observation Point, but the road was plowed just to Penney's Tavern.[5]

With the ESSC's McGee tow out of commission, on Wednesday afternoons and weekends, Dave set up his portable tow for the Bishop High racers to train. Thirty miles north, Lee Vining High School racers practiced daily using electric tows installed on a hill behind town. Thanks to this collective diligence, these two teams won the majority of the 1942 California Interscholastic Federation competitions. Unfortunately, by the end of the school year, wartime gas rationing made school travel prohibitive. California Interscholastic Federation (CIF) canceled races for the duration of the war, and school ski teams disbanded. Lee Vining High closed completely. Mono County students boarded in Bishop and attended Bishop High until further notice.

In early March 1942, most of the top ski racers in the country competed in the first U.S. National Championships ever held in California. The competition, staged at Yosemite, would not be held again until after the war, nor would the Inyo-Mono Championships, Sun Valley's Harriman Cup, or Sugar Bowl's Silver Belt. However, rather like a grand finale to ski racing during the war, Sugar Bowl did host the 1942 California Class "A" Championships, a race that Dave decided to enter. He and Roma, now almost seven months pregnant, drove to his mother's house in Reno, where Roma would stay while Dave competed.

Early Saturday morning on the way to Sugar Bowl, Dave noticed a hydrographer working along the Truckee River. He stopped to visit, lost track of time, and arrived at the race too late for his mandatory nonstop training run. Dave asked the race committee if they would make an exception to the rules and allow him to race anyway. Aware of his competent racing history, the race chairman granted permission.

Despite not having seen the course, Dave raced with confidence. Near the bottom, a section of rotten snow, weakened by hours of direct sunlight, unexpectedly gave way. Dave's left shin smashed into the edge of the collapsed hole. He screamed in excruciating pain and threw all his weight onto his right ski. Unable to turn, he careened toward a group of scattering spectators. To avoid hitting the crowd, he slammed into the snow, then flipped and tumbled in a terrifying crash.

Within moments, Sugar Bowl's Hannes Schroll was at Dave's side waving people away, calling for a toboggan, and helping a ski patroller stabilize the leg with a splint. The patroller tobogganed Dave down to the train station near the lodge, where he lay on a stretcher, waiting in agony to be transported to Reno. Finally, the train arrived. Riding to the city alone in a baggage car, he clutched the edges of his stretcher as each bump in the tracks shot a nightmare of pain through his leg. Arriving at the train station, he found Edna and Roma waiting with the ambulance. At the hospital, X-rays revealed at least 30 breaks between the tibia and fibula. The physicians agreed. The leg was inoperable.

Dave's shattered bones hadn't broken through the skin, but the blood that had rushed to the injury swelled his leg so much that it looked ready to burst open. In those days, medical experts believed such severe internal bleeding would lead to gangrene. Sulpha drugs, designed to prevent and treat bacterial infections, weren't yet approved for use. Concerned about the risk of gangrene, the shortage of nurses, the difficulty of obtaining drugs, and their belief in the impossibility of surgery, the doctors recommended amputating the leg.

Dave refused to give permission. He had witnessed the pain and suffering both his uncle and his grandmother endured from their amputations. The doctors asked Edna and Roma for their consent. For the first time, these two women united as allies. They stood firm. If Dave said his leg would not be cut off, it was *not going to be cut off.*

Day after day, Dave lay in the Reno hospital bed without saying much but cringing with pain at the slightest movement. Roma stayed by his side, massaging his good leg to facilitate blood flow, taking care of his personal needs, reading to him, her soft voice soothing him to sleep, and praying for a miracle. As if in answer to her prayers, three weeks later, a surgeon named Dr. Stoddard, on rotation from San Francisco, became interested in Dave's case.[6] Infuriated that no action had been taken on the leg, and disagreeing with the Reno doctors' prognosis that surgery would be futile, Dr. Stoddard obtained permission to operate. After five hours of wiring and screwing the shattered bones together, he deemed the operation successful. Dave's left leg would be an inch shorter than his right, but if he followed the rehabilitation protocol, he could have two functioning legs.

During the three weeks of post-surgery hospitalization, waiting for his bones to heal, Dave was fighting a personal battle over the implications of his injury. The pain he could endure; the worst would pass. What tormented him was that he was *not* fighting in the war. Ever since Pearl Harbor, he had wrestled with his desire to be protecting his country, fighting as a Navy fighter pilot with "the Boys in Blue." He had secretly clung to the hope that enlistment rules would change, and he could join the military. But now, his broken leg would prohibit him from ever serving his country in combat. He kept his thoughts to himself and focused on healing rather than self-pity. The least he could do was get back to his DWP job where he could continue his contribution to the war effort.

DAVE's friends occasionally dropped by the Reno hospital to see him. During Nan Zischank's visit, she gave an entertaining, quite possibly embellished, description of the 1942 Flying Skis on Carson Peak. Nan assured Dave he wasn't the only racer injured that spring. In fact, every one of the eleven competitors who entered the Flying Skis suffered an injury of some kind—dislocation, fractured ribs, a sprained ankle, bruises, and even a ski pole through the leg. The drama of Nan's day had started with the terrifying hike up to the starting gate, so steep it took all her courage to keep putting one boot in front of the other. On top, as the last racer to go, she wondered why she was even there. Rather than racing as fast as she could, she sideslipped and snowplowed through the turns, trying to hold her speed back. When the finish gate came into view, she saw a group of people standing on the course in her way. As she recalled:

> *Those folks were trying to help the racer before me, Frank*
> *Springer. He'd broken through the snow—just like you*
> *did Dave, at Sugar Bowl—only he'd caught his ski on*
> *some sagebrush and was lying there howling like a wild*

animal because he was hurt so bad. Well, here I came, and you know, when you're going pretty fast, the tears get in your eyes and mess with your vision. All I could see were people. They were yelling, "Don't come down," but I thought they were shouting, "Come on down!" The closer I got to the mess of people, the less I could find a spot to get through, so I sideswiped the whole thing and took everyone out, Springer and the whole bit! The two of us went through the finish gate together with our bodies clanging against each other. While we got untangled, someone borrowed a mattress from a local motel and drove Frank and me to the hospital in Bridgeport in their station wagon. Dr. Denton took X-rays of both of us and pronounced me whole, even though I was black and blue from head to toe, and then went to work setting the eight spiral breaks on Frank's leg.

Hearing Nan's hilarious rendition of what took place that day, Dave laughed out loud. He hadn't laughed that way since before his accident.

Six weeks after Dave's crash, Dr. Stoddard released him from the hospital with strict orders to use crutches and not to put any weight on his casted left leg until the bones had fully healed. DWP offered Dave further sick leave, but he asked to return to his regular assignment. That was a big mistake. Even with crutches, cast, and Dave's iron will, his leg couldn't tolerate the physical demands of his job.

George Lewis arranged with a co-worker for a temporary exchange of positions and living quarters. Working at a desk job in the Independence office would facilitate Dave's healing and shorten his weekly trips to a DWP insurance company doctor in Los Angeles. Also, the Lone Pine hospital was only a half-hour drive from Independence, and Roma was eight months pregnant.

Sure enough, on July 2, 1942, Dave sat on the edge of Roma's maternity ward bed holding their firstborn. Wrapped in a swaddling blanket, six-pound Gary Robert McCoy slept peacefully in his father's arms. Dave's heart swelled with affection. Fatherhood was far more powerful than he had imagined. Roma smiled at him and asked, "What do you think of our little punkin?" From that moment until the day he entered Bishop High, Gary McCoy would be known as Punkin.

EVENTUALLY, Dave graduated from cast and crutches. Though he walked with a limp, he was able to work in the field. One of his responsibilities was to monitor wells in the Manzanar War Relocation Center, located just south of Independence.[7]

SKI TRACKS
Manzanar War Relocation Center
1942

Established in March 1942, Manzanar was the first of 10 highly controversial government-mandated wartime camps housing over 120,000 Japanese Americans. These people had been forcibly relocated, swept from their homes with only the personal belongings they could carry on their backs, stuff under their arms, or hold in their hands. After weeks of waiting in assembly centers, they were transferred to relocation centers, one of which was Manzanar in the Owens Valley. The first internees to arrive helped build the facility. By July, the population of the camp neared 10,000. Over 90 percent came from the Los Angeles area; the rest were from Stockton, California, and Bainbridge Island, Washington. Many were farmers and fishermen; two-thirds were native-born American citizens.[8]

To know these Japanese Americans had been torn from their homes and interned in the desert upset Dave. These people were not his enemies. They were kind, generous people who befriended him. He, in turn, admired their strong spirit and how they were making the best of their situation. Whenever he visited, they loaded his arms with bags of pears and apples from the Manzanar orchards they'd rejuvenated, and with fresh vegetables they'd cultivated. To Roma's surprise and delight, they even shared rationed wartime commodities such as butter, eggs, sugar, and flour distributed in bulk to the relocation camp. Each time Dave left the camp for Independence, he struggled in turmoil about the tragedies of war.

ONCE U.S. troops had been fighting on foreign soil for a few months, the predominant sentiment among skiers was that on the grand scale of things, skiing was out. It would be inappropriate to enjoy the leisure of a ski vacation while fellow countrymen were in battle. Gas rationing had practically eliminated resort operations through lack of attendance, rail and car travel were at a new low, and the military closed mountain areas considered strategically critical. The *National Skiing Weekly* had gone out of print and the *Los Angeles Times* had discontinued Ethel Van Degrift's *Ski Slants* column.[9] In October, the California Ski Association met to decide how they should handle wartime affairs.[10] Many ski clubs had lost entire memberships and maintained skeleton organizations in name only. The exception was defense plant ski clubs, which still enjoyed large programs.

Sun Valley resort closed and converted its lodge into a Naval convalescent hospital. A similar conversion took place at the Ahwahnee Hotel in Yosemite. In this case, the Navy kept the road open from the hotel to Badger Pass Ski Area by providing funds to override gasoline rationing and a shortage of manpower. Yet, even in these two exquisite settings, men were restless. Some longed for their homes and a more city-like environment. Others were afraid to ski, either fearing an injury or dreading that if they skied well enough, they might be considered healthy and ready to be sent back to war.[11]

AFTER a year of living in Independence, Dave's left leg had healed enough for him to return home to Crowley and resume his hydrographic duties. Though chronic pain and limited movement prevented him from working at his usual pace, he didn't complain about his limitations. Instead, he focused on an idea he had about a way he could contribute to the war effort. He would build a small ski area on McGee and offer free skiing to returning veterans, servicemen on leave, and their families. In the beginning, there would only be his portable tow. In time he would build larger, more efficient permanent tows, and eventually a warming hut with food service.[12]

All Dave needed to get started was the Forest Service permit that Corty Hill had given Ma Yerby when he disbanded his McGee sling-lift before the war. Dave shared his vision with Ma and asked if she would be willing to pass the permit on to him. Ma knew his intention was genuine. She responded with one question. "How are you going to finance your dream?"

Flashing his trademark grin, Dave replied, "Why, you know how that goes, Ma! When you put your mind to something and work hard for it, what you need just comes around." Dave left Toms Place that afternoon with Ma Yerby's blessings and, in his pocket, the Forest Service permit to build a permanent ski tow on McGee Mountain.

About that time, Stover Lowe, who had previously been working for the DWP in the Mojave Desert, moved in next door to the McCoys with his wife Zola and daughter Sarah. Right from the beginning, the two families became fast friends. According to Zola,

> *The thing to do was to go to war, and both Stover and Dave felt terrible they couldn't go. They'd have been the kind who would've gone out and gotten shot because whatever they did, they didn't quit. To compensate, they'd take on-leave servicemen fishing or hunting and then invite them over for a hot dinner. If anything was worrying Dave, he didn't show it. All he talked about was how he wanted to have rope tows ready for the soldiers when they returned. He had a dream and all the confidence in the world he could make that dream come true.*

Stover helped Dave tear down the tiny ski hut Corty had left behind, and the two men used the materials to build a new shelter in a spot Dave thought would be out of avalanche paths. He set up his portable tow once there was enough snow on the ground to ski. In December 1942, signs of a brewing snowstorm prompted Dave to park his car at Toms Place and limp back to the Crowley house. That night, ripping winds and whirling snow pounded the walls and windows. The next morning, as he shoveled pathways around the complex and completed his duties at the dam, he listened for the sound of the state Sno-Go clearing Highway 395. Once he heard the machine rumble by, he strapped on his skis and cut a trail through the virgin snow to Toms Place. With each step, Dave found a new appreciation for snow. On skis, his leg didn't hurt. And, he didn't limp.

At Toms Place, Dave warmed up the car and drove toward McGee, but due to an avalanche that had plummeted off the high chutes of the mountain, Highway 395 was impassable. As the crashing snow blasted down the mountain, it had picked up energy, ripped apart the Eastern Sierra Ski Club's hut, and destroyed their up-ski. The avalanche also uprooted three of Southern California Edison's electric power poles, tore down almost 2,000 feet of telephone cable, and left a 500-foot-long wall of avalanche debris on the far side of McGee Canyon Road. Dave's portable tow and small ski hut, located northwest of the avalanche, were buried by the snowfall, but unscathed by the avalanche. Within a week after the storm, Dave had them dug out and running. In January, he organized his first ski party for servicemen on leave, offered visitors the use of ski gear he had borrowed from his friends, and, of course, allowed them to ski his tow free of charge.

Similar "ski therapy" was taking place north of Mono County near Donner Summit.

SKI TRACKS

Military Men Ski Soda Springs

1943

A group of Royal Dutch Air Corps men from Holland and Java were stationed at a camp near Donner Summit waiting for new planes to fly back to the South Pacific battlefronts. The Army bused them to Soda Springs each day to enjoy the skiing. When they finally left for the South Pacific, the corps flew over Soda Springs in formations of three, each in his turn peeling off with a final buzz that seemed to say, "So long, thank you, we'll be back someday."[13]

Two years after his operation, Dave's limp and the pain he endured had worsened to the point where people recognized his lone figure hobbling along the highway near Toms Place, trying to rebuild leg muscles.[14] Finally, Dave acknowledged that his leg hadn't healed properly. He made two appointments in Los Angeles, one with his DWP doctor, the other with Corty Hill's physician. Both doctors agreed. Only the surface layer of Dave's bone had regenerated. They suggested an experimental surgery that would involve both legs.

The surgeon would drill numerous holes through the outer layers of bone in Dave's left leg and remove the unhealed bone, leaving the holes open to encourage blood circulation. He would then extract solid bone from the healthy right leg and graft it onto the unhealed bone of Dave's left leg. Lastly, the surgeon would crush the weak bone he'd removed from the left leg and pack that into the right leg where he had taken the bone graft. Dave would need to recuperate in the hospital for three months post-surgery. Nurses, still in short supply, would monitor for signs of infection, but due to a limited inventory of drugs, pain management would be minimal.

Putting the risk and potential complications aside, Dave signed the release to operate. Punkin and Roma, now pregnant with her second child, moved in with Frances and her family, whose North Hollywood home was located conveniently close to the hospital. Roma could visit Dave daily, leaving Punkin at the house to play with his cousin, Mike Martin. That was until the day she noticed some attractive nurses having a fine time flirting with her handsome husband, and he was smiling right back at them. Roma started taking Punkin to the hospital with her, setting him right on Dave's lap along with baby bottles and diapers, and making sure her pregnant belly was noticeable. She bought Dave a set of knitting needles and yarn, and taught him how to knit "soakers," an outside covering for the diapers.

Three months post-surgery, Dave's doctors released him with strict instructions to wear a full-length metal brace on his left leg *and* use crutches for a year. If all went according to plan, he would eventually be able to move around with physical competence. However, if he pushed too hard or too fast, he could be crippled for life.

BACK home at Crowley, Dave readied for the 1945 winter by adjusting his leg brace so he could wear it with ski boots, cutting a pair of old wooden skis down to size for Punkin, and tuning up his portable tow to welcome veterans, starting with Max Zischank.

After an 18-month tour of duty in the Aleutians, Max returned to his Long Valley Resort with an honorable discharge from the Navy Seabees. He envisioned one day adding a cocktail lounge and Union 76 gas station to his resort, but for the present, he just needed to be open for fishing season, still a few months away. His wife Nan had yet to complete her employment at Manzanar where she drove Japanese American internees to their appointments off-premises, so Max had plenty of time on his hands. He offered to help Dave with his portable tow on McGee for as long as the snow lasted.

Meanwhile, Nyle and Ruth Smith returned to the Eastern Sierra after completing their obligations at the U.S. Naval Special Hospital in Yosemite. They purchased the old Steffen Fox Farm, refurbished the building, opened for business as Crowley Lake Resort, and advertised Nyle Smith Ski Lessons at Dave's tow.

Marc Zumstein moved his wife Ethel and their daughter Charlotte from Southern California to Bishop. Their son Don was still fighting in the Pacific, and the Zumsteins were constantly concerned about his safety. Marc hoped that being in the mountains would bring his family solace, even laughter. They opened an upholstery shop in Bishop and spent their weekends helping Dave with his tow. Charlotte became the first female to race on the Bishop High School team.

As soon as a snowstorm finally hit, about 30 skiers arrived at Dave's tow, eager for a weekend of skiing. His portable provided a ski run that was only long enough to make five or six turns, but that didn't seem to matter. Animated faces spoke of fresh mountain air, alpine scenery, and time spent with family and friends. No one complained. No one spoke of war.

Roma hung Dave's fishing creel on a willow pole next to her hand-written sign, "Donations Here." Six-months pregnant with child number two, she skied as elegantly as if she had never missed a day. Punkin, almost three years old, shuffled around on his little skis, looking like a miniature version of his father. Former Bishop High students, now veterans of the armed forces, whizzed down the slope, each trying to ski faster than the other, while off to one side, Nyle Smith instructed a group of beginners.

Dave stood at the bottom of the slope, resting all his weight on his right leg and jutting his left hip out for stability. Visiting with the skiers, he'd point out where he planned to install a second 650-foot-long tow and explained, "You'll soon have the pleasure of skiing down 1,300 feet without stopping." He also let everyone know that if a group of skiers could round up a total of $7.50, he and Max would operate the tow on a weekday.

Young Eddie Riley, who had come up from Bishop to ski with his father, watched Dave from the top of the tow. Eddie thought, "This guy sure looks top drawer with his pants tucked into his boots. He must be a real skier!" But what impressed Eddie most was that Dave let all the kids ski for free.[15]

Driving back to Crowley after a day of running the rope tow, Dave ruffled Punkin's hair with affection. He caught Roma's eye, and teased, "Hey Toots, don't you think this was the best day ever?"

Roma nudged Dave's shoulder. "Oh, Honey, you always say that!"

On May 8, 1945, just over a week after Hitler committed suicide, the Allies accepted Germany's unconditional surrender, and Winston Churchill pronounced V-E Day for Victory in Europe. War raged on in the Far East, until August 6 and 9, when the U.S. dropped atomic bombs over Hiroshima and Nagasaki, respectively, causing unprecedented destruction. On September 2, representatives of the Empire of Japan signed formal surrender documents.

World War II was officially over.

CHAPTER TWELVE

Roma: War Days

Roma and Punkin in DWP truck.

After the initial shock of Pearl Harbor, we tried to keep some normalcy in our lives, but thoughts of war were ever-present. The sense of security Dave and I had taken for granted was gone. Who knew what was going to happen from day to day? No one.

I was sick with worry over the boys who were fighting, especially my brother. Marshall had been drafted in November 1941, just before Pearl Harbor, and now he was stationed in North Africa. I wanted to support the cause, so I joined women across the nation who were making scarves and socks for the troops and taught myself to knit. Believe me, I put my prayers for the men into every single stitch, along with my gratitude that Dave's job kept him from enlisting. Yes, I knew he had a desire to be fighting, but I was selfish. I don't deny that. I did *not* want my husband to go to war.

Dave stayed busy with his usual DWP duties plus operating our portable tow on Wednesday afternoons and weekends, helping with the Bishop High race team. He even ran courses himself, which was one of his *most* favorite things. In fact, in early April, he was feeling so good about his skiing he decided to enter the 1942 California State Championships at Sugar Bowl. He didn't want me to be alone at Crowley so, I went to Reno with him. I was six months pregnant and if I needed help, I'd have to ski out to Toms Place, no matter what the weather, and hope someone there could get me to a doctor.

I had a plan about how to handle Edna if she criticized the way I was dressed in Dave's shirt and Levis, the only clothing we owned that would fit around my pregnant belly. I would say in my sweetest voice, "Why, Edna, don't you think it would be inappropriate for me to spend money on luxury items during wartime?" But Edna didn't mention my outfit, and we got along just fine, which meant the world to me.

Saturday afternoon, we were having such a pleasant visit that I barely noticed when the telephone rang. Edna answered the call, and I looked up from my knitting just in time to see her face turn pale. She was asking, "What... Where...?" She hung up the phone, fighting tears and said, "Come on, Roma, we've got to get to the train station. Dave broke his back!"

When we arrived at the station, an ambulance was already there, ready to carry Dave to St. Mary's Hospital. What a relief to find out his back was okay; it was his leg that had broken. But when the attendants transferred him to the ambulance, I swear, I'd never seen such anguish on his face. Then, just when the vehicle began to move, the back door flew open, and Dave's stretcher started to slide out. I screamed so loud the sound could have broken windows. The ambulance stopped just in time, and the attendants pulled Dave back in. If that wasn't carelessness, I don't know what was.

At the hospital, the doctors tried to get either Edna or me to give them permission to amputate Dave's leg. No way! As if we would go against Dave's wishes. They got so frustrated. Right to our faces, they called us "obstinate women" and told us, "The tissue will die, gangrene will set in, and you'll be wishing you'd listened to us."

I cried out, "Are you serious? What do you mean, you're just going to *wait* for gangrene?" There was nothing else they could do, or so they said.

The nurses tied four corners of a sheet to the bedposts and rested Dave's leg on the makeshift sling. Dave was accustomed to being in control of his life, so he was *not* happy about lying in bed day after day, useless, with no plan of action and in constant pain. I spent my days sitting by his side, keeping him company, and trying not to think about gangrene. One week passed, then another. At the end of the third week, there was still no sign of gangrene. Thank heavens!

Around that time, we met Dr. Stoddard, an angel who came into our lives to save the day. He was sure he could stabilize the broken pieces of bone in such a way they would heal, so Dave signed the permission papers. After the surgery, the doctor outlined a slow, conservative rehabilitation. The patient must use crutches, heed all caution, and avoid all risks putting *no* weight on the left leg. Of course, when Dave awoke from the anesthesia, he was filled with confidence he would be back to normal in no time.

Three weeks later, Dr. Stoddard released Dave to go home. Our friends, Bruce and Grace Morgan from Toms Place, drove to Reno to pick us up. What a sight we were: Dave in a full-length leg cast using crutches to walk, and me, almost eight months along, trying to get him onto a mattress in the back of the station wagon. But we did it.

We ended up in Independence where the local townsfolk went out of their way to make me feel at home. I appreciated their kindness, but I've never been good at socializing with strangers. Dave was the only company I wanted. I was happy to fill my time caring for him, tidying the house, cooking our meals, knitting for the soldiers, and making preparations for our baby.

The news depressed me, so I stopped listening to the radio. Why couldn't the war just go away? Everything about it was horrible and emotional and complicated. Just the mention of the fighting made Dave's jaw go square. I knew that the fact he was not fighting overseas haunted him, but I couldn't help with his struggle. I was grateful that every afternoon, I got to hear the sound of his crutches coming up the cement pathway and home to me.

One hot July day, I was standing in front of a fan I kept on the kitchen table, peeling potatoes, trying to cool off from the relentless desert heat of the Owens Valley, when all of a sudden, my water broke. You'd think I'd have known what was happening, but I didn't. I raced into the bathroom and stayed there until Dave came home. When he found me, I was all worked up and afraid. As usual, he calmed me down. My labor pains began after we went to bed but were pretty far apart until around midnight. That's when Dave grabbed my bag of personal items, and off we drove to the hospital in Lone Pine. The nurse told Dave he might as well go home and get some sleep because labor for a first child usually lasts a long time. Indeed, it wasn't until about 7 p.m. on July 2, 1942, that Punkin was born. Dave was sitting in the waiting room when the nurse opened the door and announced loud and clear, "It's a boy!"

Back then, new mothers and their babies remained in the hospital for ten days, but once I got home with my baby and my husband, I felt a happiness I'd never known. Frances came up to help me and brought along her first child, two-month-old Mike Martin. Here we were, two sisters and best friends who were now young mothers, so glad to be together, helping each other with our little boys, laughing away at everything we did.

After Frances left, Edna came down from Reno. Based on how close we'd become over Dave's broken leg, I thought her visit would be a joyous occasion. But as soon as she arrived, I could feel that old tension between us. She didn't even ask to see Punkin. I couldn't believe it. Still I was determined to keep a good attitude and *not* take her comments as personal criticisms. I lifted Punkin from his crib and carried him to her. And do you know what she said? "Oh, he's so small. You should've seen how strong and healthy my Sonny was; twelve pounds, twice as big as this one." I wanted to yell out, "Isn't your own grandson good enough for you?" But Edna had already gone into the kitchen. I was sure I saw her looking behind the refrigerator to check for dust. She might as well have been throwing knives at my heart. It took all I had to keep from bursting into tears. I wanted her to love me and be proud of me, but I was beginning to think a close friendship between us was hopeless.

WHEN we finally moved back to Crowley, Dave still walked with a limp, but at least he could get around. Punkin had just learned to walk, and we thought it was so funny the way he dropped his shoulder every other step, imitating his dad's uneven gait. The memory makes me sad. The fact that Punkin had never seen his dad walk correctly wasn't funny at all. Nor was the pain Dave was enduring. But Dave never, and I mean never, complained. I'd ask how he was doing, and he'd grin at me and say, "I'm feeling better than ever." I think he believed if he ignored the pain, it would go away; if he just worked a little harder, carried a little more weight, or walked the extra mile, everything would be fine.

My biggest fear was that Dave's leg might give way when he was far from the house without anyone to help him. So, when Stover Lowe moved next door with his wife Zola and daughter Sarah, I was thrilled because Stover liked to go with Dave on all his activities.

Stover was born on August 24, 1914, exactly one year before Dave. He liked to say the two of them had never been strangers. What a pair. They both had high moral standards, chose to live quiet lives, and didn't drink alcohol. The main difference between them was the amount of energy they had. Dave woke up every morning at five and stayed in constant motion until he went to bed. Stover was a slender, red-haired, six-foot-two desert rat kind of guy content to spend the day sitting still in the open air. Zola said she was afraid he might kill himself, trying to keep up with Dave. Sometimes when he'd be relaxing in his living room, Dave would walk by the window and beckon. Stover didn't want to show how tired he felt, so he'd pull his boots on and go outside. You see, Dave thought the rest of the world was on the same schedule he was and that everyone worked just as hard as he did. But not many people could do that.

Zola and I shared everything from our phone party line to babysitting. In the summer, we'd go to Bishop and she'd do the grocery shopping while I babysat the kids in the air-conditioned drugstore. Boy, was I spoiled. Back at Crowley, she'd keep me company while I sunbathed out on the lawn. I'd tie one of Dave's handkerchiefs around my chest as a halter top, rub baby oil all over my skin, and try to get as tanned as possible. Zola sat in a chair protecting her skin from the sun while we visited. After it snowed, Dave would shovel out a sunbathing pit for me and lay boards across the bottom. Zola would come outside dressed in her coat, hat, and gloves, and read her newspaper while I lay there soaking up the sun. Now that was friendship.

Stover and Zola had adopted little Sarah, who was not much older than Punkin. Coming from a Paiute family of eight children, Sarah missed all her brothers and sisters, so once she saw Punkin, she decided he would be her little brother. She played with Punkin, took care of him, and stood up for him, hardly letting him out of her sight. When he was learning to talk, the two of them made up their own language and Sarah was the only one who could understand what Punkin was saying.

One day Zola heard me scream, ran over to the house and found me crying over my white dress shoes. Sarah had marked them up with my lipstick, and I was furious with her, poor little thing. It's just that I wanted my dress shoes to last a long time. You see, during the war, we were rationed one coupon for one pair of shoes per person per year, so I was saving my coupons for Punkin's fast-growing feet. Well, Zola got me calmed down, and I felt bad about getting so upset with a child. I tried to make amends by letting Sarah help me polish the shoes until they were presentable.

Rationing had become part of everyday life.[1] But even with food rations, we never went hungry. Dave kept our freezer stocked with wild game: trout, venison, rabbits, ducks, geese, and sage hen. Once you taste wild sage hen, you'll never settle for chicken again. We'd trade game for a lamb from a local sheepherder, and come harvest time in Bishop, Zola and I would swap game for crates of fruits and vegetables. Together, we'd can pears, applesauce, green beans, tomatoes, and whatever else we came across. If either of us ran out of money or food before the next paycheck or ration book arrived, we shared what we had.

Dave wasn't boastful about his hunting and fishing skills. It was just that whenever he got interested in something, he'd give his full attention to it. He had an excellent eye, steady aim, and a sense for tracking wild animals. To conserve ammunition, he'd wait until three geese lined up in such a way that he could hit all three with one bullet. I'm not kidding. And fishing, why he was beautiful to watch, casting his rod with such a light, accurate touch.

Dave and his boss George Lewis had an ongoing fishing competition. George liked to fish the slow waters below the Gorge, casting his spinning rod from his canoe. Dave preferred to fly fish, casting from shore behind the dam where the river was swift and rough. When he hooked a fish, he'd run in the water without caring that his shirt, Levis, and boots got soaking wet as he bounced over the rocks and through the big water holes trying to pull in his 20-inch rainbow.[2]

In those days, there was so much waterfowl on Crowley Lake that when the ducks and geese took flight, the sky darkened. I mean it! There were times Dave and Stover came home carrying 20 ducks between them. The four of us would pluck feathers until past midnight, freeze the meat, and pack up the down fluff to mail to Ducks Unlimited in Seattle to be used in sleeping bags and clothing for the soldiers.

Whatever I cooked, I always tried to have enough food to feed the unannounced visitors Dave might bring home. He liked to invite people to share our meals, especially U.S. military servicemen on leave, and that was fine with me. Having people around eased my loneliness.

So many days, Dave worked all morning, came home for lunch, grabbed warmer clothing, took off with Stover to go hunting, and didn't return until eight or nine at night. I'd sometimes wake Punkin from his nap just for his company. Or I'd go next door and talk to Zola. She enjoyed her quiet time alone and tried to teach me to do the same, reminding me I had plenty of things to do to stay occupied. She was right, of course. When you're raising children and keeping house, there's always something to cook or clean or iron, not to mention knit or crochet. So, I started making a big rag rug for our living room floor, and that helped.

I didn't dare complain about my loneliness, what with the war and all. Still, I think Dave noticed. He knew I loved to walk outside, and Punkin did too, so he built us a stroller with extra big wheels that could roll on the dirt roads. Sometimes I'd walk Punkin to Toms Place just to pick up a newspaper and the mail. Oh, how happy I was when I'd see Frances' handwriting on an envelope, or I'd find a battered letter from Marshall.

Dave and I looked forward to weekends when the Lowes' friends, Donald and Eloise Dawson, would visit. Donald was an instructor for the Air Corps in Las Vegas. He would bring cases of #9 skeet-load ammunition that they used on the base for target practice, and the men would hunt, while the ladies sat around and talked. One afternoon at Zola's house, we decided to bake a chocolate cake. Eloise and I were both pregnant and both craving sugar, and you know how that goes. Just the smell of baking chocolate and sugar made our heads spin. So, we ate the entire cake in one sitting. Then we felt bad that we hadn't saved any for the men, so we scrounged for enough ingredients to bake another one. The following weekend, Eloise resupplied us with shortening and cocoa from the Air Corps commissary, and that's how our multi-family, ration-sharing, cake-baking tradition began.

Occasionally Edna came down from Reno with friends. There was still an awkwardness between us, but we had reached an unspoken truce. On one of her visits, Dave took her over to the dam. She waited on top while he walked down to the river. Just after he reached the bottom, an earthquake shook all of Long Valley. Edna saw room-size rocks crashing down the hillside and screamed at Dave. He looked up, saw what was coming, and started dodging rocks like a kangaroo jumping around. Back at the house, I grabbed Punkin, ran outside, and the two of us huddled on the lawn. I was praying for the earth to stop shaking and worrying about Dave and Edna at the same time. Of course, Dave didn't understand why we got so frightened. He thought the earthquake was sensational!

Dave just wasn't the kind of person who worried. He even had a relaxed attitude about money. One time when money was short, rather than get all upset, he said to me, "Toots, we ought to take advantage of living here at Crowley Lake. I could build a landing and start a fishing guide service, and…" There he was, once again, figuring out how to turn an activity he loved into a profitable business. Nothing I said was going to stop Dave, so I supported him. Besides, sitting in a boat might be good for his leg.

Using empty barrels and scrap wood, Dave built his dock, the first one on Crowley Lake. A dealer in Los Angeles sold us a rundown, flat-bottomed boat for $40. Boy, we must have looked raggedy, rattling along the highway with that boat on its rickety trailer. Dave chinked all the cracks with tar, tuned up the engine, and opened for business. He then fished every corner of Crowley Lake, studying where the trout migrated and what food sources they liked. One of his favorite fishing spots was McGee Bay, where the browns fed. He'd pull the centerboard up, row through the shallow water, and drift back out skimming over the weeds, landing one trout after another with his fly rod.

Dave tracked the *Los Angeles Times* classified ads in search of afford-able boats. At one point, he bought a frame, planking, and a boat cabin, built the boat himself, and installed an outdated four-cylinder Star engine. Eventually, Dave built his fleet up to six rental boats. Then he figured, why not moor and maintain boats for clients? That inevitably led to other mis-cellaneous jobs. One wealthy Southern Californian who kept his boat at our landing paid us $20 to clean his cabin at McGee Creek. He also hired Dave to cut, split, and stack his winter firewood.

As time went on, Dave's leg got worse. Even though he didn't say anything about it, you could see the pain as he moved. He tried everything he could think of, even soaking his leg in five-gallon buckets of Mono Lake's salt-water, hoping the water did have healing power. Nothing helped. His leg had become so unstable that with just a touch of the hand, his knee joint would move back and forth. Sometimes he came home with dirt all over his jeans, a telltale sign his leg had given out and he'd been crawling. I'd say, "Honey, where *have* you been today?" He'd laugh or joke as if crawling across the ground was perfectly normal.

One day, Dave sat me down and said, "Roma, I've got to fix this leg of mine." For him to admit that something hurt meant the pain had become unbearable. Off we went to Los Angeles for medical advice, which evolved into Dave enduring an experimental surgery on both legs. The procedure was risky and the recovery slow, but we had to try.

By the time the doctors released Dave from the hospital, he'd gotten extremely thin. His left leg was still over an inch shorter than his right, but his bones were mending. He was disciplined about wearing his full-length metal brace, and thank heavens Stover was there to help him because I was busy getting ready for our second child.

As my due date approached, the warmth of spring was melting the snow off the top of McGee, sprouts of green grass were poking their heads out from our dormant lawn, our blue irises were getting ready to bloom, and our climbing rose was creeping up the trellis preparing to burst with pink blossoms. Dave was back at work and running his fishing guide busi-ness, so we designed a system to alert him if my time came.

Sure enough, Dave was out on the lake when my labor started. I squeezed myself behind the steering wheel and drove to the back of the house out of his view. As soon as he noticed the car was gone, he raced home. We grabbed my bag and the bassinette Zola had made for the baby and drove down Sherwin Grade to the Bishop Hospital, which in those days was a house on Elm Street. On May 27, 1945, Dr. Mason delivered nine-pound Dennis Marshall McCoy. Holding this innocent child in my arms, I prayed he would grow up in a peaceful world. Later that afternoon, Stover and Zola came to see us. Stover took one look at our husky boy and chuckled, "Why, howdy there, Poncho!" Everyone in the room laughed. What a good start, I thought. A roomful of laughter welcoming our second-born son into the world! Little did we know that the name Poncho would stay with him for life.

After Poncho's birth, I was as happy as I had ever been. Two precious little boys, Dave's leg getting stronger and stronger, the war coming to an end, and friends we hadn't seen for years beginning to drop by. One day, I opened the front door and saw our friend, Carl Grebe, standing there, so thin that he was barely recognizable. My mouth dropped open in surprise. He was reluctant to tell us what had happened, but at least I got him to eat some nourishing meals.[3] Only later did I learn that he'd spent two years in a German prisoner of war camp.

Oh, how the war had stolen the innocence of our lives. Besides all the other terrors and horrors of war, we learned that the atrocities of the Holocaust were more horrific than any of us ever could have imagined. My heart ached, and my eyes filled with silent tears that wouldn't fall.

If I wanted to truly honor the millions of people who had faced suffering, in their memory, I needed to be brave in my own life. There was nothing I could do to fix the harm done. Dave was different than me. He was a true believer that the joy of skiing could help heal the wounds of war, and he had a plan to make that healing happen.

INTERLUDE

"This is Skiing"

Mammoth Mountain, undeveloped.

The following article by Larry Thackwell, which was first published
in *Western Skiing,* October 1945.

F our of us left Los Angeles right after work on Friday, July 13, 1945.
After 320 moonlit miles through sage-scented mountains and desert, the car finally poked its way into the Mammoth Campground
at 1 a.m. Down went the sleeping bags, and into them we dove, pine needles and all.

It took the combined effect of the sun in our faces, and the absurd
chattering of the blue jays, to get us up. But then we saw the snow on
the peaks! That did it. We doused our heads in the stream, maneuvered
through a pile of hot cakes and sausages at the lodge across the road, and

tore off toward our mountain. A mile more of the paved road toward Mammoth Lakes, then to the right through park-like forests with ever closer glimpses of the high snow fields, and then, with a turn onto the pine needles by a swift snow stream, we were there! Less than a half mile away the snow rose dramatically above us like a vertical wall to an altitude of nearly 12,000 feet.

For two days we had incomparable skiing, with Saturday night spent among the trees near the edge of the snow. Let me tell you about our last run. As we climbed out of our sleeping bags… we looked up toward the mountain. There, far above, were our tracks of the day before, curving down from the highest rock, out of the sun, and into the long blue-pink shadows, which were drawing slowly back into the East. Hurriedly we waxed. In a few minutes our stream became the snow and looking down on our boots crunching one after the other, we could still hear the rush of water underneath.

There is something rather wonderful about climbing, something both physical and spiritual, an intermingling of strange exultation and inner happiness. Our minds and movements gradually become one, we feel the surge of strength in our legs as they take us upward, our lungs and hearts perform in unison, and all is wonderful in the world.

Now we were in the sun and on the broad curving face of the mountain. Look at our shadows! The long legs, then the rucksacks, and last, the crisscrossed skis and poles showing above all. A similar picture flashed to mind, one that had deeply thrilled me long ago, a scene in an Austrian mountain film. But this scene was real, and I was a part of it!

Ahead and above was our route. It passed along the lower reaches of the tremendous snow slope to our right, up and across three long islands of grass and rock to the foot of a rounded knoll: and above this, up a steep headwall-like rise to our 11,000-foot goal—Mammoth Saddle.

At a flat rock on the second island we paused… A thousand feet and nearly an hour below… the road wound through the trees up to Minaret Summit, and then, out of sight in the deep valley of the San Joaquin… the sun flashed along the airy precipices of Banner, Ritter, and the needle-like Minarets, sending showers of gold cascading down their hanging snow fields to wither and die on the rocks below. A moment like this to be ours, to keep, to cherish—Romance, Music, Paradise!

Onward and upward! The sun was becoming warm and our bare arms felt it. Each boot now formed a shallow trough in the glaring wet crystals. Our shirts were wet where the skis pressed on our shoulders. Everywhere was sun and snow. We moved more slowly now, tiny figures high on the face of an immense headwall. Where was our strength? Each leg trembled as the other kicked a step above it. We steadied ourselves with our poles in one hand, and delicately balanced the skis on our shoulders with the other as we fought desperately up the last curving pitch. And then, with the blood pounding in our foreheads and our lungs straining in the thin air, we reached the top!

The breeze hit us even before we topped the rise and finished the last few yards to the crest. It came laden with the icy fragrance of far off summits. It went through our thin shirts and we breathed it deeply and exultantly. We grinned at each other as we flopped down on our skis. We were calmer for we were there!

We tightened our boots. As I tugged on the ankle straps, my heart beat faster and the old familiar tingling sensation once again enveloped me. "Let's get out of here, gang!" I cried. Hurriedly we returned to the edge and put on our skis. A dizzy feeling came over me upon straightening up; and then, looking over and down, faint thoughts of apprehension ran through my mind. Nervously, my skis slid back and forth in the snow. They were really fast. "Time to go," someone said. I took a deep breath, gripped my poles, and shoved off.

Even as my shoulder came back and the tips leaned into the fall line, I knew the snow was perfect. And then as I swung, the skis came around and together almost without effort, their edges literally carving out the turn. Oh, what ecstasy! No slip, no chatter, just that rare sensation of snow spraying from under bent tips, the slithering hiss of the edges and the slope whirling round and accelerating towards me.

As I swung steeply into the next turn, around and down, with the thrill of the speed and the wind in my face, there came an exquisite feeling of utter abandon. Never had I felt like this! Another turn, and skiing became soaring over the snow crystals. Faster and faster, leaning out and forward with arms outstretched, one diving turn became another as my skis carried me down, down off the headwall, across the knoll, and with a fantastic sweeping curve, into a headlong schuss.

As I looked back at my tracks, flowing down out of a world of mountains, sun, and sparkling snow, I could see the others, starting down. First they were just scurrying specks 2,000 feet above me and over a mile away, making small white puffs of smoke-like snow with every turn and yet crisscrossing each other's tracks. Down they came, faster and faster, weaving long daisy chains on the white snow wall before me, and then, one-two-three, they swept over the knoll and into the schuss.

What a beautiful sight! As my friends rocketed toward me, poised on their skis with arms outstretched, I could hear the loud cracking of their trousers flapping in the wind. And then, quickly, one after the other, they turned upward in a cloud of snow, came down from my right and christied to a stop around me. We looked at each other and broke into yells of pure joy. This was the life.

CHAPTER THIRTEEN

McGee Tows

Dave's McGee Warming Hut and Rope Tows.

Respected and honored by their countrymen, the World War II generation stepped into peacetime with resilience. Most survivors chose not to talk about what they had seen, what they had lost, and what they had done in the war. Instead, they devoted their energies to rebuilding their lives, creating new opportunities, and appreciating each moment.

Accordingly, American skiers revived their favorite sport out of its wartime dormancy. As published in *Ski Illustrated*, "it takes more than a war to dampen the enthusiasm for skiing... the fires of ski adventure are burning even more brightly." Ski resorts recorded an exponential increase in the number of visitors compared to before the war. Thus began a trend that would continue for the next 70 years, as skiing grew into a recreational industry with new significance in American culture.

Those who had skied before the war, generally the wealthy or adventurous, returned to the slopes with joyful abandon. Others, who had previously considered skiing prohibitively expensive, found they could now afford to learn the glamorous sport. Quality, low-cost ski equipment ordered for the 10th Mountain Division was piling up in sporting goods and war surplus stores. Civilians could purchase long, white Army skis; bamboo poles with sewn leather straps and webbed baskets; leather boots; and baggy, but warm and durable military suits.[1] If skis or poles were too long, skiers sawed them down to size. As for bindings, traditional non-releasable "Bear Traps" with leather long-thong straps wrapped around the ankle now competed with the new favorite: a combination double-cable front-throw with a toe iron.[2]

During the winter of 1946, most U.S. ski areas—except for Sun Valley, Idaho, which remained a Naval Convalescent Center through December—resumed full operations and reinstated their annual ski races. New ski areas and ski schools opened, many of them built by veterans of the U.S. Army's 10th Mountain Division. For example, Friedl Pfeifer, who had first skied the mountains near Aspen, Colorado, during his 10th Mountain wartime training at Camp Hale, believed Aspen had all the makings of a world-class ski resort. By November 1945, he had met with the City Council, outlined a business plan, secured investor funding, installed two means of uphill transportation, opened the Friedl Pfeiffer Ski School, and cut ski trails on Ajax—the mountain that rose from the center of town.[3]

Further west in California, with skiing on the rise, so too was the demand for a ski area in the Eastern Sierra. District Ranger Fred Meckel and Dave McCoy agreed that of all Inyo National Forest mountains being considered for development, only Mammoth warranted a significant investment. In that regard, Meckel prepared a six-page preliminary plan for winter development of the Mammoth Mountain area, in which he summarized local knowledge, past studies, and estimated future trends and needs. Meanwhile, as the Forest Service analyzed Meckel's report, Dave spent the summer of 1945 improving his McGee ski operation.

THOUGH still using his metal brace and walking with a limp, Dave scouted the terrain of McGee, his senses alert for rattlesnakes as he moved through the sagebrush, determining the best slopes away from avalanche paths. He planned to rig his portable as a beginner tow at the bottom. For intermediate and advanced skiers, he would install two heavy-duty permanent tows—which he had fabricated in a Long Beach shipyard—in succession, accessing 3,000 vertical feet of uninterrupted downhill skiing. To achieve maximum power and load capacity, Dave would place the engines at the top of the tows. That he would need to climb the slopes to start the engines *and* carry fuel did not trouble him.

Using a pick, shovel, and crowbar to remove sagebrush and rocks, Dave cleared access roads near the tow lines.[4] In the DWP workshop at Crowley, he built components for two 10-foot by 12-foot motor houses, hauled the components to McGee, and assembled them on site. Each motor house was large enough for an engine, a radiator, a seat by the window for the operator, and enough space for one skier to come in from the cold.

On his way to LA. to pick up the engines, Dave stopped at a car dealer and traded his '38 Chevy coupe for a '41 Chevy sedan that would better accommodate his growing family. He then picked up an old flatbed trailer he'd purchased through a newspaper ad, hitched it to the car, continued to the shipyard, loaded the engines onto the trailer, paid his bill in cash, and headed home.

Dave's friend, Jim Wilson, drove the engines up the McGee access roads in his four-wheel-drive truck. Using physical strength and knowledge of mechanical leverage, the two men installed the engines in the motor houses, set the wooden towers in the tow line, then strung and spliced the ropes.

One day in the heat of the summer, while Dave was shoveling a septic pit near the base of the ski run, a guest of Nan and Max's carrying a six-pack of Budweiser wandered over to see what was going on. He sat down in the dirt, pulled a bottle opener out of his pocket, and drank a beer while he watched Dave work. When Dave leaned against his shovel to take a break, sweat dripping down his dusty face, the man offered him a cold one to quench his thirst. Dave guzzled the entire bottle. Within minutes he had a splitting headache. That was the last beer he ever drank.

To complete his outhouse, Dave threw lime over the hole he had dug, built a redwood enclosure over the hole, and installed high windows and wooden seats. On the day he was shingling the roof, a couple parked their car along Highway 395 and walked toward him. Dave's first words to the strangers were, "Hey, would you mind handing me that bundle of shingles?"

The man introduced himself as he lifted the shingles. "I'm Don Redmon, and this is my bride Gloria." The newlyweds were on their way to visit Gloria's parents, the caretakers of Convict Lodge, just a few miles up the road.[5] Don had just been released from the U.S. Coast Guard and had secured a job with the telephone company out of Ridgecrest. The two couples, the McCoys and the Redmons, soon became close friends. As Gloria recalled:

> Once a week, Don and I ate a spaghetti dinner with Dave and Roma, and then we'd all go to a movie. Dave was the personality kid, always happy-go-lucky, outgoing, strong, and handsome. Actually, he was gorgeous, like a muscular Robert Redford. Roma had a quiet personality and a special knack for making delicious home-baked pies. She always looked beautiful and sexy, even though she was pregnant most of the time. No one had any money or fancy clothes, so no one was jealous of each other's financial status. I remember sewing Punkin his first pair of ski pants using material from an old pair of Dave's ski pants. Everyone donated their time to make the ski tows successful. Dave asked Don if he'd help him build a warming hut on McGee the next summer. Dave didn't have cash to pay for labor, but he offered us unlimited free skiing. That was fine with us, even though Don could only work on weekends.

LIVING at Crowley, Dave and Roma decided to join the Mammoth Ski Club. With officers such as Lloyd Nicoll, Nan Zischank, and Nyle Smith, this had to be a fun group. Sure enough, at their first meeting, the McCoys met Toni Milici, a newcomer to Mammoth whose enthusiastic, vibrant personality reflected the flair of his Italian heritage.

During the war, Toni had served as a military photographer on limited-service stationed in Riverside, California. His wartime work schedule allowed him to pursue his real passion: skiing. Whenever snow fell in the mountains surrounding the Los Angeles Basin, he would round up bootleg gas ration tickets and drive his '41 Clipper Packard into the San Bernardino Mountains to ski at Snow Valley.

When the war ended, Toni and his wife Jenny ventured north to Mammoth and rented a room at Penney's Tavern. Toni secured a summer job with the Forest Service picking up garbage, cleaning picnic tables, issuing fire permits, and cutting firewood for campers. Not long after being assigned to Rock Creek Station, his marriage to Jenny fell apart, and that's when he met war veteran Roger Link.

Roger had come to Mammoth in search of a cure for post-war aimlessness. Having been discharged from military service after surviving over 30 missions as an airplane gunner, he felt idle and unhappy in Los Angeles. One month of breathing fresh mountain air convinced him to stay in the Sierra. With a graduate degree in forestry, he landed a Forest Service job working with Toni.

The two bachelors moved into a rustic, non-insulated cabin at Rock Creek Station, and offered to help Dave with his rope tow operation on McGee. Dave was glad to have their help, but, of course, had no money to pay them. So, as was his pattern, he let them ski for free and frequently invited them for dinner at the Crowley house where they would gobble up Roma's hot dinners and freshly baked pies, often staying overnight, sleeping on the living room floor.

As Roger recalled, "Dave made everything we did enjoyable, whether it was building the lodge or fixing the tows or skiing or hiking. I would have worked for him the rest of my life for nothing if I could have figured out how to survive financially."[6] Toni added, "Dave was like Flash Gordon, a big, tall, blond, athletic muscleman. He worked like mad, and everybody liked him. Roma was beautiful, blond, tanned, and usually pregnant with one of those cute McCoy kids!"

ON the Wednesday before Thanksgiving Day 1945, two feet of fresh powder covered McGee Mountain in an inviting blanket of soft whiteness.

Dave and Toni tracked through the snow to the top of each tow and dou-blechecked that everything was ready for the expected rush of holiday ski-ers. As they climbed, the two men laughed about how skiers had trimmed the sagebrush with their metal edges the prior spring, inadvertently prep-ping the slopes so that two feet of snow was adequate coverage for opening day.

By the time Dave and Toni tested all three engines, thick, wet snow-flakes had started to fall. The men skied to the bottom, then looked up to admire their tracks. Dave mused, "Tomorrow we're gonna christen these permanent tows with a lot of happy skiers having a lot of fun. The great thing is, we won't have to take anything down at the end of the day. Now, let's get on home and see what Roma's cookin' for dinner."

As they drove to Crowley, dense raindrops splashed on the windshield. Dave rolled down the driver's window and felt the air outside. The warmth caused him to grimace. Rain like this would destroy the snow on McGee. But there was nothing he could do to lower the air temperature. With one deep exhale, he relinquished his agenda to Mother Nature, turned to Toni, and said, "Well, there's always Plan B!"

Throughout dinner and into the night, raindrops slapped against the Crowley house. Dave rose early, stepped out the back door, and looked across the valley. The skies were blue, but the slopes of McGee were brown, making the rope tows appear misplaced amid the sagebrush. He turned his gaze to Mammoth. Snow covered the mountain in white.

Dave hoped the snow on Minaret Road wasn't too deep because that day, he didn't have access to the DWP's jeep.[7] His '41 Chevy would have to suffice. As usual, he would drive the car forward a bit, shovel out the snow that had piled up in front of the tires, then push forward a bit more, inch-ing along. There would be enough of a track left behind him that other vehicles could follow. If Dave only got partway up the road, he'd pile the supplies for the day onto his toboggan tow and drag the load as he skied the rest of the way to the slope.

Dave hustled to complete his rounds at the dam and planned to fin-ish his other DWP duties that evening. He put his roving permit into his wallet, joined Toni and Roger eating Roma's scrambled egg breakfast, grabbed the picnic lunches she'd prepared for them, kissed her goodbye, and stepped outside. Toni and Roger helped load the tow, supplies, and ski equipment, and the threesome took off for Mammoth for a work-filled, fun-loaded day of skiing.

A full year after his risky double-leg surgery, Dave no longer wore the metal brace. His doctors gave him permission to ski, but *not* to run courses. That was okay with Dave. He was happy to be open for business. He felt strong and free of pain as he skied around making sure his tows were running smoothly.

One afternoon in February 1946, Dave joined his Bishop friends skiing fresh powder on McGee. The weather was unseasonably warm, so Dave took off his shirt. His friends rolled up their sleeves. Bishop school teacher, Aim Morhardt, offered to document the day. He set up his camera while the others rode to the top of the tow, traversed south, and waited above an untouched snowfield. When Aim waved his arm, the skiers took off. With one click of his camera, Aim captured the foursome schussing virgin powder with their shadows stretched out before them and rooster-tails of snow spraying from their wakes.[8]

On a typical weekend at McGee, Max Zischank and Howard Cooper manned Dave's tows, undeterred by how the engines sputtered and back-fired when starting up. At any given time during the day, an average of 20 to 30 skiers queued up at the bottom in the tow line. With Dave's powerful new engines, the line moved quickly, even though the high speed of the ropes made them difficult to hold. Still, skiers managed, the more experienced using rope-tow grippers.[9]

Meanwhile, Toni Milici and Frankie Stevens gave ski lessons, dressed in matching black-and-white sweaters. They loved being in the heart of the action, so ski instruction was their dream job. Roger Link preferred to stay in the background, happily sideslipping the towline and carrying fuel to the engines. Three-year-old Punkin zoomed around the lower slopes, already trying to ride the beginner's tow by himself. Off to the side of the main run, the Bishop High team ran courses.

Aim had revitalized the post-war high school ski team and even per-suaded the school to purchase a Chevy wagon for hauling the kids to training sessions and races. The "Woody" became a familiar sight on the streets of Bishop, ski gear tied on top, racers leaning out of the windows, and Aim at the wheel wearing his earflap hat and white poplin jacket, puffing on his ever-present pipe.

Dave assisted Aim, not so much as a designated coach but as a passionate skier who cared about kids. With nothing formally organized, when the racers noticed Dave grabbing an armful of willow branches from the pile he kept stacked at the bottom of the hill, they would ski over to help. The group carried the makeshift poles up the tow, then sideslipped down alongside Dave, tossing him a few willows at a time as he set a course. Dave would then stand to the side and watch the kids ski the course, replacing poles that got knocked down and occasionally giving helpful advice.

Though Dave's verbal compliments were few, his smile and approving nod let the athletes know they were on the right track. His criticisms were constructive and delivered with a positive spin. Instead of pointing out that a racer was sitting back too far, Dave might suggest, "feel your shin touch the front of your boot." Rather than tell racers they were over-turning, Dave would direct them to make little jump turns that kept their body facing down the fall-line so they could quickly get on and off their edges. Instead of pointing out that a racer was dropping their arm, Dave would suggest keeping their hands in front so they could see them.

To practice for the jumping events, which in those days were a component of school competitions, the team helped Dave build a jump at McGee. The racers took turns using the one pair of jumping skis—triple-grooved, 8 feet long by 5 inches wide—they owned while Dave stood on the out-run calling out the distance jumped. Some of the kids soared over 40 feet.

In the spring of 1946, U.S. Forest Service Recreation Officer James Gibson flew from Washington, D.C. to discuss various proposals for recreation in the Eastern Sierra.[10] He came to the same conclusion as Fred Meckel and Dave McCoy. Mammoth Mountain had potential to become a top California ski area.

At that time, two temporary tows were operating on Mammoth, both on the south side near Observation Point. One was Dave's portable, which he had set up because there was too little snow to operate McGee and too much snow to get to the north slope of Mammoth. The other tow, initially installed by Lloyd Nicoll but purchased by Nyle Smith before the war, was barely being used.

Gibson met individually with each of the operators to learn their visions of development. Dave proposed two or three rope tows on the north slope and emphasized that the key to developing Mammoth was maintaining Minaret Road. He also urged Gibson to house the District Ranger in Mammoth year-round to better understand winter challenges. Gibson agreed with Dave on all points. He wrote, "I believe McCoy's application should be given consideration as it is an expedient temporary approach pending largescale developments, which must come sooner or later. He is willing to accept a temporary permit, which would be subject to cancellation at such time as permits are issued for the ultimate development."[11]

In Nyle Smith's meeting, Gibson reminded him he had to operate his tow, or the Forest Service would terminate his permit. But first, the tow needed to pass inspection. Rather than dealing with Forest Service protocol, Nyle passed his permit on to Hans Georg.

Recently released from military duty, Hans had returned to Mammoth with the desire to build a life around skiing. For him, operating the tow at Observation Point would be a dream come true—he could manage his ski business, run his ski school, and live in the shelter of his rock hut.

When Hans met with Gibson, he advocated building a chairlift from his rope tow up the south side of Mammoth. Gibson tabled Hans' proposal on the grounds that "no expensive improvements should be made until a complete plan is prepared." However, Gibson assured Hans, when the ultimate development happened, he would be able to either participate or sell any improvements he had made for their actual value.

Hans left the meeting downhearted. Ever since Pearl Harbor, life's twists and turns had worked on him. When he enlisted in the U.S. Army during World War II, he wasn't allowed to carry a gun because he was German. The Army, therefore, trained him as a medic and eventually assigned him to teach skiing to 10th Mountain Division troops based at Camp Hale, Colorado. In January 1945, he deployed with the 10th

Mountain troops for what turned out to be four months of heavy combat in the Northern Italian Alps. As a medic, Hans saw the worst.[12] He returned to the Eastern Sierra with a Bronze Medal for meritorious service and a determination to block out the past. But to go forward with the lifestyle he envisioned in the Eastern Sierra, he needed support from the Forest Service, which he didn't feel he had.

WITH Mammoth Mountain still snow-covered in the spring of 1946, Dave got the grand idea of organizing a Memorial Day Race to honor U.S. servicemen and women killed in the war. Roma loved the concept, but eight months pregnant with their third child, she told Dave, "Don't even *think* I'm going to be racing. Besides," she said, "I've already got plans for that day." May 27 was Poncho's first birthday.

Dave ordered trophies, notified California ski writers, and made arrangements for the Forest Service to plow Minaret Road. Toni and Roger helped him haul five portable tows, slalom poles, timing equipment, and several watermelons to the upper slopes of Mammoth. On race day, close to 200 racers and spectators showed up. As one ski journalist reported:

> *A highlight of this admirable McCoy career came when Dave brought weeks of planning to a close and personally conducted, unaided, his Memorial Day Slalom Race (a combined two-day event with giant slalom and slalom). A smooth, swinging 28-gate giant slalom originated about 50-feet from the top of the 11,000-foot Mammoth Mountain and wound down a 3.4-mile course to a beautiful finish in the draw. A select field of contestants dubbed the course the best they had ever run in their lives.[13]*

At the awards, Dave praised participants for their celebration of skiing, mountain air, and competitive spirit. He then thanked the Forest Service for clearing snowdrifts off Minaret Road and creating a parking area for some 100 cars. Before handing out trophies, he invited his guests to share a minute of silence to honor those who had perished in the war.

DAVE'S friend Corty Hill had been unable to attend the Memorial Day Race because of his busy schedule.[14] Most recently, he had spearheaded and financed a two-month Ski Area Survey to photograph, map, and analyze the ski area potential of mountains from Southern California to Central Oregon.[15] On May 31, European skiing experts Hannes Schneider and Luggi Foeger joined the Forest Service's James Gibson and Corty on a two-day, 1,775-mile aerial reconnaissance portion of the survey. After the flight, Gibson returned to D.C. while the others continued on a six-week, 6,500-mile trip surveying the mountains by foot, boat, and on horseback.

On one leg of the journey, Corty invited Dave and District Ranger Fred Meckel to guide the survey team through seven locations in Mono County. Both extremely familiar with the region, these two men made their case that Mammoth Mountain's favorable terrain, accessibility, and snow conditions provided the most potential as a major ski area. The survey team, minus James Gibson, disagreed.

The final report of Corty's Ski Area Survey concluded that Mammoth was too windy, received too much snow, the altitude was too extreme, and the location too isolated. Some of the slopes were in avalanche zones, the irregular shape of the terrain would make funneling skiers to a central terminus difficult, the lower slopes were too timbered, and there was inadequate room for parking at the base. Essentially, some of the most knowledgeable figures in American skiing advised against developing Mammoth.

ON June 28, 1946, Roma and Dave celebrated the birth of their third son, Carl Dean McCoy, named after their friend Carl Grebe from Michigan and Dean Kiner, a "Bishop boy" who had raced with them before the war. Following tradition, Dave and Roma gave their tiny six-pound son a nickname: "P-Nut."

All that summer, if Dave wasn't completing his DWP duties, guiding fishermen, or hunting wild game to restock the freezer, he could be found working on a warming hut for McGee Mountain. One day he might be shoveling aggregate or pounding nails. Another day he would be scrounging for materials or splitting and stacking firewood.[16] Rather than taking out a loan, he financed the project with creative thinking, hard work, and rope-tow money saved during the previous winter. For materials, he scrounged and bartered, often putting to good use what others had discarded. In his words, Dave said, "I guess I was recycling." For labor, he relied on the help of friends like Toni Milici, Roger Link, Don Redmon, and the Bishop High racers.[17]

Equating hard work with having fun, at the end of the day Dave sometimes drove his helpers up Rock Creek Canyon maneuvering around the nine-foot boulder that blocked the road at Mosquito Flat.[18] They had to push the Chevy to get up a section of road they called "Crank Case Hill" because of how the car banged on the rocks. Dave would say, "Oh, those sharp ones, they don't hurt."[19]

Some of Dave's friends thought his ideas about skiing were crazy, but they liked him, so they went out of their way to help. Moffet Lumber Company allowed him to salvage lumber and plumbing from the old shacks at Mono Mills just south of Mono Lake. Mono Mines Company offered him discarded materials from abandoned mining claims. And his DWP superiors lent him equipment, set aside surplus materials such as cement and rebar for his use, and gave him a key to their aggregate pit near Toms Place along with permission to use all the rocks, gravel, and sand he needed. DWP allowed him to collect underground plumbing materials they'd left at the West Portal barracks, where employees had lived while building the Mono Tunnel.

Dave staked out the McGee warming hut about 50 yards off Highway 395. He dug the footings by hand and purchased cement to mix with the DWP aggregate. Downstairs, he constructed a large basement, public bathrooms, and some bedrooms. Upstairs, he built a small kitchen in the corner, and an oversized sunken fireplace against one wall with rocks collected from Rock Creek Canyon, leaving the floor open for tables and chairs. He installed three sets of windows facing the White Mountains to the east. To the west side, he built double doors that opened onto a wooden deck and the ski run. According to Dave's records, construction costs amounted to $12,750.

With all Dave was trying to achieve that summer of 1946, he frequently lost track of time and rarely made it home to tuck his three young boys into bed. Occasionally, he wondered if Roma felt neglected. But she didn't complain, and no matter how late he came home, she waited to share her evening meal with him. During dinner, she would pummel him with questions about his day as if starved for adult conversation. Dave answered her inquiries with as much energy as he could muster, but as soon as they finished eating, he'd reach across the small table, take her hand, and side-track the conversation. "Come on, Toots," he'd beckon, "let's go to bed."

MEANWHILE, Hans Georg was refurbishing his tows at Observation Point and building a small rock ski hut with an expanded porch that provided a panoramic view of Long Valley. With a fireplace, cooking facilities, a din-ing area, and a bedroom, he could live year-round in the hut. Hans made a point of leaving a bowl of milk on the porch, befriending feral cats who soon adopted him as family.

An artist at heart, Hans designed the Hans Georg Ski School logo and a brochure featuring his handsome portrait.[20] Along with attending California Ski Association's examination at Mt. Rose to become a fully certified Arlberg instructor, he wrote weekly snow reports and articles for ski magazines.[21] Various ski publications praised him as an "internationally known ski stylist," a "true maestro," a "great analyst of any style," and an

Hans Georg.

"ingenious instructor who knew how to pass the art of skiing on to his pupils." Uplifted by such glowing compliments, Hans wrote the Eastern Sierra Ski Club to thank them for "trying to revive the old spirit and summon the old gang... and for starting a campaign to combine all clubs and wake everybody up, as there are quite a few small difficulties of local jealousies to overcome."

Recently a conflict had flared up between Hans and Dave. With about 20 kids waiting to train, having no snow on McGee, and with Minaret Road buried, Dave had rigged his portable on a slope near Hans' tow. Hans ran outside of his hut, yelling that Dave was intruding on his lease. Dave lost his temper and shouted back that he only wanted a place for the kids to train for free. The racers were dumbstruck. They'd never seen Dave so angry or heard him use such brash vocabulary. In silence, they helped him move the tow down the road. After everyone calmed down, the team skied for the rest of the day without incident.[22]

In reality, Hans and Dave faced the same challenges, mainly road access and variable snow conditions. Still, Hans felt threatened by Dave. In a letter to ski writer Ethel Van Degrift (formerly Ethel Severson), Hans vented his frustrations:

> *Dave didn't want to cooperate with me this year but announced his own ski school with Frankie Stevens and Toni Milici. As you may know by now, he didn't show up for the certification or instructors meeting, and this kind of leaves him out to direct a school, and, in fact, [at the meeting] it was motioned that noncertified instructors shouldn't get publicity. Frankie didn't pass the test, just Toni, so he would be the only authorized instructor in Dave's setup. I hate to mention all this, yet it took me many hard years to build a school up in this area, and I told Dave that I still will be at McGee [across from McGee Creek Lodge] this coming year yet would give it up to him entirely if I can make it go at Mammoth. This means mainly as soon as I can fully depend on the road [to Observation Point] being open.[23]*

Later that winter after a storm covered McGee and closed Observation Point, Hans asked Dave if he could teach skiing at McGee independent of Toni Milici and Frankie Stevens. Dave sympathized with Hans' situation. Their argument belonged to the past. He told Hans to come on down. The financial arrangement would be the same as Toni and Frankie's. Every cent Hans made teaching skiing would belong to him.

ALTHOUGH Dave wasn't one for sitting down and reading a book, he occasionally perused ski magazines to get a glimpse of what was going on outside Mono County. According to the *National Skiing Guide*, there were now 30 ski areas in Southern California and 10 more in the High Sierra.[24] The *Los Angeles Times* had reinstated Ethel Van Degrift's biweekly "Ski Slants" column, and the CSA started selling one-dollar annual subscriptions to *The Skier*, its new weekly ski report. Austrian Sepp Benedikter had opened a ski school at Southern California's Big Pines. Friedl Pfeifer was now directing two ski schools simultaneously, one in Sun Valley, Idaho, and the other in Aspen, Colorado, then home of the world's longest chairlift.

Dave learned that boot suppliers were expanding their inventory even though leather was still a scarce commodity. With restrictions on wood finally easing, ski manufacturers were increasing production and taking their wooden skis on sales tours. Revolutionary ski wax and ski bindings hit the market, and new skiwear designs were attracting notice, as were made-to-order handknit sweaters.[25]

One day, an advertisement for a "Tow-Mobile" caught Dave's attention. Invented by Howard More, who before the war had built a rope tow for ESSC, the portable tow was 3 feet wide by 5 feet long. Powered by a 30-horsepower Wisconsin motor, a set of chains revolved around tracks beneath the base.[26] Using lawnmower-type handles, the operator could drive the Tow-Mobile to a desired location on its own power, then disengage the chains and redirect the power to run the rope tow pulleys. Thinking the Tow-Mobile could facilitate moving portables around Mammoth, Dave ordered two units.[27]

BY the winter of 1947, Dave's doctors granted him permission to start skiing through courses, but not to enter a race. How fantastic it was to be running courses with his Bishop team! And how much progress they had made from finishing dead last in the first CIF race of the season to winning the final meet. *The Inyo Register* reported that their impressive performance was "a testament to the excellent skiing and coaching these kids had received."

Dave hosted the Inyo Mono Championships at June Lake and then focused on his annual Memorial Day race, once again setting up five portable tows on the upper slopes of Mammoth. Fifty racers showed up, traveling from as far away as Aspen, Reno, and, of course, Southern California.[28] Dave foreran, skiing conservatively and in control. Passing through the finish gate that day, he felt like the skier he had been before the accident. Next year, he pledged, he would race again.

That afternoon, Corty helped Dave pull the race course. The high-altitude sun warmed their shoulders as the two visited, Corty complimenting Dave on the event and sharing his amazement at the amount of snow Mammoth held so late in the season. Though the tone of their conversation was playful, they both understood the irony of their situation. Corty had the finances and desire to build a California ski area but doubted Mammoth's potential. He was involved in discussions about two other promising mountains—San Gorgonio in Southern California and Mineral King in the Southwest Sierra Nevada. In contrast, Dave's belief in Mammoth never wavered; only a lack of financing kept him from submitting a proposal to the Forest Service.

Dave accepted the fact that a financial investor would eventually develop Mammoth. When that time came, he would pack up his portables and focus on McGee. He loved his job as a hydrographer, and he loved his life with his growing family. Looking ahead, he purchased a piece of property near Hilton Creek, across Highway 395 from Crowley Lake, where he and Roma could one day retire. All was fine in his world, or so he told himself.

The truth was, deep in Dave's heart, Mammoth was his jewel and his dream. No matter what he verbalized—and regardless of what other people thought—he could not imagine anyone other than himself, Dave McCoy, developing Mammoth Mountain into a ski area.

CHAPTER FOURTEEN

Roma: Home at Crowley

Roma, enjoying her life at the Crowley house.

After the madness of war ended, Dave and I tried to get our lives back to normal. We were grateful for our situation, yet we felt terrible for those who hadn't been as fortunate. Some returning veterans couldn't even find a place to live because of a housing shortage in the Owens Valley. Even worse, so many people had loved ones who would never be coming home, just like Marc and Ethel Zumstein who had lost their son, Don, in Okinawa.

I wanted to help the Zumsteins, but I didn't know what to do except to encourage them to come skiing with us. Ethel liked to sell tickets with me and help Dave with the races. Their daughter, Charlotte, loved skiing on the Bishop High Race Team, which now included girls. Marc put his heart and soul into organizing a volunteer ski patrol of dedicated skiers, mostly from Avalanche Ski Club. These volunteer patrollers drove from L.A. to

Mammoth every weekend. In exchange for free skiing on Dave's tows, they took care of first aid, safety, and injured skiers. I don't know what we would have done without them.

Just as Dave predicted, veterans and civilians alike started returning to the ski slopes, which kept him as busy as ever. As soon as he accomplished one goal, he'd start in on another. Of course, I'd be wondering how we were going to pay for his latest idea, but not Dave. Nope. A lack of money never slowed him down. He just worked harder.

When people saw all the effort Dave was putting into his tows, they'd offer a helping hand and would end up being our closest friends, like Roger Link and Toni Milici and the Redmons. Roger was a serious person, kind of quiet, while Toni was a talkative little guy of Italian heritage who had us in stitches most of the time. When his marriage broke up, he said in his bouncy voice, "It's no big deal. Jenny and I had a difference of opinion about lifestyle, so we separated, split everything right down the middle. She took the record player because she liked to sing, and I took the couch."

Now the Redmons, they were a handsome couple. I was so embarrassed when I first met them. I heard a knock on our front door, and when I opened it, there stood a tall, good-looking guy and a glamorous woman with perfect make-up, wearing a crisp white blouse tucked into fitted blue slacks. There I was, wearing Dave's shirt and shorts as my maternity clothes, walking around without any shoes on, my long hair tied back to keep the strands from falling into the pie I was making. Later on, Gloria told me that when she first saw me, she thought, "Wow, here's this beautiful woman with gorgeous long legs, looking sexy in her husband's clothes." I think she was trying to make me feel good. Anyway, Don ended up helping Dave almost every weekend, and Gloria became one of my closest friends and knitting partners.

Dave appointed Toni Milici as Ski School Director for McGee Mountain, and the first thing Toni did was design a "company" ski sweater—black on the bottom and cabled white on the top. He had a woman from down south knit a sample, and boy, that sweater looked sharp. So, I knitted one just like it for Dave, and someone else knitted one for Frankie Stevens and wow, three top-notch skiers zipping down McGee in matching sweaters was a sight to see!

ONCE Dave and I had rope tow businesses on both McGee and Mammoth, we decided to join the Mammoth Ski Club. At the first meeting we attended, Dave volunteered to take charge of everything that had to do with racing. That way he could stay involved even though his leg had not healed enough for him to race. I think Dave loved ski racing more than anything else in life, except for his family.

When Dave reinstated the Inyo-Mono Championships, I was bound and determined to enter. Dave looked at my tummy, six months pregnant with our third child, and asked if I was sure. I said, "You better believe I'm sure!" Well, any worries about me falling and losing the baby were for nothing. I won everything. The women's slalom, downhill, and combined. At the awards, Dave tried to bring back the European tradition of the crowd cheering *"Ski Heil!"* for each trophy winner. But no one wanted anything to do with the word *"Heil!"* because of its association with Hitler.

AT the end of June 1946, I gave birth to Carl Dean McCoy. Yep, another boy. He was so tiny, it was natural for us to nickname him P-Nut, but oh, how his big smile and happy laugh filled our house with joy. Three little boys. What a family! I was utterly content, well, except for wanting to have more time with Dave. It seemed like we rarely saw each other, with him up at the crack of dawn and then sometimes working on the McGee warming hut until after midnight.

Now, don't get me wrong, I loved being a mom, feeding and bathing the little ones, playing with them, and putting them to bed. It's just that being a 26-year-old woman, I craved adult conversation. But Dave couldn't build a ski operation and be home entertaining me at the same time. How silly of me to want more. So, what did I do? I knitted.

After the boys went to sleep, I'd turn on the radio and position my chair in such a way that right through my window, I could see the lights at the McGee building site. I'd pick up my knitting and get so absorbed in working those needles and watching the colors and patterns emerge, that I barely noticed the time pass. When the lights of McGee turned off, I knew Dave was on his way home. I'd put my knitting down and warm up our dinner, my whole being just bubbling with excitement to see him.

I'd come a long way from teaching myself how to knit scarves for soldiers. Now, I could design my own patterns with reindeer and snow-flakes and hearts. Sometimes I created different designs for each person in the family, and other times I made identical sweaters for all of us like the black and white patterned sweaters the junior racers wore. One of my favorite projects was knitting matching yellow cable-knits for Dave and me. I thought we looked quite fashionable wearing our sweaters tucked into our pleated wool ski pants, and leather belts around our waists.

Of course, Dave didn't always work late. If he had people helping him at McGee, he'd invite them home for something to eat, and that was fine with me. While I was setting out food, the men would get engrossed in conversations about rope tows or the Forest Service, and I would feel like part of the program.

That same summer of building the McGee warming hut, Roger got a job at Lloyd Nicoll's Mammoth Lumber Company, and we suddenly had *the* inside scoop on local news.[1] How sad we were to learn that Frank and Nora "Ma" Penney sold their tavern in Mammoth and moved down to Bishop. Penney's Tavern had been the only place open in the winter where a person could go inside to warm up. And Ma Penney had always welcomed skiers, whether they stopped for a hot meal, an awards ceremony, a night's lodging, or to just use the old payphone that had a slot for silver dollars. Dave and I usually stopped by to visit with Ma Penney after we skied Mammoth, but we left before the heavy drinking started.

The new owners named their business Mammoth Tavern, and the bar got even wilder than before. I always thought a perfect ad would have been, "Mammoth Tavern: Rough lodging, lots of alcohol, and a raucous nightlife!" Rumor had it that one of the new owners got mad about some stupid thing, pulled out his pistol, put it in the face of a young kid, and then fired a shot through the ceiling. The kid fainted. I mean, I only heard about this. You know, stories travel fast.[2]

As soon as we saw frost around the Crowley house, Dave and I invited Toni and Roger to move in with us. Sure, our house was small, but we couldn't let those two bachelors spend another winter freezing in a shack at Rock Creek Station. Well, they didn't put up much resistance. So, there we were, seven of us cozied together for the winter in our little home with

Toni sleeping on the couch, Roger on the extra bunk bed in the boys' room, and on Saturday nights, the racers spread across the living room floor. It's funny. I was thrilled to have the company. I loved all the conversations and all the craziness, even if the paper-thin walls made it so you could hear every sound between the rooms.

One evening when we were all talking together, someone started laughing about the time a well-built woman—that's how they described her—got her shirt twisted in the tow and ripped right off her. Well, it so happened she wasn't wearing a brassiere, so Howard Cooper, who was operating the tow, came to the rescue, threw his jacket over her shoulders, and led her into the warmth of the engine room.

Then Dayton McDonald brought up the time his shirt got tangled in the rope. He said he felt like a fish on a line hanging from the tow about two feet off the ground as it pulled him uphill. Once again, "Coop" saved the day, shutting down the engine just in time. As far as Dayton was concerned, Coop saved his life.

Every time another story came up, like the time the rope ripped Dave's new pearl-buttoned shirt off his back, and it went around the pulley and came out in shreds, we laughed even harder. Then, in all seriousness, someone remembered the time little Dale (Buzz) Coons almost got hurt riding a portable Dave had rigged near Observation Point. Everything happened so fast. Suddenly, Buzz was being sucked up the hill with his shirt caught in the rope, and no operator to shut the tow down. But I swear, Dave always had his eyes on those kids. He skated over to the tow, pulling his knife out of his pocket as he skied, and cut the rope just in time. Dave was already a legend in those kids' eyes, but rescuing Buzz sure turned him into a hero.[3]

Those teenagers with their youthful capers were so much fun to have around, and they never caused any trouble. Either they were too tired from skiing all day, or they had too much respect for Dave to misbehave. One time, we were driving down Minaret Road after a day of skiing at Mammoth. I was in the front seat next to Dave and young Dayton was sitting on the hood when Dave saw something move in the snow just ahead of us. He yelled at Dayton to grab it. Dayton didn't hesitate, just blindly dove into the snow and came up with a half-frozen duck. We drove that little semi-conscious bird to the Tavern, warmed her up by the fire, and let her go. So, there you are. By following Dave's orders without even thinking, Dayton saved a duck!

After dinner on Saturday nights, I'd put on a record and teach the high schoolers to jitterbug, or Lindy hop, or waltz. If June Lake Lodge or Toms Place was having a community dance, we'd sometimes get a babysitter for Punkin, Poncho, and P-Nut, and go dancing for a few hours, but we didn't stay out late. I didn't like being away from my kids for too long, and everyone wanted to be up early, ready to ski their hearts out. In the mornings, Dave would wake the sleepyheads by bouncing around the room and tickling them. Then I'd cook breakfast while the racers made stacks of sandwiches to take to the hill and helped Dave load the car.

Dave was such a good role model for those racers. When they saw him hanging diapers on the line, they'd run outside to help. Later, they'd bring the "freeze-dried" diapers inside, spread them out all over the furniture for the few minutes needed to finish drying, and then fold them in neat stacks. They were happy to wash dishes, play with the boys, or wrestle with each other. But by nine, they'd have their sleeping bags lined up across the living room floor and be settled in for the night.

THERE was something magical about our life at the Crowley house. We were all so happy to be together, family, friends, and racers. Dave was the pied piper, our motivator, and our inspiration. He had this way of making each one of us feel special, and in turn, we were all drawn to him. If you had a positive attitude, Dave welcomed you. If you were negative, he didn't give you much attention. He wasn't mean; he just didn't have time for anyone who wasn't supportive of what he was trying to accomplish. So, negative people drifted away.

Sad for them. They missed out on all the fun.

CHAPTER FIFTEEN

Mammoth Tows

Rope Tow Two at Mammoth.

Dave's first project during the summer of 1947 was to replace the gas engine on his McGee beginner's tow with an electric one. He called his friend Jack Smith—a frequent Eastern Sierra skier who worked at his family's electric supply company in Southern California—and asked if he could purchase an electric motor on credit. Payment might take a while, Dave explained, because he had to put most of his cash back into the rope tows to keep them running.

"Not a problem," Jack replied. With complete trust that Dave would honor his word, Jack found a used 30-horsepower motor with miscellaneous electrical supplies and hauled the load to McGee. The total bill was $360, to be paid at a later date. Dave had already shoveled a 100-yard ditch through the rocky soil from the rope tow site to the county power pole. He then buried electrical cable in the ditch, connected it to the new engine on one end and the power pole on the other, and started the tow. Bingo! Everything went according to plan, except for one small detail...

Jack's father Burt was a strict businessman. After several months without Dave paying a single penny on his outstanding bill, Burt was displeased. Jack tried to convince his father that Dave was a unique individual, a reliable customer who would pay the bill in due course, but Burt was having none of it. He decided to drive north and find out for himself about this "so-called" extraordinary circumstance.

Jack awaited his father's return with trepidation, praying that Burt's impatience wouldn't jeopardize his friendship with Dave:

> *When Dad didn't show up at work on Monday morning, I panicked. When he didn't arrive on Tuesday, I was terrified. Those days it cost too much to call long distance, so I didn't even think of trying to telephone. Then Wednesday morning, Dad came in looking sheepish. He said to me, "Jack, I can tell this guy's going to be something. He's got three kids, and he's working hard on accomplishing his dream, so we'll support him." Come to find out, Dave was just being Dave and taking Dad fishing every day.*

Dave's second summer project was making improvements at Mammoth's north side. With permission from the Forest Service to limb and clear small trees off a slope near the parking area, Dave sharpened his double-bladed axe and went to work. Bishop High racers assisted him by dragging the slash into an open ditch that ran down the center of the run. As ever, Don Redmon worked with him on weekends. Dave purchased another double-bladed axe and the two men, both in their early thirties and competitive to the core, limbed everything up to 10 inches in diameter, pushing each other to their limit. As Redmon described, "Dave kept those axes so sharp we could sever a three-inch diameter branch in one swing. It was all in fun."

When the first snows fell that November, Dave rigged his portable tow on the newly-cleared slope and arranged for two friends to transport skiers in their four-wheel-drive trucks from where they parked their cars to the rope tow. Two hundred skiers arrived. Somebody joked that the run looked as crowded as the streets of Manhattan. That was it! Mammoth's first cleared ski run would be called Broadway.

On Thanksgiving Day, "No Vacancy" signs hung in the windows of almost every winterized lodge in Mono County.[1] As skiers laced their boots in the Mammoth rope tow parking area, they noticed dark clouds filling the sky and realized a warm Sierra snowstorm was brewing. By noon, large, heavy snowflakes were clinging to jackets, hats, and goggles. Some skiers called it a day and drove through the deteriorating weather to the warmth of their lodgings. The diehards stayed on, resolved to ski until Dave closed his tow.

By late afternoon the wind picked up, the temperature dropped, and Minaret Road transformed into a slippery mess of half-frozen slush. Dave knew that even with tire chains, cars were bound to slide and spin. He envisioned darkness approaching with tired, hungry skiers stranded inside automobiles stuck in the frozen snow. To avoid such a disaster, he needed to rally teamwork. Dave gathered the remaining skiers in the parking area and asked them to work as a unit to get every car safely to the Tavern. Though cold and tired from their long day of skiing in the wet snowstorm, everyone agreed to help.

The biggest challenge would be getting the cars over two hills about a mile down the road.[2] But Dave had a plan. He repurposed his tow rope by cutting it into three lengths and loading them into his Chevy. The other skiers drove their cars close behind him until they reached the bottom of the first hill, then he pulled his car to the side, stepped out, and tied the three lengths of rope to the front bumper of the first car in line.

Dave assigned several men to each rope, instructed others to push the car from behind, and told the driver to give just enough gas to create momentum without spinning the wheels. With this coordinated manpower, the group inched the car up the slick road. Cresting the first hill, they let out a joyful cheer, then hustled back down to the next vehicle. Warmed by physical effort and inspired by victory, the skiers toiled, grunted, and laughed until all the vehicles were safely up and over the first hill. Then they repeated the process on the second hill.

According to Dave, the group reached the Tavern around midnight. With a slightly different memory, Ethel Zumstein recalled, "We got to the Tavern about four in the morning, and Dave bought us all breakfast." From that night on, those who knew what had happened referred to the double-summit as Thanksgiving Hill.

IN their December meeting, members of Mammoth Ski Club unanimously voted Dave in as president, Don Lutes as vice-president, and Toni Milici as secretary-treasurer.[3] With gavel in hand, Dave announced the first item on the agenda: winter access on Minaret Road. This subject was pertinent to the problem Dave faced when there was too much snow to get up Minaret Road and too little on McGee Mountain.

Dave gave an update on the recently passed Collier-Burns Act, hopeful the new law would designate either the state of California, Mono County, or the Forest Service to finance appropriate equipment and enough workforce to clear snow off Minaret Road.

SKI TRACKS
Collier-Burns Act
1947

In an attempt to provide monies to improve California's transportation infrastructure, the Collier Burns Act of 1947 raised the vehicle automobile licensing fee from $3 to $6 and increased the gasoline and diesel fuel tax to 4.5 cents per gallon. Money raised was to be applied to building California's freeways, highways, and some county roads, and consolidating of county road administration.

Though the Act sounded good in theory, the reality was that Mammoth Mountain, the most popular skiing in the region, would be inaccessible once snow arrived. Club members shouted their frustrations. Dave hit his gavel to call the meeting back to order and waited until the room was quiet. Determined, as always, to divert negativity, he spoke with a spark of enthusiasm. "I don't see a problem here. We just need a little cooperation

A weasel going to the saddle.

between Mono County, the Forest Service, and myself, reinforced by some grassroots support from you." Laughter broke the tension.

A club member raised his hand to address the audience. "Has anyone heard about the upcoming Army surplus auction in San Diego? They're going to be selling Weasels." He went on to describe the amphibious all-terrain tracked vehicles built by Studebaker during World War II. Weasels looked like big bathtubs sitting on tracks, but with their six-cylinder engines, they had proven to be good at traveling over snow.[4]

Dave was stunned. After watching skiers drive by his new McGee Warming Hut searching for snow at higher elevations, he had been feeling discouraged. Yet his heart had told him not to worry. Now, he wondered, could Weasels be the solution he needed? If so, skiers might never again have to be snowed out of Mammoth because Dave would be advertising, "There's an eight-foot snowpack at Mammoth with Weasels operating from the Tavern!"

By the end of December, Dave was transporting skiers up and down a snow-covered Minaret Road in three Weasels he'd purchased at the auction. Each Weasel carried 15 passengers in the compartment and pulled ten more who were holding onto two knotted ropes tied to the back. With this success, Dave bought two more Weasels, increasing his fleet to five.[5]

One drawback of Weasels was that their tracks frequently broke, sometimes several times during one trip. The driver had to jump out, fix the broken track, and climb back in before continuing on. Fellow ski area operator Howard More had the same problem with his Army surplus Weasels at Table Mountain Ski Area.[6] To solve the problem, he designed a unique hinge. Dave purchased several and found them to be an improvement. The tracks no longer broke, they just bent. He noted the hinges were misaligned and let Howard know. "From Dave's insight, I corrected the problem," Howard recalled. "I shipped those hinges all over the world, and Dave was the best customer I ever had. He would order about 1,500 at a time, at the cost of a dollar apiece."[7]

Between broken tracks, bent hinges, and engine breakdowns, Weasel rides could take hours. Rather than wait, skiers occasionally attempted to ski down Minaret Road, sometimes getting dangerously lost. Once, when a Los Angeles skier didn't show up at the Tavern as expected, a search party set out to find him. Three stormy hours later, at about 9 p.m., the rescuers spotted the lost skier in the dark traveling the wrong direction along Highway 395, heading toward Crestview, some six miles north of Mammoth.

Another time, Dave got word of a lost skier and instructed Eddie Riley to ski down to the Chevy, drive up Highway 395, and meet him south of Crestview. He grabbed a Coleman lantern and took off, following the man's tracks through the woods. Eddie felt anxious as he watched Dave disappear into the storm:

> *I knew Dave was brave, but something about the way he took off alone in the darkness of the storm really got me. I was surprised he didn't ask me to go with him. The wind was blowing like heck, but I guess Dave knew the terrain so well that he was confident where to go, even in a snowstorm. I drove up and down 395 in the dark, and finally saw Dave, still alone. The guy turned up eventually, sitting at the Tavern bar.*

Though volunteer rescuers accepted the hardships and danger of a search—darkness, fatigue, cold, and disorientation—no one wanted these incidents to recur. If Minaret Road had been maintained, those "lost" skiers would have driven away in the warmth and safety of their automobiles. In a plea for funding, June Lake's Chuck Osborn wrote a letter asking the Forest Service to accept responsibility for clearing Minaret Road.[8] Their reply was discouraging at best. The Forest Service had replaced their RD-7 CAT, which they had previously used for occasional clearing of Minaret Road, with a smaller D-4 CAT that would be of little use in heavy snow. The agency wanted to cooperate but was greatly handicapped and could only offer incidental assistance in opening up part of Minaret Road before ski racing meets.[9]

Meanwhile, Mammoth Ski Club circulated a petition asking Mono County to keep the four miles of Minaret Road open to Dave's north slope operation.[10] But the county was no more helpful than the Forest Service had been. They replied, "To make Mammoth succeed as a winter playground, we are aware our help is needed to keep Minaret Road open. However, we don't have the manpower or the machinery to make that happen."

RATHER than feeling paralyzed by the road issue, Dave focused his energy on the Bishop High Race Team. The kids had recently gained notoriety in articles Hans Georg wrote about them, praising the team's preseason efforts:

> *I saw the Bishop High School boys training on Wednesday afternoon, chasing each other in pure mud and rainstorm conditions, running behind the Bishop High School station wagon driven by Aim Morhardt... the boys worked hard all summer on the construction of ski facilities to earn their free ski tow rides... outsiders envy them for being able to ski at least three times a week... you will probably recognize them by their white and black sweaters...they look sharp and ski sharp... they have been very fortunate in having Dave McCoy take them under his wing.[11]*

While Roma welcomed the racers into her home and considered them family, Dave inspired them with his skiing ability and his love for adventure. They admired how he moved rope tows from place to place and spliced ropes with his bare hands in the coldest of weather. They experienced Dave's diligence as they helped him repair Weasels at night with a wrench so cold it stuck to their hands. They enjoyed his free spirit when they accompanied him as he monitored clock stations in the dark using the headlights of the City Jeep for light and rode with him in the Jeep as he drove straight across the frozen surface of Crowley Lake to get home.

Whoever skied with Dave helped him out, and in so doing, received his support. Once, Dave bought new skis for the entire team and arranged for them to purchase wholesale ski boots from the Canadian Ski Team. There were times Dave and the racers spent the whole weekend getting the slope ready to ski, pulling toboggans loaded with a rope tow, fuel, water, food, ski equipment, and 200 feet of ¾-inch coiled rope, finally getting the tow strung by Sunday afternoon. The kids went home exhausted but in good spirits, looking forward to the following weekend, even knowing that when Saturday came around, there might be so much new snow that they'd have to spend another half day digging out the rope.[12]

Bishop High's 1948 Ski Team. From left: Dayton McDonald, Bobby Cooper, Beth Garrigues, Bob Autry, Eddie Riley, Charlotte Zumstein, and Don Coons. Aim Morhardt is kneeling in front.

In February 1948, Dave hosted a California Interscholastic Federation (CIF) competition and invited all out-of-town racers to lodge in his McGee Warming Hut. According to Aim, "The meet was a personal triumph for McCoy, whose training has been instrumental to the Bishop team's success."[13] Indeed, at the final CIF race of the season, Bishop won the league title, and received high praise from the *Reno Gazette*:

> *Bishop High School Team evoked much admiration during the CIF meet on Mt. Rose last Saturday. The well-dressed, well-trained group arrived at the ski slopes in a school station wagon. Outfitted entirely alike from their boots on up they made a flashy contingent in their dark trousers topped with hand-knit, two-toned sweaters. The youngsters all skied in the same style and at about the same speed, which indicated they all had received an equal amount of instruction. They traveled as a team and performed as a team. Their spirit during the races showed they were more interested in team accomplishment than individual honors. Charlotte Zumstein, a member of the Bishop High girls' team, ran the slalom gates like an up and coming champion. Her speed and smoothness served notice to the competitive ski world that her name will be heard often in the future.*

THE inaugural Junior Nationals, organized by the National Ski Association, were scheduled for Bogus Basin, Idaho, in March. Each of the seven regional divisions would be sending their best junior racers to compete. When the Far West Ski Association—previously called the California Ski Association—named Eddie Riley and Dayton McDonald to their team, Eastern Sierra residents chipped in to pay expenses. The Zischanks drove the boys to Reno to join their Nevada teammates traveling north.

Ski Tracks
Bishop Boys Compete at Bogus Basin
1948

In Boise, the Bishop boys housed in the mansion of a
wealthy radio station magnate. Out of their comfort zone,
they had to bite their cheeks to keep from laughing when
their host rang a bell to have his servants remove the food
from the formal dining table. Out on the mountain, the
boys felt more at home. Since Bogus Basin didn't yet have
an up-ski, racers hiked to the start. About noon, an airplane flew over the course and dropped lunches for the
competitors and officials, but no one could find where the
food bags landed.[14]

Both Eddie and Dayton placed in the top 20 out of more than 65 of
the best junior racers in the United States. Two weeks later, Sun Valley
hosted the Western States Championships, an inaugural junior competition sponsored by the American Legion and known affectionately as the
"Legions." With Aim as their chaperone, the California team lodged in
the resort's iconic Challenger Inn along with the entire field of racers.

On race day, bright red, yellow, and blue flags tied to bamboo poles
marking the slalom course on Dollar Mountain waved in the breeze.
Outfitted in colorful team uniforms, the athletes sidestepped up to inspect
the course and then waited for their turns to race down. The downhill, by
contrast, was held on Baldy Mountain, towering behind the town, and
included sections of the renowned Harriman Cup. So giant was Baldy that
racers rode three single-person chairlifts in succession to get to the start.
Due to lack of experience, especially in the jumping events, California
placed 8th out of 10 teams.[15]

Six years after shattering his leg in the 1942 State Championships,
33-year-old Dave McCoy, a respected ski tow operator and father of three,
was ready to compete again. He entered the Silver Dollar Derby giant
slalom and the 1948 Class A California State Championships, both held

the same weekend on Slide Mountain and Mt. Rose.

In the long and demanding Silver Dollar giant slalom, Dave came in just behind 1940 U.S. Olympian Hal Codding, who won the race with a time of 2:32. In the State Championship downhill, described by the *Reno Gazette* as "… spectacular with men and women skiers rocketing down the wide-open expanse of Slide Mountain, some reaching speeds of 70 miles per hour on the fast schusses… ," Dave placed 13th.

Pleased with his results, Dave focused his attention on Sunday's State Championship slalom. Climbing the course, he memorized each combination of gates, periodically pausing to close his eyes and move his hand, visualizing the line he planned to take. Since the total time of two runs would determine the winner, Dave raced his first run with precision. He skied a high line as he entered each turn and then cut his skis straight past the gates rather than chattering sideways and losing speed. Dave's time placed him among the fastest in the field. He knew if he had a strong second run, he had a chance to win.

As his turn to start neared, Dave felt calm. He took three deep breaths and exhaled slowly. When the starter called his bib number, he pulled into the gate, clicked his ski poles for luck, and planted them firmly in the snow. Like a cat preparing to spring forward, he bent his knees and let his body gather energy. The starter chanted, "Racer ready…" and Dave focused inward. On "Set…" he reached forward with his arms. At the word "Go!" he burst toward the first gate.

Dave's only conscious thought was the course before him; the only sound his skis moving against the snow. He held nothing back but took an even straighter, faster line than he had in the first run, and skated through the finish gate as the 1948 California State Slalom Champion.[16] Joy sparkled in his eyes as he accepted his 1st place trophy, and a grin spread across his face as the emcee announced, "McCoy's second run was three seconds faster than any slalom mark made during the two-day meet."

At the banquet, Dave sat by fellow ski racer—and budding ski filmmaker— Warren Miller.[17] According to Warren:

> *Dave was walking around with a limp, but by the end*
> *of the races, he'd gained high esteem in the eyes of all the*

> *competitors. At the time, I was traveling to ski races,*
> *working my way from being a C racer to racing in*
> *the Harriman Cup. I was excited about racing at Mt.*
> *Rose because the year before, prizewinners at the Silver*
> *Dollar Derby had won belt buckles with real silver*
> *dollars in them. But this year, the Far West disallowed*
> *the belt buckles and gave us trophies because someone*
> *thought the racers might remove the dollars and spend*
> *them, which would make us professionals.*

DAVE closed out Mammoth's 1948 season by staging his annual Memorial Day and Fourth of July races. He then drove north to Mt. Lassen, passing through the heat of Central California and then winding up a road that at times tunneled through 30-foot drifts of snow. Arriving at the dormant volcano, Dave joined up to 5,000 spectators and other elite racers to compete in the Inferno, an annual midsummer ski race. *The San Francisco Examiner* reported:

> *The race started at the lip of the crater at 10,300 feet*
> *elevation and dropped to 8,500 in less than a mile and*
> *a half. First to the finish would win. Competitors hiked*
> *to the top of the ridge, lined up, and at the countdown*
> *turned loose in a mass start. They twisted and turned*
> *through the control gates off the 1,000-foot headwall*
> *that carried them down toward Devil's Nose. On the*
> *sheer face of the protuberance, the greatest speed was*
> *developed causing many to check. This was followed by*
> *a leap over a cornice causing many to withdraw with*
> *splintered skis.*[18]

Donner Summit's Dick Buek, nicknamed "Mad Dog" for his reputation as a risk-taker on and off skis, won the race by skating out in front of the field at the start and then schussing straight down. Dave was in awe of Buek's skill and nerve. He felt sure the young man would soon be winning national races.

By June 1948, the U.S. Forest Service had completed the GENERAL PLAN FOR RECREATIONAL DEVELOPMENT OF MAMMOTH AND REDS MEADOW AREA but was still undecided about the best way to develop the mountain. This indecision guaranteed that for the time being, Dave would have no competition on Mammoth. In fact, on January 1, the Forest Service had issued him a special use permit to operate a temporary tow in a permanent location on the north side.[19] By accepting the permit, Dave agreed that during the summer, he would install two heavy-duty rope tows, a small shelter, and an outhouse to service people skiing Broadway. He acknowledged that the permit could be renewed or terminated at any time, and any grading, clearing of brush or timber, or building of additional structures required the District Ranger's approval.

Per Forest Service regulations, Dave paid his annual $10 fee, purchased public liability insurance, and installed a required automatic shutoff device to his portable tow. Toni Milici agreed to take charge of the ski school, and Marc Zumstein committed to being the first-aid man on duty. As such, he gathered first-aid supplies.

As soon as the snow on Broadway melted, Dave began leveling out access roads and digging footings. Lacking heavy equipment, he used hand tools. That was fine with him. He claimed his best thinking happened while he was shoveling. The repetitive movements allowed him to ponder how to accomplish all he needed to without spending money.

The A-Frame, Dave's portable hoist.

An example of Dave's creative thinking was when he needed a portable hoist to place heavy-duty engines at the top of rope tows in difficult to access locations on the mountain. Using equipment he had on hand, he fixed a winch to the front of his Army surplus flatbed truck and attached a fabricated metal A-Frame structure with two rope guidelines to the back. With the help of a friendly welder and a minimal amount of cash, Dave soon had his hoist, which he fondly called the "A-Frame."

Building heavy-duty tows on Mammoth, as always, Dave depended on the help of his friends and the racers. Eddie Riley had just graduated from high school and was working on a Forest Service summer crew sculpting the Shadow Lake Trail.[20] But Friday afternoons, he'd scramble down the cliffs near Shadow Creek and hike the River Trail out to Agnew Meadows where Dave picked him up in a DWP Jeep. He'd work all weekend helping Dave build the 10-foot-high motor house for Number One tow, installing motor mounts, and setting poles and sheave wheels. Sunday evenings, Dave would drive him back to the trailhead.

By autumn, Eddie was off to college, the racers were in school, and Milici and Redmon were only occasionally available. Still having plenty of work to complete, Dave tackled what he could on his own. The motor house at the top of Number Two tow needed to be built on a steep pitch and stand tall enough to rise above the deep snow that collected there. Therefore Dave built a platform 16-feet high on the uphill side and 20-feet high on the downhill side, which made the top level. He secured the structure to the hillside with a cable and a Deadman anchor.

Next, Dave used his A-Frame to load a stack of railroad ties onto a Weasel. He drove the load straight up Broadway to the ridgeline and then out to the knob directly above the platform.[21] Preparing to ease the loaded Weasel down the slope, he cautiously put the transmission in gear and inched toward the edge. The moment the Weasel's tracks crested the rim, gravity took over. Within seconds, Dave, the Weasel, and the railroad ties were heading straight down the fall line, completely out of control.[22] As Dave recounted:

> *I was hanging on for dear life. Then we hit a bump.*
> *The ties flew out and the Weasel kept going. I was lucky*

*I didn't have my head cut off by flying railroad ties. I
hung on until the Weasel slowed down in a flatter area
where I could regain control and bring it to a stop. I
looked back up the hill and could hardly believe my eyes.
The ties had landed just above the motor hut, exactly
where I wanted them.*

Stunned by his unexpected Mad-Hatter ride and thankful to be alive,
Dave maneuvered the empty Weasel to the bottom of Broadway, chuckling to himself about the surprisingly good result. He then drove the
A-Frame to the motor house and stacked the ties neatly along the edges
of the platform, purposely leaving a large opening.

Back at the bottom again, Dave hoisted the tow engine onto the
Weasel and drove back up Broadway and along the access road until he
could park it directly beneath the platform opening. The engine was now
in the perfect position to be hoisted into place. Dave turned off the Weasel
and walked down the slope.

That evening, Dave invited Punkin to work with him the next day,
playfully adding, "You can learn to work a hoist!" There was nothing the
six-year-old would rather do than spend the day with his father. In fact,
Punkin often accompanied Dave on his outings. Waving goodbye the next
morning, Roma, who trusted Dave unconditionally to keep Punkin safe,
called out for the two of them to have fun, whatever they did.

Punkin rode shotgun while Dave drove the A-Frame up Broadway
and backed up to the Weasel he'd left in place the day before. He engaged
the emergency brake, had Punkin climb into the driver's seat, showed him
how to work the winch, let him practice a few times, and told him to wait
for further instructions.

Dave strung the winch cable from the A-Frame up and over the side
of the platform, and down through the open floor. He then anchored the
cable to the engine and scrambled back up onto the platform. From there,
he called out step-by-step directions.

Ever so slowly, following his dad's instructions, Punkin hoisted the
engine up through the opening until it hung suspended above the platform. He waited while Dave slid the railroad ties into place under the

Top of Rope Tow Two, summer and winter, if they can dig it out!

engine to close off the opening, then he slowly lowered the engine to rest on the railroad tie floor. Dave let out a holler of success and declared to his son, "You're a darn good co-pilot, aren't ya?" Punkin beamed with pride.

NEXT on Dave's summer list was the construction of two outhouses and a 16-foot high, 200-square-foot warming shelter at the base of Broadway. He shoveled out the foundations, and then mixed pumice, an abundant material on Mammoth's volcanic slopes, with cement and water. Using pumice rather than sand was an experiment, but from experience, Dave felt sure the pumice would work.[23]

Without electricity at Mammoth, Dave and his carpenter friends Jim Wilson and Andy Anderson fabricated components for the warming shelter in the workshop at Crowley. They hauled the sections to Mammoth, assembled the building, placed windows, and put up siding. The following weekend, Bishop High ski racers painted the building.

For the two outhouses, Dave dug pits off to the far side of the rope tow line with the doors facing the woods. He deliberately made the buildings large enough for a person to keep their skis on while taking a "nature break." In the end, the cost of the warming shelter and the two outhouses totaled about $1,500, plus an undetermined, yet priceless, amount of sweat equity.[24]

WITH his Mammoth tows prepared for winter, Dave took his family on a road trip to visit his grandparents, Bob and Katie Cox, in Washington. He hadn't seen the Coxes since his motorcycle trip 12 years earlier, and they'd never met Roma and the boys.

Grandpa and Granny Cox welcomed Dave and his family with open arms. During their visit, Dave learned his father Mac had married Grace, the woman for whom he had abandoned Edna and himself. Mac was now living in Northern California with Grace's two boys from her first marriage, Wayne and Richard, and two children they'd had together, Kathy and Bill. This news re-opened a wound of painful feelings that Dave had long repressed.

Lost in thought while driving south from Washington, Dave barely said a word. He was glad to hear that Mac had a good job running a logging crew in the Greenville-Quincy area. Still, sorting through his emotions, he swayed between wanting nothing to do with his father and longing to see him. Roma encouraged him to stop by Mac's house.

Somewhere in Oregon, Dave reached in his shirt pocket, pulled out a folded paper, and glanced at Bill Cox's handwritten directions to Mac's house. This time, Dave's family answered his knock on the front door and welcomed him. From the moment father and son saw each other, they acted as if nothing disconcerting or painful had ever come between them. Rather than delving into the "whys and wherefores" of 17 years of separation, they started anew.

The Snake Pit.

When Mac learned that Dave was using double-bladed axes to clear timber, he shook his head, "Not an easy job. I tell you what, you can borrow my chainsaw on weekends, just as long as you have it back to me before I leave for work on Monday mornings." Dave accepted the offer. Soon, he was spending his Friday nights driving 10-hour roundtrips to borrow the saw in Greenville. Saturdays and Sundays he would fell trees, and on Sunday night, he would drive another 10-hour round trip to return the saw. Sleep became a rare indulgence.

Offering Dave the use of his chainsaw might have been Mac's way to apologize for the past, but it didn't take long for him to become genuinely interested in what his son was accomplishing at Mammoth. Mac gave Dave helpful tips on logging techniques and took over sharpening the chainsaw blade. He sometimes even drove the saw down to Crowley for the weekend, bringing along his oldest son, Wayne, whom he set to work helping the Bishop racers drag slash to the ravine that ran down the center of Broadway.

On a stormy 1948 Thanksgiving eve, northbound skiers drove through white-out conditions, trying to avoid sliding off the steep banks of Sherwin Grade above Bishop.[25] The self-proclaimed Sno-Spiders, a group of avid skiers from West Los Angeles, arrived at Nan and Max's Long Valley Resort well after dark. They struggled to carry their gear through the blizzard into the lodge. Convinced the bad weather would prohibit skiing the next morning, they started partying.

Near midnight, Sno-Spider Clifford Scott noticed the storm had let up. Thanksgiving skiing might be possible, after all. Scotty thought, why not ask "the man" himself? He dialed Dave at his house in Crowley and asked about skiing the next day. Dave didn't hesitate. If Scotty could assemble a group, Dave would run his tows, snowstorm or not. As Scotty remembered:

> *The next morning, Dave met us with his Weasel. About half of us got in, and the rest held on to ropes attached to the rear. When we arrived at the tow, after what seemed like a tremendously long ride, we had to dig out the rope. It's funny—that Thanksgiving Day was*

*cold and full of hard work, yet it was one of the best
Thanksgivings I ever had! We skied hard until about 3
p.m. Someone had a bottle of rum that we all enjoyed.
And, for the first time, Mammoth had a shelter where
we could warm up.*[26]

Dave's new shelter had its share of challenges. There were times he
spent half a day shoveling down through the snow to get the door open.
The volunteer patrollers nicknamed the building the "Dynamite Shack"
because Dave kept his avalanche control supplies in the far corner. Other
skiers called the shelter the "Snake Pit" because they had to slide down
the snow on a curved track to enter. Once inside, they took turns huddling
around the potbelly stove. To get back outside to ski, they clawed up steep
steps shoveled into the snow.

DESPITE having limited facilities, Mammoth's excellent north slope conditions lured so many skiers that on the weekends, Dave needed all five
Weasels to transport skiers up and down Minaret Road.[27] By Saturday
afternoons, some Weasels had inevitably broken down, which meant Dave
would be working into the night trying to repair them for the next day.

One such afternoon, Dave pulled into the Tavern parking area with
a load of passengers returning to their cars. Just then, Rich Thompson, a
newcomer to town, walked up to Dave, introduced himself, and said, "I
heard you could use some help maintaining your Weasels."

Dave looked at Rich and nodded. Rich continued, "If you can get
your Weasels to the station, you're welcome to work in the warmth of my
garage. You can use my tools, and I'll help you with the repairs."

Dave had heard about "Rugged Rich the Roadside Wrecker," who had
purchased Bill Reed's garage and gas station across the street from the
Tavern. Now, here Rich stood, a stranger offering him the assistance he
desperately needed. Dave had no doubt Rich and his family would fit right
into the Mammoth lifestyle.

Rich's wife Gertrude had written her friends about how friendly the
people in Mammoth were. She said there were about 26 residents—
including the Barkers at the Manahu Lodge, the Clarksons at Mammoth

Creek Lodge, and Hugh and Alice O'Connell at the Alahu Resort—and ten party lines, five on each side of the street. Dean Crow, who now owned the Tavern, was known for having a beer in one hand, a cigar in the other, and his ear against the crank phone, eavesdropping. When he'd hear that someone's relatives were coming to visit, he'd interrupt the conversation and suggest they rent a room at the Tavern.[28]

When Rich decided to keep his business open as Mammoth's first wintertime service station and garage, he didn't realize how high the demand for his services would be once the temperature dropped below freezing. If he wasn't busy helping a stranded skier with car trouble, he was thawing out frozen pipes or repairing a home generator—the only source of electricity in Mammoth at that time. When it took him 11 hours to thaw out Joe and Bonnie Zwarts's frozen pipes, Rich billed them his going rate, then deducted morning coffee, donuts, lunch, and companionship, barely charging the Zwarts anything.[29]

Having Rich's warm garage and mechanical assistance gave Dave a tremendous boost. It was not uncommon for the two men to work straight through a Saturday night. Dave would catch a few hours of sleep on the Thompsons' couch and then take off to meet Sunday morning skiers at the snowline. Rich described Dave as "the toughest man I ever worked with. He didn't cuss or get angry and when things went wrong, he would just say, 'That's fate, let's go out and lick it.'" About Roma, Rich added, "She was too busy with the kids to do much socializing, but never too busy to help out at the hill. She worked right alongside Dave, fixing a thrown Weasel track, shoveling snow, or selling coffee."

Even with Rich's help, by the heart of the 1949 winter, so much snow had fallen that Dave closed down his Mammoth tows and returned to McGee Mountain.[30] Being back at the lower elevation and closer to home simplified his life. Suddenly, he had more time to ski, coach, complete his DWP work, and devote to Roma, who was now carrying their fourth child. Dave had to laugh. Life was abundant.

CHAPTER SIXTEEN

Roma: The Weasel Era

Dave awarding Roma her Memorial Day trophy.

D ave believed that a problem wasn't really a problem. It was just a temporary inconvenience with a solution waiting right around the corner. Time and again, something would happen that made me a believer too. Take Minaret Road. Just when we'd had enough of skiers getting their cars stuck while driving to or from the Mammoth tows, Dave heard about some crazy open-aired Army Surplus contraptions designed to transport people over deep snow.

Well, I could tell Dave thought he'd come across the answer to his prayers, but of course, I asked him how we were going to pay for one of those things. He got a mischievous look in his eyes and a singsong bounce in his voice, and said, "Toots, we're not gonna buy one. We're gonna buy three!" Then he opened our dresser drawer, gathered up all our rope tow savings, crammed the bills into a bag, twirled me around, and said, "Pack your toothbrush and grab that cash you stashed away for Christmas presents. We're on our way to the Army surplus auction in San Diego! I've already arranged for a babysitter." I tell you, when Dave gets an idea in his head, it's hard not to get caught up in his enthusiasm.

At the auction, Dave examined each Weasel on the lot and picked out the ones he wanted. Once the bidding started, he tracked the numbers while I made the bids. Well, the place turned into a madhouse. The auctioneer was speaking so fast I couldn't understand him. People were waving their cards in the air, and auction assistants were running around to the bidders. I got completely flustered. Still, we somehow ended up the proud owners of three Weasels, a flatbed truck, and a single-axle trailer to carry the goods home. Our "new" Weasels needed work, but work was something we could handle.

From then on, every weekend morning we'd welcome skiers at the snowline with our Weasels. As skiers loaded, we'd give them a numbered card corresponding to the order they arrived. In the afternoon, they could either catch a ride back to their car when we called their number, or swap numbers if they wanted to ski longer or quit earlier. If I do say so myself, this was a good system.

The good thing about the Weasels was that we could now get skiers up and down Minaret Road. The bad thing was that we couldn't make a schedule because we never knew how many tracks we'd have to fix along the way. We didn't even know if the Weasels would make it back at all. But even if the ride took a long time, the skiers loved the adventure, and that's what counted.

One afternoon when there were about a hundred skiers at the tow and only one Weasel operating, a snowstorm blew in. At that time, we still didn't have a shelter to keep people warm, so we needed to get everyone down Minaret Road on a single trip. Dave knotted lengths of his tow rope to his two permanently attached ropes, making the extension long enough for the entire group to hang on. Once every skier found a spot on the rope, Dave started the engine. Under his breath, he whispered, "Come on, girl, you can do this!"

As the Weasel inched forward, Dave heard people singing. He looked behind and could only see the first skiers in line because the others hadn't come around the bend yet, but their happy voices grew louder as more people joined in. They were having so much fun on their "rescue ride" they forgot how cold they were. So, there you are. We discovered the downhill capacity of a Weasel was at least 100 singing skiers, maybe more.

ONE of the skiers that afternoon was Nick Gunter, an accountant from Los Angeles who carpooled to Mammoth every weekend to ski with his buddies from Edelweiss Winter Club. Nick was entranced with our operation, so he naturally asked us who was doing our bookkeeping. Dave and I exchanged looks of surprise and answered him in unison, "What bookkeeping?"

Nick offered to stop by the house on his way back to the city. When Dave opened our dresser drawer where we kept our rope tow business papers, Nick burst into laughter and said, "You've got to be kidding. What a mess!" He kept shaking his head as we stuffed the cash, receipts, and unopened envelopes into a paper bag for him to take home.

The next weekend, Nick handed us a stack of receipts organized by date, a ledger listing expenses and income, a bank deposit slip that reflected the money he had sorted, and a list of correspondence to be answered immediately. With a teasing look in his sky-blue eyes, Nick asked Dave point-blank, "Do you have something against opening envelopes?" We all broke out laughing. That moment, Nick Gunter became our accountant and lifelong friend. To this day, every time I see him, I burst with love.

Dave and I could always count on Nick's allegiance. His clear thinking and conservative way of managing finances were part of the reason we succeeded in the ski business. Nick knew how to curb Dave from overextending financially or just flat-out giving money away. Well, except when it came to ski racing. There wasn't anyone who could stop Dave from ordering the biggest trophies or organizing his whole life around skiing with his racers.

Ski racing. It's funny how important this sport gets to be in your life. When the first winter Olympics since the war was to be held in 1948, we got so excited we might as well have been going to Switzerland ourselves. Corty Hill called before he left for St. Moritz—he was the U.S. team manager—and gave us the inside scoop that the American women had a chance to shine in St. Moritz. He was right. Gretchen Fraser won gold in slalom and silver in combined.[1] Her signature blond braids dangled over her shoulders as she stood on the podium holding the first alpine skiing medals ever won by an American, man or woman. We were all so proud of her.

Back in Mammoth, the Olympic spirit was alive and well, inspiring us to set personal goals and overcome challenges. There Dave was winning the 1948 State Championship Slalom after the odds had been that he might never walk again. And I wanted to push myself to higher limits too. I entered the Inyo-Mono Championships held at June Lake, *not* pregnant for a change, and planned on skiing all out, which was exactly what I had to do if I wanted to beat Bishop High's rising star, Charlotte Zumstein. Char was about ten years younger than me, and we were close friends, but still, on the course, we raced to win. I came in just ahead of her in both the slalom and the downhill, but we both knew she could just as easily have been the faster one.[2]

WHEN the Far West asked Dave to host their 1948 instructors' convention at Mammoth, he welcomed the opportunity to show off the mountain's expansive spring skiing.[3] While shuttling instructors to the saddle beneath the cornice in one of his Weasels, he pointed out different options for skiing down. Skiers could descend via St. Anton, the open bowl they'd just come up, or they could ski Dry Creek, a gully that ended up on Minaret Road about a mile away from the tow. The more adventurous could hike to the top of the cornice for a steeper descent, or climb a rope Dave had hung off a cliff to ski a slope, later called Face of Three, which funneled toward Broadway. If skiers arranged for a car shuttle, and possibly a guide, they could traverse south from the saddle and ski to Twin Lakes either down an intermediate slope or an advanced route through Hole in the Wall.

After the instructors' convention, Dave organized his third annual Memorial Day Race. To add to the festive tradition of this spring race, Dave and I wore matching red-checked shirts. When Dave announced the awards at the end of the day, he teased, "Young lady, these 1st place trophies have gotten to be a habit with you." Well, as you can imagine, I was delighted.

—W. A. Southworth, Jr. Photo

At the April, 1948 meeting of the California Ski Instructors, at Mammoth Mountain. L. to R.: Sepp Benedikter, Toni Milici, Dave McCoy, Otto Steiner, Bob Mason, and Herb Brook.

THE racers had taken to calling us "Ma "and "Pa," but I swear, sometimes Dave acted just like the teenagers. One Saturday afternoon back at the Crowley house, Dave got in a water fight with the kids, all of them against him. Well, right in the middle of the chaos, he disappeared. The kids snuck inside, thinking they were in a safe place, but the next thing they knew, Dave blasted through the kitchen, squirting water from the garden hose, drenching everyone and everything. We couldn't stop laughing. How many husbands would spray the garden hose inside his own house to win a water fight against a bunch of teenagers?

After Eddie Riley left for college in Flagstaff, Arizona, Dave wrote a letter about how much we missed him. Eddie saved the letter, then later on, he sent it back to me, and I kept it in a box with my treasures. For a man who rarely put pen to paper, Dave sure had a lot to say to Eddie. He wrote, "There's a pending storm I hope won't come because there're a million trees I still need to clear off the hill, but the wind is about to move this shack off its foundation, and the sky is black as coal. My bet is a foot

241

or two tomorrow." Wanting Eddie to know he hadn't been sitting around,
Dave added:

> *We took a ride to the top of Mammoth last Saturday
> and really had fun hurtling the thing [the car] around
> in about six inches of snow. Roma and the kids were
> along. Don [Redmon] and I went deer hunting and got
> two good ones. It didn't take long to get them, but we
> worked six hours hauling them to the car, which was a
> good workout for the legs. Roger [Link] is staying with
> us now. He and Fido [the dog] sleep together. We all
> send our best and here's to better skiing.[4]*

THAT fall, Dave and I loaded our three boys and our camping gear into
our '41 Chevy and took off on a family vacation to Washington. I looked
forward to meeting Dave's grandparents. They'd given him the home life
his parents had failed to provide, and I already loved them for that. Well,
meeting the Coxes, hardworking people who weren't demonstrative about
their feelings, helped me understand why Dave had such high expectations for himself and everyone around him.

While we were visiting, we let the kids go outside to play. Then suddenly, the screen door slammed, and the sound of tiny footsteps came
running toward us. Little Poncho was screaming, "P-Nut's in the creek!" I
hadn't even known there was a creek in the backyard. We ran outside and
saw Punkin lying on his stomach, hanging on to P-Nut's shirt, trying to
keep his little brother's head above the water. Thank heavens for Punkin
and Poncho's fast thinking! The whole thing shook me up so much I don't
remember much else about our visit.

Driving home, Dave told me his father Mac had reconnected with
his grandfather Bill Cox. Well, you should have seen me bristle up. I was
ready to rattle on about how horrible Mac was for abandoning his family,
but then I noticed the saddest look on Dave's face. Knowing that for 17
years, he hadn't heard one word from his father, I stopped myself. "Honey,"
I suggested in a soft voice, "let's go see him."

Dave was reluctant. "Roma, my dad left a long time ago. I'm doing fine.

He's doing fine. I don't want to intrude on his life." Of course, Dave would feel this way. Why take a chance on being rejected again? But something told me that trying to reconnect was worth the risk. He finally agreed.

The house was easy to find, and Grace welcomed us like we were long lost friends. I'd been harboring such resentment about how she'd treated Dave that I was surprised to find her to be a kind and friendly person. I even got the feeling that she felt horrible about having closed Dave out of their life. Anyway, I stayed with the kids while Grace and Dave drove to Mac's job.

As far as I know, neither Dave nor his dad ever mentioned the past to each other. Men don't like to talk about old wounds, regrets, or disagreements. At least Dave doesn't. So, he and Mac got reacquainted by conversing about Mac's logging job and Dave's rope tows. Back in the car on the way home, Dave radiated a lightness I'd never seen in him before.

ONCE winter rolled around, Dave and his friends worked on the ski slopes while we ladies babysat each other's kids and sold rope tow tickets. We used our fishing creels as cash boxes to carry the tickets, a single-hole punch, and wires to attach tickets to skiers' zippers. We'd take turns standing in line and punching the tickets each time a skier came through. Oh yes, they counted their punches to total how many runs they took, like an old-fashioned tracking of vertical feet. Some tried to bribe us into giving them extra punches, you know, for bragging rights, but we wouldn't give in.

Selling tickets was actually just a way for us girls to spend time together and be part of the team. None of us had money for new ski clothes, so we'd fancy up those big warm Army surplus parkas by embroidering hearts and flowers along the edges, then we tied ribbons in our hair and let our curls fly out from under the fur-lined hoods. And we got to go skiing too. I even traveled to some races with Dave.

My biggest challenge at the 1949 Class A State Championships was when Dave and I were hiking up to inspect the downhill, I kept having to ski over to the trees to be sick. Yes... I was two months along with our fourth child. Anyway, Dave showed me the fastest line through a narrow, bumpy section under some tree branches and warned me, "Toots, you better duck your head when you come through here." Well, I did just that and placed 6th.

The next day, my first run of slalom surprised everyone, especially Clarita Heath, who'd been a member of the 1936 Olympic Team. Between slalom runs, she skied over to Corty and asked who I was. "Don't worry about who Roma McCoy is," Corty chuckled. "Just know, if you don't put the speed on, she'll beat you."[5] Well, maybe I didn't beat Clarita, but I came in 2nd place. Not bad, I thought. Just one second behind an Olympian! Back at Crowley, Dave was so proud, he set up all my trophies on the front steps of our house and had me pose for a photo. I was kind of embarrassed.

Then, more trophies. At the Inyo-Mono Championships, Dave won the slalom and placed 2nd in the downhill. I won the downhill and placed 2nd in the slalom, right behind Charlotte. Char and I were a good match, always pushing each other. Even though she was just 16 years old, she had won the 1949 Junior Nationals at Mt. Rose and placed 2nd in the Legions at Sun Valley. She took her accomplishments in stride, crediting her dad for teaching her to ski, Aim for managing the Bishop team, and Dave for inspiring her to become serious about ski racing.

CHAR wanted to race against the experienced senior racers, so Dave and I invited her to go to Mt. Rose with us and race in the U.S. Senior National Giant Slalom. "Why not try?" That was our attitude. Char applied for her "Senior A" race card from Far West, but when her new card arrived, she saw that the Far West had classified her as "Senior B." She called the office to point out the error, and the secretary said there was no mistake. Far West had their own agenda for Charlotte. They wanted her to represent them as the "best from the west" in next year's *Junior* Nationals and according to their new rules, if she raced as a "Senior A," she would become ineligible to compete in junior sanctioned races. Char's heart sank.

When Dave heard this news, his jaw squared right up. He telephoned the Far West office and explained that other divisions allowed *their* strongest skiers to race "Senior A," regardless of age. The Far West refused to budge. In disbelief, Dave barely contained his anger. But there was nothing he could do. So, Char held her head high and raced the spring competitions as a "Senior B," consistently beating most of the "Senior A" women.

I sure did look forward to Dave's Memorial Day race because it was always so much fun. The highlight of the weekend turned out to be that our buddy Toni Milici proposed to Norma Watterson, my dearest friend from Bishop, and Norma said yes. They set the date for October and invited Dave and me to be witnesses at their wedding in Carson City. But just as we were getting ready to leave, my labor started. Dave asked the Zumsteins to fill in for us, then he loaded the boys and me into the Chevy and off we went to Bishop.

On October 9, 1949, I gave birth to Penny Marie, our first daughter. We named her "Penny" for how we used to sing "Pennies from Heaven" when we were riding on Dave's motorcycle. We chose "Marie" for my sister and grandmother who were both named Frances Marie, and for Marie Carter, one of my favorite girlfriends, fellow ticket-seller, and babysitter.

After three boys, how wonderful to be holding a little girl in my arms. It's funny, but from the moment Penny opened her eyes, I felt like she was saying to me, "I know, Mom, my brothers are a lot of work. But don't you worry. I'm going to be such a good girl that you'll never even have to spank me."

So much had changed in our life by the time we brought Penny home. Toni and Norma were married and living in Bishop, and Roger Link was working in Southern California. Our house seemed too quiet. I missed our friends, and I even missed all the teasing, like Roger getting such a kick out of saying he was moving because he was tired of listening to Dave and me populate Long Valley. How embarrassing.

I was happy at least one thing hadn't changed. On weekends, our house was still bursting at the seams with the racers.

Roma and Dave at McGee.

PART THREE

Love Prevails

1950–1955

CHAPTER SEVENTEEN

Charlotte

Charlotte Zumstein.

As the first half of the 20th century came to a close and memories of WWII receded into the past, the sport of skiing gained credibility as a business opportunity. In California alone, ski area operators spent over a million dollars improving at least 60 locations with over 95 tows. Southern California boasted new ski trails, chairlifts, and warming huts at Big Bear, Snow Valley, Mt. Baldy, Blue Ridge, Table Mountain, Green Valley, Kratka Ridge, and Mt. Waterman. In Northern California, Donner Ski Ranch added a $100,000 lodge, and Soda Springs spent the same amount installing a double chairlift. Wayne Poulsen from Reno and Alex Cushing from New York partnered in a business venture to create Squaw Valley, a top-flight ski resort near Lake Tahoe. The ski area boasted beautiful scenery, a magnificent lodge, a $150,000 double chairlift, and a ski school headed by French ski champion Emile Allais.[1]

In the Eastern Sierra, J. Landry, an experienced European skier and renowned mountaineer, submitted a written proposal to the Forest Service to finance a ski area in Rock Creek Canyon, about 20 miles south of Mammoth.[2] Landry praised the location as "... a most happy combination of cold clear weather, deep powdery snow, excellent terrain, and a scenery of rare grandeur." However, possibly due to negative comments about Rock Creek in Corty Hill's Ski Area Survey, Landry's proposal never came to fruition.

Meanwhile, though the U.S. Forest Service envisioned a development on Mammoth Mountain, the agency remained conflicted about how to proceed. Supervisor Charles D. Peyrone urged caution, advising, "To jump immediately from rope tows to chairlifts seems too great a risk."[3]

Hans Georg felt the Forest Service's indecision restricted him from making an honest living. On the other hand, Dave considered their lack of action an opportunity. He spent the summer of 1949 installing two new tows: one, a beginner's tow at the bottom of Broadway, and the other, an advanced tow at the top. That summer, for the first time in 20 years, Mac McCoy celebrated Dave's birthday. He surprised his son with a "*XXX Power Tool*" chainsaw, easily the most treasured gift Dave had ever received. Dave immediately put his new saw to use, clearing trees off a new run called Powder Bowl.

By this time, Don Redmon had a full-time position with Bishop's Interstate Telephone and Telegraph Company. Because he loved working with Dave, Don completed his five-days-a-week telephone company responsibility in four days and then worked with Dave on Fridays through Sundays.[4] As Don explained, "Dave and I were like brothers: competitive, but always having fun. Everything we did was heavy, uphill, or out of gas. I admired that Dave didn't drink or smoke or swear. The way he lived his life exerted a tremendous positive influence on my well-being."

Dave welcomed and appreciated Don's assistance. He didn't have money to pay an hourly wage, but he invited Don and his family to live in the McGee Warming Hut. As a bonus, he gave Don $27 for gasoline each week.

One day, after Dave and Don had spent hours using rakes and shovels to smooth the intersection of Powder Bowl and Broadway, Dave decided to ask a friend to give them a boost by bringing up his TD14 Army surplus tractor. Dave and Don sat on the ground watching in awe as the 12-foot-long blade pushed a half yard of dirt in one sweep. Without a second thought, Dave set his sights on purchasing a bulldozer of his own.[5]

In February 1950, Aspen, Colorado, gained worldwide notoriety for hosting the first FIS (*Fédération Internationale de Ski*) World Championships to be held outside of Europe. The FIS, as the race was called, carried almost as much prestige as the Winter Olympic Games. For the world's leading ski organization to assign this event to an emerging American ski area meant the U.S. was now officially accepted into the elite ranks of international skiing.[6]

Dave's longtime friend Corty Hill, who was then managing the U.S. Women's FIS Team, offered Dave and Roma guest credentials for the races in Aspen. Dave would have loved to watch the best racers in the world compete, partly because he wanted to get an idea of how Charlotte would stack up against the women.[7] But leaving the four McCoy children with a babysitter for a week, especially with little Penny still nursing, was something Roma would not do.

Charlotte dreamed of making the 1952 Olympic Team, and Dave wanted to help her. He suggested she devote her high school post-graduate year to ski racing. Such focused training would give her the best chance to qualify for the team. College could wait.

That winter, since the 1950 Junior and Senior Nationals were scheduled for the same weekend, up and coming young racers would have to choose which competition to enter. Hoping to gain notice as an Olympic candidate, Charlotte decided to race the seniors in Sun Valley. The Senior National Race Committee accepted her entry even though her race card designated her "Senior B." In their analysis, Charlotte's race results had proven her merit.

On a training run at Senior Nationals, Charlotte sprained her ankle and was thus unable to race her best. Placing 8th in downhill and 13th in slalom, she told Dave, "I got the pants beat off me and learned about losing a race." To her surprise, even racing with an injury, her skiing impressed the race officials. They invited her to spend the following winter training in Sun Valley with the other women trying out for the '52 team. Charlotte was honored and thrilled, yet she questioned whether she wanted to leave the spirit of the Mammoth team and Dave's coaching. Fortunately, she would have all summer to decide. Following Dave's advice, she competed in the spring races as a "Senior B," regularly sweeping the events, including the prestigious Silver Dollar Derby at Mt. Rose.[8]

ONE afternoon in May, Charlotte received a letter from the Far West. Curious and slightly apprehensive about this unexpected correspondence, she sat down before opening the envelope. As she read the letter, her stomach turned in disbelief. The Far West accused her of disobeying their rules by competing in the Senior Nationals. As punishment, they disbarred her from their organization, banned her from racing in Far West sanctioned races, and mandated she return the three trophies she had won at the Silver Dollar Derby.

Neither Charlotte nor Dave had any idea she'd broken Far West rules. As her coach, Dave had encouraged her decisions. Once again, he called the Far West office. The slow and deliberate tone of his voice revealed the depth of his anger. Any blame for an unintended breach of rules should fall on him, not her. But the Far West would not relent.

Dave hung up the telephone, walked outside, and looked across Long Valley. He thought of his Bishop racers, their innocent laughter, and their love for skiing. In so many ways, he had encouraged them to devote themselves to ski racing. Had this been a mistake?

In an editorial *The Inyo Register* came to Charlotte's defense:

> *How the FWSA can so smugly make an example of Charlotte for breaking the so-called rules when no one in the FWSA had taken the time to guide her in her endeavors is more than we can tolerate. She has never seen these "rules." It's hard for a skier of her caliber to be denied entering major meets when other skiers from Nevada, Idaho, Utah and Colorado, who are even younger than she is, are allowed to compete.*[9]

FOR his Memorial Day race, Dave rigged five portable tows in tandem up to the top of Mammoth. On race day, he set a 1.75-mile-long course with a vertical drop of 2,000 feet. Seventy racers from as far away as Canada entered. Since the Far West had barred Charlotte from racing, Dave encouraged her to forerun.

At the awards celebration, Dave handed out medals for 3rd place, trophies for 2nd place, gold and silver belt buckles for the winners, and two-foot-high trophies for men's and women's fastest time of the day. He thanked the Forest Service for making the race possible by clearing Minaret Road of snow and then invited the racers to close out the season by returning to compete in his Fourth of July race.[10] In closing, Dave wished Charlotte the best for the following season in Sun Valley and held up a sheet cake decorated, "Good Luck Charlotte." The crowd gave a standing ovation. Charlotte might be moving away, but she would always be *their* Inyo-Mono girl.

ON Sunday, July 2, Punkin rose early to celebrate his eighth birthday. His dad had invited him to forerun the annual Fourth of July ski race. As father and son walked out the door of the Crowley house, Roma called out, "Have a great day, you two. You'll have lots of fun."

A note of sadness in Roma's voice gave Dave pause. Envisioning her home all day with the three little ones—five-year-old Poncho, four-year-old P-Nut, and nine-month-old Penny—while he was on the mountain laughing, talking, and skiing with their friends in what had become an annual community celebration, guilt stung him. But unwilling to spiral into worry over a situation he couldn't change, Dave ignored his intuition. He called out affectionately, "Okay, Toots. You be sure and have fun too!" Roma knew that it was up to her to raise her spirits.

Dave carried bundles of willows on his shoulder as he rode up the rope tows. To set the course, he punched holes in the snow with a crowbar and then inserted the willow slalom poles that Punkin tossed him. As they moved down the slope, gates with red, yellow, and blue flags designated different combinations known as hairpins, flushes, elbows, and the occasional side-hill "sneak gate."

As forerunner, Punkin shot through the gates with quick, fluid turns, skated through the finish, and looked over to his dad. Dave's satisfied expression mirrored the consensus of the onlookers: if Gary McCoy had this much talent at eight years old, then watch out, world!

In the finish area, Dave treated the crowd to slices of watermelons he'd buried in the snow the day before.[11] After the awards, everyone pitched in to collect the race supplies. They offered to help Dave dismantle the rope tows, but he planned on leaving them rigged for as long as the snowfields lasted, just in case someone wanted to ski.

The racers loaded their backpacks, skied to the bottom of the snowfield, then walked down the dirt slope toward the parking lot. They talked about how spending the day skiing with their friends on a 10,000-foot-high snowfield in the hot July sun was as good as life gets. Those with a six-hour drive back to Southern California ahead of them counted on their high spirits to keep them awake.

DAVE turned his eyes to the rocky cliffs off the top of the mountain. The snow had receded, but there was still enough in the chutes to make some turns. He resolved that within the next few days, he would climb to the top, lower himself down through the rocks to the snowfield below, and ski a run. "No," he corrected, "I'll make two runs. One for me and one for Roma. I'll figure-eight my turns like she would do if she were with me. Then I'll drive her and the kids up here to show them the tracks. She'll like that."

Dave looked over to Punkin who was sitting on a rock waiting for him. "Come on," he called out with delight, "Let's head home. We've got a birthday to celebrate!"

CHAPTER EIGHTEEN

Roma: Not to Worry

From left: P-Nut, Poncho, Punkin.

L
ooking back on raising a family, I'm surprised I didn't worry more than I did. The good thing for me was that I had Dave's discipline to back me up. If the kids disobeyed, all I had to say was, "Stop right now, or I'll tell your father," and they shaped up. Their obedience kept me from worrying about their safety and I guess I just assumed that whatever came up, Dave could fix it.

Lord knows, things still happened! Like the day Dave was driving home on an icy road, in the City Jeep, with little four-year-old P-Nut by his side when this fierce wind kicked up. I'd never seen anything like it. Dave parked the Jeep behind a huge boulder, pulled P-Nut from the passenger seat, and huddled behind the rocks. When the wind calmed just a little, he picked P-Nut up and ran toward the house. As soon as they got inside, we heard a noise that sounded like a bomb. The garage had exploded, and sheet metal was flying in all directions. In tears, P-Nut cried out, "Mommy, are we going to die?"

After the wind passed, we looked around to see the damage done, and found that the Jeep had blown over, Dave's axes and chains had scattered everywhere, and our flat-bottomed boat had had been blown to the bottom of the Gorge, ripped apart into a million pieces that are probably still there today.

That windstorm was bad enough, but even worse was the time P-Nut woke up in the middle of the night crying that a wild animal was pacing outside and had stopped at the window by his bottom bunk and stared at him. We thought P-Nut was just having nightmares, but the next night a horrible screeching noise woke everyone in the house. Dave ran outside and saw a cougar lunging off into the darkness. Before we'd gone to bed that night, we'd forgotten to bring our dog, Pluto, inside. And now, there he was, dead on the ground, his neck ripped open.

The next morning while Dave was completing his rounds, P-Nut and Poncho took Dave's fishing knife and set out to kill the cougar. They didn't find the cat, thank heavens. To their surprise, instead of being praised for their courage, they received a severe reprimand from their father. Dave made it clear that the boys were *never* to venture out unsupervised again, with or without a knife. Then he took off through the rocky bluffs and it wasn't long before we heard a gunshot. When he got back home, he assured us the big cat would never bother anybody again.

After the cougar scare, our boys had a better understanding of why we insisted they follow our rules. Not that we lived in a dangerous place, but there were a lot of things for us to be careful about, from wild animals to the dam, the cliffs, Crowley Lake, and the Owens River. And, if something happened to one of us, we were a long way from help. So, we set boundaries. The kids could play in the yard and climb around the boulders behind the house, but that was it. They were absolutely *not* allowed to go down to the lake without an adult.

Now money, that was something I could have worried about, but then again, no matter how tight things might be, I knew Dave would take care of us. I remember one Thanksgiving when we were basically broke and I was spending the four-day holiday at home with the little ones while Dave and Punkin were at Mammoth keeping the tows running and the skiers satisfied.

As soon as those two waltzed into the house late Sunday afternoon, I could see their spirits were high. Dave walked right into our bedroom and dumped a sack of money into the rope tow drawer saying, "Toots, we had a lot of skiers these last four days." I nodded, waiting for him to continue. "You know those cowboy outfits you've been eyeing in the J.C. Penney catalogue? The ones you hoped to buy for the kids? Why don't you go ahead and order them? And while you're at it, buy something for yourself too."

I looked at Dave with surprise, only to find he was dead serious. You see, early on, we had agreed that money received from the rope tow business was out-of-bounds for family expenses unless we had an emergency. So, for Dave to tell me to go on a catalog shopping spree could only mean that we had brought in *a lot* of money over the long weekend. I decided then and there, as long as we were in the ski business, I would wait until after Thanksgiving to shop for back-to-school clothes and Christmas presents.

ANOTHER thing that almost worried me sick was knowing that the Forest Service and some high-stake investors would eventually take Mammoth right out from under us. But Dave told me the Forest Service wasn't anywhere near issuing a prospectus, so our permit was safe. "Besides," Dave said, "no chairlift is going to be built on Mammoth until someone is willing to spend some $300,000 improving Minaret Road and it's gonna be a long time before that happens."

Dave assured me we had the same right as anyone to submit a bid, but I had my doubts. As if we would magically become rich enough to outbid some highfalutin investor. But Dave was sure of himself. "Roma, there's no problem," he said. "The Forest Service and I understand each other. They know what I can do."

That was true. A few Forest Service guys had even been encouraging Dave to believe he had a chance to develop Mammoth. How crazy! Where did they think the money would come from? But, as usual, Dave had a plan.

The next thing I knew, we were down near Lone Pine having a family picnic, checking out an old tramway at the abandoned Cerro Gordo mine.

When I saw that tram, I knew just what Dave was thinking. I warned him nobody in their right mind was going to ride anything built out of that rickety wood. Well, Dave must have agreed with me because he never mentioned the Cerro Gordo idea again.

Dave put his focus on a different kind of investment. For $1,500, he purchased some empty lots near the bottom of Minaret Road. On a few of the lots, he built a small garage where he could work on his Weasels and trucks, and he put in a Texaco gas station so we could save money on fuel. He eventually gave those lots away to friends who were in a position to develop them.[1] That's my husband, so generous and supportive. Some people criticized him for being naïve about money, but Dave didn't care what they said. He liked to support the people who were working hard to enhance the community of Mammoth.

CHAPTER NINETEEN

Prospectus

Dave McCoy and Toni Milici jumping at McGee.

By the early 1950s, the California ski craze had exploded. Hordes of skiers of all ages and abilities crowded the Southern California slopes.[1] Two hundred youngsters attended a dryland learn-to-ski event in Griffith Park. John Jay ski films were so popular in Los Angeles that during one showing, 2,000 viewers were turned away.[2] On the western slopes of the Sierra, Dodge Ridge spent $130,000 on a single chairlift. In Southern California, Holiday Hill doled out $150,000 on a double, and eleven Angelenos partnered to develop Kratka Ridge. By that time, 70 ski clubs had registered with the Far West Ski Association. Their members gathered for mountaineering outings, ski jumping events, beach parties, surf safaris, and folk dances. At some point during each gathering they joined together singing rowdy lyrics and boisterous melodies from *The Skiers' Songbook*.[3]

DURING the 1950 Thanksgiving holiday, only high elevation rope tows had enough snow to operate. Skiers who drove to Hans Georg's tows only saw that rain had washed the snow off his lower slopes and didn't realize there was excellent coverage on his upper slopes. Frustrated once again, Hans wrote Ethel Van Degrift of the *L.A. Times* and complained that "the McCoys got it pretty much tied up."[4] He asked Ethel to remind her readers that he now taught the popular French Parallel System and that his slopes were easier to access than McCoy's, although, he admitted, Dave's ski terrain was "probably better for hot shots."[5]

Meanwhile, Dave had shoveled like a madman to get his higher elevation rope tows operable and the Snake Pit shelter dug out before skiers arrived. Fortunately for him, Mono County had sent a bulldozer to work through a wintry Wednesday night clearing Minaret Road.[6] On Thursday morning, an estimated 400 cars jammed Dave's parking area and lined Minaret Road for at least two miles.

Dave asked four of his friends to use their trucks to shuttle skiers up and down the road.[7] He told the drivers whatever money they collected was theirs, but, he added, "Just don't charge too much." Skiers helped each other climb aboard, stack their skis in the middle, and then unload and distribute the equipment to their rightful owners once they were in the parking area. The "cattle trucks," as they nicknamed the shuttle system, proved so successful that Dave purchased three Army Surplus trucks at $250 each and attached tall wooden rails to the sides.[8]

Skiing Mammoth that Thanksgiving weekend was Warren Miller, a young and fledgling ski filmmaker from Southern California who frequented Mammoth. After framing houses in Los Angeles all week, Warren would drive north in his red paneled delivery truck, which was usually filled with friends who paid for the gas and oil. For accommodations, Dave let Warren's group sleep on the floor of his McGee Warming Hut. One evening Warren tried to show his first ski film, "Deep and Light," but the projector kept blowing out the generator.[9]

Undaunted, the next day, Warren asked Dave if he could film him skiing near Gravy Chute. Dave happily agreed, so they rode to the top of Number Three Tow. Wearing a white short sleeved T-shirt, no hat, and no gloves, Dave waited while Warren set up his camera. Just as Dave took off,

Warren Miller's photo of Dave.

Warren ran out of film, grabbed the still camera hanging around his neck, and in one timely click, captured a classic image of Dave framed by the Minaret Range as he cut through the powder. That photo would soon be featured on the cover of the January 1951 issue of *The Skier*.

In December 1950, Barney Sweatt took over Fred Meckel's position as Mammoth District Ranger. For the first time, the ranger would live in Mammoth year-round rather than moving down to Bishop for the winter. According to Dave, Barney was tall and gangly, walked with big steps, and always wore his uniform. Dave said, "Barney looked at problems straight on, seeking solutions rather than just pointing out what was wrong. And," Dave added with a smile, "his kids joined the race team."

On Barney's first official inspection of Dave's operations, he noted discrepancies between the Forest Service permit, which was for *two* temporary tows, and the fact that Dave was actually operating *five* tows *and* selling food and drinks. Barney's solution: revise Dave's permit to cover the actual developments in place. Next, just after approving the safety gates at the top of Number One Tow, Barney watched an experienced skier fall while riding up. His gripper had failed to release and the tow dragged him 50 feet uphill, not stopping until he hit the safety gate on top. The skier picked himself up, brushed the snow off his pants, and took off for another run. Barney's reaction: request that Dave install a shutoff connection and make sure there is an attendant at the bottom of each tow.

In his report, Barney wrote, "Mr. McCoy has some capable men working for him and the operation appears to be well run although conditions are sometimes adverse." Barney offered to provide signs warning against dangerous grippers and unsafe practices, courtesy of the Forest Service, and he asked Dave to place more garbage cans in the area, build better outhouse facilities, and relocate the Snake Pit to provide more runout at the base of Broadway.

Dave assured Barney he would comply. As he later recalled, "When the Forest Service asked me to do something, I did it. That's how I kept a good relationship with them. And, if I had an idea about doing something, I'd drop the thought into their ears, then give them a few weeks, or a month, or a year, and they'd come back to me suggesting my idea, thinking it was their own."

IN contrast to Dave's diligence maintaining his rope tows, he was remiss about paperwork. Preoccupied with other responsibilities, he would carelessly toss letters, unopened, into his rope tow dresser drawer where they got buried amidst miscellaneous cash and paperwork. When his accountant, Nick Gunter, opened unread mail, he inevitably discovered what Dave had neglected. For example, Dave had forgotten to show proof of his public liability insurance. His annual rope tow permit fee was overdue, as was the minimum occupancy fee of $50 per annum. Dave had also neglected to pay an outstanding $459, which he owed the Forest Service as 1.5 percent of net sales and other income. Nick found an unopened envelope from Ethel Van Degrift. Inside was a letter begging Dave to send her ski reports.[10]

Nick reprimanded Dave: "David, you do *not* want to jeopardize your reputation with the Forest Service or the media. No matter how good you are as a ski tow operator, if you don't read your mail and pay your bills, you're done." Nick had started to use the name "David" when the two friends disagreed on financial matters.

Nick was right. Some Forest Service representatives were openly criticizing Dave. Supervisor Charles Peyrone complained that since Dave was unable to build either a chairlift or a better warming hut, he should *not* be considered a potential developer. Peyrone emphasized, "It does not appear sound to select an applicant on his promise that improvements will be made at some future date when materials are available."

WHILE Dave was struggling to manage the responsibilities of his growing businesses on McGee and Mammoth, Todd Watkins, owner of *The Inyo Register*, had been petitioning his government friends—some of whom had a direct line to Washington D.C.—to remove the main obstacle that was preventing Mammoth Mountain from being developed by anyone: maintenance of Minaret Road. Watkins arranged an exchange whereby Mono County would accept responsibility for clearing Lake Mary Road and the state would take over Minaret Road. With the state in charge of maintenance, Minaret Road would qualify for Federal Aid improvement funds.[11]

As a result, plans were made to grade two flat lanes in a more direct route to Dave's tows, cutting into the hills around Sunshine Corner and Thanksgiving Hill. At last, Minaret Road would be improved. Moffet Lumber won the contract to fell trees along the route. Dave and now nine-year-old Punkin worked as a team clearing the slash and dragging it to the side. Now, if only Caltrans would keep the road cleared of snow.

ON April 30, 1951, after 10 years of studies, debates, and feasibility reports, the Forest Service issued its PROSPECTUS FOR A PROPOSED SKI DEVELOPMENT AT MAMMOTH MOUNTAIN.[12] The prospectus was essentially an advertisement for investors to come forward with a bid to develop Mammoth. Bidding would remain open until April 30, 1953. The permittees on Mammoth, Dave McCoy and Hans Georg, would be allowed to continue their ski operations until that date.

Dave didn't miss a beat. Guaranteed two more years as the operator of Mammoth Mountain rope tows and still working for DWP, he continued to improve his tows. That summer, he cleared three new ski trails, lengthened his third rope tow to add more terrain for advanced skiers, and installed a higher capacity beginners' tow on a gentler slope. Perhaps Dave couldn't offer skiers a chairlift or full-service warming hut, but he would make sure they had excellent skiing, race courses, and trophies.

Acknowledging the deficiencies of the Snake Pit, Dave submitted to the Forest Service his design for a 200 sq. ft. food service building elevated eight feet off the ground with a 16-foot by 16-foot sun porch. Within a week of obtaining approval, Dave and friends constructed the building. Dave then subcontracted Al Whear and his family, who for the past few years had lived at the Sportsman's Lodge near Crowley Lake, to handle food and concessions.

NEXT, Dave spearheaded the formation of a new Mammoth Ski Club, one with ski racing as its focus. [13] With Dave as President, Don Redman as Vice President, Marc Zumstein as the Director of Sports, and Roger Link and Toni Milici as board members, the Club charged $3 membership dues and patterned its constitution and bylaws after the Sun Valley Ski Club. Dave then petitioned the FWSA to sanction three long-standing, well-attended competitions: the Inyo-Mono Championships, Dave's Memorial Day race, and his Fourth of July competition.

By November, with the new Minaret Road graded, his rope tows tuned, his ski slopes groomed, and local competitions listed on the official FWSA race schedule, Dave felt prepared for snow. What he didn't know was, *nobody* was truly prepared for the upcoming winter of 1952.

CHAPTER TWENTY

Heavy Snows

Rich Thompson's garage, winter 1952.

D uring the winter of 1952, a series of storms hurtled down from Alaska and raged over the Western United States unleashing snow in the worst winter rampage in 60 years. By the time the storm series subsided, a fatal avalanche in Sun Valley, Idaho, had thundered down a 1,500-foot bowl on the ski slopes of Baldy Mountain; Southern California ski areas had closed down, some buried under nine feet of snow; and snowstorms had knocked Squaw Valley's chairlift out of operation for at least 10 days. Outside Reno, snowplow crews fought in vain to keep highways open. On Donner Summit, drifts mounted to 50 feet high as swirling powder tried to swallow up even the most powerful snow removal machines.

SKI TRACKS
Train Rescue
1952

An avalanche wedged a plush streamliner, the San
Francisco, in its tracks as it was crawling up Donner
Summit. The streamliner tried to extricate itself from
the snow but ran out of fuel leaving 221 passengers
and crewmen without heat in sub-freezing weather.
A second avalanche buried the rescue train, killing
the engineer. The storm continued to beat down in a relentless fury of 100 mile-per-hour winds that whipped through
the canyon with no indication of quitting. Twenty-six
hours after the first avalanche, Southern Pacific Railroad
called on Soda Springs ski resort for ski volunteers to carry
food to the train. Among the rescuers was Mammoth's
Bobby Cooper who was teaching skiing at Soda Springs.
That night, the rescuers made two snowcat trips through
a vicious wind traveling seven miles in three hours each
way to deliver 600 pounds of food.[1]

IN Mammoth, the wild winter began with an eight-foot snowfall that
ensured excellent skiing over Thanksgiving weekend. In her *Ski Slants* column Ethel Van Degrift wrote, "There's no need to order a turkey. Just
sharpen up your skis and get one for free in a turkey chase at Squaw Valley
or Mammoth."[2] Over the long weekend, Hans Georg operated all three
of his tows and Dave estimated people took at least 2,000 runs a day at
his operation. Skiers chattered about how Mammoth needed a chairlift
and joked that Dave must have done snow dances to summon the storm
clouds.

At Dave's new food and concession stand—which was elevated off the
snow—skiers could purchase gloves, rope tow grippers, Chapstick, goggles, food and beverages. As managers of this new "warming hut," the
Whear family sold sandwiches, brownies, sweet rolls, and buckets of chili
they'd made at home. They also grilled hot dogs and hamburgers and sold

cups of spiced cider as fast as they could pour them. Pam Whear recalled that snowy winter. "We carried the food through hip-deep snow heading in the general direction of the building. Dave called the building a warming hut, but I don't know why, because we never got warm."[3]

After Thanksgiving skiers departed, the storms refused to let up. Concerned that the weight of the accumulating snow might break his towline, Dave cut the ropes and temporarily closed his Mammoth operation. Meanwhile, Caltrans was having trouble keeping Highway 395 open. Once they lost Minaret Road, the deal was sealed. Mammoth shut down.

Over the December holidays, the few ski enthusiasts who visited Mammoth ended up snowed in, their cars buried and food supplies dwindling down to canned beans, flapjack mix, and used coffee grounds. The only way to travel was by skis, snowshoes, or Weasels. Those living in Mammoth shoveled trenches to get from one house to another.

Dave heard that townsfolk were low on food, so he purchased groceries in Bishop, loaded the boxes onto his Weasel at Toms Place, and made the long slow journey to the Tavern. Residents pitched in to unload and distribute the desperately needed provisions. When the Weasel was at last emptied, Dave was shocked to overhear someone complain, "Where's the liquor?" Liquor hadn't entered his mind. He stood by the Weasel, perplexed and angered. Didn't people appreciate what he had just done? On his cold and arduous journey back to Toms Place, alone with his thoughts and the humming of the Weasel engine, Dave decided to ask Roger Link to take over the food delivery trips.

To avoid being snowed in at Crowley, Dave temporarily moved his family to a pair of cabins at Bill and June Kinmont's Rocking K Guest Ranch in Bishop.[4] Newcomers to town, the Kinmonts had purchased 80 acres of sagebrush just north of Bishop where they planted seven acres of alfalfa, built a main house, cabins, ponds, tack room, corrals, and a roping area. When the ranch closed down for the winter, the Kinmont children, Jill, Bobby, and Jerry, took up skiing and joined the Bishop Ski Team.

With Roma and the McCoy kids settled warm and safe inside the Rocking K cabins, each morning Dave drove up the Sherwin Grade to complete his DWP rounds at Crowley. There was too much snow to even consider getting into Mammoth, so he focused on getting his McGee tows operational. With a few of his friends and the Bishop racers helping, he shoveled out the towline, tuned the engines, adjusted the rope tow poles—made from Aspen trees with 18-inch wheels attached to the top—and strung and spliced new ropes. Before long, despite the continuing stormy weather, Dave had two battered but sturdy tows running.

As soon as Ethel Van Degrift caught wind of Dave's effort, she reported, "The McGee Creek area, so popular in the late '30s and early '40s, with skiing sometimes lasting until May, has suffered a dearth of snow for six years, but suddenly pops into the limelight again this weekend... McCoy has two lifts operating... Many old-timers will be glad to see McGee return to the picture."[5]

Dave's racers were ecstatic to be back skiing McGee and training for the races. They dug out the pile of willow slalom poles stacked next to the Warming Hut, carried them up the tow, and tossed them to Dave as he set courses in the soft snow. As young Jill Kinmont described, "Dave would stand quietly at the top, the sleeves of his black parka pushed up to his elbows, no gloves, leaning forward against his ski poles, sighting down the slope and imagining a line in the snow where he would set the course.[6]

Generally, the racers spent half their training session running courses: Kenny Lloyd in his nimble, bouncy style; Audra Jo Nicolson precise and in control; Bobby Kinmont carrying speed without effort, and his sister Jill pushing to go faster. After clearing the slalom poles off the hill, they'd usually free ski for a few hours, yipping, hollering, and yodeling as they zipped down the slopes with Dave in the lead. If the snow was settled and conditions were safe, he might guide them on a 20-minute climb to the two pines beneath the McGee cliffs for the final run of the day. As Kenny Lloyd described those training sessions:

We all wanted to ski with Dave because everything was so much fun. Each day was an adventure. We wouldn't have thought of doing anything else. Dave didn't say much but it was inspiring to be with him. He knew how to talk to each person, telling us what we were doing wrong and how to correct it. If he was angry with us, his jaw got square and that was enough. Just his look could make you feel disappointed in your-self and you wanted to try harder and do better the next time. He didn't push anyone to perform. It didn't mat-ter who won, just that we did the best we could.[7]

Meanwhile Don Banta, the Lee Vining High School coach, worked with his racers five afternoons a week on the electric tow behind town. Just before dark, Banta trained them for cross country races by having them run to the edge of Mono Lake, loop up to the high road past the water tank, and back into town. For gear, the team used a table saw to rip old wooden alpine skis into narrow cross-country skis, and the group all chipped in to purchase a single pair of jumping skis to be shared among them.[8]

Though Lee Vining High and Bishop High racers competed as archrivals in school competitions, on weekends they all skied together as the Mammoth Team.[9] With Dave coaching, and Don Banta assisting, together they pursued the ultimate goal for junior racers: performing well enough in divisional point races to qualify for Junior Nationals.

In January, Dave caravanned the team south to Big Bear to compete in the first point race of the season. The Mammoth racers shined. Skiing strong and steady, Jill placed 2nd in the slalom. Kenny sped down the course in his wild style, arms flapping, balancing on one ski at a time, and placing 2nd against the older boys. Then, starting almost last out of 60 entrants, Bobby skied his smooth style, letting his skis run fast across the icy ruts, winning his class with a time that was faster than Kenny's.[10]

The next weekend, Dave drove his racers to a point race at Badger Pass in Yosemite and returned home with 17 medals.[11] June Lake's Dennis Osborn won overall, a victory that identified him as one of the top junior racers in the Far West Division.[12]

WHILE Dave was coaching his Mammoth racers, America's Winter Olympians were preparing for the 1952 Games to be held in Oslo, Norway. In early February, Charlotte Zumstein, who at age 18 had been named a team alternate, received a telephone call inviting her to fill in for

Katy Rudolf, who had been injured. Here was the opportunity Charlotte had worked so hard for, had longed for, but she was forced to decline. There was no funding available and she couldn't pay her own way. So, Char remained in Sun Valley and heard from a distance about Vermont's 19-year-old Andrea Mead Lawrence's winning performance.

SKI TRACKS

Excerpt from
"Here's A New Look at Mrs. Lawrence"
1952

> Oslo, Feb 23 (AP) – The first woman ever to win two gold medals for skiing in a single Winter Olympics is a slim, level-eyed American named Andrea Mead Lawrence. The world is turning for a second look at this extraordinary 19-year-old girl. At first, because you usually see her in ski pants – with her hair pulled back tightly into a barrette so it won't fly in her eyes when she skis – you think of her as a slender and handsome but almost boyish young thing. Her feminine charm is underplayed not by design but because she is entirely unaware of it. Her attractiveness, like her personality, doesn't strike you all at once. It grows on you.[13]

INSPIRED by Andy Lawrence's gold medal performance, eight Inyo-Mono high school racers qualified for Far West's 1952 Junior National Team. Dave accompanied the Mammoth contingent to Winter Park, Colorado, where they would race against the top juniors in the nation.

Dave suggested the team leave Bishop a day early so they could ski Aspen, Colorado, en route. Carrying a wallet full of money and a bag full of sandwiches, fruit, and banana bread, he strapped the team's ski gear to the top of the Lloyds' new Packard sedan and crammed their baggage into the trunk. Off Dave drove with the Kinmont siblings, Audra Jo Nicolson, Kenny Lloyd, and June Lake's Dennis Osborn taking turns riding in the front seat.[14]

From left: Dave, Audra Jo, Jill, Kenny, Dennis, and Bobby.

Everything about the trip was fun and exciting. In Nevada, where gambling was legal, Dave stopped for gasoline, put a few coins into a slot machine, and won enough change to pay for the fuel, awing the kids with his "talents," and starting a tradition. On another trip, he won $40 off of one quarter, and once on Montgomery Pass, he hit the jackpot and took everyone out to dinner on the winnings.

In Aspen, Dave and his racers learned they weren't alone in their love for the sport of skiing. Impressed by the high-level of Colorado skiers, they rode chairlifts supplied with blankets to keep them warm, then chased each other down long, steep slopes and through mogul fields. They explored the streets of the old mining town and ate their meals in small restaurants filled with late 1800s ambiance, savoring each new experience.

Once at Winter Park, the tone grew more serious. Facing difficult courses and first-rate competition, Dave coached his skiers not to worry how they placed, but rather, to do their best to make it to the finish. During the training runs, Dave studied the skiers who were favored to win. Standing together with his team on a free-skiing run, he saw Buddy Werner, a racer from Steamboat Springs, Colorado, skiing down, and he told his racers to watch. Buddy made three quick turns, jumped off a rise, playfully caught some air, and then leaned into a new turn before his skis even touched the snow. Awestruck by Buddy's skiing, Jill took to watching him every chance she could. She soon understood why he and his sister,

Skeeter, were already in the national limelight.[15]

On race day, Dave stood near the starting gate, massaged his racers' shoulders to relieve the tension in their muscles, and reminded them to have fun. Dennis Osborn placed 7th in the slalom as the top result for the team. Unfortunately, Jill crashed in the downhill and bit her tongue. For a while, she couldn't eat solid food and she could barely talk, but she had finished the race, and Dave seemed as proud of her as if she'd won.[16]

Skiing the Colorado resorts and viewing the Junior Nationals first hand fueled Dave with energy about his coaching. "With the right training," he told his racers, "you can be just as good as the top U.S. juniors." They believed him and trained all spring, putting forth their best effort toward reaching the goals he set before them.

Dave pointed out how Upper Broadway was just like the bottom of the Winter Park downhill. He led the racers down as they schussed sections of the slope, building their confidence until they were comfortable skiing straight down the run. Dave then had them increase their speed by skating on top and holding a low body position as they continued down. Next, he shoveled a series of rolling bumps for them to speed over while working their knees to adjust to the terrain. And, always foremost on Dave's mind was that everybody had fun.

AFTER Dave's Fourth of July race, the racers waxed their skis for storage and put them away until the following winter. Jill settled into summer vacation working alongside her best friend, Audra Jo, at the Rocking K Ranch. One afternoon, Audra Jo abruptly sat down, too tired to move. Within a day, she had lost the strength to get out of bed. Her head pounded in pain. An ambulance transported her to Los Angeles where doctors diagnosed poliomyelitis and put her in an iron lung to assist her breathing.

Fortunately, Audra Jo regained the ability to breathe on her own, but the polio permanently paralyzed her from the waist down. She moved into a rehabilitation center in Santa Monica, where she worked diligently on her recovery, her indomitable spirit never faltering. By June she was able to visit Bishop and graduate with her high school classmates. At the time, Jill confessed, "I could never be as brave as Audra Jo. If I lost the use of my legs, if I couldn't ski, or ride, or walk, I would just give up."[17]

CHAPTER TWENTY-ONE

Roma: So Much Snow!

Punkin and the new Sno-Go.

As soon as the Redmons heard about the impending December blizzards, they moved from our McGee Warming Hut to Bishop so Don could get to his telephone company job on weekdays. Next thing I knew, a storm had dumped over five feet of snow on the road to the dam and had buried Highway 395 for 20 miles. Dave was stuck in Bishop and our next baby's due date was approaching. Dave didn't want me to go into labor at Crowley, so as soon as Caltrans cleared the highway, he drove to Toms Place and skied the three and a half miles to our house. We dressed the kids in their ski gear, wrapped two-year-old Penny in Dave's knapsack with a blanket around her, and skied out to the car, me right behind Dave and Penny, P-Nut and Poncho following, and Punkin bringing up the rear.[1] Welcome to the winter of 1952!

The Kinmonts invited us to stay in their cabins at the Rocking K

Ranch until the storms subsided. Our quarters were tight, but we were together, safe and sound rather than out in the storm freezing to death.

On Saturday morning, February 2, not long after Dave and the older racers had left for McGee, my contractions began. Typical me. I was determined to wait for Dave before I delivered the baby, so most of the day, I sat on the bed, trying not to move. Punkin was an angel helping take care of his brothers and sister. About six that evening, Dave walked in the front door and announced we were all going to the Kinmonts' main house for a spaghetti dinner. Well, there was no way I was going to a party. I told Dave I needed to rest, and he should take the kids and go.

By the time they came home, I was a wreck. I yelled out, "Honey, I'm in labor, and I need you to take me to the hospital *right now!*" Well, little Kandi Kay McCoy was born about 2:30 that morning, February 3, 1952. Her middle name was a tribute to the Rocking K Ranch. What a beautiful bundle of energy. Right from the beginning, we knew we had a strong-willed, bright-eyed, free-spirited little girl. In fact, from a young age, Kandi reminded Dave of his favorite aunt, Millie.

WE finally moved back to Crowley at the end of March. What a surprise to see such high snowbanks in the springtime. With the community of Mammoth still buried, Dave couldn't even consider running his north slope tows, so it was good he had his McGee operation in full swing. And actually, I was glad he was working closer to home at McGee. The McGee Warming Hut made it much easier for me to take the kids skiing. I told Punkin he couldn't go above the second pole on Rope Tow Number One, but he was skiing so well I *had* to let him take laps on Number Two. Soon he was sailing off the jump that Dave and the racers had built. I swear Punkin owned that jump. Meanwhile, Poncho and P-Nut were whizzing up and down the lower tow, and Penny was wandering around the flat on her tiny skis.

Even with my own big family, I still loved having the racers stay with us. As soon as one batch graduated from high school, we'd inherit another. I remember when Jill and Bobby Kinmont joined the team. There wasn't anyone who worked as hard or had as much team spirit as they did, spending the entire season trying to catch up to the more experienced racers.

I became close friends with Jill, just like I'd been with Char. Jill liked to tell me about her adventures traveling to races and flirting with the boys. She loved how Dave set the spirit of the Mammoth team, like the time they all stopped at a small restaurant for breakfast. When the owner saw two carloads of *hungry* racers, he looked shocked, as if he was wondering how he could possibly handle this bunch of kids. But good ol' Dave took control and said, "How about if we all order pancakes?"

Another time, in Walker Canyon on the way to Reno, Dave came around a sharp corner and saw a car flipped over on the side of the road. He pulled over, all the racers jumped out, and in one big heave, they turned the car right side up. The stunned man barely had time to say thank you before Dave and the kids were once again on their way to the races.

I have to admit, although I loved hearing about all the fun Dave and the racers were having, I felt kind of sad and left out that I couldn't go on their weekend trips. Then some parents asked Dave to travel with the Far West team to Junior Nationals, which meant he'd be gone a whole week at Winter Park, Colorado. Well, actually, longer. He said if they were going through Colorado, they might as well take a few days to ski Aspen. You can imagine my mixed feelings.

I told myself to be patient. I knew as much as anyone what a great coach Dave was. He brought the best out of people and he didn't play favorites. So even if I did feel sorry for myself, I was proud of him and happy for the racers. And I was sure that as soon as our children were old enough to travel to races, I would once again be in the midst of the fun.

Something I want you to know about Dave is that when he had the money, he paid for the racers' entry fees, food, gas, lift tickets, and lodging. Most local families lived on limited budgets and Dave didn't want a lack of money to get in the way of opportunity. He told me he had no intention of being paid back. He just hoped those he had helped would someday assist others in turn. Also, he appreciated how much the racers helped him with the tows. He'd grown to count on them. And as a surprise benefit of his coaching, his racers' achievements were giving his ski tows free advertising in newspaper and magazine articles.

GETTING Minaret Road cleared between the town and the rope tows after that heavy winter of 1952 seemed impossible. So, when Dave heard that the Navy was selling a used Klover Sno-Go in Reno, he decided to buy it, sight unseen.[2] His line of thinking was that if Caltrans couldn't clear snow off Minaret Road, he would do it himself. The only drawback was we didn't have $12,000. So, Dave went to Nick.

Nick said, "I can draw up spread sheets and profit-loss schedules to help you get a loan. But David, you *have* to make the payments on time." Based on the financial statements Nick prepared for Dave, the Bank of America financed the full amount for the Sno-Go and Dave proudly drove the heavy-duty machine home. At his garage on Minaret Road, he replaced the auger motor with a bigger, more powerful diesel engine that could blow tremendous volumes of snow over exceptionally high snowbanks.

Once Dave could get up Minaret Road, he shoveled out his Mammoth rope tow lines and re-strung the ropes, preparing to open on May 10. That just happened to be our 11th wedding anniversary. There we were at Mammoth, in business again and enjoying the spring skiing. When Dave's Memorial Day race rolled around, I entered, and guess what? Roma McCoy, mother of five, was the fastest woman down the hill.[3] I was so happy to be out there on the mountain with our friends once again. A funny thing was happening though. I noticed my feelings about racing were shifting. The boys were wanting to enter races, and I felt more interested in cheering them on than I did in worrying about how I might do.

When Sun Valley closed for the season, Charlotte came back to Bishop, partly to visit her parents, but also to ski with Dave and the team. After a day on the mountain, she stopped by to visit me. Since Kandi was napping, we sat in the kitchen drinking tea while she told me about her winter. Racing in Sun Valley had been tough. She missed the team spirit she'd known in Mammoth. In Sun Valley, the attitude had been "everyone for themselves." Now, once again, seeing how dedicated Dave was to his racers and how fairly he treated everyone, she was reminded of how she had felt when Dave coached her. Char said that only now had she realized she'd been Dave's protégé. And, she added, it looked like Jill Kinmont was following in her footsteps. I think Charlotte was right.

CHAPTER TWENTY-TWO

Gaining Momentum

Roma and Jill.

Duting the summer of 1952, not a single bid on the Mammoth prospectus had been received, yet several financiers invested in ski areas within 100 miles of downtown Los Angeles, all easily accessible via well-kept roads.[1] Corty Hill and three partners spent $350,000 at Mt. Baldy in the San Gabriel Mountains, and hired renowned Frenchman Emile Allais, who had been teaching at Squaw Valley, to direct the ski school. At Snow Valley, Johnny Elvrum built a 20,000 square-foot ski lodge costing nearly $200,000.[2] Just up the road, Big Bear invested $150,000 in a mile-long chair lift. At Mammoth, Dave tuned his rope tow engines, raised the sheave wheel poles so his tows could handle deeper snows, and purchased components to assemble 3,000 rope tow grippers that he could sell or rent.

THAT autumn, the Far West Ski Association asked Dave to be the official coach of their 1953 Junior National and American Legion teams. He happily accepted and arranged for a hydrographer to cover his rounds while he was traveling. A week before Nationals, he said goodbye to Roma and the kids, and drove off to Brighton, Utah. Dave's spirited racers didn't bring home any medals, but their sportsmanship and team spirit stood out.

Coaching the California racers at the Legions competition in Sun Valley that winter marked the first time Dave ever visited the famous ski area. He took the racers to Idaho a week early so they could ski the entire mountain *and* watch some of the top skiers in the world compete in the Harriman Cup.[3] Dave brought along a borrowed movie camera to film the competitors and use the footage as a training tool. He also arranged for his racers to gatekeep the competitions in exchange for lift tickets, and he prompted them to pay close attention to each competitor, noticing how passion and desire were as important as technique.

For the Mammoth kids, a highlight at the Harriman Cup was cheering on their own Dennis Osborn, fondly called the "June Lake Jet." By this time, Far West had adjusted its rules so that outstanding junior racers, such as Dennis, could compete as Class A seniors. Sadly, Dennis' first season on the senior circuit had not been fun. In his own words, he had felt like "a little frog in a great big pond." Though in excellent physical condition, Dennis was unaccustomed to the mental challenge and the physical strain of such demanding courses.

But now, having the support of his Mammoth teammates, Dennis' spirits lifted, his focus returned, and his energy revived. He placed 9th in the downhill. To have a top-ten finish in the Harriman Cup was a notable accomplishment. The *Inyo Register* reported, "With this sudden surge to prominence in big time events and his steady improvement, Dennis is being mentioned by ski experts as a bright prospect for the 1956 Olympic team."[4]

The American Legions took place right after the Harriman Cup. Kenny Lloyd placed 2nd in the downhill and proudly brought home the first trophy ever won by a Californian in this well-respected junior competition.[5] Jill Kinmont fell in every event and returned home disappointed. She was tired of hearing, "If Jill hadn't fallen, she'd have won." Even receiving the

Sportsmanship Award didn't make her feel better.[6] But instead of moping around, she made a plan.

Jill knew she had the guts to go fast. She just needed to feel more comfortable at high speeds like the boys did. If she imitated their attitude, their body position, and their movements on the snow, she might be able to stay up with them, maybe even one day pass them. Yes, to ski like the boys would be her goal for spring training.

SHORTLY after Dave and his team returned home from the Sun Valley races, the closing date for the MAMMOTH MOUNTAIN PROSPECTUS, April 30, 1953, arrived with no bids received. There were no last-minute bargain pleas, no late offers, nothing. However, within the local Forest Service, a campaign had begun to give Dave the opportunity to develop Mammoth. Not being part of the decision-making, Dave focused on his racers while the Forest Service debated over how to proceed.

Early one morning near the end of June, Dave drove Toni Milici, Jill and Bobby Kinmont, and another racer, Dave Taylor, to the Sonora Summit Summer Slalom.[7] Near the parking area, he placed a small pressure stove on a rock, melted a concoction of mothballs and wax in a coffee can and painted the hot wax in overlapping layers on the bases of each of their skis. The group then joined the 100-some other competitors hiking up and studying the course.

Near the start, Jill made a few warm-up turns and swiveled to a quick halt. Suddenly, another skier stopped by her side. She looked up to see an attractive man wearing a navy-blue racing jacket with a 1952 Olympic patch. Jill recognized Dick "Mad Dog" Buek's angular face and high cheekbones from seeing him race at the Harriman Cup. Though they'd never met, Buek grinned at her as if they were old friends and said, "You know, you're going to win today."

Embarrassed, Jill blushed. Here was one of the best skiers in the country paying attention to her. She didn't want anyone to know what he had just said or how his words had affected her, especially not Dave because he might disapprove. Buek was well known for his outrageous athletic feats, and Dave wasn't impressed with "big time" people.

When it was Jill's turn to race, Dave said, "Just have fun!" She let the sound of his encouraging voice flow through her, as if having fun was the key to everything good in life. Her neck and shoulders relaxed. Her body resonated with energy.

Skiing against a strong field of females, Jill crossed the finish line with the fastest time of the day for women.[8] She cheered for Bobby as he won the junior boys' division, Dave Taylor as he won the senior men, Dick Buek coming in 2nd, and Dave McCoy for placing 3rd.

That afternoon on the way home, worn out from the high-altitude sun and all the excitement of the day, Jill sat quietly, lost in thought. Spring training had served her well. She was prepared to ski her best. Winning felt right. And when she thought about Dick Buek, her heart felt happy.

After the Sonora Pass race, Jill lost interest in the boys at Bishop High. She didn't care about going to dances, not even the senior prom. All she wanted to do was win ski races. Almost as if Dave could read her mind, one afternoon he blurted out, "Jill, I think you can make the '56 Olympic team. If you work hard, ski hard, and keep on the way you're going now, there's no reason why not." Jill about jumped out of her seat. She promised Dave she would do whatever was needed to reach that goal. Dave knew she would follow through. He talked to Jill's parents about letting her postpone college for a year, and they agreed.

All summer, foremost on Jill's daily schedule was performing a series of exercises Dave had designed for her to build endurance, timing, strength, and agility. Every day she jogged a few miles, did sit-ups and push-ups, hiked up hillsides of sagebrush and ran back down, darting back and forth to mimic running slalom. She walked barefoot to toughen her feet, did sets of one-legged squats, and jumped through a series of automobile tires placed flat on the ground as in a football drill.

Dave believed tire drills were among the best exercises for ski racers. He had Jill jump through two rows of tires with one leg, then both legs; fast, then slow; starting slowly and then speeding up; and then repeating the series with the tires spaced uneven distances apart. By the end of summer, Jill had gained physical and emotional strengths she never before knew existed.

CHAPTER TWENTY-THREE

The Permit

Hans Georg's ski hut at Observation Pt.

S
ince the 1930s, the U.S. Forest Service had been responsible for managing public forests in a way that satisfied the winter and summer recreation needs of all Americans. This mandate included developing ski areas and promoting skiing. When April 30, 1953, the closing date of the Mammoth prospectus, drew near, tension in the regional Forest Service mounted. Lack of investor response could be interpreted as the agency's failure to fulfill its duty to the public.

Meanwhile, Mammoth District Ranger Barney Sweatt had been campaigning for the Forest Service to retract its prospectus and issue Dave McCoy a term permit that would allow him to build a full-service warming hut and clear more slopes. Barney reminded his superiors that for the past 13 years, in response to Forest Service encouragement and suggestions, Dave had put forth a tremendous amount of energy—and $40,000 of his own money—to meet the public demand. He'd established a volunteer ski patrol, hosted ski races that attracted hundreds of skiers to the region, maintained an excellent relationship with the Forest Service, and provided ongoing service to the public. Now, due to the prospectus, Dave faced elimination. In Barney's view, such treatment wasn't logical, and it wasn't right. Despite Barney's plea, the Forest Service ruled that, according to policy, the prospectus would continue to be advertised. Dave's permit would remain temporary.

At this pivotal moment, Wilfred S. "Slim" Davis arrived in Bishop as the new Inyo National Forest Supervisor. Once familiar with the situation, Slim joined Barney's campaign. Believing that Dave had the heart, soul, and skills to develop Mammoth Mountain, Slim approached Dave and bluntly asked him, "Dave, can you do it?"

With a confident ring to his voice, Dave responded, "I'd give it my best." On a blank piece of paper, he sketched an outline of Mammoth with lines delineating where he would erect three chairlifts, if given the opportunity.[1] Beginning mid-April 1953, a four-month dialogue ensued. Fittingly, the discussions resembled the twists and turns of a slalom course:

> **April 15** Following Slim's advice, Dave penned a proposal to the Forest Service offering to develop Mammoth on a looser timeline than the prospectus required.

> **April 21** Slim wrote Barney Sweatt that if no bids were received by the closing date, they should immediately alert Forest Service Chief John Sieker in Washington D.C. of Dave's handwritten proposal.

> **April 30** Bidding on the two-year prospectus closed without a single offer to develop Mammoth Mountain.

> **May 1** Slim mailed Dave's handwritten proposal and lift-line sketch to Forest Chief Sieker along with a two-page cover letter establishing his case for McCoy.

In his letter to the chief, Slim explained that while operating with a temporary annual permit, Dave McCoy had not been in a stable enough financial position to add amenities (sanitation, warming hut, parking, and lift facilities). Even so, Slim argued, ski attendance under Dave's management had continued to increase. Skier visits for the current season already numbered more than 20,000 with an expected 25,000 before the snow melted. Most of the visiting skiers were Southern Californians, indicating that even with chairlift-served ski areas nearer their homes, they appeared to prefer skiing Mammoth.

Slim suggested that any potential criticism for departing from the prospectus standards could be met with the argument that since there were no takers on the original proposal, it was in the public interest to let the current permittee expand his operation and provide the facilities that were badly needed. In conclusion, Slim wrote that Dave could finance the warming hut himself and claimed to have a backer for a chairlift.

AFTER much debate, on May 27, the Forest Service ruled to negotiate a 25-year permit with Dave, provided he agreed to eventually construct the lifts planned for Mammoth's ultimate development. The permit should tie construction of the lift to the date the county or state assumed responsibility for clearing snow off Minaret Road because a lift enterprise would not succeed if the operator also had to handle snow removal.

Thinking Dave had won the race, Slim wrote him a letter stating that by July 1, he hoped to issue two permits, one for five acres of base area facilities, buildings, and parking lots and the other for 480 acres of actual ski terrain. However, before these permits could be issued, Dave had to provide evidence he had the funds to construct a full-service warming hut, parking area, and the first lift.

DAVE asked Nick to draft a loan proposal for $125,000 that would liquidate his outstanding small debts and provide adequate financing to move forward.[2] With Nick's financial analysis and repayment schedule in hand, Dave felt sure he could secure a loan. Unfortunately, the bankers, who apparently were non-skiers, didn't understand the growing sport of skiing, didn't consider the ski area to be sufficient collateral, and didn't trust Nick

Gunter's income projections that were based on a six to seven-month ski season. According to the bankers, a ski season couldn't possibly last more than three months a year.

Unable to secure a bank loan, Dave took to the streets of Bishop. He walked door to door, asking friends and merchants for contributions, raising some money, but not nearly enough.[3] He contacted skiers who had previously offered him financial help, but it turned out that anyone interested in investing wanted to form a partnership. To Dave, a partnership would spell defeat before he even got started. As he later explained. "Without a formal education, I knew I could end up as low man on the totem pole and I never wanted to let myself get in that position."

Dave called his friend Corty Hill, but Corty was tied up trying to develop a ski area at Mineral King in the southwest Sierra Nevada. Turning the tables, Corty seized the opportunity to ask Dave to join *him* as a partner. Believing there was no one more qualified than Dave McCoy to make his venture a success, Corty flew Dave to Mineral King, gave him the grand tour, and offered to buy out Dave's investment at Mammoth plus more. Dave tried to be open-minded to Corty's offer but no, Mammoth was where he wanted to be.

DAVE and his advocates refused to give up. In a persuasive presentation, Slim Davis convinced his superiors to approve a more feasible two-phase development plan. Phase I would require Dave to raise only the $25,000 needed to build the warming hut before the coming ski season. Phase II would give Dave two more years to erect a chairlift and have it running by the winter of 1955-56. With renewed hope, Dave revisited his five most loyal supporters.

The next time Dave walked into Slim's Forest Service office, he carried a large manila envelope tucked under his arm. Without a word, he emptied the contents onto Slim's desk. Bills, change, and a series of checks, each written for $5,000, scattered across the tabletop. Dave stood back and watched as Slim read the names on the checks and added up the figures: Nora "Ma" Penney, Nick Gunter, Corty Hill, Carl Grebe, John Grebe (Carl's brother, now a renowned scientist with Dow Chemical Company), and devoted Mammoth skiers Les Burt and Sid Cooke (president of

Cummins Diesel). When Slim reached $25,000, he stopped counting. Slim looked up at Dave, smiled and said, "I do believe it's time you start building that warming hut you've been dreaming about. Let's get her up and running before the first snowfall." The two men exchanged a firm, robust handshake.

ON August 11, 1953, the U.S. Forest Service issued Dave McCoy a 25-year term permit for the further development and operation of the Mammoth Mountain Ski Area. Slim drove to the Long Valley Dam to offer Dave his personal congratulations. He knocked on the wood siding of the screen door, and Dave welcomed him inside. Roma was standing in the kitchen, leaning over a mixing bowl, wearing an apron over her six-month pregnant belly. In a casual voice, Slim said, "I'm glad to find you both at home. Roma, I thought you'd like to be the first person to hear that your husband is now the official developer of Mammoth Mountain Ski Area!"

Roma set the mixing bowl down and walked into the living room, her mouth opened in wonderment. She raised her fingertips to her lips, softly gasped, then whispered, "I knew it. I just knew it."

CHAPTER TWENTY-FOUR

Mammoth's Warming Hut

Mammoth Mountain Warming Hut.

In preparation for winter 1954, ski media tantalized skiers with ads for John Jay and Warren Miller ski films, offers to get in ski shape on a Bongo Board, and invitations to ride new chairlifts at Reno Ski Bowl and Edelweiss. There was also the lure of visiting Squaw Valley's new $75,000 lodge and riding Sugar Bowl's $250,000 Magic Carpet aerial tramway running between the train station and the lodge.

Southern California skiers talked about Kratka Ridge's single chairlift and Snow Summit's new Ski School Director, Doug Pfeifer, who would be teaching the parallel Emile Allais technique.[1] But the loudest preseason buzz was that Dave McCoy now held the permit to develop the north slopes of Mammoth Mountain.

Dave's reality was that his friends had loaned him $30,000 to build a two-story 30-foot by 60-foot, full-service warming hut, later known as

Main Lodge, and that he had promised the Forest Service to have the building operational by winter. September was upon him, days were getting shorter, and the pressure was on.

The warming hut plans called for the lower story to house a small ticket sales and administration office, rental and repair shop, first aid room, flush toilets, and a few employee bedrooms. The second floor would showcase a rock fireplace, spacious lobby, cafeteria, dining room, and sport shop. Generator-driven electricity would supply radiant heat to the floors and ceilings. Skiers entering from slopeside would walk up a steep wooden ramp and across a sundeck past the rock fireplace chimney featuring an arrow made of black rocks pointing down symbolizing, "This is the place to ski!"

FOR a water source, Dave accessed a spring about a quarter mile west of the building site, located high enough that gravity would flow water down to the building.[2] About halfway between the spring and the warming hut, he shoveled a hole to house a donated 20,000-gallon water tank he had refurbished with rivets and tar. He then buried 600 feet of pipe in a three-foot deep trench to connect the tank to both the spring and the building. According to his calculations, this water system would provide the warming hut with 7.5 gallons per minute.

Dave hired Lloyd Nicoll, owner of the local lumberyard, to be his building contractor. Together they formed the foundation based on stakes the Forest Service had placed in the ground to mark the approved location of the building. When local Forest Service representatives checked on progress, they saw that the foundation was some 30 feet closer to the ski hill than their stakes had marked, an "error" that shortened the ski slope's outrun but made a larger parking area. The rangers walked to where Dave was shoveling on the other side of the building. He put his shovel down and came over to inspect. With a mischievous twinkle in his eyes, he concluded, "Gosh, you're right about that." The rangers chuckled knowingly. They made no change orders, charged no penalty fees, and caused no delays.

Still having access to the DWP gravel pit, Dave and his friends frequently made evening aggregate runs. Though P-Nut was too young to go along, he paid close attention to what was happening, later recalling:

> *One night when I was on my way to bed, the men folk,*
> *most likely Redmon, Eddie Riley, and Autry, disap-*
> *peared in the dump trucks and went down to Toms*
> *Place where Dad had keys to get in the gravel pit. Those*
> *trucks weren't licensed to be on the highway and only*
> *had little lights in the front. As I heard the story, Mr.*
> *Sherry, the Highway Patrolman drove up, looked at*
> *the aggregate and the trucks, and said to Dad, "This*
> *doesn't look quite legal. You guys get back in the trucks*
> *and on the road. I'll tail you back to Mammoth and*
> *make sure no one notices."[3]*

Inspired by a building he had seen in Sun Valley, Dave constructed the lower story exterior out of brown-stained concrete that resembled rustic wood siding. On top of the second story, he built a flat roof so that he could eventually add a third floor. In the meantime, he believed the wind would sweep most of the snow off the roof and thus prevent the formation of dangerous icicles and ice dams. Leftover snow would melt to the center and be collected in drainpipes built within the interior construction.

WITH costs for constructing the Mammoth Warming Hut being over budget and his house overflowing with children, the time had come to make a change. Dave's youngest member of the family, newborn Randy Lewis McCoy, was sleeping in a crib next to Roma and Dave's bed. The five older children occupied the other bedroom.

No matter how much Dave loved working as a DWP hydrographer, he needed more time to meet the demands of being a family man and a ski area operator. On a pad of blue memo paper he composed a personal note to his longtime DWP supervisor George Lewis writing, "Well, I don't know just how to say this after 16 years of the best working relations I could hope for, but now I would like to apply for a one-year leave of absence to try my hand in my own business, which for so many years has been my hobby." Dave filled out the DWP *Request for a Leave of Absence,* folded the form and memo together in the shape of a diaper, closed the correspondence with a safety pin, and delivered it to the Bishop office. By the end of November 1953, DWP had granted Dave a leave, bought his fishing boats, and held a retirement dinner.

AFTER moving his family into the McGee Warming Hut, Dave devoted his energy to preparing his Mammoth Warming Hut for winter. He sawed trees into rounds, split and stacked the wood near the rock fireplace. Dave unloaded boxes of goggles, gloves, grippers, ski pants, sweaters, and jackets that he'd ordered for the sport shop. He inspected a shipment of Northland skis, put aside the best pairs for his racers, and designated the rest for rentals and retail.

Dave hired a local girl, Beth Kinney, to run the cafeteria and asked her to look into a hot dog machine that Eddie Riley had told him about, one that kept wieners warm while revolving around a roller system. Dave offered volunteer patrollers overnight accommodations sleeping on cots in the new first aid room and told Beth she could use one of the employee bedrooms downstairs. Beth's assistant, who went by the nickname "Swiss Freddie," and his St. Bernard, Queenie, moved into another downstairs bedroom, although Queenie spent most of her time sleeping in front of the fireplace with an adopted house cat purring on her head.

Over Thanksgiving vacation, the Warming Hut buzzed with excitement.[4] Since the weather was warm, guests didn't notice that the radiant floor heating system failed. However, after the vacationers went home, the air temperature dropped and the water line between the spring and the water tank froze, rendering Dave's water system useless. He located another water tank, which he secured to the flatbed on one of his trucks, then drove down to Rich Thompson's garage and used a garden hose to fill this "portable" water tank. Dave drove the filled tank back up Minaret Road to the Warming Hut and operated an electric pump to transport the water from his "portable" water tank up to the "buried" water tank. In order to keep the toilets flushing and the faucets running, Dave continued to make "water runs" throughout each day. Unaware of how close they had come to a water calamity, skiers deemed the new Warming Hut a smashing success.

CHAPTER TWENTY-FIVE

Roma: Living at McGee

From left: Kandi, Poncho, Punkin, Randy, P-Nut, Penny.

Leave it to me to go into labor with our sixth child while Gloria and I were washing dinner dishes at the Redmons' house down in Bishop, getting ready go to a movie. I whispered to Gloria, "Don't tell Dave because he'll make me go to the hospital." She kept my secret, but before we put the last dish away, my contractions were coming fast and furious. Dave rushed me to the hospital as fast as he could. We got there at 6:55 p.m. and 10 minutes later I gave birth to a beautiful, healthy, nine and a half pound not-so-little boy. We named Randy Lewis McCoy after George Lewis, who'd been teasing me that one of our kids should be his namesake.

Randy wasn't more than a few weeks old when Dave asked for a leave of absence from the DWP. I could hear the excitement in his voice as he told me, "We'll live in the McGee Warming Hut. I've already got Bob

Schotz separating the downstairs into bedrooms, building more kitchen cupboards, and closing off a laundry room and an extra bedroom upstairs for live-in help. That way, you'll be able to go to the races with me." So there you are. We were moving to McGee.

On a chilly November day, Dave and Eddie Riley, who was home from college, hauled our household goods and gads of ski equipment from Crowley to McGee. All I had to do was pack up six children and 12 years of memories. Oh my!

When the house was finally empty, and the men had driven off with our last boxes. I stepped back inside, alone. My footsteps echoed as I walked through the barren rooms. I swore I could hear the sound of my heart aching about leaving behind this chapter of my life. But what could I do? Standing at the back door, I whispered, "Thank you," as if I were saying goodbye to a dear friend. I let the screen door slam shut and walked down the steps.

When I arrived at our new home, Bob Schotz was installing a big black butane stove, his tools scattered around him, and Dave was standing on a ladder, stuffing newspapers into cracks in the wall for insulation. He already had a fire burning in the sunken fireplace and the oversized room was heating up. The kids were running around the house dashing upstairs and downstairs, chattering about how they could walk out the *back* door to ski and out the *front* door to catch the school bus. I laughed. I'd forgotten about the excitement of new beginnings.

Bob was an excellent helper. We arranged our couch, two rocking chairs, and a few tables around the rag rug I'd made, and together we measured the windows so I could sew curtains to match our ruffled lampshades. When he was ready to start upgrading the kitchen to meet our family's needs, I told him I'd like to have two ovens. He looked at me like I was crazy and told Dave about my request. Dave just smiled and said, "Bob, go ahead and give Roma whatever makes her happy. If she wants two ovens, put in two ovens."

WHEN we first moved in, Bob arrived early each morning and sat at the counter while I fixed him breakfast. After a while, I started making him lunch too, and eventually he was staying for dinner. Dave finally said, "Hey

Bob, why don't you just move into one of those downstairs bedrooms?" I think this was just the invitation he'd been hoping for.

Our life turned out to be just as fun at McGee as it had been at Crowley, except now we had more space for family and friends. It didn't take long for toys to be scattered across the floor and leather ski boots to be lined up drying by the fireplace. Our biggest problem was our water pump kept going haywire and we'd be out of water until Bob or Dave fixed the problem.

About the time Bob moved out, Dave invited his dad to move in. "Grandpa" had been in a terrible logging truck accident. The tie rod had broken, and the steering had locked, sending his truck crashing off a bank and into a tree. Grandpa survived but was hospitalized for three months with a broken neck and several broken vertebrae. Mac McCoy's logging days were over. He would no longer be the "Bull Buck of the Woods" as they called him in Quincy. But Dave, with his big, kind, generous heart, offered his dad a place to live and a full-time job operating the beginner tow at Mammoth.

Everybody loved Grandpa. He was such a playful, happy-go-lucky guy with his big barrel chest and shining eyes. It didn't take long for him to fall in love with the Eastern Sierra, then find a place of his own, and move his wife Grace and Dave's half-siblings Kathy and Bill down from Quincy. Grace's two older boys were already living on their own.

After Grandpa moved to his own place, our extra bedroom didn't stay vacant for long. One Friday night on his way to Mammoth, Nick stopped by to deliver some bookwork. It was snowing pretty hard, so we invited him to stay with us. I guess he had a lot of fun at our house that weekend, because Monday morning he called his accounting firm and told them he was snowed in at McGee and couldn't make it to work. The truth was, Nick preferred mountain life over city life. The next week he returned to L.A., quit his job, packed up his belongings, and never looked back.

After Nick moved in, Tom "T.J." Johnston started hanging around our house, entertaining us with his constant chatter, and eventually moving into one of the downstairs bunks.[1] T.J. had started skiing after the war when his surfing buddy, ski filmmaker Warren Miller, sold him a pair of Lund and Northland Army surplus skis for $5. Oh, I can just hear T.J.

Randy, Kandi, Poncho, Punkin, Penny, and P-Nut.

telling us, "That was when Warren had a head of hair!" Anyway, Nick and T.J. spent their evenings playing with the kids and bantering about what kind of pie I would bake for dessert.

My boys loved living at McGee, playing in the meadows behind the house, having rock throwing contests, making up cowboy and Indian adventures, and running and jumping along the irrigation ditches, catching fish with their hands. Punkin spent a lot of time taking care of a black horse named Lightning that he kept down the road at the old Fox Farm where Nyle and Ruth Smith now lived.

One thing that scared me at McGee was rattlesnakes and there were lots of those. Once, Dave found one asleep in a motor house. He hurried down to get the boys. When they opened the door, the rattler was coiled in a corner, shaking its rattle and hissing a terrifying warning. Dave told the boys to stay calm, move slowly away, and no matter what, never run.

A few days later, Poncho and P-Nut were walking down the road to buy candy at Lovejoy's Store when they found a bright blue glass bottle. They hid their treasure under a rock ledge to pick up on the way back. When they reached in to grab the bottle, they heard a rattle. They jumped backwards and ran all the way home. Dave was *not* pleased to hear they had done just the opposite of what he'd told them.

One day I was working inside but keeping my eye on Kandi who was playing on the porch. I heard Nick drive up and only seconds later, I saw him madly waving his arms. I stepped outside to see what he was carrying on about and my gut turned inside out. A rattlesnake was right where Kandi was playing. As quickly and quietly as I could, I scooped her into my arms and carried her inside before the snake even knew what was happening. Nick was a wreck. He was just as afraid of rattlesnakes as I was. From then on, I kept the door closed and the little ones inside unless I was right there with them.

DAVE was always teaching self-reliance skills to the children, especially the boys. He showed them how to cast a fly rod, where to fish, how to read moving streams, and how to figure out what the fish were eating. He taught them to make mental notes of landmarks they passed when they were hiking so they could find their way back to camp, how to build fires from bits of brush and kindling, and how to signal for help using smoke from burning green branches.

As soon as each boy was old enough for a hunting license, Dave sent him through hunter safety training and then gave each a gun of his own. They were eager to learn. They'd seen Dave down a quail on the fly with his .22, and they wanted to be able to shoot like he did.

Learning to hunt was a rite of passage for the boys, as well as an opportunity to be with their father. Dave taught them to use common sense and stay quiet while stalking wild game, to honor the ethic that any game killed was to be eaten, and to respect that no matter how many trips it took, how late in the day it was, or how tired they might be, they were to locate a downed animal, gut it, bring it home, and prepare it for eating or storage.

Early one morning when Punkin was still just 12, he hiked up the rope tow access road carrying his rifle. Near the top of Rope Tow Two, a couple of does leapt out of the high brush. Following his instinct, Punkin quietly reached for a couple of rocks and threw them at the bushes where the deer had appeared. Sure enough, a three-point buck bounded out. Punkin aimed his rifle and shot his first deer. He cleaned the buck just as his dad had taught him, then grabbed it by the horns, and dragged it down to the house. When Dave got home, he helped Punkin skin, hang, and butcher the meat. Talk about one happy kid, so proud to be supplying the family with meat.

After scoring that first buck, you couldn't stop Punkin from hunting. He even traded a pair of Stein Erikson skis for a shotgun. After school, he'd hunt along McGee Creek toward Crowley Lake, usually bringing home two or three ducks. Sometimes, I'd load all the kids in the car—by then we had a Pontiac station wagon—and drop Punkin off at North Landing where we kept a kayak. He'd paddle the shoreline toward the white chalk columns, hunting ducks or fishing, depending on the season, making sure he was back at our meeting spot at a given time. Whatever wild game he brought home, Punkin made sure to have the meat packaged inside our big freezer before going to bed.

In the winter, all our kids wanted to do was ski, even little four-year-old Penny. On nights before going skiing, she'd set out her red-and-white-striped long johns, her knickers, and her favorite dark glasses that had little plastic guns on the frame. With Dave's half-sister Aunt Kathy watching over her, Penny would ski on the beginner tow all morning. Meanwhile

Penny riding the beginner tow.

the boys raced around the upper slopes chasing the other junior racers.

Jill Kinmont moved in with us for the winter of 1954. Since all the downstairs bedrooms were occupied, she slept on a mattress in front of the fireplace. She didn't mind. She just loved being with our family, helping me do housework, baking chocolate chip cookies and chocolate cakes with sprinkles, feeding the little kids, making giant stacks of tuna or chopped olive and egg sandwiches for lunches. I think she glamorized my lifestyle. She imitated everything I did, even started talking like me.

Early each weekday, Jill would leave for Mammoth with Dave and spend the day running courses and free skiing with Dennis Osborn. They were both such good-natured kids and so dedicated to ski racing. They made perfect training partners.

On weekends, by the time I got the kids to Mammoth, Grandpa would already be snowshoeing up to the engine house of the beginner tow, carrying his knapsack with his lunch and two bottles of beer. Jill would ski a few runs before the crowds arrived and then help sell tickets. About 11 a.m., we'd eat a candy bar, tighten our ski boot laces, grab our parkas and dark glasses, and ski for an hour. Jill loved to follow right behind me and that made me feel good. I'd challenge her by making precise slow turns, then accelerating into wider radius giant slalom turns. After skiing, we'd sit on the sun deck, eating our sack lunches, the big rock fireplace chimney at our backs, our faces turned toward the sun.

I'd take Penny back home to McGee in the afternoons so I could start cooking dinner and Dave would ski with the racers until he shut down the tows. They'd either run gates or free ski in a serpentine line. Jill stayed right on Dave's tail as the others pushed for a spot somewhere in the lineup. Linda Meyers, a young Bishop High racer who was determined to follow in Jill's footsteps, always tried to ski right behind her, imitating her every movement.

BACK then, Jill couldn't stop talking about her crush on Dick Buek. She made me promise not to tell Dave what she was feeling, but Dave probably knew anyway. He had a sense for such things. And with all that had happened to Charlotte, he didn't want anything to hurt Jill or distract her from her personal goals.

Anyway, Dick almost died in a terrible motorcycle accident, injuring his spleen, head, and leg. He had something like 250 stitches in his body and was so weak he couldn't even raise his head. Jill couldn't get the accident out of her mind. I guess the doctors had told Dick he would never walk again, much less ski race. But Dick's attitude was, "Just wait and see!" By the next winter he was flying his airplane and ski racing, wearing a bent-knee leg cast he and his doctor had designed.[2]

Jill couldn't figure out her feelings. Dick's courage and confidence attracted her, but also scared her. "Ma," Jill would say to me. "You wouldn't believe how fast Dick skis, jumping off bumps so carefree and nonchalant, even though he walks lopsided and uses his ski poles as a crutch. He's such a daredevil, it's hard not to worry about him."

When Jill asked me for advice, I didn't know what to say. True, she was young and inexperienced, and Dick was older and unpredictable, but I remembered how people used to worry that Dave was too wild for me and am I ever glad I didn't listen to them.

Dick Buek and Jill.

CHAPTER TWENTY-SIX

Olympic Dreams

Jill, spring training at Mammoth.

D ave coached ski racers the same way he approached all aspects of his life. He wasn't a scholar or a trained coach, just a self-taught skier who trusted his judgment, used his intuition, and taught by example. To the racers, their coach was bigger than life, a man of "rugged individualism" who spoke in the simplest form without using too many words. He didn't push his racers but encouraged them to determine the seriousness of their own desires. In turn, they ignored any shortcomings they might have seen in him.[1]

In a sense, Dave didn't allow himself to really know others, but communicated on his own terms, intense, not frivolous. He lacked a desire to relate to people who weren't just dead serious about what they were doing. This was odd, because he also made everything the racers did so much fun. Jill later recalled that being one of Dave's racers was like being in the

299

middle of an exciting romantic era:

> *It was wonderful to feel that we were a good enough*
> *racer to stay with the McCoys. We felt special and*
> *the competitiveness was exhilarating. The family had*
> *magic about them, and it was exciting with all the kids*
> *around. Roma and Dave were always together, sitting*
> *beside each other or with their arms on each other's*
> *shoulders. We all felt welcome at the big dinners Roma*
> *made, eating all the home-baked cakes and pies, and we*
> *wanted to be like them.[2]*

To help his racers develop into well-rounded competitors, Dave coached his team to conquer every course, every slope, every situation. He purposely set courses on varied terrain and snow conditions, making some too fast, slow, steep, or flat. Some contained complicated combinations without rhythm, others had perfect rhythm.

To improve quickness, Dave set 20-gate flushes that forced the racers to make tight turns down the fall line while controlling their speed. To improve downhill racing skills, he shoveled snow into different sized bumps for the kids to practice pre-jumps—lifting their skis off the snow right before the lip of a bump, floating over the crest, and landing softly on the other side. If they flew in the air, he taught them to reach their hands toward their boots to regain stability before landing.

But always, no matter what drill the racers were doing, Dave set the tone: laughing, hollering, and having fun were the most important parts of each day.

In December, Dave hosted the first Far West point race of the season. Since little snow had fallen, he spent days shoveling snow onto the course. By race day, he was ready for the 60 senior racers and 125 juniors who had sent in entry forms.

The Mammoth racers—including Punkin, Poncho, and P-Nut—dominated the event, looking sharp in their slim-fitting black jackets with yellow stretch inserts.[3] In mid-January, Dave drove his Mammoth junior team to compete in the point race at Dodge Ridge and brought home 25 medals.[4] In Yosemite for the next point race, the team won 14 medals, followed by similar results at Edelweiss.[5] They won again at Big Bear, this time racing through "rain and sleet in a test of fortitude... [where] the youngsters carried pounds of water in their clothes and the parents shivered and dripped at their posts."[6]

After this run of success, five of Dave's racers—Bishop's Jill and Bobby Kinmont along with Lee Vining's John Murphey, Gus White, and Dickie Miller—qualified for the 1954 Junior Nationals, to be held at Jackson Hole, Wyoming. During the few weeks before the race, the boys were in school and Dennis Osborn was off competing on the senior circuit, so Jill trained alone. By the time the group left for the races in early March, she felt prepared to perform her best against the best junior racers in the country.

Dave invited Roma to accompany the team to Nationals. Nick encouraged her, saying, "It'll be good for you. T.J. and I can take care of the kids." So, Roma went along, traveling 750 miles with chains on the tires. Once in Jackson, while the kids were training on the mountain, Roma wandered through the western town with its wooden sidewalks and arcades. She admired the elkhorn arches that adorned the central square, and the big banners welcoming the competitors. During the opening ceremony parade and flag raising, she stood in the crowd of onlookers applauding the seven uniformed teams and the marching band.

Back at the motel, Dave transformed the garage into a wax room by setting up a table with wax pot and a traveling iron. He melted a concoction of cold weather waxes on each racer's skis, then painted their bases with overlapping layers. The athletes stood by, ready to scrape and cork their bases between layers.

The next morning, cold air, nervous energy, and a challenging course heightened everyone's senses as they inspected the downhill. Afterwards, Dave had his racers ski the course in sections to become familiar with the terrain and to gradually build up speed. When the time came to take their mandatory nonstop training runs, they were able to attack the entire course with confidence.

In the afternoons, Dave set a few gates on the slalom hill. When he noticed other coaches setting straight linear courses, as opposed to the rounder turns his team was accustomed to, he adjusted his course setting so his racers could practice going straighter at the gates.[7]

On the morning of the downhill race, competitors carried freshly waxed skis over their shoulders as they walked to the bottom of Jackson's Snow King chairlift. Along the way, the frozen snow crunched under their ski boots. Their breath condensed as they exhaled, adding to the anxiety of race day. Some racers nervously laughed and joked among their friends. Others focused inward. Dave called his team together at the base of the lift, and said, "Let's go have some fun skiing and get warmed up." Instantly, the mood lightened. Just the idea of skiing with friends diffused the tension.

At the start, Dave individualized his coaching to each racer, but gave everyone his same trademark wink, nod of the head, and a smile. Down at the finish line, dressed in her warmest jacket, gloves and hat, Roma clapped and cheered as each racer passed the last gate, all the while listening carefully to the announcer, Olympic medalist Andrea Mead Lawrence, who called out each racer's time over the loudspeaker.

By the end of the weekend, Dave's Far West team had won six of the 18 medals awarded. Jill won the girls' slalom and placed 2nd in both the downhill and combined. Bobby won the boys' slalom and placed 3rd in combined. Photos of the Kinmont siblings flashed across the sports sections of newspapers and reporters quoted Dave as saying, "I am exceedingly proud of the Far West team. In below zero weather they raced a rugged downhill course, many times flying into the air after hitting the bumps at better than 50 miles per hour."[8]

MEDALISTS at Junior Nationals automatically qualified to compete in Senior Nationals, that year scheduled for the following weekend in Aspen, Colorado. The *Inyo Register* reported, "For the first time in history, three skiers from Mammoth—Jill Kinmont, Kenny Lloyd, and Dennis Osborn—will clash with the nation's finest... funds are still needed to defray expenses... please send checks to..."

Since Kenny and Dennis were already training in Aspen, Jill rode to Colorado with friends traveling straight from Jackson. Roma and Dave drove Bobby, who was too young for a Senior Class A race card, back home to Bishop. Dave checked on his rope tows, refueled the station wagon, and picked up Jill's father Bill. Off the two men drove, heading across the desert to Colorado.

Before Jill hit the slopes in Aspen, her friend and fellow racer Barni Davenport warned her, "Jill, you won't believe the women. They're huge and strong and so good. We don't speak the same language."[9] Jill soon saw for herself. She freaked over how hard and steep the courses seemed, and not until Dave arrived and studied the downhill course with the team did she calm down. They discussed where to carve and where to let their skis run. Dave also pointed out that the terrain wasn't any steeper than the slopes they'd been training on at Mammoth. He equated the racing to their practices, always talking to them with confidence saying things like, "Just ski the way you ski."

In the greatest achievement of her career so far, Jill placed 3rd in the Senior Nationals downhill. Dick Buek, racing with his bent cast, won the men's race, earning the title of U.S. National Downhill Champion. In the afternoon, Dave and Jill sideslipped the slalom course and found the wind had blown the fresh snow off the top and exposed the hard surface beneath. He had to do something special with Jill's $35 Northland skis to make them hold on the slick, icy snow. As he recalled:

> I took Jill's bindings off her skis and used a skill saw to put a couple of grooves on the top of the skis to change the flex, kind of the way skis were later designed. Her skis had really thin edges, so I filed them differently than I would have done to heavier ones.

Jill's skis held perfectly. On her first run, she turned in the fastest time by three seconds. Before the second run, Dave told her, "Just make it pretty, Jill. Do it how you can do it."[10] She raced her second run with a good enough time to win the race and become, at age 18, the Senior National Slalom Champion and the first racer to win both the Junior and Senior National slalom titles in the same year.[11] Dave beamed with excitement. As Jill described, "I'd never seen him like that. He couldn't take this big grin off his face and his eyes were misty. He kept saying, 'I knew you could do it. That's just the way you ski.'"[12] Ski writers credited Dave McCoy, applauding him for spending a week in Aspen training his charges.

FOLLOWING the Aspen races, Jill, Dennis, and Kenny drove to Sun Valley to compete in the Harriman Cup. The Lloyds, Zumsteins, and Bishop High School racer, Linda Meyers, drove from Bishop to cheer on their friends. Dave headed back to Mammoth to take care of business.

Dennis tied for 9th in the Harriman downhill and did well enough in the slalom to place a respectable 8th in combined. Kenny finished 13th in slalom but crashed in the downhill, eliminating him from combined. Jill had the second fastest time in the first run of slalom but fell in the second slalom run and in the downhill. All the glory and success of her prior two weeks seemed to dissipate into Sun Valley's cold, thin air. Keenly aware that Dave was absent, Jill worried her success was dependent on his presence, encouragement, and advice.

The following weekend, Dave drove from Mammoth to Reno to coach his racers at the National Giant Slalom Championships. Dennis stunned officials with a 2nd place that beat out other Olympic hopefuls.[13] Jill placed 3rd. These results were an improvement, but they still weren't good enough for Jill. She had tasted winning and she wouldn't settle for less.

To wrap up the whirlwind month of racing, Dave and the California junior team traveled back to Sun Valley to compete in the Legions. Roma

Kenny Lloyd.

Dennis Osborn.

and 12-year-old Punkin came along. Dave wanted Punkin to experience a real downhill course, so he arranged for him to forerun. Roma argued that Punkin was too young for such a treacherous race course, but Dave was so confident in Punkin's ability and Punkin was so excited that she changed her mind and agreed.

Dick Buek was then living in Sun Valley, as were many of the top racers in the country. It didn't take long for him to seek Jill out and invite her to dinner. Jill enjoyed their meaningful conversation and respected his attitude about skiing. When he offered to prep her skis for the next day's downhill, Jill, unthinkingly, let him.

Preparing skis for his racers was Dave's domain. At races, he would work late into the night, filing edges, filling screw holes with wax, and painting shingle-like steps on the ski bases to break the suction and thus create more speed. That night, when he saw that someone else had prepared Jill's skis, a chill ran through him. The next morning, he asked Jill who had worked on her skis. She told him the truth, that she'd given them to Buek. Dave went silent. Drowning in guilt, Jill asked him, "Pa, could you go over my edges again?" Dave didn't answer. His silence and square jaw spoke of his disapproval and disappointment.[14]

By the time the team assembled at the start of the race, to Jill's relief, Dave was back to his positive self. When her turn to race came, he gave her his usual nod of encouragement and she pulled out of the start with confidence. Jill swept the field that weekend, winning the downhill, slalom, and combined. "All right! This is more like it," she thought. Her only letdown was that Bobby had fallen in both events.[15]

RETURNING home after a winter of travel, competition, and unprecedented success, Dave appreciated how his employees had kept the ski area running smoothly during his absence. However, he noticed a sadness in Roma. At first she claimed she was just tired, but before they closed their eyes that night, she confessed, "Honey, I missed you." For Dave, the time away had passed quickly, meeting new people, seeing new places, and enjoying new adventures. But he knew that for Roma, time at home without him was lonely. He silently vowed to give her the attention she deserved. But as he drifted off to sleep, he was thinking about drills he wanted to put his racers through while the spring snow lasted.

That season, Roma had watched Dave grow into his role as a respected coach. The April issue of *The Skier* acknowledged his coaching, saying that the Junior FWSA team had significantly benefited from some six weeks of intensive coaching at Jackson Hole, Aspen, Reno, and Sun Valley. Roma recognized her husband's dedication to the team, and she saw how racing had become an integral part of their family life.

THROUGH all the joy of spring skiing, Jill remained concerned that her race results were too inconsistent. One day on the mountain, she shared her worry with Dave. But he wasn't bothered. He told her all she needed was some competitive seasoning and a few more victories, and there was plenty of opportunity ahead for that. "Now, come on!" He said, "I'll race you down!"[16]

THAT evening after all the kids had gone to bed, Dave and Roma sat together on the couch. With logs crackling in the fireplace, Roma knitted while Dave glanced through the stack of ski magazines on the side table. He picked up a copy of *The Skier* and let his eyes linger admiringly on the cover photo of Jill edging past a slalom gate.

"Toots," Dave said, "If any of our Mammoth kids make the '56 Olympic Team, we're going to support them all the way to Cortina d'Ampezzo in whatever way we can."

Roma rested her knitting on her lap. "So, besides building a chairlift, what else do you have on your mind?"

"You and me, taking a trip to Italy," he grinned.

CHAPTER TWENTY-SEVEN

Summer 1954

Dave, clearing ski runs.

B y accepting the Forest Service permit to develop Mammoth, Dave
agreed to have a chairlift operating in November 1954. However,
as summer approached, he had neither lined up a chairlift nor
located the financing to build one.[1] To make matters worse, even though
Nick had helped with bookkeeping, Dave's miscellaneous business affairs
were a mess. His Forest Service permit stipulated that he pay the agency
1.5 percent of gross sales and provide an adequate set of books to verify
his accounting. However, Dave still hadn't submitted his 1952-53 gross
statement for his rope tow permit, nor had he provided the cash register
receipts to support his 1953-54 report of over $10,000 total sales for the
cafeteria and $1,300 for the ski school.

Dave had also been dragging his feet about the Forest Service requirement to form a corporation. If he had to incorporate, which ran against

his intuition, he at least wanted to find an attorney who would ensure he retained the value of existing improvements and kept controlling interest in the ski area. As of yet, with only one month remaining to meet the Forest Service deadline, no such attorney had materialized.

As one more act of negligence, Dave hadn't complied with "clause 23" of his permit, which stated that "under no circumstances shall any tow be allowed to operate unattended." District Ranger Barney Sweat had admonished Dave in a written memo dated February 26, 1954:

> *On Saturday, I found the safety gate so poorly set that if a skier were to be dragged through it, the gate had a 50-50 chance of not working… about 30 "Ski Bunnies" [beginners] had been exposed unknowingly to the possibility of a pretty disagreeable accident or death. I understand why the "Bunny Tow" was ignored in the past, but this many Bunnies should be considered a good omen of what is to come. I do not want an accident to occur due to negligence.*

When Supervisor Slim Davis reprimanded Dave about these pending matters, Dave knew he needed to rise to the occasion. He also knew he wasn't going to be shuffling papers. There was too much to do managing the tows and coaching the racers. As a solution, Dave asked Nick to take complete charge of the ski area paperwork. In exchange for his services, Nick could have free room and board in the new Warming Hut. "Sounds pretty good to me," Nick responded nonchalantly. "As long as I can ski during my lunch break." Dave called Slim and gave his word that from then on, his bookkeeping would be in perfect order. Then he walked outside where he wanted to be and went to work doing what he wanted to do, while Nick made a list of supplies necessary to set up a business office.

Always needing to increase his cash flow, Dave took on whatever side jobs he came across. That spring of 1954, after local residents pooled their money to bring electricity to Mammoth, Dave contracted to clear trees along the proposed pole line from Highway 395 to town. He felled the towering trees with his "*XXX* chainsaw" while 13-year-old Punkin followed a distance behind clearing slash under the supervision of Bob Bumbaugh, a newcomer to town.

Bumbaugh had arrived in Mammoth from Southern California in early May. Between jobs and recovering from a divorce, his intention was to spend a week skiing in the mornings, fishing in the afternoons, and sleeping in his convertible at night. Within days, he knew everyone in town. Bumbaugh liked that feeling, so he extended his stay.

Already aware of Dave's reputation, Bumbaugh approached him, mentioned his background as a machinist, and asked if he could work in exchange for rope tow tickets. Dave replied with a smile. "See me in the morning and we'll go from there." Bumbaugh spent the next day shoveling bumps out of the towline and carrying fuel to the rope tow engines. Within a few weeks, he was working side by side with Dave, morning to night, hauling portable rope tows to the uppermost slopes of Mammoth for his Memorial Day Race. After the race, Bumbaugh drove south, picked up his belongings, and moved to Mammoth.

That summer of 1954, Dave improved the Mammoth Warming Hut by refurbishing the water system, installing a permanent railing around the sun deck, closing off the area beneath the deck where he'd been storing firewood, and remodeling that space into rooms for employees to live. He also expanded the ski repair, rental, and merchandise shops. Finally, he tore down the old Snake Pit and concession stand, cleared a new trail east of Bowling Alley, and paved the parking area.[2]

With Nick's guidance, Dave purchased two used bulldozers—a D4 CAT and a TD International 14—and secured a $12,000 loan to buy a new Ford Tractor skip loader. "Puff," as Dave called the skip loader, was the first piece of *new* heavy equipment Dave had ever purchased. Word about the dozers and Puff spread quickly and residents started calling on Dave for favors. Guinn Davison asked him to grade what he called Davison Road, a steep access from Lake Mary Road to the top of his property. Neither Dave nor Bumbaugh had ever sat in a dozer before, so they made a quick decision about who was to do what: Dave would direct while Bumbaugh drove. In return for grading, Guinn gave Dave nine lots of land.[3]

To fine-tune the slopes of Lower Broadway, Dave had "master blaster" Eddie Riley dynamite a gigantic rock that sat in the middle of the ski run, then bull-dozed the smaller pieces of rock into an erosion gully. One day while working near the bottom of Broadway, the weighty swing of a large tree stump flipped the A-Frame onto its side. Just then, a man approached. Dave asked him to wait a minute. Once Puff righted the A-Frame, Dave turned to the man, who didn't seem fazed at all about the incident, and asked, "What can I do for you?" The man said he was an insurance agent and handed Dave a policy. As Dave described, "I sat down in the dirt and signed my name. It didn't cost me too much, but the agent was recognized for a million-dollar sale and got a trip around the world."

ONE summer day in 1954, a stranger walked into Dave's small business office in the Warming Hut, introduced himself as Walter Martignoni, and announced, "I have a chairlift for you to buy."

Dave looked at Martignoni with surprise. Could this be for real? Just as the Forest Service had granted him an extra year to install a chairlift, here appeared a man who had one for sale.

Martignoni owned United Tramway Engineers, a ship salvaging company in San Francisco that also built tramways for mines. Partially due to a personal interest in skiing, Martignoni had recently signed contracts to build three chairlifts, one at Snow Summit in the San Bernardino Mountains, and two at Sierra Summit, near Boreal Ridge. However, financial difficulties had forced Sierra Summit to reduce its order from two to one. Suddenly, by default, Martignoni had an extra chairlift for sale. Therein was his plan.

"Walter," Dave said, "I don't have the necessary financing."

Martignoni didn't flinch. He told Dave he would carry the finances with a payment plan that wouldn't begin until after the chair was up and running. Dave resisted. He didn't even have money to make payroll during installation. Martignoni stood his ground. He would advance money for labor as well as materials. On a handshake, the two men closed the deal.

Two weeks later, a distraught Martignoni returned to Dave's office. Neither Snow Summit nor Sierra Summit had come through with their promised payments, forcing Martignoni to declare bankruptcy. He would have to back out of the Mammoth deal.

This time, it was Dave who didn't falter. He looked Martignoni straight in the eye and said, "Walter, you made a promise."

For the next few minutes the men stood in silence. Walter spoke first. "You're right," he said, "A deal's a deal." The men shook hands again. By mid-August, the two had signed an 11-page contract stating that United Tramway would finance the estimated $95,000 chairlift cost.[4] Construction would begin as soon as the snow melted off the slopes the following spring.[5]

AFTER Walter Martignoni's timely entrance, good fortune seemed to rain on Dave. Foremost, he found an attorney who convinced the Forest Service to rescind its incorporation requirement and to allow him to continue as the sole proprietor of Mammoth Mountain Ski Area.

Next, Clyde Pearson, foreman of the Mono County Highway Department, indicated that its Blade-Grader snowplow and two County Sno-Gos, along with McCoy's personal Sno-Go, could keep the 4.3 miles of newly paved Minaret Road open to the Warming Hut, no matter the snow depth. Then he added, "That is, within reason." Pearson also stated that during holiday periods he would clear enough snow from the newly paved parking area to accommodate 400 vehicles, and he would plow a half mile of an extra wide lane on Minaret Road for another 100.[6]

THANKSGIVING Day 1954, Dave watched happily as car after car came up Minaret Road to the cleared parking area. Skiers carried their gear to the bottom of Broadway and stuck their poles into the snow and their skis through the pole straps, the bases facing the sun. Those who walked up the wooden ramp to enter the Warming Hut passed the rock chimney on their way into the second floor. There, Beth Kinney stood behind the counter selling coffee, pancakes and fried eggs, while Queenie the St. Bernard snoozed in front of the fireplace, her friend, the cat, asleep on her head.

Downstairs in the rental shop, Howard Cooper fitted skis and boots. In the first aid room, Mark Zumstein gave instructions to his volunteer patrol. Toni Milici scampered around outside organizing ski school students. Grandpa McCoy took charge of the Bunny tow while Dave, Don Redmon, Eddie Riley, and Bob Bumbaugh hiked to the top of Number One and Number Two tows to get them going. The ski team boys sidestepped up the rope tow lines to make sure they were in good shape. The race team girls helped Roma, Gloria Redmon, Norma Milici, and Ethel Zumstein with ticket sales, while Nick Gunter made the rounds to see that employees were properly tracking receipts.

Throughout the day, the junior ski racers scooted up the rope tows and chased each other down the slopes, taking time to help Dave whenever he asked. In the afternoon, he set a course off to the side of Broadway. As he watched the racers ski, he gave them each bits of advice, but mostly, seeing how well they were performing and how much fun the skiers were having on his slopes, he just smiled.

Punkin running slalom.

CHAPTER TWENTY-EIGHT

Jill

Jill on the cover of Sports Illustrated.

I n early December 1954, Dave's race team competed in a Far West sanctioned point meet held at Mammoth. Kenny Lloyd came home from the University of Nevada in Reno to race and ended up tying for 1st in the downhill with Dennis Osborn.[1] Jill crashed in both the downhill and the slalom. Falling in the first two races of the season shook her confidence, but Dave encouraged her, "You're skiing really well. All you have to do is concentrate on what you're doing right, which is plenty. Now, let's see how straight a line you can take on this 20-gate flush I've set!" Dave's positive mindset lifted Jill's spirits. As soon as she shot by the first gate of the flush, she felt her confidence returning.

As hopefuls for the 1956 Olympic team, Jill and Bobby Kinmont received invitations from the National Ski Association (NSA) to attend a three-week training camp at Sun Valley, Idaho, beginning the week before

Christmas. Dennis Osborn was also invited, but why Kenny Lloyd and Charlotte Zumstein weren't was a mystery.[2]

During the week leading up to the Sun Valley camp, Dennis, Jill, and sometimes Charlotte, who was now married and living in Bishop, skied and ran courses together. Still in high school, Bobby could only day-dream about how much he wanted to be training with the others. On the afternoon before their departure for Sun Valley, the three older racers climbed with Dave to the top of Mammoth Mountain, then wove in and out of each other's turns as they descended to the Warming Hut. Out of breath and exhilarated after dropping from 11,000 feet to 9,000 feet, carving turns the entire way, they came to a stop and leaned on their ski poles. Dave laughed, looked at his racers, and teasingly delivered one of his favorite sayings. "We just might learn to ski if we keep having fun like this!"[3]

Jill thought to herself, "If I can hold on to how good I feel right now, I'll do fine in Idaho!"

THE first day in Sun Valley, Buddy and Skeeter Werner, a talented broth-er-sister team from Steamboat, Colorado, befriended the Kinmont siblings. Almost immediately, a romance sparked between Buddy and Jill. Before long they were skiing together, eating meals at the same table, going to chalk-talks with each other, and sitting side by side riding the shuttle bus from the Sun Valley Inn to Baldy Mountain. In the evenings, Jill watched as Buddy prepared their skis in the wax room at the Challenger Inn.[4]

Self-assured about her skiing and joyful in her growing feelings for Buddy, Jill exuded happiness. She admired how Buddy balanced his seri-ousness about racing with his pure joy for skiing and his lust for life, just as Dave did. Jill was sure Dave would approve of their relationship, partly because of how humble Buddy was. Only through other sources had she learned he was the first American to win the famed downhill in Norway's Holmenkollen Ski Festival, and as such was considered one of the best skiers in the world.

PHOTOGRAPHERS from *Sports Illustrated* and *Time,* who were covering the training camp, caught wind of the "Jill and Buddy" romance and began

Buddy and Jill skiing at Sun Valley, 1954.

chasing them around, clicking their camera shutters everywhere they went. The lack of privacy became maddening. To add to Jill's growing anxiety, two days before Christmas, Dick Buek arrived in Sun Valley on leave from the Army. Jill felt awkward and unsure of her feelings. She continued to spend most of her time with Buddy, but in the afternoons, she'd walk with Dick over to Ed "Scotty" Scott's shop and talk ski equipment. At times she felt people might wrongfully be thinking she was more interested in boyfriends than in the Olympic team.

Jill's mind struggled with indecision about Buddy and Dick. She felt comfortable and confident with Dick, but with Buddy she shared goals and likes and dislikes. Dick was excitingly wild and restless while Buddy was good-hearted and wholesome.[5] Jill wished she could discuss her conflicted emotions with Roma, even though she knew what Roma would say, "Just push those boys out of your head, both of them, and don't let anything get in the way of your dreams. Boyfriends will fall into place in time."

DURING the training camp, the coaches were talking about a new up and down technique. Jill ignored them. "Now, of all times," she thought, "just a

315

month before the most important racing season of my life, I don't want to change my skiing style." But still, she tried to please the coaches, and her skiing began to fall apart. Instead of accelerating out of the gates like she usually did, her timing was off, and she was skidding through the low line. She had lost her natural flow.

Jill started to dread the daylight hours on the mountain. All she could think about was that something bad had happened to her skiing. She couldn't wait to get back to Mammoth and the positivity of Dave's coaching. The Alta Snow Cup, a giant slalom qualifying race for the Olympic tryouts, was only one month away and Jill had set her sights on winning this end-of-January competition. She wanted to go home where she knew Dave would get her back on track.

Back at Mammoth, Dave told Jill to ski just for the sake of skiing. So, she did. Skiing without worrying about technique, having a blast with Dennis and Charlotte, Jill regained her composure and confidence. Whether free skiing, running slalom courses, or practicing pre-jumps and floating weightless through the air, she felt great. In her words, she had renewed her friendship with the mountain.

Jill's experience at the Sun Valley Christmas camp had taught her how easy it was to get off track and she didn't want that to ever happen again. When *Life* magazine featured her in a multi-page article about Olympic hopefuls, she ignored the hype and stayed focused on her training. It did trouble her that whenever she mentioned Buddy or Dick's names, Dave didn't say much in response. Roma reminded her, "Dave is your friend, but also, he's your coach. As long as your goal is to make the Olympic Squad, he doesn't want anything or anyone to get in your way, certainly not boyfriends or publicity."

Meanwhile, travel plans to the Alta Snow Cup took shape. Bobby planned on skipping the race so he could take an important high school exam. He would travel with his parents and his younger brother Jerry to a junior competition at Kratka Ridge. Roma decided to stay home, leaving more room in the packed station wagon for Dave and his protégés.

ARRIVING at Alta, a short drive from Salt Lake City, the Mammoth team was awestruck by the beauty of everything around them: the Wasatch

Range, Little Cottonwood Canyon, the historic Peruvian Lodge at the
base of the chairlift, and the inviting ski slopes above. The racers carried
their gear to their rooms, met for lunch, and then, as a group, hustled out
to explore the mountain and loosen up their travel legs.

The next morning, the entire field of racers gathered on top of the
giant slalom for inspection. Right out of the start, a tight steep section
widened into a series of fast open turns. About two thirds of the way
down, there was a sharp bump just before a U-shaped gully called the
Corkscrew, and then a short plateau leading toward the finish. Overall, the
course looked fun, but everyone agreed the most challenging part was the
bump at the top of the Corkscrew. It would be impossible to not catch air.
Dave showed his team that all they needed to do was control their speed
coming into the bump, just as they had practiced at home.[6] Standing on
top of the bump, Jill overheard Andy Lawrence say the race would be won
or lost at this point.

Giant slalom rules in the 1950s allowed racers to "shadow" the course
during inspection, essentially ski the turns with speed alongside the gates,
but not through them. When Jill was shadowing, she let her skis run as she
approached the Corkscrew, made a quick speed check before the lip, and
went over the bump with her skis parallel. Caught off-guard by her speed,
her knees slammed against her chest before she launched about 15 feet in
the air. But just as she had done so many times back home in Mammoth,
she reached for her boots, stayed in balance, and landed without a problem.

Carrying her skis over her shoulder as she walked back to the lodge,
Jill wondered if she really needed to check her speed before the Corkscrew.
She decided she would study conditions in the morning and then make a
decision about what to do.[7]

THAT evening, Buddy invited Jill to dinner with a group of his friends.
Someone brought along the latest edition of *Sports Illustrated*, which had
just hit the newsstands. The cover featured a portrait of Jill holding her
skis and wearing Skeeter Werner's yellow sweater. Jill's closed lips lent
a seriousness to her expression, softened only by strands of blond hair
falling across her forehead.[8] She thumbed through the magazine, and the
photographs brought back the magic of being with Buddy. Then suddenly,

doubt crept into her mind. Could she live up to the praises written about her? The memory of Dave's words echoed in her mind, "We've never cared much for publicity. We'd rather earn it first."[9]

That night, Jill returned to her room later than planned but fell asleep quickly and slept soundly. In the morning, she awoke happy, energetic, and ready to race. Her only sign of nervousness was a lack of appetite. On the warm-up run with Dave and the team, she saw that the snow was firm enough to ensure that ruts would be minimal, but soft enough for her skis to hold. The wax Dave had applied the night before ran perfectly. Her legs felt limber and light, yet strong and quick. Being accustomed to wind at Mammoth, the windy morning didn't bother her at all. Inspecting the course, she gave careful attention to the bump before the Corkscrew, the spot where she could separate herself from the field. She decided to go straight into it, but, she didn't mention her decision to Dave.

Andy Lawrence was to be the first racer down the course, however, after her final inspection, she got stuck in a long lift line and the lift operator wouldn't let her move to the front. The referee on top finally had to start the race without her. When Andy at last arrived, she was told she would run last.[10]

Wearing bib number three, Charlotte planned on skiing conservatively. She feared the bump at the entrance to the Corkscrew. Just before she slid into the starting gate, Dave scraped the snow off the tops of her skis, gave her a big smile with his usual, "Have fun!" Jill called out, "Go for it, Char!" Charlotte skied smoothly and cautiously, just as she had planned. At the finish, she skied directly over to the chairlift and made it to the top in time to wish Jill good luck and ski down to the Corkscrew to watch.

Waiting her turn, Jill felt as if she owned the world. She wasn't anxious, just ready. Dave had told her to make it smooth and pretty, of course, adding, "Have fun!" If he felt any anxiety, he didn't show it. Like Jill, he felt sure she would qualify for the Olympic trials, and she had a good chance of winning. Just before the countdown, Jill glanced over at Dave. He smiled and nodded his head.

At the word, "Go," Jill skated out of the start, setting up for the top section of the course with total concentration. Nothing else in the world existed but the gates in front of her. The snow was faster than the previous day, but she felt solid on her skis and negotiated the first two turns with ease. She misjudged the next turn, went too straight and slid low. Reacting quickly, she cut back onto her chosen line and settled into a rhythm.

Nearing the Corkscrew, Jill let her skis run parallel and headed straight toward the bump without checking her speed, exactly as she had decided to do during inspection that morning. But, just before the lip, she realized she was traveling *much* faster than she had anticipated. There was no time to slow down. She missed the timing of her pre-jump by a fraction of a second, a mistake that sent her flying farther and higher than she had ever experienced:

> *I was in the air heading toward the trees. I used my body to try and adjust the direction but got off balance. When I hit the ground, I started flipping head over heels down the gully and got tangled up with a spectator. When I finally stopped, I couldn't feel anything. I thought my arm had broken off. I told someone to sit me up so I could watch Andy, but no one would move me. Then I saw Charlotte and Sally Neidlinger, and then there was the ski patrol and a cardboard collar supporting my neck and the ambulance. I remember so clearly, I wanted Dave and Andy to be with me.*[11]

Charlotte witnessed Jill's crash. She skied immediately to her side, put her face close to Jill's, and lightly touched her cheek. Their eyes met. "What's the matter with my legs, Char? I can't feel anything, not even the snow." Then Jill's voice turned to a desperate whisper. "Please," she pleaded, "Don't tell my parents." Charlotte told her not to move.[12]

Sally Neidlinger, an East Coast racer, skied over, took off her parka, and slid it under Jill's head. Dick Movitz, a member of the 1952 U.S. Olympic team and a National Ski Patroller, knew immediately that Jill's lack of feeling indicated her condition was critical. He held her head stable while he waited for more patrollers to arrive. Together they placed Jill in traction and delicately transferred her into a toboggan.

On top of the course, when the news that Jill Kinmont had fallen crackled over the radio, Dave strapped on his skis and sped down to the Corkscrew, arriving just in time to help stabilize the toboggan and assist with the arduous task of inching Jill down the mountain. Blinded in disbelief, in shock, and worried, Dave's heart pounded.

Though Jill didn't outright cry, she could feel tears flowing down her cheeks. "At least," she thought to herself. "I have feeling in my face." She wanted to wipe the tears away, but her arms didn't seem to exist. Gripped in fear, she closed her eyes and prayed she would wake from this terrible nightmare and be fine. But when she opened her eyes, all she could see was white clouds floating across the sky. She was still flat on her back in a toboggan unable to move. She couldn't even feel the bumps and roughness of the ride.

Was this it? Was her life over? Would the loss of feeling creep up through her head? Jill concentrated on the sound of the toboggan moving across the snow as if the noise might bring the feeling back to her arms, legs, and back. She pleaded with herself, "Don't cry, Jill, don't cry."

After finishing her run, Andy searched for Dave and found him in the parking lot standing alongside Jill's toboggan, waiting for the ambulance. Jill smiled at Andy and asked who won. Andy said she had, that Charlotte was 4th, and that Jill's time had been estimated 10 seconds ahead of the field before she fell. Jill hesitated, then asked Andy to ride in the ambulance with her and Dave.[13]

On the way to Salt Lake City, the ambulance crept down the narrow road of Little Cottonwood Canyon, held back behind a line of skiers driving home. Rather than discussing Jill's terrifying condition, Dave, Andy, and Jill made small talk, mostly about the race. No one knew what to say. Nothing could ease their fear for Jill's life.

Not being able to see the expression on Dave's face, Jill clung to the sound of his voice. The reality was, he felt as if his heart was being squeezed into a small box. His face had turned square and his body tense as he relived the last few days, searching for something he could have done differently that would have prevented this accident.

Andy struggled silently with her own fear that on some level, her presence had contributed to Jill's accident. If she, Andrea Mead Lawrence, Olympic gold medalist, hadn't been in the race, Jill might not have pushed so hard or taken so much risk.[14]

Jill kept asking herself over and over why she hadn't followed Dave's advice and checked her speed before the bump as she had in the shadow run? Couldn't she rewind the tape and be back in the starting gate?

At the hospital, the doctors diagnosed that Jill's fourth, fifth, and sixth cervical vertebrae had been crushed.[15] She was able to turn her head and shrug her shoulders, her biceps still functioned, and she had a minor muscle reaction under her arms and on the tips of her lips. She was otherwise paralyzed from her shoulders down and would most likely never gain back the feeling she'd lost. That was it. With surgery, there was a slight possibility of a different prognosis, but the outlook looked dim.

Since Jill was underage, the doctors couldn't legally give her medical attention without her parents' permission. But the Kinmonts could not be reached. They were with their two boys at the junior race at Kratka Ridge where there was no telephone service. Outraged, Dave grabbed the *Sports Illustrated* sitting on the waiting room table and waved the magazine in the air. His voice thundered through the room, "Are you going to let this girl go without even doing something?"[16] Jill later remarked:

> *Dave made them help me. When he means business, he means business. I remember them cutting into my ski pants to take my clothes off. I think I was going in and out of consciousness, but I was awake when they took me into surgery. They gave me a local anesthetic to drill the holes in my head for the tongs. I heard the knife as it cut into my back and could feel warm blood dripping down my neck and onto my collarbone. I couldn't feel anything else in my body.*[17]

During the four-hour emergency operation, the surgeon painstakingly removed pieces of fractured bone that were pressing against Jill's spinal cord, trying not to cause more injury. Jill remained conscious the entire time. She was afraid if she went to sleep she would never wake up.

Meanwhile, June Kinmont had heard about Jill's accident via a radio call to Kratka Ridge. Worried over her husband's heart condition, she decided not to tell Bill the severity of Jill's condition until they had driven off the mountain to a lower elevation. Once they arrived at the Pasadena home of their ski racing friends, the Davenports, June gathered her family together, told them what had happened, and made plans for Bill and her to depart for Salt Lake City. The boys would stay with the Davenports. That night, Jerry crawled into a dark corner of the dining room and didn't stop crying until sleep overcame him. Bobby fumed in anger. How could this be?

When the Kinmonts arrived at the hospital, Jill was still in surgery and Dave was crouching against a wall near the swinging doors to the operating room, taking a break from hours of pacing the hospital halls. The staff finally wheeled Jill out of surgery, and Dave stood up. He leaned over the gurney, so he could have eye contact with her. In a faint voice, she murmured "Hi" and Dave smiled at her with every bit of tenderness he had. He told her that her parents were right down the hall. She whispered, "Hi Mom, Hi Dad," and then drifted off.[18]

MONDAY morning, Jill awoke to her new reality. Steel tongs had been attached to her skull to prevent her from moving her head. The rest of her body was stretched lengthwise down a Stryker Frame.[19] Her ski clothes had disappeared. A white sheet rested across her skin, leaving her shoulders bare. She lay on her back, hooked up to numerous tubes. An oxygen machine waited in readiness at her bedside. After Jill had spent two hours facing the ceiling, her nurse attendants rotated the Stryker Frame 180 degrees so that she faced the floor for the next two hours. This would be her schedule for the foreseeable future. The only way she could see the faces of people talking to her was if they leaned far over the bed when she was facing up, or flat on the floor beneath her when she was facing down.

By evening, Jill's head hurt where the tongs were rigidly attached. Dave, June, and Bill stayed by her side through the night, taking turns trying to relieve the pressure of the tongs by supporting her forehead with their hands when she was facing down, and holding the back of her head when she faced the ceiling. Just before dawn, less than 48 hours since Jill had pulled out of the starting gate at Alta, Dave left the hospital to drive back to Bishop, pick up Roma and Bobby, and drive back to Salt Lake.[20]

WHEN Jill's accident hit the national news, America's ski world went into shock. The idea of their young, beautiful athlete Jill Kinmont unable to move a muscle, triggered a silent scream of denial. Letters, telegrams, flowers, donations, and phone calls flooded the hospital. The *Inyo Register* reported that Inyo and Mono County residents were "rocked more severely than they had been by almost any other tragedy in recent years."

When Dick Buek heard the news, he was in the service in Germany. He called the hospital for details, then tried everything he could to get back to the States. He even lied to the Red Cross, telling them that his fiancé was dying. No luck.

Meanwhile, conflicting rumors flew around. One report claimed the wind had increased Jill's speed so much that she flew out of control, landed on her back, and then bounced forward, somersaulting down the slope, striking trees, and hitting a bystander so hard that the man suffered broken ribs. Another report said she'd hit one knoll, launched high in the air, and landed on another knoll, out of control and crashing into the ground. Some said that knee-deep powder snow caused the fall. Jill acknowledged pieces of truth in each description but insisted that the crash was the result of her misjudgment alone and could not be blamed on the course or the weather.

Reports about Jill's prognosis were likewise contradictory. Most newspapers claimed Jill was bouncing back and regaining feeling throughout her body at a rate of about an inch a day. This was the story people wanted to believe, that "their" Jill *would* heal, that she *would* walk again, that she *would* ski again. They could not accept the sobering truth that she was now facing.

During the long hours Jill lay stretched out in the Salt Lake City hospital, she learned that her body was like a lamp with a damaged electrical cord unable to produce light. Her mind was as sharp as ever, her internal organs, while compromised, still functioned. The only muscles with which her brain could still communicate were those above her armpits. The amount of independence she might eventually gain depended on how much she could strengthen her few responsive muscles. With hard work and the assistance of a few mechanical tools, she might learn to feed herself, comb her hair, brush her teeth, and maneuver an electric wheelchair.

THE only people Jill shared her fears and disappointment with were those closest to her, especially her mother. That was, until a group of the girl racers called her from Stowe, Vermont. A nurse held the phone to Jill's ear. At the sound of Skeeter Werner's voice, Jill had to fight away tears. She could hardly speak. She wanted to be smelling the sharp winter air, laughing with her friends, hearing the starter's countdown, and racing in the trials.

When the nurse retrieved the phone, Jill broke down. She cried for the first time since the accident. She cried because she wasn't going to the Olympics. She cried because she wasn't going to be skiing on Mammoth Mountain next month in the toasty sun and corn snow. She cried because she wasn't going to be skiing again. Ever.[21]

Alone in her hospital room, Jill's tears gradually subsided. She slowly calmed down, even though her heart still ached. Her mind clung to treasured sensations, especially the smooth graceful feeling of gliding over snow on skis, a feeling she would never experience again. She wondered how she could face the life that lay ahead of her.

Jill thought of her family, how brave and loving they were. In spite of the sadness they must feel and the challenges the accident brought them, they didn't complain. Jill needed to be strong for their sake. But how?

Then, the strangest thing happened. Jill thought she heard the voices of Dave, Andy, and Dick, as clearly as if they were standing by her bed. Each voice, with its own distinct tone of love and command, was telling her the same thing, "Okay Jill, you've had your cry. Now pick yourself up and get on with it." Jill let the voices resonate within her. With strength she didn't even realize she had, she willed herself into a Zen-like state of being and let her memory of skiing float through her mind as she repeated to herself, "Let it go, Jill. Let it go…"[22]

CHAPTER TWENTY-NINE

Roma: Resilience

Jill, leaving the hospital.

I refused to accept what the doctors were telling us about Jill. As far as I was concerned, my friend would be walking again, skiing again, and no one was going to convince me otherwise. I can only imagine what Dave was going through. Of course, he didn't talk about his feelings, just struggled in silence, moving around with a heaviness I'd never seen. Even the kids, the older ones especially, felt the strain and sadness of our loss, but at least they would ask questions about Jill and I could explain to them what was going on. One thing for sure, none of us could shake off our grief.

It turned out that Dennis, Kenny, Bobby, and Charlotte all qualified to compete in the Olympic tryouts that were to take place on the East Coast. Bill Kinmont drove the teammates home to Bishop and then back to Salt Lake so they could visit Jill before taking the train to New Hampshire. Of course, Jill mustered up her biggest smile, wished everybody good racing, and lent Char her good luck sweater. Then off they went, trying their best to get their spirits up.

On the train ride back east, Dennis started feeling under the weather. By the time he got to New Hampshire, his fever had skyrocketed, and his joints were aching. He had no energy to do anything but check into a hospital. The doctors diagnosed rheumatic fever and confined him to a hospital bed for two weeks. There went Dennis's Olympic dreams. All his hard work blew up in smoke, just like that.[1]

Bobby was so upset about Jill that he couldn't focus. At the Cannon Mountain race in New Hampshire, he accidentally kicked over his wax pot. Then, so I heard, Bobby stared at the mess in a daze as if he didn't know what to do next. He fell in the downhill, fell in the slalom, and missed a gate in the giant slalom, which was so unlike him. I bet he would have given up right then and there if it hadn't had been for Dick Buek. Dick had gotten leave from the Army to compete in the tryouts. When he saw what was going on with Bobby, he took the young man under his wing, studied the course with him, directed him to ski behind him in the training runs, and plain ol' gave him encouragement.

But still, things didn't go right. At the races in Stowe, Vermont, Bobby was the eighth American to finish in the giant slalom. He broke a toe-plate in the slalom and broke a ski in a downhill training run. On race day, a thick fog rolled in and the lack of visibility shook what little confidence he had left. Dick told him it was okay *not* to race so Bobby pulled out. Dick went ahead and raced, but took a horrible crash, broke his back, and ended up in the hospital. Can you believe that? Fortunately, his injury wasn't anything like Jill's. He was going to recover.[2]

The good thing about the tryouts was that Kenny and Charlotte were both named alternates to the 1956 U.S. Olympic Squad.[3] We were all delighted for them, but we were still so upset about Jill that it didn't feel right to celebrate anything.

As for me, between the racers' accidents and Dave's silence, I was wiped out. I tiptoed around as if I were walking on eggshells. It seemed like Dave blamed himself for the accident and I got the feeling he might never coach again. But it's odd how life works out. A few weeks after Jill's accident, we hadn't been at the mountain more than a half hour when about 20 of the junior racers, including our own kids, were skiing up and down the rope tows, ready to have a normal day of Saturday training. Essentially, they took a stand as a group. Jill wouldn't have given up so why should they? You could almost feel Jill's spirit in the air encouraging them. Dave couldn't resist their enthusiasm. Ski racing might have caused Jill's accident, but it was also a way for the Mammoth team to recover from her accident.

Dave's return to coaching broke the ice between us. Thank heavens. One evening, he just started talking about how to coach racers to go for the win yet keep them from taking unnecessary risks. I told him he'd know what to say once he was out on the slopes. And that's what happened. Even with added caution, that winter three of Dave's racers placed in the top-ten at Junior Nationals.

WHILE life continued on at Mammoth, Jill was making progress, too. I saw a photo of her when she was being transferred from the Salt Lake hospital on her way to a rehabilitation center in Southern California, and she looked so pretty, smiling as if nothing were out of the ordinary. Her makeup was perfect, and her hair was brushed softly around her face. Later on, I asked her how she could keep such a positive attitude at such a difficult time. She teased, "Oh, you know, Roma, it's important to wear fresh lipstick when photographers are around."

Believe it or not, Jill moved into a facility right near the famous Muscle Beach at the Santa Monica pier, the same place where her friend, Audra Jo, was still rehabbing from being paralyzed by polio. What a strange world! Two beautiful girls who had been best friends and teammates in high school were now learning how to perform basic motor skills and using wheelchairs for mobility.

What really impressed me about Jill and Audra Jo was that they didn't sit around crying or complaining. No, they each put smiles on their faces and found something positive to concentrate on while they faced their challenges. I swear, these two young women were the most resilient people I'd ever met. Just watching them made me want to change how I was handling my own problems.

You see, I'd gotten in the habit of feeling sad and lonely and sometimes angry that Dave was gone so much of the time. But really, he was just taking care of business. I was healthy and strong, and as Dave reminded me, I should appreciate that I could get out of bed every morning and take care of myself. Now that the kids were older, I could even go skiing whenever I wanted. If I just took pride in keeping a clean house and preparing delicious meals for the family and the constant flow of guests, like I had always done, I would be happy, and Dave would surely give me the attention I craved.

I went down south to visit Jill and Audra Jo whenever I could, and I enjoyed every minute we spent together. We mostly talked about girl stuff. If one of them wanted a new blouse or different lipstick, I'd go out and find it for her. You know, things like that. Of course, conversations with Jill always included the latest news about Buddy and Dick. Even though Buddy had come to see her a few times and had been faithfully writing her letters while he was off ski racing, Jill said their relationship was no longer working. Buddy couldn't accept what had happened to her. That made *me* furious. For heaven's sake, Jill didn't deserve more hurt. But Jill would calm me down saying, "Roma, don't be mad. Buddy's doing what he can. He's a wonderful person. That's why I fell in love with him. And honestly, if I were in his shoes, I might feel the same way he does." How Jill could be so kind and sympathetic was beyond me. Still, I thought about what she said, and I understood. The reason her accident was so hard on Buddy was because of how much he cared for her. I tell you, Jill was not only resilient, she was wise.

Then there was Dick Buek. Between the Army and his broken back, he couldn't make it to California until June, but when he finally got to Jill's hospital room, boy, did he ever put a spark of joy in her life. The first thing he did was to close the hospital door and give her a tender kiss. Then he drilled her about her condition. He wanted to know exactly what she was going through.

Jill's hands were frozen in a clenched position. Using a combination of gravity, the muscles above her chest, and tools the therapists had designed to stay put between her fingers, she was learning how to comb her hair, put on her make-up, feed herself, and even paint by number. There was

328

hope that she could learn to write, pick up a glass of water, and turn pages in a book.

Dick Buek wasn't fazed one bit about Jill's limitations. Without permission from the hospital staff, he wheeled her outside into the salty ocean air. Basically, he kidnapped her. Then he pushed her through the streets of Santa Monica at an unruly speed. When Jill told me about this spontaneous outing, her eyes twinkled with happiness and she laughed. I mean, really laughed, like I hadn't seen her laugh since before the accident. How grateful I felt to Dick. He made Jill Kinmont realize that even though she would never ski again, she could still have fun.[4]

Jill attending college at UCLA.

CHAPTER THIRTY

Those Durn Fools

Ralph Batchelder and Tom Dempsey.

S
ummer 1955. Dave pulled together a small but dependable crew of hard-working men to build the Eastern Sierra's first chairlift. With tanned biceps bulging out of short-sleeved T-shirts and white teeth grinning through dust-covered faces, these ridiculously handsome men weren't afraid of flirting with the inherent dangers of managing heavy equipment on a rocky mountainside. As they labored in the high-altitude heat, wind, and occasional rainstorm or snow flurry, they took ownership of their boss's confidence in his semi-ancient fleet of Army surplus vehicles. The men grew fond of how the temperamental brakes, cut-off cabs, missing bumpers, and low-powered engines gave each vehicle a personality of its own, and they hoped this used equipment still had enough guts to transport 6,000-pound chairlift towers up the steep slopes. How the men would raise and set these towers was yet to unfold.

DAVE had come to believe that whenever he needed someone with a particular skill, that person would appear. Take Eddie Riley who shared dynamiting skills he learned while working at the tungsten mine outside of Bishop. Or Don Redmon's telephone company survey experience proving to be invaluable in monitoring the alignment of the 14 lift towers. Then there was Grandpa McCoy who managed the tool shed as carefully as if he were taking care of his grandchildren. And Dave's racers, Kenny Lloyd and Rhubarb Marcellin, driving dump trucks, shoveling sand and aggregate, and clearing slash while Linda Meyers claimed the title Chief "Go-Fer" as she shuttled between Bishop and Mammoth resupplying misplaced nuts and bolts.

Just when Dave needed more laborers, his friend Carl Grebe telephoned from Michigan in search of summer work for his nephew and two of his nephew's friends. Dave told Carl, "If they can shovel, send them out." Within a week the three boys were living with the McCoys at the McGee Warming Hut and shoveling alongside Dave's half-brother Bill who was about their age.

AFTER a season of helping Dave with his rope tows, Bob Bumbaugh asked Dave for a more permanent position. In his previous life, Bob had worked as a machinist building tools to retrieve objects accidentally dropped into oil wells. Dave told Bob he couldn't afford a full-time person who had such experience and knowledge. "Well, maybe you can and maybe you can't," Bumbaugh responded. "I have enough money in the bank to take care of my expenses, insurance, and things like that. All I need is room and board and a bit of spending money." Dave hesitated. Bumbaugh didn't. He moved his few belongings into one of the small rooms on the bottom floor of the Warming Hut.

Bumbaugh quickly earned a reputation for his exacting work and his willingness to share knowledge with younger employees. In the eyes of his peers, he was the glue that held everything together. Co-workers teased about how he always had 10 innovative ways to fix things, and that "whatever Bumbaugh built wasn't coming down in this lifetime without a wrecking ball and three torch welders."

RALPH Batchelder, better known as Batch, had moved to Mammoth—population about 20—after giving up an engineering job in Burbank.[1] When Batch located Dave at his garage on Minaret Road, all he could see was greasy Levis and a well-worn pair of boots sticking out from under an International TD 14 dozer. Batch cleared his throat and, in a determined voice, addressed the boots, "Mr. McCoy, I just moved my family to Mammoth and I'd like to work for you."

With no idea who was talking to him, Dave answered, "I can't pay enough for a man to feed a family."

Usually a soft-spoken man, Batch replied assertively, "You don't understand, Mr. McCoy. I'm *going* to work for you."

Dave scooted out from beneath the engine to get a look at this person. Hesitantly, he agreed to employ Batch when he could, so long as he understood money was tight. Early the next morning, Batch showed up at the Warming Hut, clean-shaven, carrying his sack lunch and a pair of well-worn work gloves.

At this time, Batch had purchased property on Berner Street and erected a parachute tent to lodge his family while he built their home. They blew up air mattresses for insulation, used Army surplus canned heat for warmth, and bathed in a wheelbarrow. When winter arrived, most of Batch's offspring joined Dave's junior race team and spent their extra time skiing on the Mammoth rope tows free of charge. Since the new house wasn't yet habitable, Batch located extra sleeping bags and stuffed one inside another for warmth. During storms, the family would get up in the middle of the night to brush snow off the tent. One night, they didn't wake up in time, the snow-laden tent collapsed on them, and they scrambled in the cold darkness to salvage their "home."

Batch applied his strong work ethic to any job asked of him. As a skilled engineer, he understood the complicated patterns and engineering parameters required to install three diesel engines in the bottom terminal: a large one to run the lift; a medium-sized one to serve as a back-up; and a small one to provide electricity for the Warming Hut. There was no question, Batch was an invaluable addition to Dave's summer crew.

MEANWHILE, Dave had taken notice of Tom Dempsey, a young man from Southern California who had been frequenting the Mammoth rope tows on weekends. Though small in stature, Dempsey's strong will, quiet focus, and fiery temper more than compensated for his size. Prior to his introduction to skiing, he'd been a self-described "frustrated baseball jock." After his first ski trip, he called himself a "penniless high school ski bum." To his mother's chagrin, he had ruined her clothes iron when he tried to waterproof his Levis by ironing paraffin wax into the denim.

Longing to ski Mammoth at any opportunity, Dempsey often tagged along on weekend trips with members of the Avalanche Ski Club. If he couldn't find a ride, he hitchhiked. One miserably cold winter night, he stood at the only open service station in Bishop, praying for a ride, but not a single car drove by. Shivering with cold, Dempsey spied some empty cardboard boxes stacked against the building. He carried a few into the men's restroom, crawled inside them, and went to sleep. Early the next morning, he doused his face with cold water from the bathroom sink and resumed hitchhiking. A trucker dropped him at the Highway 203 turnoff to Mammoth, and Dempsey walked the three miles to town carrying his skis and poles on one shoulder and his knapsack on his back.

Immediately after graduating from high school, Dempsey packed a suitcase and a nail pouch, and left his home for Mammoth riding in the back seat of volunteer ski patrolman Bob Clow's VW bug. He landed a summer job working for Lloyd Nicoll at his lumberyard, and as soon as the snow fell, volunteered to help Dave on weekends in exchange for free skiing.

From the beginning, Dempsey wanted to impress Dave. He also aspired to be part of the group of hotshot racers who followed Dave down the mountain in their matching handknit sweaters, laughing and carrying on while they trained. Clearly, this clique would not be easy to break into, but Dempsey was undeterred. By 8:30 each winter morning, after helping Dave get the tows running, he could be found on his way to set a course, balancing slalom poles on his left shoulder and gripping the rope tow with his right hand. His diligence made a good impression.

By mid-winter, Dempsey was traveling to senior races as a member of the Mammoth race team. He was surprised to learn that while Dave rarely accompanied the senior racers to competitions, he sent them off with gas cards, cash, and a directive to have fun, which meant they should do their best to ski well and be happy. No questions asked. In appreciation of Dave's trust and generosity, when Dave asked him to work on his summer crew, Dempsey didn't hesitate to join in. In fact, he promised himself that no matter how much dirt and rocks other employees might shovel, he would shovel more.

In need of even more helping hands, Dave turned to Bob Edwards, a Southern Californian who had been skiing since 1950, eventually joining the National Ski Patrol so he could ski for free. As Edwards described, "Skiing was instant gratification. I loved it! Every turn was a big accomplishment, and a series of turns was even better." In the summer of 1954, he moved to Mammoth, settled into the Shady Rest Campground on the edge of town, and worked for Caltrans making $2.50 an hour paving Minaret Road. The following summer, he moved into an unfinished house with Tom Dempsey. When Dave offered to match the state wages if Edwards joined Mammoth's summer crew, he switched jobs and ended up doing whatever Dave asked of him, from refueling trucks at Bill Banta's gas station in Lee Vining to hammering nails and shoveling pumice.

One June morning when Dave met his work force outside the Warming Hut, he noticed one of Batch's sons, 16-year-old Harry Batchelder, standing by his father's side. Dave took one look at the sturdy young man and told him, "You can drive the cement truck. Talk to Bumbaugh. He'll set you up." Harry thought that was pretty good. Dave trusted him with his equipment, without even having him go for a test drive.

The cement truck turned out to be a 4 x 4 Chevy dump truck that Dave had converted into a portable, do-it-yourself, cement-mixing contraption. He'd attached three 50-gallon drums on top of the cab for carrying water. Above the drums, he'd built a rack large enough to transport 12 sacks of cement. He then separated the bed into two sections, one for aggregate, the other for sand, and at the back, secured a gas-powered cement mixer that could be positioned to mix, transport, or pour a quarter yard of concrete at a time.

Bumbaugh introduced Harry to his work partner, Dick Hunt, an athletic 19-year-old who would later compete on the 1960 and 1964 U.S. Olympic Speedskating Teams. Harry and Dick's first task was to help Dave's other employees unload a semi-truck and trailer full of 94-pound cement sacks, and stack them near the Warming Hut.

WHEN Dave heard that an experienced heavy equipment operator named Sam Basch had arrived in town, he immediately sought him out. Sam had zero interest in skiing. He just loved the region. A quiet man, he came to be known around Mammoth as the rare bachelor who abstained from alcohol. Well-matched to his chosen trade, Sam was a little rough around the edges, but laughed right along with his friends when they joked that he couldn't get a comb through all the dust and gravel in his long hair.

Dave asked Sam if he was interested in maneuvering a bulldozer across a steep hillside, cutting switchbacks to reach the rocky cliffs of Gravy Chute. The primitive roads needed to be stable enough to handle the weight of fully loaded dump trucks, and wide enough for them to back in and out with ease. Dave pointed out the potential danger of loose rocks rolling down on Sam as he worked, and the lack of space to build functional turnarounds. In a soft but confident voice, Sam assured Dave, "Yes sir, I can put roads in there for you. And I can also excavate your tower site holes."

EACH of the 14 tower holes needed to be dug 8 feet deep and 12 feet square. Sam drove Puff, the skip loader, straight up the slope to the lowest tower site and scooped Mammoth's air-filled pumice to make a rough hole. Unfortunately, the sides of the hole kept collapsing inward. To keep things rolling, Sam backed off, and a few crew members jumped in. With hammers pounding and nails flying, they framed the sides of the tower hole with scrap lumber and fine-tuned the inside edges by tossing shovel-fuls of pumice over their heads and out of the hole.

Once the first tower hole was dug, the crew formed the footing by wiring rebar into a 2-foot thick by 12-foot-square mat, which they placed into the bottom of the hole. Next, they lowered a 3-foot-square steel plate—which had 11-foot-long bolts welded to each of its four corners—onto the center of the mat. With the four long bolts extending vertically above the

The cement truck.

surface, the men wired the steel plate to the wire mesh mat. Then, Redmon and Batch used a transit to direct the crew as they nailed a crisscross pattern of 2-foot by 4-foot boards to stabilize the long bolts in perfect vertical alignment with the centerline of the planned chairlift. This step was critical. A slight error could cause catastrophic stresses on the towers. Once Redmon and Batch triple-checked their work, the tower hole was ready for concrete.

Meanwhile, Harry Batchelder and Dick Hunt had filled the water barrels on Dave's portable cement factory, tied cement bags to the rack, shoveled gravel and sand into the bed, and headed up to the tower site, Harry at the wheel, Dick riding shotgun. The steep pitch and heavy load required every bit of horsepower the six-cylinder engine could provide at 9,000+ feet altitude.

Lumbering upward in low gear, Harry made it to the lower tower sites without a problem. But the first time he headed up the steeper slope toward the higher sites, the truck's engine ran out of power, sputtered, and died. Still in first gear, the truck started to roll backwards. Panicked, Harry stepped on the brake and the clutch simultaneously, causing the truck to lose compression and roll back even faster. Harry and Dick had no choice but to "enjoy" the ride until they reached the flat and slowed to a stop.

On the next dying-engine incident, Harry was prepared, or so he thought. When the truck started traveling backward, he eased the clutch out slowly. The truck slowed down, but because it was still in gear, its front-end reared up. Not a problem when the front wheels landed straight down, but this time the truck tipped sideways, landed on two left wheels, and almost flipped over—an undesirable thrill!

Harry eventually figured out the best thing to do when driving a loaded truck with a dead engine rolling backward in first gear on a steep and rocky hillside was to turn the ignition off, jam on the foot brake, pull on the parking brake, and ride out the backward roll until the truck eased to a stop. Harry and Dick could then climb in the back, lighten the load by shoveling out excess rocks and sand, and take another run.

Each time Harry reached one of Sam's access roads, he had to turn around, and then back the truck to the very edge of the tower holes. If he wavered too much toward the downslope side of the narrow access road, the truck would be a goner. One of the crew, shaking his head with a laugh, put it this way, "Backing up those roads you felt like if you made a mistake, you'd have just enough time to get airsick before you died."[2]

At each tower site, cement dust filled the air as Dave monitored the ratio of sand, aggregate, cement, and water shoveled into the gas-powered mixer. The ratio of materials would determine the strength of the concrete. Only when the viscosity passed Dave's quality test did the crew rotate the mixer into the outpour position and deliver enough cement to cover the rebar and steel plate with a 2-foot-deep slurry.

Once the concrete slab at the bottom of the tower hole had set, Dave and his crew latched a 3-foot-high cylindrical steel form around the 11-foot bolts, reinforced the inside of the cylinder with rebar, and filled it with concrete. After this second pour hardened, the men unlatched the form and set it aside to be reused at the next tower. Lastly, they positioned a 3-foot-square steel plate—that matched the bottom plate—over the concrete cylinder with the tops of the 11-foot bolts sticking through the four corner holes. The site was now ready to receive a tower.

On July 21, 1955, ski instructor Lester LaVelle reported to the *Inyo Register* that the lift construction job was a full 30 days ahead of schedule:

... or so declared George Lodvick, head engineer and vice president of United Tramway, after completing a two-day inspection. He praised the tramway engineer, Victor Tchelistcheff, and Dave McCoy. Tchelistcheff added, "I've never worked with a crew which has accomplished so much per man-hour. The equipment which they have assembled has so far performed perfectly. Some of the foundation holes have been dug by the backhoe digger in less than an hour. We have been lucky to locate towers where we have encountered no rocks, and if our luck holds, we will certainly break all records for any similar project." Lodvick returned to San Francisco to try and keep the factory and supply end of the project abreast of the actual field accomplishments.[3]

The tower sites on the rocky cliffs of Gravy Chute were even narrower and more precarious than those below. Nudged up against the cliffs, there was barely room to walk around, much less to grade a proper footprint on which to operate heavy equipment. The slightest disturbance dislodged unstable rocks and sent them crashing downward.

Since Puff couldn't break through the volcanic rock to dig the tower hole, the crew prepared to dynamite. The men crank-started a generator to run the air compressor that would power a jackhammer to drill holes into the rock. Then they packed the holes with dynamite powder, wired a long fuse, scrambled a safe distance away, and ignited the blast. After the dust and rocks settled, they tossed out the loose rock and detailed the edges of the hole with picks and shovels.

ONE afternoon, Dave was working on an upper tower site when a man wearing cowboy boots and a cowboy hat hiked up the slope toward him. In a heavy Swiss-German accent, the stranger introduced himself as Gus Weber. Gus had sent Dave a letter of inquiry about applying to be the Mammoth Mountain Ski School Director but had never heard back. So, he decided to drive from Jackson Hole, Wyoming, and apply in person.[4]

Dimly recalling a letter with a recommendation from French Canadian

Ski Champion Ernie McCullough, Dave thought, "If this guy went to the trouble to walk up the mountain to find me, he should work out just fine." Dave welcomed Gus with a smile of approval, told him his first day of work would be Thanksgiving morning, and offered accommodations in the trailer behind the Warming Hut. And yes, Gus's Belgian sheepdogs could stay there, too. The animals would help keep the trailer warm, which turned out to be an excellent benefit because the only heat source was from electricity and the generator shut off at 10 p.m.

ON days that 13-year-old Punkin, 10-year-old Poncho, and 9-year-old P-Nut went to work with their dad, the group left the McGee house early, all four of them crammed onto the bench seat of the Jeep pickup. Dave assigned his boys duties as if they were part of the crew. They tamped freshly poured concrete and threw rocks off the access roads and into holes that were being backfilled. When the lift towers were being moved around, Dave let them watch from a distance.

One day while P-Nut and Bill McCoy were linseed oiling the Warming Hut siding, they watched Sam Basch bulldozing boulders, downed trees, and massive stumps into the 30-foot ravine where Dave kept a fire going, burning off slash to create space for more fill. With a nine-year-old boy's curiosity about the combustion of oil and fire, P-Nut hauled a half-filled 5-gallon can of linseed oil to the ravine—a worthy effort in itself— dumped it on top of the burning stumps and ran as fast as he could off to one side. To his delight, the explosion shook the slopes and rattled the Warming Hut windows, making P-Nut's endeavor worth the disapproval he received from his dad that afternoon.

IT took teamwork to unload each of the fourteen 6,000-pound cylindrical lift towers—varying in length from 22 feet to 45 feet—off the semi-truck. Dave attached his A-Frame's pulley cable to the center of "the beast" and assigned men to the guidelines at each end. As soon as Bumbaugh began winching the tower upward, it swayed dangerously out of control. A few guys ran to each end and with sheer muscle strength tried to stabilize the tower while Bumbaugh lowered it to the ground. As Eddie Riley remarked, "That old A-Frame required good skill to keep it from tipping

Bob Bumbaugh driving to a tower site.

over. It was doing way more work than it ever should have."

To transport the first tower up to its site, Bumbaugh constructed an elevated saddle bracket on the side of the D4 CAT dozer. Once the tower was lifted onto the bracket with the top end resting on the dozer blade, he inched the unstable, off-balance dozer to the tower site. Dave followed in the A-Frame so they could use the hoist and guidelines to maneuver the tower off the dozer and onto the ground, placing it directly above the footing.

Dave and his crew then bolted the angle iron components to the upper end of the tower, used the A-Frame to pull the tower up vertically and then lower it down over the four 11-foot bolts that extended up from the footing. They secured the bolts with massive heavy-duty nuts, then stood back and admired their work. The first chairlift tower on Mammoth Mountain had been raised and set in one try, and no one had been hurt.

By September 1, three towers had been erected and several of Dave's workers had returned to school and other commitments. Since the footings for the other 11 towers were already prepared, Dave projected that his skeleton crew could raise and set them within a week.

The most challenging tower would be the one on Gravy Chute, but Dave had a plan. He directed Bumbaugh to back the A-Frame along the Gravy Chute access road until the hoist was next to the tower site. With Puff stabilizing the A-Frame from the front and a dozer from the back,

Don Redmon tightening a bolt.

the men attached the A-Frame cable and guidelines to the tower, then they climbed up between the cliffs and roped off onto the most stable rocks they could find. Bumbaugh steered the boom, as the others manually worked the guidelines, inching the tower to vertical until the bottom was positioned over the long bolts. They then lowered the tower over the bolts and tightened the nuts. Each man, in his own way, breathed a sigh of relief. Chair One might become a reality after all.

ONCE all the towers along the chairlift line had been set, the time had come to raise the 54-foot-high counterweight tower at the top terminal.[5] The function of this massive cement counterweight was to ensure the proper amount of tension on the haul rope—as they called the main cable—when the chairlift was operating. Dave's small crew built the footings, set the anchor bolts, and poured the cement without a hitch. Next, they assembled the angle-iron components of the *gigantic* tower while it lay in a horizontal position on the ground, making sure that two legs were up against the footings in direct alignment with the anchor bolts where they would be attached. But how were they going to raise the monstrosity and then lower it down in precisely the right place? The counterweight tower was twice as tall as Dave's 25-foot-high A-Frame. Even adding a telephone pole extension, the A-Frame still looked too small for the job. A mistake could be disastrous.

Standing at the top terminal, United Tramway engineer, Victor

Tchelistcheff, and Dave discussed options of how to raise the bulky tower. As they talked, the wind picked up, the temperature dropped, and snow-flakes began to blow across the landscape obstructing their view. Dave called out to his crew, "Let's go home. We'll leave the equipment here. Better dress warm tomorrow!"

Dave drove Victor down to the Warming Hut in his Jeep. Bouncing along the rocky dirt road, Victor pulled his collar high and folded his arms across his chest for warmth. He decided to drive to San Francisco for the weekend to seek advice from fellow engineers.

THE next morning, Dave's three eldest boys and one of their friends, Dennis Agee, stood by Dave's side as he gathered his crew near the Warming Hut. The men joked about the newly fallen snow, slapping their hands together to keep warm. Though the cold bit their cheeks, the autumn air hinted that the temperature would rise as the day progressed. Dave greeted the crew with his usual enthusiasm, "Let's go raise that tower and give Victor a surprise." Once again, he had a plan.

Driving to the upper terminal, the men were unusually quiet. Keenly aware if anything went wrong that day the result could be ugly, they avoided serious conversation and used laughter to break tension. Danger was something they chose not to discuss.

As an adult looking back on those days, P-Nut would recall, "This is how it was at Mammoth. There wasn't a feeling of desperation or fear, but more determination and fortitude. Everyone wanted to achieve the goal set before them. They each planned on giving 110 percent to get the job done, no matter what. If they didn't, there could be severe consequences. I was pretty young, but the building of Chair One had a heavy imprint on me. It was the foundation for the subsequent years of work I put in on the mountain."

At the upper terminal, the crew gathered around the ominous counter-weight tower lying on the snow-dusted ground. Dave instructed the four boys to stay outside a designated perimeter, and then, with Don Redmon as his assistant, proceeded to give directives. The men cleared snow off the footing bolts and attached cables to specified points along the tower. Dave placed scrap wood at the base of the tower to keep it from sliding forward once they began to raise it. He stationed two men to work the guidelines and another to operate a "come-along" stretched down one side of the tower. Sam Basch drove the D4 to the north side of the tower, Dennis Osborn steered the TD 14 to the west, and Bob Bumbaugh motored the A-Frame midway down the south side. When all three vehicles were in place, Dave and Don hooked cables from the tower to each vehicle.

Using hand signals and commands—"Back a few inches farther!" "Pull up a little bit!" "Whoa, stop!"—Dave and Don directed the operators to tighten the slack of their ropes and cables as Bumbaugh winched the middle of the tower about 18 feet in the air. With everyone keeping the ropes and cables taut, Bumbaugh slowly released his cable. He then drove the A-Frame to the top end of the tower, hooked onto a longer cable that was connected to the tower midway up and backed away until this cable was taut.

On Dave's command, Osborn slowly pulled the tower toward his TD14 and Bumbaugh gently let out slack from the A-Frame while everyone else stabilized the tower with their lines. Once the tower was near vertical, the group lowered the base onto the anchor bolts of the concrete foundation. Dave and Don rushed in to fasten the heavy-duty nuts. That was it. The men stared at the standing tower, amazed. Nobody said a word. Then Dave let out his signature yodel and everyone relaxed.

With slaps on the back and bursts of laughter, heartbeats slowed down to a reasonable rate for the first time that day. Like grown-up kids on an oversized Jungle Jim, a few of the crew scrambled up the tower to release attached cables. The others collected scattered tools, coiled the ropes and cables, and loaded pieces of debris into the dump truck. Osborn drove the TD-14 down the mountain. When he reached the Warming Hut about 40 minutes later, he glanced at his watch. Not yet 3 p.m. Not even quitting time.

Monday morning, Victor returned from San Francisco. Stunned to learn the counterweight tower had been raised, he asked Dave how they'd done it. Dave replied with a sly grin, "The sky got cloudy, snow started falling, and when the storm passed, I looked up and saw the tower standing there."

Raising the counterweight tower.

To chairlift builders, tall black towers standing erect against the sky were an invitation to scurry up steel ladders and perch on a piece of angle iron 30 feet in the air while handling heavy awkward items without fear of looking down or worry of falling. As Dave and his crew pushed through the final stages of building Chair One, there was no doubt they had joined the ranks of this small community.

Dave put Tom Dempsey in charge of building the lower terminal to match the look of the Warming Hut. Though Dempsey knew little about construction, he qualified to take on the task because he owned a nail bag. His roommate, Bob Edwards, qualified as his assistant because he knew less about construction than Dempsey did. Soaking up the last of the Indian summer sun, the men started hammering, shirtless. When they stepped back to admire the finished building with its steep wooden loading ramp, they felt as proud of their work as they did of their suntanned backs. Not until the first winter storm filled the building with snow did they get called back to fix the windows which they had unknowingly framed in backwards.

After building the terminals, the crew installed the engines and the top and bottom bull wheels. Next they assembled the sheave trains—wheels over which the cables would roll—on the ground, then scrambled up the towers carrying ropes to pull the awkward trains along with them. With the strength and balance of acrobats, they perched on top while maneuvering the sheave trains into place and bolting them down.

Now the crew had to string the 7,000-foot cable that would carry the chairs. Starting at the top terminal, they unspooled a 1.75-inch cable called a "sand line" which they would pull down the chairlift line. The man in the lead carried the end of the sand line to the top of each tower, threw it over the cross arm, and fed it to the ground. Then he climbed down, grabbed the end of the rope again, bounded down to the next tower and repeated the process. Once the end of the sand line was tied down at the bottom terminal, the men went back to the top and pulled the rope down the other side of the chairlift line the same way.

The next step was to scramble up each tower and place the sand line on the sheaves, removing as much slack as they could by hand, preparing for Whitey Reyer, the professional splicer from Carson City, Nevada. Whitey then spliced the sand line to a gigantic spool of the actual chairlift cable, which the men winched around the towers. Finally, Dave's crew supported both ends of the cable, while Whitey wove the strands into an intricate splice.

Once the cable was in place, Dave hung the one double chair in his possession, started the Cummins engine, and put his new chairlift to its first test. Everything worked perfectly. Hoots and hollers echoed up the mountain. Now he just had to wait to hang the remaining 84 chairs, which didn't arrive until mid-November.

EARLY morning on the scheduled day for the State of California safety tests, volunteer ski patrolman Bob Clow, who had driven from Southern California on a weekend trip, stopped by to check out the last-minute progress on Chair One. Seeing Dave's crew carrying 90-pound bags of rock up the wooden ramp to the loading area, Clow joined in to help. On each double chair they stacked four bags—360 pounds, approximating the weight of two full sized skiers.

As Clow recalled, the inspectors tested the lift to full capacity with repeated starts and stops. Chair One passed the safety test with flying colors. The inspectors signed their certificate of approval and left for home. Enjoying a feeling of relief, Dave restarted the lift to unload the bags of rocks, but the cable derailed. One more challenge to address before Opening Day, which was creeping closer and closer.

Before heading south that afternoon, Clow stopped by the Warming Hut to say hello to Jim Farnsworth, a ski tech hired to run the retail and rental shop. "Farnsy" was scrambling to get his merchandise organized before the Thanksgiving opening. Clow paused to admire a blue and black parka, one he could never have afforded. Just then, Dave happened to walk by and casually asked Clow if he liked the parka. Clow confided, "Yeah, it's neat."

Dave smiled and said, "It's yours." Clow skied in that parka for the next 40 years.

JUST before Thanksgiving, the *Los Angeles Times* published a full-page photo spread on Dave McCoy and his new chairlift, detailing how this "affable, good looking guy in his early forties, sort of a small edition of Paul Bunyan" had completed the complicated construction job despite having no previous experience on a project of such magnitude. Dave credited his father Mac McCoy's construction and engineering influence. He said the rest just seemed to come naturally. The article went on:

> *Working at least 12 hours a day, seven days a week, McCoy fore-manned his eight-man crew with such proficiency and speed that they outstripped by a large margin the record of similar projects that utilized far greater labor forces... he has almost completed the entire operation inside of three months... only through his amazing inventiveness and ingenuity was the major portion of the construction completed in this short span... Dave designed, on the spot, special tools, rigs and gimmicks to transport the 6,000-pound towers up the steep mountains for placement in the rock-hard ground... the speed and accuracy startled even those professionally in the tramway business. United Tramway who supplied the materials was unprepared for the resourcefulness of the man.*

The morning the article hit the newsstands, Dave stood in front of his crew holding a rolled-up copy in his hand. He waved the newspaper in the air and said, "We all know the credit for building this chairlift goes to you, all of you. It's because of your hard work, your time, your energy, and your accomplishments that Mammoth Mountain is going to have a chairlift this winter."

WHEN ski instructor Lester LaVelle started writing his own article about Chair One, he struggled to understand why Dave's crew worked so hard for him. Lester decided to ask the men for their explanation. Bob Bumbaugh replied that the summer spent building Chair One was one of the best times in his life, mentally and physically. True, he'd made less money in one year working for Dave than he'd paid to the IRS the year before, but he said, "I was happy. Feeling good was a fringe benefit far more valuable than dollar bills."

Harry Batchelder told Lester that Dave didn't stand back and watch but worked right alongside the crew as if he were one of the guys doing the grunt work. "He doesn't get mad," Harry went on, "and never makes you feel like he thinks he's better than you. You wouldn't even know he was the boss, except he's the one who makes sure everything goes right."

Bob Edwards laughed when he tried to describe Dave to Lester, "He was a maverick. His energy rubbed off on everybody. He'd ask how you were doing, which just put a fire in you. You didn't want him to show you up. Whether it was conscious on Dave's part or not, I don't know."

In the end, Lester wrote, "The durn fools are so enthusiastic about the area and so loyal to their boss, they work from sunrise to dark. No outsider understands it and attempts at explanation are wide of the mark."[6]

One thing everyone agreed on, if they were "durn fools," then Dave was the biggest "durn fool" of all.

CHAPTER THIRTY-ONE

Jill Comes Home

Dave showing Jill the new Chair One.

Noticeably missing from the Eastern Sierra during the summer of 1955 was Jill Kinmont. While Dave was raising towers on Mammoth Mountain, she was living in a Santa Monica rehabilitation home, learning how to function without the use of her arms and legs. Every now and then Dave telephoned her, each time reminding her to let him know if she needed anything. He invited Jill to come to Mammoth as soon as she could travel in an automobile for the six plus hours the trip would take, and he offered her a job managing his newly remodeled ski shop. Dave thought that this position would be a perfect way for Jill to stay involved with the ski world and to share in the growth of Mammoth. But she turned down the offer. She had already decided to enroll in college and become a schoolteacher.

In mid-October, just nine months after her accident, the doctors gave

Jill permission to travel to Mammoth. Her mother June, who had learned to transfer Jill and to take care of personal needs, would drive them. When the women passed through Bishop, they would call the office at Mammoth, so that Dave could be waiting in the parking lot when they arrived.

Dave lifted Jill's wheelchair out of the car and unfolded it next to the opened front door. When he reached inside to transfer her, she told him exactly what to do as if communicating her needs allowed her to take a more active part in what she was doing. Once Dave had settled Jill in her wheelchair, he gave her a grand tour of his new yet unfinished chairlift, carrying her to places where the wheelchair couldn't go. He then asked if she'd feel safe riding in the Army Jeep to the top of the chair. "Of course," she smiled. "I wouldn't miss that for the world!"

Once at the upper terminal, Dave carried Jill to the ridge above Gravy Chute where the top tower stood. From there, she could see down the chairlift line and take in the entire panorama of Long Valley. She studied the landscape with pleasure and enjoyed the light breeze as it softly waved her curls. Closing her eyes, she breathed in the scent of mountain air and absorbed the sun on her face, soaking up all she loved about Mammoth.

When Jill opened her eyes, she looked up at the chairlift tower, felt its heavy presence, and then said softly, "You've done really good, Pa. I'm proud of you."

Dave shook his head in astonishment and replied, "Now, let's get this straight. Who's proud of who? You're the one who's always teaching me about life."

Jill turned her head to meet Dave's eyes. She smiled and then said with firm confidence, "You know, Pa, I'm okay."

He returned her smile. "I know."

Alone together on Mammoth Mountain, Dave and Jill made an unspoken agreement. Sadness and pity would not be part of their relationship. What had been was then. What was now was now. The only constant between "then" and "now" was the bond of how much they cared for each other.

As the Kinmonts' car disappeared down Minaret Road, Dave's mind filled with gratitude to see Jill's progress, yet an aching pain gnawed at his heart.

CHAPTER THIRTY-TWO

Opening Day

Rope Tow One and the lower terminal of Chair One.

Thanksgiving morning, November 25, 1955, Opening Day for Chair One. Crystals of snow sparkled like diamonds in the brilliant blue Eastern Sierra sky while final preparations took place. Using county snowblowers, Clyde Pearson and his crew had spent most of the night clearing Minaret Road and the parking area of snow that had fallen the previous day. Down in town, the local restaurants were already selling out of food. It was later reported that during the busy morning, one restaurant alone cracked 49 dozen eggs for hungry skiers, and by the end of the day sold some 90 pounds of burgers.[1]

Dave and his men had risen at dawn to shovel the entrances and sundecks of the Warming Hut. They were now hiking the chairlift line to make sure chairs could pass over the crest of Gravy Chute without skis getting caught in drifts of fresh snow. Ralph Batchelder had cleared the lower terminal, then packed a layer of snow onto the wooden ramp that led up to the loading platform.

Dave and Roma gathered their children, all dressed in matching black and yellow Mammoth Race Team parkas, and arranged them on and around the double chair with the number "1" stenciled on its back. Dave balanced on the far edge of the platform, Brownie camera in hand, trying to capture a moment when all six kids stopped wiggling and faced him.

In the cafeteria, the new managers Chuck and Doris Osborn served their first customer, Ski School Director Gus Weber. Late the night before, Gus and his two Belgian sheep dogs had arrived from Jackson Hole—where he'd spent the summer cowboying for Pete Mead, Andrea Mead Lawrence's brother. He caught a few hours of sleep in his station wagon before being awakened by the sound of tires crunching against the snow. Gus quickly donned his ski clothes, took his dogs on a short walk, then headed over to the Warming Hut cafeteria.

After a satisfying breakfast of ham and eggs, Gus found his new boss, and received a warm welcome. Dave introduced him to Bill (Sigi) Farrell, Lester LaVelle, T.J. Johnston, and Toni Milici, who would be his assistants and then addressed the group in a festive voice, "We're expecting a lot of skiers today, so go on out there and have fun with them!"

As the morning sun warmed the air, automobiles packed the parking area. The overflow lined Minaret Road for at least a mile. Throughout the day, Dave's cattle trucks, each winterized with chains on all tires, shuttled skiers between their cars and the tows. Inside the Warming Hut, Nick Gunter set out a cash box and stacks of tickets he'd printed for the occasion, all the while wondering if skiers were going to complain about the $4 lift ticket price. He showed Mammoth ski racers, Linda Meyers and Alice Batchelder, how to use the new "wire ties" to attach the tickets to the skiers' parkas. Upstairs, Farnsy strolled through the ski shop and rental room, adjusting displays of dark glasses and Chapstick, checking for any last-minute details he might have forgotten to address.

THE formal dedication of Chair One was scheduled for 11 a.m. when Jill Kinmont and Roma McCoy would become the chairlift's first official passengers. Until the christening, only the rope tows would operate. Skis and poles covered the open area at the bottom of Broadway while a disorganized "line"—at least six skiers wide and 30 skiers long—inched forward toward Number One tow. The skiers were laughing and talking. Some played a traveling game of bridge. Those skiing down Broadway turned every which way trying to avoid hitting each other before joining the line again. The fact that almost everyone knew each other created the feeling of an extended family reunion.

To secure a bird's-eye view of the upcoming ceremony, skiers stood shoulder to shoulder across the Warming Hut's flat rooftop and below on the sundeck. About 20 skiers waited on the wooden ramp to the chairlift loading zone, standing side by side with their skis on, holding their place in the line that extended out to the parking area. No one complained about the crowds or the cost of lift tickets. Rather, excitement mounted about riding the long-awaited chairlift and about seeing Jill Kinmont. Whether people knew Jill personally or not, her accident had deeply affected anyone who was aware of her story. To think that America's "Sweetheart of Skiing" had the courage, strength, and desire to join them in celebration of this special day at Mammoth touched them deeply.

THE previous day, local pilot Bill Symons had flown Jill and her mother June from Santa Monica to Bishop, while Bill Kinmont had driven his youngest son Jerry. Bobby was in Colorado attending Denver University on a skiing scholarship and couldn't make it to California. Sadly, in order to meet Jill's medical expenses, the Kinmonts had been forced to sell their Rocking K guest ranch in Bishop. The new owners invited the family to stay at the ranch over the long weekend, and though the Kinmonts graciously accepted, coming back to the land and the home they loved so dearly was bittersweet.

Thursday morning, longtime Mammoth skier Frank Zila picked up Jill and June at the Rocking K and drove them to Mammoth. He pulled into the parking area around 10:30 a.m., right on cue. Roma and Dave worked their way through what seemed like a forest of skis, poles, and people to greet their friends. "Oh, Jill," Roma exclaimed, her voice filled with love, her eyes misty with emotion. "We're so glad you're here. This day wouldn't be right without you."

Dave looked at Jill with a mischievous smile, and teased, "Did you notice? There're a few people here who are looking forward to seeing you."

Jill laughed and said, "Let's go!" Dave lifted her into his arms and carried her over the snow toward the lift with June and Roma walking right behind. Skiers parted to let the foursome pass. Someone started clapping. Others joined in, and the applause turned into a joyful roar. Folks called out, "Hi, Jill," "Welcome home, Jill," "We love you, Jill." From the assuring strength of Dave's arms, Jill responded to the welcoming crowd with her vibrant smile, as radiant as ever.

Once at the loading zone, Dave nodded to Batch that the time had come. Batch skipped down the steps and into the engine room below the ramp. He grabbed a rag, sprayed it with starting fluid, stuffed it into the intake, and switched on the engine. The Cummins sputtered to a start and emitted a cloud of thick smelly black smoke, a telltale sign that the engine was working just fine.

Knowing the smoke would dissipate once the engine warmed up, Batch hustled back up the loading ramp to where Dave had gently set Jill onto the left side of Chair #1 and Roma had taken her place on the right. Filled with excitement about the ride, Roma leaned over to Jill and whispered, "Are you afraid? We're going to be pretty high off the ground."

Jill laughed, "What do I have to be afraid of?"

Dave pulled the armrest down, which automatically raised the footrest into position, and then lifted Jill's sheepskin after-ski boots onto it. In a quiet voice, she asked, "Pa, would you cross one of my legs over the other, so I look more natural?" He made the adjustment, and then curved her arm around the center pole in a relaxed position.

After attaching a cord to a bottle of champagne, Dave placed the cord between Jill's teeth. Only then did he look out at the crowd. In his loudest voice, he called out, "Are you ready?" Skiers answered with a hearty cheer. Dave then raised his arm in the air, looked at Jill, pointed one finger to the sky, and counted down, "Five, Four, Three, Two, One, Go!" Jill released her grip on the cord and the champagne bottle crashed into the lift tower, officially christening Chair One. Batch pushed the green "On" button to advance the gearbox into forward drive. To the roar of the crowd, Jill and

Roma floated into space and up Mammoth Mountain.[2]

LATE that afternoon, long after the Kinmonts had departed for Bishop and the last diehard skiers were driving down Minaret Road, Roma stopped by the Warming Hut business office. There she found Nick sitting at his desk with stacks of cash neatly arranged in front of him. He smiled at Roma, his blue eyes twinkling, and asked, "Can you guess how much money this is?" Too energized to wait for her answer, he declared, "Right around $7,000. You oughta go upstairs and buy a few pairs of those Bogner stretch pants Farnsy's got displayed in the ski shop window!" Roma started laughing. She figured Nick was thinking, "Oh, good, now we can pay the bills." And, she felt sure that when Dave saw all that cash, he'd have visions of Chair Two swirling around in his head.

Roma stared at the money, thinking about how it comes and goes. Then, for no reason at all, in one spontaneous motion she stepped toward Nick and tossed a handful of the cash into the air. Nick looked back at her in wonderment, grabbed a handful of his own, and flung it into the air. In reckless abandon, the two of them burst out laughing and continued to throw bills into the air and watch them scatter across the office. Roma twirled around as if she were dancing across a ballroom floor and stopped at Nick's desk, breathless. "You know, Nick," she said. "I always wanted to be a dancer. I just didn't realize what kind of dance I'd be doing."

Just then, Dave walked in. He glanced from Roma to Nick, and then at the money on the floor. Grinning with approval, he said, "Looks like a bunch of green confetti! That's a pretty good way to celebrate!"

What did it matter that Chair One frequently stopped, or that to keep the cable from derailing Batch was limited to loading every other chair causing an exceptionally long lift line, or that the rubber sheave liners on the tower tops *were already wearing out*. What was important to Dave was that Mammoth skiers had enjoyed an entire day riding up Chair One and skiing down the expansive ski runs now open to them.

Roma hugged Nick, then threw her arms around Dave's shoulders and kissed his cheek, crying, "Honey, I knew you could do it!"

"No, Toots," Dave corrected. "*We* did it. *All* of us. Together."

Epilogue: After Chair One

Roma and Dave, 1980s.

"It wasn't a job. It was a love affair."
–Dave McCoy

The epilogue consists of excerpts from
Tracks of Passion, Eastern Sierra Skiing, Dave McCoy, & Mammoth Mountain.

After building Chair One, Dave's optimism, physical stamina, ingenuity, and steadfast belief in what a person can accomplish continued to inspire those around him to achieve more than they ever thought possible. Each summer, without taking on a partner or long-term debt, Dave and his small but dedicated crew, which for many years included his children and some of his racers, sculpted Mammoth's ski slopes and eventually erected 26 chairlifts, two T-bars, and a two-stage gondola that accessed the top of the 11,053-foot mountain. They also expanded the warming hut at Main Lodge and added Mid-Chalet, Canyon Lodge, and Eagle Lodge. Using old Army surplus equipment, common sense, and brute force, the crew lived by the motto, "The impossible is simply something that takes a little longer." Improvisation served as the rule of each day.

In Dave's own words, "It's hard to remember all that we did, putting in power lines and substations, fixing the ski runs, digging wells, installing water tanks...it goes on and on. We operated by the seat of our pants without making long term plans or budgets, didn't have to wait around a year or so for approvals, worked with what we had, took care of our people and the cost of materials."

According to ski racer, ski instructor, and close friend Eddie Riley, "Dave had the ideas, and he had the personality and stature to influence people to back him. He wasn't social...there was no icing on the cake. He never lost sight that he was simply promoting the experience of skiing."

Dave's immediate family felt his powerful influence more than anyone. Watching from the sidelines, living out her role as Dave's partner, Roma often marveled, "There's no one like my husband." No matter what youthful interests the six McCoy children might have nurtured while growing up, it was to Mammoth Mountain Ski Area and to ski racing that they dedicated most of their time and energy. "We were proud of what we did at Mammoth, of being Mammoth ski racers, of how hard we worked in the summers," reflected Dave's third son Carl "P-Nut" McCoy. "The same spirit we had as racers carried over to the workplace on the mountain. The other employees were proud of us. Their camaraderie and friendship made us feel like we belonged to something."

The people who worked with Dave developed an allegiance to him, and their loyalty, in turn, created the energy that built Mammoth Mountain Ski Area. Mechanic Wally Mann reminisced, "Dave was out there; he worked with us, mingled with us, ate his lunch with us, told us his stories. He was one of the crew, that was all. We were a family." Ski Patrolman Joe Maruca added, "There was just something about Dave that commanded respect. He worked hard and wouldn't ask anyone to do something he wouldn't or couldn't or didn't already do. I would have done anything to impress him, would have gone to the end of the earth for him."

Longtime employee Don Rake recounted, "I don't think you can say we worked for Dave. I know we did, but it didn't come down like that. People were allowed to do their jobs their own way, with nobody telling them what to do. You'd wake up in the morning, and instead of thinking, 'I have to go to work,' you looked forward to what each day would bring. That came from Dave."

"What we did at Mammoth forced the industry to open their eyes," fabricator Chic Gladding recalled. "On the mountain, Dave could see what other people couldn't see. When he wasn't satisfied with what the industry was giving him, he would say, 'If they won't do it, we will!' " Among other revolutionary industry innovations, Dave and his team built a high-tech snowcat, experimented with winch systems that could groom steep slopes, and pioneered height-adjustable terminals that could handle variable depths of snow.

In 1969, Dave met Yan Kunczynski of Lift Engineering and the two visionaries hit it off. Yan described Dave as a natural leader, saying, "Dave's understatement was stronger than any overstatement could have been. I've never worked for anyone harder than I worked for him, and there were about 40 or 50 other people doing the same thing. In the 1970s, Mammoth was selling 23,000 tickets a day, so Dave had the resources to do what he wanted and that was to put money back into the ski area! He could single-handedly decide to spend hundreds of thousands of dollars on a project, building prototypes without even having drawings or engineering. Almost anything we built at Mammoth was on the cutting edge, and the industry later adopted our ideas."

Clifford Mann, one of Dave's junior racers who would eventually become a vice-president of the ski area, recalled the summer of 1969: "We worked from dawn to dark building Chairs 7, 8, and 9, essentially opening up 40 percent of the acreage on the mountain. By 1994, we'd built 18 more chairlifts at Mammoth, upgraded three others, remodeled lodges, built a 100,000-square-foot garage, Hut Two, a 'people mover,' and reconstructed much of June Mountain." Dave had purchased June in 1986 with the idea of connecting both resorts by a series of chairlifts and small villages, modeled after interconnected ski resorts in Europe. This vision did not come to be.

As ever, Dave loved ski racing as much as he loved building his ski area. In the years following Jill Kinmont's accident, Mammoth junior racers, including the McCoy children, were intent on carrying Jill's spirit forward. From their dedication, Dave's program expanded. Along the way, he insisted that ski racing at Mammoth Mountain, above all, be about building people with character. One of his young racers, Paula Page, once said, "Every positive thing about me can be linked directly back to my being a member of the Mammoth Mountain Ski Team."

Throughout the 1960s, the consistency and fairness of Dave's soft-spoken, fun-loving coaching style became well-respected in the ski racing world and a majority of the top women skiers in the United States trained at Mammoth. In those days, male skiers generally stayed in college and represented their school teams. Team member Cathy Allen, who raced on the 1966 U.S. World Championship Team, said, "Dave coached from the heart and what he thought of you mattered. It was a lot to live up to—a privilege to be training on the same hill with Olympians and medalists such as Jean Saubert, Linda Meyers, Joan Hannah, and Penny McCoy."

When Mammoth Race Department hosted the Masters National Alpine Ski Championships in 1987, Dave not only competed but also staged an event to be remembered, including a Hollywood-style banquet extravaganza and crystal goblet awards, never mind a six-foot snowfall closing out the downhill.

On the opposite end of the spectrum from ski racing, Dave offered essentially free recreational ski programs to accommodate local school children. He hoped the free local bus system and the fun of skiing would draw kids to the mountain and keep them occupied in a healthy environment while their parents were at work.

Dave motivated his employees the same way he coached his ski racers. "I listened to people tell me what they *wanted* to do, then said right back to them what they'd just said and watched them go out and do it." Many individuals considered their employment at Mammoth Mountain one of the best periods in their lives, a time of learning by practical experience. Dave's close friend, accountant, and financial advisor Nick Gunter once commented, "It certainly wasn't for the money, because they didn't make anything. I think it was how Dave treated them. Employees were always first on his mind."

"Dave understood people better than anyone I've ever known," said attorney Dave Slavitt. "He had the ability to communicate in a way that helped him succeed. His presence was powerful, and he dealt with difficult events without getting ruffled. He knew his business completely and could successfully put together the complexities of dealing with the Forest Service, banks, accountants, attorneys, employees, customers, construction intricacies, and suppliers."

WHEN Dave saw a need or became aware of a difficult circumstance, his generosity abounded. In the early years, he supplied firewood, helped with snow removal, provided ski equipment, and paid expenses for his ski racers. As Mammoth grew into one of the most successful ski areas in the country, he helped families with medical emergencies, college expenses, down payments on homes, and materials and labor for building houses.

By the early 1970s, Dave was volunteering his resources to make the Mammoth Motocross a stand-out event. For 35 years, he raced in this annual home-grown competition that drew some of the country's best motocross riders to the Eastern Sierra. In the 1980s, at the age of 65, he was National Motocross Champion in his age group. On the final day of the 2004 Mammoth Motocross, escorted by friends and family riding alongside him, Dave rode the track one last time. He was 88 years old.

Recognizing the need to establish Mammoth Lakes as a sustainable community, Dave donated his time, money, and creative energy to provide ball fields, a town transportation network, a high school, and a hospital, as well as to support road bike and mountain bike races, and other such ventures. In 1989, he founded the Mammoth Lakes Foundation as a conduit to bring arts and higher education to the Eastern Sierra. Cerro Coso Community College, the Gateway Student Apartments, and the Mammoth Lakes Repertory Theatre all exist because of Dave's dedication to this cause.

In 1967, Dave was inducted into the United States Ski Hall of Fame. For many years, this award, along with numerous others—including the 1989 Ernst & Young's Entrepreneur of the Year of California, the 1993

Southern California Edison's Environmental Excellence Award, and the 1999 National Ski Area Association's Lifetime Achievement Award—decorated his office.

In 2005, at the age of 90, Dave, along with minority interest partners taken on in a previous transaction, sold his share of Mammoth Mountain Ski Area to Starwood Capital Group. Though Dave had carefully thought through this decision, he wasn't prepared for the painful emotions he felt when he signed the final papers. But he was not one to stay down. In a conversation we shared sometime after the sale, he told me:

> *As far as the ski area, I'll always care. It's been my heartbeat. It was hard to hand off the torch, but it was time. Roma and I are still alive, and our children have the freedom to do whatever they want—be it ranching or making music, training horses, driving trucks, or flying airplanes. I'm a happy man. I hope Mammoth's new heartbeat is good to the people because it's the people that make Mammoth good. No, great!*

The People

From left: Tom Dempsey, Jack Smith, Toni Milici, Don Redmon,
T.J. Johnston, Warren Miller. In front: Dave McCoy and Nick Gunter. Circa, 1990s.

As I researched what had become of the people featured in *For the Love of It*, I was repeatedly reminded of how they shared extended family bonds, treasured memories, and a passion for skiing. Though most of them have now passed away, I hope their love of the Eastern Sierra lives on in my writing.

Once Chair One was operating, Hans Georg's rope tows became obsolete. However, the Forest Service allowed him to continue living in his rock hut at Observation Point. Moving forward, Hans built a business in old-world masonry work, pursued his interest in photography, and helped organize Mammoth's first art show. In the winter, he skied on Dave's north slope tows. He was working on his third book, *The New Modern Ski Systems*, when he passed away in 1965.

Several individuals made a career at Mammoth Mountain Ski Area: Nick Gunter as an accountant and trusted financial advisor; Toni Milici as the head of the cafeteria; and Bob Bumbaugh as a welder, shop man, and machinist. Tom (T.J.) Johnston took charge of tasks that ran the gamut from handling race registrations to unofficially documenting the ski area's history with his photographs.

After supervising the volunteer ski patrol through the mid-1960s, Mark Zumstein passed the torch to paid patrol. Don Redmon spent several years assisting Dave with outside management before moving on to other ski areas in California and Utah. When he returned to Mammoth, Dave put him to work again. Rather like a guardian angel, Ralph Batchelder meticulously cared for Chair One's ramp and lower terminal until the late-1970s when he joined the Forest Service. Roger Link returned to Mammoth from Southern California in the late-1960s. Fondly known as the "Gondola-Meister," he took full charge of running the gondola, which was just then being built to the top of the mountain.

Rhubarb Marcelin, Eddie Riley, and Bob Cooper all taught skiing at Mammoth through the early sixties. Before pursuing other careers, Bob spent several years managing the Sport Shop in the winter and operating heavy equipment during summer construction. Rhubarb took charge of the ski area's rental and repair shop and later rental and repairs at Kittredge Sports, still located on Main Street in Mammoth. Eddie went on to work in Southern California as an underwater diver and later owned a motorcycle shop in Reno, Nevada.

As Mammoth's Ski School Director for 15 years, Swiss-born Gus Weber spent his summers taking care of backcountry trails and livestock while living out his dream of being an American cowboy. Bob Schotz, who remodeled the McGee Warming Hut into the McCoy's home, purchased Woods Lodge at Mammoth's Upper Basin lakes, built the Edelweiss Lodge and other dwellings in Old Mammoth, and supervised construction of the Yodler near the bottom of Chair One. This lovely Swiss-themed restaurant was prefabricated in Switzerland, then shipped to America in sections. One of the biggest challenges Schotz faced when he began to assemble the building was locating a *metric* tape measure!

Tom Dempsey changed the face of Mammoth Lakes when his

Dempsey Construction Company built the Snowcreek projects in Old Mammoth, emphasizing exquisite building design and extensive, well-planned landscaping. In 1996, Tom spearheaded the building of Edison Hall as a base from which Cerro Coso College could grow. He spent hours with architects, subcontractors, and planners asking favors of various tradespeople and suppliers, donating his staff to the project, never asking for reimbursement. Tom would also dedicate much of his life energy and a small fortune trying to fulfill his dream of developing the Sherwin Bowl into a ski area. This dream was never realized.

After raising a family and succeeding at every endeavor she pursued, Charlotte Zumstein spent the last 20 years of her life working with her husband, David Lee, to protect and document ancient rock art and associated traditional knowledge. They worked with both Southwest Native Americans and the indigenous Wardaman people in Northern Australia. In 2016, Charlotte's free spirit and zest for life were still vibrant when she unexpectedly passed away at the age of 84.

Jill Kinmont left a mark of excellence in everything she did. For 57 years after her ski racing accident in Alta, she embraced a joyful, creative, productive, and inspiring life. Living in Bishop, enjoying 35 years of marriage to her husband, John Boothe, she became a highly respected schoolteacher and watercolor artist. To paint, she used a unique tool that fit between her fingers to hold the brushes. She established the Jill Kinmont Indian Education Foundation, and later, the Bishop school district named the Jill Kinmont Boothe School in her honor. Two books, *The Other Side of the Mountain I* and *II* captured her story, and two major motion pictures based on these books were produced about her life.

After breaking both legs racing in Aspen's Roch Cup, Dennis Osborn worked for 32 years as a hydrographer for Southern California Edison, and spent some time piloting safety flights for snow surveyors. Kenny Lloyd qualified as an alternate for both the 1956 and 1960 U.S. Olympic ski teams. After completing his military service, he worked at family-owned businesses and eventually purchased the Texaco dealership in Bishop.

Linda Meyers became the first Mammoth racer to compete internationally in Europe. In 1960, she tied with fellow American, Penny Pitou, for 1st place in Austria's Kitzbühel Slalom, one of the highest-level ski races of the time. Linda competed in two Olympics (1960 and '64) and two World Championships (1958 and '62), before raising a family in Colorado, and later working as a ski area risk management consultant.

For 37 years, Dennis Agee worked for Dave performing a broad spectrum of jobs that included creating and directing Mammoth's Race Department, supporting Dave at motorcycle races, and establishing and running Sierra Star Golf Course in Mammoth Lakes. In 1970, Dennis took a leave from Mammoth to serve as the U.S. Women's Head Coach, and again from 1991-93 to work as Alpine Program Director of the U.S. Ski Team.

As young competitors, all six McCoy children made their marks in ski racing. Poncho and Penny raced on the 1966 F.I.S. World Championships team in Portillo, Chile, where Penny won the only U.S. medal, a bronze in the slalom. Both siblings were named to the 1968 Olympic squad, and Poncho would go on to compete in the 1970 World Championships.

As adults, each of the McCoy offspring worked at Mammoth for various lengths of time. Gary (Punkin) spent over 40 years at the mountain, doing everything from summer construction to administration. After leaving Mammoth, he ran a small trucking business out of Bishop until he retired. Poncho and P-Nut worked a few years at Mammoth before Poncho left to run cattle ranches in Montana and British Columbia, and P-Nut moved to British Columbia to raise his family and run livestock. Penny competed as an accomplished Iron Man Triathlete and mountain bike racer, later authoring Christian inspirational books and song lyrics. She has been a companion to her parents through their life transitions since selling the ski area. Kandi managed June Mountain for several years and then bred, raised, and trained hunter-jumpers on her horse ranch in Camarillo, California. When the ski area owned a plane, Randy worked as the company pilot, and later operated the Winnemucca Airport in Nevada, giving lessons and building stunt planes.

In January 2020, besides their six children, Roma and Dave's family included 15 grandchildren, 34 great-grandchildren, and one great-great-grandchild.

Acknowledgements

There are so many people—professionals, family, friends, and strangers—who are part of the team that helped create *For the Love of It*. I thank you all. If by chance you are not listed below, I apologize. Please know that my appreciation and gratitude run deep.

Roma and Dave, I thank you for being who you are and for how you have supported my life endeavors. In the same breath, I give thanks to your many friends who shared their stories with me.

I thank Poncho McCoy for reading the manuscript early on, for giving me support and guidance to go forward, and for encouraging me along the way. Penny McCoy, I thank you for always being so openly appreciative and grateful of my work and for coining the title, *For the Love of It*.

Rusty Gregory, I thank you for embracing my concept and securing Mammoth Mountain Ski Area's support for the project.

I give thanks to my front-line editorial team, beginning with Bea Beyer—remember when you first saw my research and told me I *had* to write this book?—and proceeding on to Ginny Chadwick, Sandy Hogan, and Maggie Egan. I loved our team meetings, and I wonder how we made it through those first drafts.

My readers, Ruth and Todd Hensley, Lee Ann Wood, Sally (Grebe) Miller, Allison Amon, Francesca Driver, Quentin Lawrence, I thank you all for your critiques. Janet Gregory, I thank you for the time and energy you spent outlining your thoughts and sharing your wisdom in telephone conferences. Kathleen Lang, I thank you for being my "stranger-in-Flor-ida-editor" who knew nothing about skiing, Mammoth, Dave McCoy, or me, but still loved the read. I thank Suzy Fontana, my go-to editor living just down the street. How fun it was to get away from the computer and run a hard copy chapter over to your house.

To my dear friend Christin Cooper-Taché. You offered to edit the manuscript, then spent the next two years applying your inquisitive mind, critical thinking, wealth of skiing knowledge, and writing skills to improve and refine it. Never letting up on your belief in the project, you helped me bring the storyline to the forefront, pulled me through my meltdowns, and guided me into the sunlight when I felt trapped behind brick walls. You relentlessly encouraged me to take the manuscript to another level, always insisting in your Olympian style (silver medal in the giant slalom in Sarajevo) that I reach higher. Will I ever be able to thank you enough for all the energy you gave to *For the Love of It?*

I thank Demila Jenner for sharing research files from the 1970s, Chris Lizza for sharing research completed in the 1990s, and Eddie Riley for sharing heartfelt memories of Roma and Dave, along with fact-checking the manuscript.

Michael Lella, I thank you for sharing your experiences working on your father Pino Lella's book, *Beneath a Scarlet Sky,* and for confirming that I was capturing Dave and Roma's personae as you recalled your time living with them.

I thank Tom Johnston for advising me that if I promise the reader I'm going to give them something, I better give it; John Allen for being overwhelmed by the original table of contents (you'll be happy to see how I have trimmed it down!); John Fry for fact-checking the *Ski Tracks* in my "Opus" as you called the early drafts; Bill Cox for sharing your knowledge about routes to Wallace Lake; Jim Stimson for being my angling fact-checker; and Pat Armstrong for reviewing my snow survey sections. I thank the LADWP crew who took the time to read the pages about Dave's work with the Water Department. Clifford Mann, Heimo Ladinig, and Chris Bulkley, thank you for your chairlift-building expertise.

My thanks goes out to my sister, Katie Morning, and sister-in-law, Susan Morning, for sharing your invaluable photos and advice; to Heidi Vetter for your kind and precise help with graphic arts; to Jennifer Crittenden, Ann Gimpel, Curt Carpenter, Eve Gumpel, Debbie Boucher, Laura Patterson, Kirk Stapp, Marianne O'Conner, and ski historian Ingrid Wicken for sharing your respective expertise whenever I called; and to Dick Dorworth and Peter Shelton for your comments and eloquent writing. Rosi Fortna, my devoted friend and fellow member of the Mammoth Team and the U.S. Ski Team, I thank you for modeling your Olympic persistence and for believing in me. Eric Clark, I thank you for believing in the value of preserving and passing on our local history.

I thank my finish line editing team of Lesley Byberg, Rosanne Higley, Robin Conners, and Tom Coat (who also helped with photo enhancement). On a sunny day of Nordic skiing when the end was in sight but still oh so far away, you each came to me and offered fresh eyes to edit. I thank Diane Eagle whose editing and laughter walked me toward the end; Sydney Quinn and Charley Spiller who both were willing to double-check what I thought was the final copy; and Dallas and Alistair Veitch, Judy Burgenbauch, and Nordic Olympian Nancy Fiddler for yet another "last proof."

Steve Hylen, thank you for cleaning up battered photographs to give them a new life, for artful colorization of old black and white photos, for designing the original cover and graphics, and for tirelessly adjusting the initial layout to solve the complications my "bright ideas" created.

I thank Will Thackara who appeared in my life just as the demands of bringing this book to closure were making my head spin with confusion and doubt. You took me under your wing, answered my endless questions, and guided me through the scary experience of publishing.

Joe Reidhead, thank you for waiting, and waiting, and waiting, for my final edit so you could apply your design and publishing skills to transform the manuscript into this lovely book. It has been a delight to work with you.

I thank my Ukelele Club and Wild Mountain Thyme for keeping music in my life, and I thank all my friends and family who have been so patient.

And Ueli. I thank you. This book would not exist without the quiet support you give me every day, for the love of it.

Endnotes

PART ONE: *Falling in Love*

CHAPTER ONE: *A Meandering Youth*

1. Owen Cooper, interview by author, San Diego, CA. The letter is fictional.

2. Alaska was not yet a state.

3. Sammy Griggs was one of these hydrographers. In 1928, Sammy and his co-worker Orland Bartholomew had been the first stream gaugers to use skis on assignment. That winter, Sammy also supported Orland Bartholomew's 100-day, solo winter ski-traverse along the Sierra Nevada, including the first solo winter ascent of Mt. Whitney. [Gene Rose, *High Odyssey*, Fresno, CA: Panorama West Publishing, 1987, p. 24.] Forty years later, in March 1970, Carl Dean "P-Nut" McCoy and Doug Robinson would be the first skiers to repeat Bartholomew's feat. Using innovative lightweight Hexcel skis designed at Mammoth Ski Area for alpine skiing, P-Nut and Doug would take 36 days to ski the 210 miles from Whitney Portal to Yosemite Valley.

4. Bill Berry, "Snow-Shoeing... to Skisport, 1850–1930."

5. Paul C. Johnson, *Sierra Album*. Snowshoe Thompson carried 50 to 100 pounds of mail strapped to his back, covering the one-way 90-mile trip between Genoa, Nevada, and Placerville, California, in just three days.

6. E.M. Halliday, "When the Forty-Niners Went Sixty." After hiking to the start with their long heavy skis on their shoulder, the racers slid their work boots under leather toe straps and grabbed a long stick of wood as a rudder. At the gong of a loud bell, they tucked low and shot their skis straight down the slope in fierce pursuit of the prize money. Race referees clocked one miner at a speed of over 90 miles an hour, thus making him the "fastest man alive."

7. Gary Caldwell, *Mammoth Gold*.

8. Norman DeChambeau, interview by author, Lee Vining, CA. DeChambeau salvaged boards off old buildings in the nearby mining town of Bodie, heated and bent the wooden tips in the 12-gallon water tank of his wood stove, and then attached his trademark, a hand-carved knob facing downward off the tip.

9. Demila Jenner, *McCoy and Mammoth Mountain*, Benton, CA: 1979.

10. T.H. Watkins, *California, An Illustrated History* (New York: American Legacy Press, 1973), p. 313.

11. Cooper, interview by author.

12. Walton Bean and James Rawls, *California, An Interpretive History* (New York, NY: McGraw Hill, Inc., Fifth Edition, 1988), p. 283.

13. Richard Coke Wood and Leon George Bush, *The California Story* (San Francisco, CA: Fearon Publishers, 1957), p. 274.

14. Watkins, *California Illustrated*, p. 341.

15. Throughout the West a rampant infestation of rabbits was causing extensive crop destruction. Folks organized roundups similar to Native American rabbit drives. They formed a large circle, then banged on drums and cans to frighten the rabbits out of the bushes. So many rabbits ran out that the ground appeared to be moving. Unknowingly, the animals scurried into long nets or pens, where they were slaughtered with sticks or clubs. This socially accepted practice was later prohibited on the grounds of animal cruelty.

16. Watkins, pp. 380–7. In spite of ten years of Prohibition, insurance companies claimed that deaths from alcoholism had increased tenfold. Sales of cigarettes in the U.S. had increased by a billion dollars in one year, paralleling an upswing in tuberculosis.

17. *The Wilkeson Record*. During the early 1900s, the company thrived as one of a group of mines in the Wilkeson-Carbonado Coal Mining District. Although the mines had been in operation for over 30 years, vast mountains of coal beds with hundreds of millions of tons of coal remained to be mined.

18. Carl Sandell, interviewed by Demila Jenner, Enumclaw, WA, 1978.

19. The author double-checked with Dave that $7.50 was the cost of the used Model T. Further research indicated that the price of a new touring-car Model T was $850 in 1908 but less than $300 in 1925.

20. Originally dammed in 1915, Grant Lake collected the waters of the Rush Creek watershed. Due to the needs of local irrigation, the dam was enlarged in 1926. LADWP began its Mono Basin Tunnel Project in 1935.

21. Originally known as Pumice Mountain, by the early 1940s, Mt. Mammoth was being called Mammoth Mountain.

22. http://www.alpenglow.org/skiing/silver-skis-2005/

23. Morten Lund, *Skiing Heritage*, September 2009, "America's First Olympic Trials and Tribulations," p. 10–12.

24. Hannes Schroll, the yodeling racer, spoke no English. He had come to America after winning Italy's Marmolada downhill shortly before the Silver Skis took place.

25. On a ski-racing trip to Washington in the 1960s, Dave McCoy drove his racers past Mr. Phillips' house. Philips repeated the exact details Dave had shared.

26. As part of his New Deal, President Franklin Roosevelt implemented the Works Progress Administration (WPA) to employ unskilled men to carry out public works projects. Between 1935 and 1943, the WPA provided almost eight million jobs. Almost every community in the U.S. had a new park, bridge or school constructed by the agency. The WPA also employed musicians, artists, writers, actors and directors in large arts, drama, media, and literacy projects. Roosevelt's Civilian Conservation Corps (CCC) operated from 1933 to 1942 for unemployed, unmarried American men from relief families. In nine years, the three million men who participated received shelter, clothing, and food, together with a wage of $30 a month ($25 of which had to be sent home to their families). Enrollees planted nearly three billion trees, constructed more than 800 parks nationwide, upgraded most state parks and forest firefighting methods, and built a network of service buildings and public roadways in remote areas.

27. Mammoth Rock.

CHAPTER TWO: *A Bishop Girl*

1. Laws Railroad Museum and Historic Site located just off U.S. 6, five miles north of Bishop, CA.

2. About 25 percent of the entire American population became sick with the Spanish flu. In the U.S. military alone, 43,000 servicemen died from this flu. The fever spiked to 104-degrees, dark spots appeared on the cheeks, and then the lungs would fill with a frothy, bloody mess, the skin turned blue from lack of oxygen, and the victim suffocated.

CHAPTER THREE: *Independence*

1. Vic & Eleanor Taylor, interview by author, Independence, CA, August 1994.

2. http://www.skilibrary.com/timeline.html and Chris Lizza, "The Development of Ski Tows in the Eastern High Sierra, 1930–1955," 2002. By 1921, Edi Juan, one of the first skilled skiers in Southern California, had arrived in Lake Arrowhead. By 1924, the first ski resort in Lake Tahoe, Olympic Hill (now Granlibakken), had been built to service guests of the Tahoe Tavern, In 1928, Yosemite's Don Tresidder tried to lure winter sports enthusiasts to the Ahwahnee, his new yet empty hotel, by hiring Swiss mountaineer Jules Fritsch to direct a ski school. In 1929, the Auburn Ski Club formed and purchased land to use as a ski hill at Cisco Grove, near Donner Summit, California. There exists a 1921 photo of Slick Bryant holding a pair of skis on a steep slope near Bridgeport, California, and a 1924 photo of Art Hess skiing into Mammoth Lakes to check on his lumber yard at Shady Rest. Also, a 1925 Mono County travel guide included skiing. In 1934, residents were reported to be skiing on the city streets of Bridgeport, California, as well as on "Indian

Hill" east of town. A year later, in February 1935, Walter Mosauer led his nascent UCLA Ski Team past Bridgeport where they were "welcomed by the lonely winter caretaker of the popular summer resort of Fales Hot Springs ... an informal intramural ski race was held on a slope near the lodge."

3. The National Ski Association (NSA, later changed to USSA), was founded in 1905 in Ishpeming, Michigan as the original governing body of United States skiing. One of its main purposes was to coordinate ski jumping tournaments and exhibitions. NSA was a parent organization to the California Ski Association (CSA). In 1949, CSA would become the Far West Ski Association (FWSA).

4. Grays Meadow, Owens Valley, Devils Postpile, Reds Meadow do not use an apostrophe. Various references on Toms Place use an apostrophe, others don't, so for consistency, the author uses Toms Place.

5. In an author interview with Dave, he did not recall knowing about other up-skis such as one of the earliest, built on Gilbert's Hill in 1934 at Woodstock, Vermont.

6. Wendolyn Spence Holland, *Sun Valley, An Extraordinary History* (Ketchum, Idaho: The Idaho Press, 1998), pp. 183–5.

7. E. John Allen, *From Skisport to Skiing*, (Amherst, MA: The University of Massachusetts Press, 1993) p.108. Also, http://trn.trains.com/railroads/2011/12/snow-trains

8. http://snowbrains.com/the-history-of-skiing-lake-tahoe/

9. Gene Rose, *Magic Yosemite Winters* (Truckee, CA: Coldstream Press, 1999), pp. 34–41.

10. Clarita Heath telephone interview by author, Mammoth Lakes, CA, November 26, 2000.

11. "Washed Out," *Inyo Independent*, 28 February 1935.

12. "Snowslide Wrecks 4 Cabins at Glacier," *Inyo Independent*, 24 February 1935.

13. "Independence Locals," *Inyo Independent*, 3 April 1936.

14. Taylor, interview.

15. Bob Vinsant interview by author, Independence, CA, August 1994.

16. In 2019, the tennis courts at Snowcreek Athletic Club in Old Mammoth

17. In 2019, next to Crawford Street in Old Mammoth.

18. Northrop jacked up one rear tire, clamped on an outrigger contraption he had built to fit directly onto the wheel. He then winched and spliced a rope which he'd looped between the wheel and a pulley he'd attached to a tree up the hill.

19. In 2019, this ski area is called Mountain High. Located near Wrightwood in the Big Pines area of the eastern San Gabriel Range, part of Mountain High used to be called Blue Ridge.

20. Marianne Rey, interview by author, Ventura, CA, 2001.

21. The courses were originally 5,000 feet long, but later condensed to 1,000-foot lengths.

22. The snow surveyors pushed a long, hollow, calibrated pole into the snow until it touched the frozen earth below, then pulled the pole out, and weighed it on a portable scale. By subtracting the weight of the empty pole and factoring in the volume, they calculated the water content. The men would later forward these measurements to the DWP to be analyzed with other data within their water management plan.

23. This second course was abandoned in 1976.

24. *Inyo Independent*, 1936. Since arriving at UCLA in 1931 as a zoology professor, the Austrian-born Mosauer had organized the UCLA ski team, led numerous ski ascents of Eastern Sierra peaks, and authored an instructional ski book, *On Skis Over the Mountains*. Just a few days prior to summitting Mammoth, Mosauer and Brinton had departed nearby Conway Summit on skis at daybreak. By early afternoon, they summitted the 12,374-foot Mt. Dunderberg, a feat never before accomplished on skis.

25. Documentation of those who climbed to the top of Mammoth Mountain before the 1950s has not been located.

26. Otto Lang had come to America in 1935 after four years of teaching for the Hannes Schneider St. Anton Ski School in Austria.

27. Milt Allen, interview by author, Enumclaw, WA, 2001.

28. Schwartz, Larry (2000). "Owens Pierced A Myth." *ESPN Internet Ventures.*

29. Daniel James Brown, *Boys in the Boat*, (New York, NY: Penguin Group, 2013), pp. 350–1.

30. "Hunters Flock into Sierra," *Inyo Independent*, 18 September 1936.

31. In 2019, Footloose Sporting Goods is in this location.

32. Barbara Chin, interview by author, Bishop, California, 28 April 2001, and "We Have Been Napping," *Inyo Independent*, 4 December 1936.

33. George Deibert of Bishop was elected president; Walter Dombrowski of Mono Lake, 1st vice president; George Francis of Independence, 2nd vice president; Jack Hopkins of Lone Pine, 3rd vice president; Slick Bryant of Bridgeport, 4th vice president; and Fred Meckel of Bishop, secretary/treasurer.

34. Bill Henry, *McGee Mountain Rope Tow Site*, 3, 1998. Peter and Hazel Steffen purchased land from Gus Schultz, where they built and operated a fox farm from 1935-45. In 1947, Nyle and Ruth Smith built Crowley Lake Resort, offering rental cabins for hunters and fishermen. All that remains is part of the asphalt driveway going under the fence a short distance.

35. "Winter Sports Plans Now Being Made In Valley," *Inyo Independent*, 14 December 1936. The term funicular—a cable railway in which two suspended cars counterbalance one another—was used incorrectly in the article.

36. Jack Northrop had designed an overhead jig-back system wherein two tracks of used oil-well cable ran above the towline. Each track had five hangers placed approximately a ski length apart. At the bottom, the operator would give waiting skiers a sling made of harness webbing, similar to the belly cinch on a horse saddle. Each sling had a long cotton rope and D-ring attached. Skiers would wrap the sling around their waist, hook the D-ring onto the hanger, point their skis parallel uphill, and prepare for take-off. Accordingly, skiers would call this up-ski a "sling-lift."

37. "Ski Courses Draw Enthusiasts," *Inyo Register*, 21 January 1937.

38. Cortlandt T. Hill, interviewed by Demila Jenner, 1978.

39. In 2019, the restaurant is called Whiskey Creek.

40. This "Scotty" is *not* the person who died on Mammoth in the 1968 avalanche. Once, when Scotty and his friends hiked to ski the upper reaches of Mammoth Mountain, Scotty fell and broke his leg. Whorff and Janes managed to get him safely off the mountain and down to his Bishop medical practice where the injured physician gave step-by-step instructions on how to wrap his leg in a plaster of Paris cast.

41. Venita McPherson promoted skiing from her Mono Inn, located on the shore of Mono Lake, about 35 miles north of McGee.

42. "The Skisters," *Inyo Register*, 11 February 1937.

43. "Bishop," *Inyo Register*, 19 February 1937.

44. "More Snow Falls as Mercury Drops," *Inyo Independent*, 5 February 1937.

45. "Superb Skiing," and "Ski Party Sunday," *Inyo Register*, 18 March 1937.

46. Taylor, interview.

47. The Inyo-Mono Championships prompted significant publicity for Eastern Sierra skiing, just as Corty had predicted. Ethel Severson, fresh off her victory of winning time of the day for women, penned an article titled, "California Ski-Scape" for the nationally distributed *Ski Illustrated*, praising the Bishop area as one of the most promising regions for winter sports. Her article featured a photo of Dave standing on his skis, shirtless with his tanned and muscular chest glimmering in the sunlight. The *Uptake*, a monthly DWP in-house magazine distributed to 50,000 Southern California families, also published an article about the race with photographs of their star employee ski racers Eleanor Taylor, Ed Parker, and Dave McCoy, the latter dubbed, "the DWP dark horse from Independence."

48. Allen Adler, "The Battle of Fifth Avenue," *Skiing Heritage*.

49. http://en.wikipedia.org/wiki/Chairlift.

50. At that time, Bishop Creek Basin water measurements were handled by SCE hydrographer Claude James.

51. Marshall Carriere, telephone interview by author, Florida, November 2000.

52. Ibid.

CHAPTER FOUR: *Still Dancing*

CHAPTER FIVE: *Getting to Know Roma*

1. The portable tow was purchased from Sweden Freezer Company, a rope-tow manufacturer.

2. Crestview and Deadman Summit were separate places that people skied, but the names were used interchangeably because the locations were near each other.

3. Crestview Lodge, located at the base of Deadman Summit on the west side of Highway 395 across the road from the Caltrans Maintenance Station, was razed in 1977 to make room for the new four-lane highway.

4. The Los Angeles May Company group sent their busload to Crestview.

5. Nicholas Howe. "Beginning With Harvey," *Skiing Heritage* vol. 16, no. 3, September 2004, p. 20.

6. John Jay. *Skiing the Americas*, (New York: The Macmillan Company, 1947), p.19.

7. Allen. *From Skisport to Skiing*, p. 140.

8. Ibid., p.138.

9. http://www.alpenglow.org/ski-history/notes/period/mtneer-a/mtneer-a-1930-39.html. The same weekend of the championships, Dave met Otto Steiner, a two-time German cross-country Olympian, and pioneer ski mountaineer, now living in Southern California. Otto had gained notoriety for skiing a multitude of Sierra Nevada peaks during the 1930s, including a solo round-trip winter traverse of the Southern Sierra. He came to McGee to guide ESSC members through the Sierra Club Ski Mountaineers 3rd- and 4th-class Ski Proficiency Tests, originally designed by Dr. Walter Mosauer in 1932.

10. Eddy Starr Ancinas, *Squaw Valley & Alpine Meadows, Tales from Two Valleys*, (Charleston, SC: The History Press, 2013).

11. ESSC Bulletin.

12. Adele Reed, *Old Mammoth* (Palo Alto: Genny Smith Books, 1982), p. 131.

13. Leonard was the son of Roma's father, Marshall Carriere, Sr., from a previous marriage. He wrote politically conscious poetry that was published in the *Inyo Register*.

14. A coupe is a closed two-door car shorter than a sedan of the same model.

CHAPTER SIX: *A Young Romantic*

1. A tree well is a hollow in the snow around the base of a tree.

2. The accident happened on Highway 395 at the north end of what is now called Crowley Lake Drive. The original Eaton Ranch included 12,000 acres including land, later covered by Crowley

Lake. In 1998, the bunkhouse of Eaton Ranch was still standing. (Henry, *McGee Mountain Rope Tow Site*, 3, 1998).

CHAPTER SEVEN: *A Leader in Local Skiing*

1. Bill Henry, *Long Valley Property History*, 1998. Built in 1926 by Hans Lof, this log house initially had a restaurant and store inside. Hans later added a Shell gas station and then sold the property to Charles Partridge, who added four rental cabins and renamed the building Happy Jack's.

2. Averell Harriman, chairman of Union Pacific Railroad, had lured Sepp from his hometown of Badgastein, Austria, to help with the December 1936 opening of his Sun Valley, Idaho ski resort. Sepp was the first person to ride the first chair of the first chairlift in the world. The following winter Sepp introduced downhill skiing to the American Midwest and organized Sun Valley Ski Weeks. When Minnesota's Corty Hill met Sepp, he recruited him to run his Wooden Wings Ski School. Sepp went on to develop Southern California's Holiday Hill ski area, in 2019 known as East Mountain High.

3. "Ski Notes," *Inyo Register*, 12 January 1939. The access road is still visible from Highway 395.

4. On May 30, 1939, along with Southern California ski legends Schatzi and Ernie Woods, Hans made one of the earliest known ski ascents of Mt. Whitney. The November 1939 issue of the popular magazine *Ski Heil* featured a cover photo of his portrait along with his two-page article titled, "Schooling in Skiing."

5. "Famed Teacher to Establish New Ski School," *Inyo Register*, December 1938.

6. "The Eastern Sierra Ski Club," *Inyo Register*, 16 February 1939.

7. One version of the exam was: Third class: Climb 500 vertical feet in one hour, returning in 15 minutes, plus a cross-country trip of at least four miles on skis. Second class: Climb 1000 vertical feet in one hour 15 minutes, returning in 20 minutes, plus a cross-country ski trip of at least twelve miles. First class: Climb 2000 vertical feet in one hour 30 minutes, returning in 25 minutes, or climb 1500 vertical feet in one hour five minutes, returning in 20 minutes plus a cross-country ski trip of at least 18 miles in one day and a "difficult" ski descent of 500 feet, without a fall, within a time limit set by the judges.

8. Jay, *Skiing the Americas*, pp. 21–2.

9. http://www.newenglandskihistory.com/biographies/schneiderhannes.php

10. "Champions at Ski Meet at Mammoth," *Inyo Register*, 16 March 1939.

11. Near the top of Cloud Nine Express in 2019.

12. Ethel Severson, "Skifully," *Ski Illustrated*, December/January, 1936-37.

13. "State Meet Run Despite Storms Over Weekend," *Inyo Register*, 30 March 1939.

14. *1940–41 American Ski Annual*, p. 209.

15. Ibid.

16. Friedl Pfeifer, *Nice Goin'*, *My Life on Skis*, (Missoula, MT: Pictorial Histories Publishing Company, Inc.), 1993, pp. 88–9.

17. Demila Jenner Collection, gleanings from Eastern Sierra Ski Club minutes. "Scotty's qualifications to run a ski patrol were that he was a good skier, had medical experience, and was interested in performing the job." He concluded that 98 percent of ski accidents rarely happen to experienced skiers but are caused by out-of-control skiing, selfishness, and insufficient physical conditioning. ESSC began requiring skiers to demonstrate they could walk on skis, change direction at a standstill with a kick turn, control speed with the snowplow, and negotiate a moving turn with a stem Christie before they could ride the tow. They also reprimanded skiers who schussed too much or who didn't fill their "sitzmarks"—holes in the snow left by skiers when they fall.

18. *ESSC Bulletin*, March 7, 1940, vol. 1, no. 3.

19. Telephone interview with Carl Grebe by author, 2002.

20. Morhardt was a poet, musician, artist, photographer, and an officially tracked genius. He composed the Bishop High School anthem.

21. "Junior Ski Club News," *Inyo Register*, 16 February 1939.

22. *Inyo Mono Bulletin*, February 16, 1939.

23. Westwood placed 2nd, Bishop 3rd, and Reno 4th.

24. In the fall of 1939, the CSA invited 13 ski instructors to a conference at Yosemite hosted by Dr. Donald Tresidder, president of the Yosemite Park & Curry Company, to plan for certification tests to be held during the winter.

25. Other club members took charge of fellowship and ticket punching. All members were encouraged to wear a Kandahar-type sweater—a woolen pullover crew neck popularized by European ski racers—with club colors of navy blue and gold. Members who had extra room in their cars were asked to stop at Bishop's Kittie Lee Restaurant or at Pinion Book Store to pick up junior skiers needing rides to the slopes.

26. Eastern Sierra Ski News, January 1941, vol. 1, no. 2. On the evening of October 27, Americans dialed their radios to hear President Roosevelt's drawing of the first lottery number for the Selective Training and Service Act of 1940, the first peacetime draft in U.S. history. This conscription bill required men between the ages of 21 and 35 to register for the draft lottery. All major radio stations across the country came on the air early. Before Roosevelt's speech began, the announcer read news blurbs. Suddenly, 70 million listeners heard that an October snowstorm was pounding California's Eastern Sierra and would guarantee excellent skiing through December.

27. In 1945, Howard More received a special use permit to assume ownership of Table Mountain Ski Area, now called Mountain High North Resort and used mainly for tubing and beginning skiing. Another ski area, Blue Ridge, is now called Mountain High West.

28. Winter guest accommodations already included Fobes 40, Happy Jack's, Rock Creek Inn, Toms Place, and McGee Creek Lodge.

29. Bill and Louise Kelsey, "Nan's Story. The Lady on the Flying Skis," *The Album,* Chalfant Press, vol 6, no 1, February 1993, pp. 2–5.

30. Ibid. The Long Valley Lodge, known as Nan & Max's, was partially destroyed by a 1969 McGee Mountain avalanche and later rebuilt as the Normandy Inn.

31. Adele Reed, notes from a scrapbook.

32. In 2019, the remains of the Observation Point rope tow hut are just beyond the Juniper Springs Bridge. Hans Georg later took over operating the tow. The ski hill drops down toward Valentine Camp.

33. Per Bob Schotz, who worked at the Woods Lodge by Lake George, Nyle lived year-round in this isolated cabin with his wife and a younger girlfriend. He wrote a letter to skiers saying "if summer skiers wish to stage an event in the Tee Jay [sic] Bowl (one mile above Lake George) where the slopes are broad and long, and the snow will last for some time to come, the Summer Skiing Committee will help, free of charge. Skiers may arrange for instructors and guides for cross-country trips. Those seeking directions, snow conditions, and the loan of slalom flags, instructors, and guides should contact us."

34. Chris Lizza, "The First Dual Slalom," www.skiinghistory.org/resources/index-skiing-history-magazine-and-skiing-heritage-past-articles-issue, *Skiing Heritage.*

35. To Dave's knowledge, Chris Schwarzenbach was also the first skier to ever hike to the top of McGee Mountain. Once on top, Chris traversed south to the next canyon and then skied down. In March, Schwarzenbach would place 3rd in the prestigious Harriman Cup in Sun Valley, Idaho.

36. The year before, on February 25, 1940, ESSC members skied down the hillside carrying red flares while two hundred spectators listened to a narration over the loudspeaker. *The New York Times, Baltimore Sun,* and *Chicago Tribune* published details about the choreographed skiing performed by ski instructors Sepp Benedikter, Gottfried Schmidt-Ehrenberg, Hans Kolb, Frankie Stevens, and Chet Janes.

37. During the 1940s and '50s, polio—one of the most feared diseases of the twentieth century—crippled an average of 35,000 people each year in the United States alone. In 1921, at the age of 39, Roosevelt himself was diagnosed with polio. In 1976, the Infantile Paralysis Fund became known as the March of Dimes Birth Defects Foundation.

CHAPTER EIGHT: *Ups and Downs of Love*

1. Mammoth Ski Club Bulletin.

PART TWO: *Passion Grows*

CHAPTER NINE: *A Rope Tow of His Own*

1. In 2019, near the base of Blue Ox.

2. www.volcanodiscovery.com/long_valley.html. The 17 km x 32 km Long Valley caldera east of the central Sierra Nevada range, California, is the result of a giant eruption about 760,000 years ago.

3. "Mount Whitney Mountain Lore," book from the Whitney Store, pp. 136–7. "Father Crowley organized street carnivals and local plays and formed the Inyo Mono Associates, a cooperative of local editors, miners, farmers and merchants. Cutting through an atmosphere of mistrust and intrigue, he joked his way into the people's hearts and saw the value of tourist attractions. When the road that joined Death Valley and Mt. Whitney was finished, he organized a media event he called the Wedding of the Waters."

4. Lynn Newcomb, Sr. began construction of the first chairlift in Southern California, the second in the state, located off the Angeles Crest Highway on Mt. Waterman. At that time, there was already a chairlift at Sugar Bowl in Northern California; one in Sun Valley, Idaho; and one at Oregon's Timberline Lodge. As far as up-skis in Southern California, Johnny Elvrum had two at Snow Valley, Green Valley had two, and Big Bear Lake had one. Lake Arrowhead had a 1,200-foot tow built four years before by Edie Jaun (although the tow never ran due to lack of snow); Table Mountain and Blue Ridge, both in the Big Pines region, each had a tow. Sierra Club's Ski Mountaineers continued to rendezvous at the ski hut they'd built at 9,000 feet on Mt. San Antonio (Mt. Baldy). San Diego Ski Club built a ski hut on the slopes of Cuyamaca and organized a first ski patrol. In Kern County, there were rope tows at Mt. Piños and Shirley Meadows. Six miles above Wolverton Meadow in Sequoia National Park, the Park Service built Pear Lake Ski Cabin to accommodate cross-country skiers.

5. *Southland Ski-View*, November 21, 1941. This magazine included an extensive article about Hans Georg and his St. Moritz style of skiing.

6. Larry Thackwell (chief instigator) staged an impromptu ski meet with the UCLA and Pasadena Junior College teams as participants.

7. Ethel Van Degrift, Ski Slants, 5 December 1942.

8. http://www.history.com/news/5-facts-about-pearl-harbor-and-the-uss-arizona

9. http://www.history.com/this-day-in-history/the-united-states-declares-war-on-japan

CHAPTER TEN: *Newlyweds*

1. Between Toms Place and the houses at the dam, the old dirt road is still visible, paralleling Highway 395 north of Sunny Slopes and then winding up a rocky hill toward the dam.

2. In 2019, the bottom of Blue Ox.

CHAPTER ELEVEN: *A Personal Battle*

1. Friedl Pfeifer, *Nice Goin', My Life on Skis.*

2. *American Ski Annual*, 1942, for the year of 1940–41, 207.

3. *Ski Slants*, 30 December 1941.

4. George Conn of June Lake Lodge organized weekly bus trips from Los Angeles including a complimentary weekend trip for 20 representatives of the press and travel bureaus. However, due to either the high cost of heating or the military, Conn closed his lodge. Also in June Lake, Don Almour of Fern Creek Lodge, planned to extend the length of his Dream Mountain tows and keep the area lighted for Saturday night skiing. He noted that 200 skiers could be comfortably lodged around June Lake even without Conn's Lodge.

5. Nyle mailed the following letter to Los Angeles publicists encouraging skiers to park at the snowline and walk to his tow:

    > *Like a lily-white snowflake, unharnessed by progress or conquest, but doing its bit towards making the skiing on the white slopes of Mammoth simply supre [sic], so comes your humble hillbilly trying to do his bit by suggesting that a weekend of fun at the Mammoth Ski Lift would help you bear the jitteriness of a world in trouble. In case you have not heard, your hillbilly is now the owner, operator, and host at Mammoth Ski Lift [purchased from Lloyd Nicoll], which is now operating. A short ski trip through the woods and an easy grade, which you will not mind, will bring you to the Lift, where we have 60 inches of snow. Do come up and see us.*

6. The author was unable to find Dr. Stoddard's first name.

7. https://en.wikipedia.org/wiki/Manzanar. Under the management of the Wartime Civil Control Administration, the location was officially called the Owens Valley Reception Center. In 2019, it is called the Manzanar National Historic site.

8. *California, an Illustrated History*, p. 432.

9. Van Degrift collection.

10. American Ski Annual, pp. 238–240. For the duration of the war, CSA decided to keep the organization alive even without active participation, so that clubs and organized skiing would be ready to reactivate after the war. It froze officer positions, carried dues, doubled up on work, and operated in

cooperation with wartime activities of the National Ski Patrol while refraining from activities that might be construed as interfering in any way with the war effort—no tournaments, no sanctioned events, no approved travel.

11. *Ski Illustrated*, March 1943, p. 4.

12. The author has used lower case "warming hut" when the building was being constructed and upper case "Warming Hut" after the building was completed.

13. *American Ski Annual*, 241, pp. 252.

14. Eddie Riley interview. While walking to the Bishop Theater with Dave and Roma, Eddie heard a stranger comment, "What a shame for such a strong young man. He'll probably never walk correctly."

15. Ibid.

CHAPTER TWELVE: *War Days*

1. Sometimes the McCoys exchanged wild game for gas stamps to supplement their fuel allotment of four gallons of gasoline per week. It was almost impossible to be approved for a new tire, but they could apply to the rationing board for retreads or recaps.

2. Eddie Riley, interview by author.

3. Carl had enlisted in the U.S. Army Corps in 1941. Two years later, his P38 fighter plane was shot down in an aerial dogfight over Vincenza, Italy. He parachuted from the burning aircraft but was injured, and then captured by the Germans. He spent the last two years of the war in a German POW camp.

INTERLUDE

CHAPTER THIRTEEN: *McGee Tows*

1. Richard Needham, *Ski, Fifty Years in North America*, 1987, p. 47.

2. Bob Seamons, interview by author, Carlsbad, Calif., 27 November 2001. According to Seamons, the double-cable front throw was made by Grosvold in Colorado and the toe iron by Dover in New Hampshire.

3. Pfeifer, *Nice Goin'*, p.130.

4. Parts of this access road can still be seen above the Clampers monument on Crowley Lake Drive.

5. Gloria Redmon, telephone interview by author, Palm Desert, Calif., 10 January 2002.

6. Roger Link, interview by Chris Lizza, Mammoth Lakes, Calif., 6 January 1998.

7. The DWP jeep had four sets of dual tires and tire chains with solid one-inch angle iron crossbars. The vehicle could power right up the unmaintained Minaret Road.

8. This photo is on the cover of *Tracks of Passion, Eastern Sierra Skiing, Dave McCoy & Mammoth Mountain*. The skiers are Dave McCoy center, Dr. C. L. "Scotty" Scott lead, Marshall "Benz" Carriere top, Chet Janes lower right.

9. Some skiers placed their right gloved hand on the rope in front of them and their left gloved hand on the rope behind their back. Small skiers either squatted down and held the rope against their knee with their elbow or grabbed the rope right behind a bigger person. The youngest skiers rode up between the skis of their parents, leaning their bodies against the knees of the adult, never putting their own gloves on the rope.

10. James N. Gibson, Office Memorandum, United States Government, 3 June 1946, Forest Service files photocopy, pp. 1–7. Areas analyzed were Whitney Portal, Onion Valley, Big Pine Canyon, Bishop Creek, McGee Mountain, Mammoth Mountain, Crestview/Deadman, June Lake Loop, and Conway Summit.

11. Ibid.

12. Dana Miller, telephone interview by author, June 2019. Dana's grandparents, Joe and Opal Miller, became close friends with Hans. Dana houses Hans' scrapbooks and plans to write a book about his life.

13. "McCoy's Memorial Day Race Huge Success," *Western Skiing*, Vol 1, no. 9, p. 28.

14. While serving as treasurer of the California Ski Association, Corty organized California's first postwar ski instructor certification, joined Hannes Schneider and Charlie Proctor as official examiners, and helped stage the First Annual Silver Dollar Derby giant slalom and the 1946 California Class A State Championships at Mt. Rose, Nevada.

15. *"Ski Area Survey of California and Parts of Nevada and Oregon,"* 1946, Chris Lizza collection, photocopy.

16. *McGee Mountain Rope Tow Site*, National Register of Historic Places Evaluation, Inyo National Forest, California, compiled by Bill Henry 1998. After Dave left his DWP job in 1952, he moved his family to the McGee Warming Hut, where they lived until their oldest son, Gary, entered high school. Dave allowed Mammoth Mountain employees to live there until 1983 when the Forest Service permit for the building expired. In 1984, the Forest Service told Dave to demolish the building and clean the area. In 2019, a Clampers' monument stands on a flat area in front of the building's location.

17. Dave said he wished he could remember all the people who helped. There was Andy Anderson, Jim Wilson, and a man named Young from Toms Place. Also, Chuck Kispert from the State Highway Department; Howard Cooper, who was living with his family at the Whitmore Hot Springs; Stover Lowe; and Pat Coons and his boys, Don and Buzz.

18. According to Dave, during those years, hydrographers had DWP permission to drive City vehicles on the Rock Creek road past Mosquito Flat and through the Little Lakes Basin. The road was kept open for the Pine Creek pit mines located over Morgan Pass. The miners lived in a bunkhouse near Morgan Lake and had their food delivered by a D8 Caterpillar that could travel over the deep snow.

19. Richard Coons, interview by author, Bishop, CA, August 2001.

20. In his brochure, Hans advertised McGee Creek Lodge, Toms Place, including rental skis and accessories; Mammoth Tavern, and Bishop Flying Service with transportation by air or auto to the ski resorts.

21. Hans Georg, "Eastern Sierra," *Western Skiing,* March 1948, p. 18. Besides teaching skiing, Hans continued to publish articles advertising the Eastern Sierra. In March 1948, he reported that Augie Hess was running a rope tow on an open treeless slope off of Conway Summit; Crestview Lodge added a glass porch where a person could watch the slopes and enjoy refreshments; Glen Jones, who worked as a seasonal forest ranger, took a job instructing at June Lake; Frankie Stevens passed his CSA certification so he could instruct at Glacier Lodge out of Big Pine, where a new Warming Hut had been built; and Vic Taylor and O.K. Kelley built a ski hut with a food counter at their Onion Valley rope tows.

22. Dayton McDonald, telephone interview by author, Reno, Nevada, August, 1998. Winter, 1946–47.

23. Ethel Van Degrift collection.

24. Minot Dole editor, *1947 National Skiing Guide,* (NY, NY), 1946.

25. Arlene Baker, interview by author, Zephyr Cove, Nevada, July 2001.

26. Mid 1960s, Stanley Voorhees invented the Power Ski that was propelled uphill by an engine. Though he worked on the project for some ten years, the Power Ski never became popular. The first prototype had the skier carrying the engine in a backpack with power controls on the ski poles. Voorhees later developed a motor for the back of each ski. Once at the top of the hill, the tracked skis could be turned over so the base would be smooth for skiing down. Voorhees hoped the Army would be interested in his invention, but among other issues, the noise from the motor was too loud. To advertise the ski, Voorhees went to the sand slopes off the Coast Highway in Southern California, had his wife Jean dress in a bathing suit, and motor up the dunes, while his daughters Gwen and Donna threw Styrofoam pieces around her to simulate snow. Warren Miller used footage of Stanley driving his power ski as comic relief in his films.

27. "Mammoth News," *Inyo Register,* 6 December 1946.

28. "600 View Mammoth Mt. Ski Meet," *Inyo Register,* 6 June 1947. Dean Kiner and Roma McCoy won.

CHAPTER FOURTEEN: *Home at Crowley*

1. Around this time, Midwesterners Frankie and Steve Stevenson built the Red Buck Lodge near the corner of Lake Mary Road and Minaret Road. Off Main Street, the Gould family built the Mammoth View Lodge, and Easterners Alice and Hugh O'Connell built the Alahu, a play on their names. Near McGee, the Zischanks added a new lounge and fireplace to their Long Valley Resort, and then about five miles farther south the Hilton Creek Lodge, the Lake View Motel, and Wally and Jo's Motel were built.

2. Shortly thereafter, Dean Crow and Elmer Stone purchased the Tavern.

3. Don Coons interview by author.

CHAPTER FIFTEEN: *Mammoth Tows*

1. Florence E. Nicoll, "Mammoth News," Bridgeport Chronicle-Union, 5 December 1947.

2. Near where Chair 2 (Stump Alley Express) is in 2019.

3. "Mammoth Winter Sports Association Elects Officers," *Inyo Register,* 26 December 1947. The board of directors included Olive Barker, Max Zischank, Dick Shefflet, Arch Mahan, Lloyd Nicoll, Dick Barker, and Dean Crow.

4. Ethel Van Degrift, "Ski Slants," Los Angeles Times, 16 December 1947.

5. Dick Barker purchased a Weasel to transport guests from the Tavern to his Manahu Lodge on Evergreen St. in Old Mammoth, and Don Lutz, who had a house on Minaret Road, purchased two for personal use and to assist Dave when needed.

6. In 2019, this ski area in the San Gabriel Mountains is called Mountain High North.

7. Howard More interview by Chris Lizza, Los Angeles, CA, 2000.

8. "Eastern Sierra Ski Club Meets; Requests Improved Roads to Mammoth Sports Area," *Inyo Register,* 15 January 1948.

9. Forest Service files, Floyd Iverson Letter, 23 January 1948, photocopy.

10. "Winter Sports Fans Ask Supervisors for Snow Clearance," *Inyo Register,* 10 November 1948.

11. Hans Georg, "Eastern Sierra," *Western Skiing,* February 1948, p. 24.

12. Later, Dave placed 4 x 4s with sheaves nailed to the top along the tow line and would hang the rope above the snow at the end of each day. Sheaves are grooved wheels often used for holding a belt, wire rope, or rope and incorporated into a pulley.

13. "Bishop Declared Winner in SNISF Ski Meet Held Friday, Saturday on Mono Slopes," Inyo Register, 19 February 1948.

14. Eddie Riley, telephone interview by author, Reno, Nevada, August, 2001.

15. Dayton McDonald, telephone interview by author, Reno, NV, August, 1998.

16. "McCoy Wins State Class A Title," *Inyo Register*, March 1948.

17. Warren Miller, telephone interview by author, Seattle, WA, April 2002. Through the evening, Warren sketched crayon caricatures of guests and handed them out as gifts. Warren reminded Dave they'd met when he passed through Mammoth with his "surf-rat ski-bum" Sun Valley friends on their way to surf in Southern California. They needed to cash a $10 check for gasoline money. Warren drove to the ski hill at McGee, didn't even pull his ski equipment out of the car, just walked right up to Dave. Dave cashed the check, no questions asked.

18. *American Ski Annual*, 1941–2, pp. 221–223.

19. Forest Service files, photocopy of Special Use Permit. The permanent location was section 31, T3s. R.27E and included the ski run called Broadway in 2019. James Gibson's conclusions about other locations were:

> At Glacier Lodge up Big Pine Canyon, permittee wants to install a chair or T-Bar lift, but there is concern about avalanches and Inyo County's road maintenance. Cross country touring trips from Glacier Lodge are thought of as the possible future use as the surrounding area is admirably adapted. Up Bishop Creek, rope tows are proposed at Cardinal Mine and slopes are being considered on Mt. Emerson, although the problem of access and of slopes being within Primitive Area boundaries is a concern. On Fern Ridge at June Lake, Mr. Osborn asked for an ultimate plan of a chairlift to serve the entire ridge with a lodge, service lodge, and parking space at the bottom. His contention is that unless they built chairlifts, customers from Los Angeles will try the rope tows and then move on to Mt. Rose where better lifts and longer and steeper runs are available. The Forest Service considered Osborn's plans a sound investment.

20. First, they blasted, then they used picks and shovels to manipulate heavy rocks into granite stair-steps, and finally, they smoothed out the blast marks with hydrochloric acid.

21. The ridgeline is the area around the top of Chair 1, and the knob is the area above a run called The Wall.

22. The fall line is the route leading straight down any particular part of a slope.

23. Several years later when tearing out this concrete, Dave cut a core of the "pumice-cement concoction slab" and had it tested for strength. His "pumice cement" tested just as strong as "sand cement."

24. Statement of Dave McCoy's assets in 1953, Nick Gunter collection.

25. "Two Mammoth Ski Tows to Operate this Weekend Following Inyo-Mono Storm," *Inyo Register*, 10 November 1948.

26. Betz Salmont, Memories of Southern California Skiers. This story was from Bob Blackmore about Thanksgiving 1948. Twenty years later, a tragic avalanche off the top of Mammoth Mountain

killed Scotty while he and his friends were skiing fresh powder. The run they were skiing was posthumously named "Scotty's."

27. "Thousands Crowd Mammoth Mt. For Holiday Weekend Skiing," *Inyo Register*, 1 December 1949.

28. Rich and Gertrude Thompson, interview by author, Bishop, CA, August 1994.

29. Joe and Bonnie Zwart, interview by author, Mammoth Lakes, CA, April 2002.

30. "Snow Fall Prepares McGee Mt. For First Skiing This Season; Storm Blankets Area," *Inyo Register*, 20 February 1949.

CHAPTER SIXTEEN: *The Weasel Era*

1. Also in the 1948 Olympics, after having been wounded and later captured by the Russians in WWII, Franz Gabl won a silver medal in the men's downhill. He grew up skiing in the Austrian Alps but when Hitler invaded Austria, Franz was sent to the Russian front and forced to fight for a cause he didn't believe in. Franz had no personal grudge against the "enemy." He didn't want to kill, to see others killed, or to be killed, but he followed orders out of fear if he resisted, the Nazis would torture or kill his loved ones, just as they had already done to other innocents in his hometown. Franz later said that his desire to ski again was the force that guided him through the darkest hours of war.

2. "Trophies Awarded in Annual Inyo-Mono Ski Meet Held Last Sunday at June Lake," *Inyo Register*, 15 April 1948.

3. "State Ski Instructors to Hold Annual Spring Session in Inyo-Mono April 19 to 25," *Inyo Register*, 1 April 1948. Instructors who attended the convention were Tony Freitas, Tommi Tyndall, Frank Ferguson, Bob Mason, Otto Steiner, Bob Seach, Tom Coles, Ed Heath, Tunette Steiner, and Mark Coates. Dave befriended Nic Fiore who had come to Yosemite Valley from French Canada to teach skiing for one season. When Nic first drove into the Valley, a snowstorm prevented him from seeing the landscape. The next morning, he gazed in disbelief at the park's towering granite walls and declared, "This is fantastic! But where in the world do the beginners learn to ski?" Nic spent the next 50 years as a stalwart of the Yosemite community.

4. Letter to Eddie Riley, McCoy collection. In later years, Eddie gave it to Roma.

5. Clarita Heath, telephone interview by author, November 2000.

PART THREE: *Love Prevails*

CHAPTER SEVENTEEN: *Charlotte*

1. Ethel Van Degrift, "Ski Slants," *Los Angeles Times*, 9 and 13 December 1949.

2. In February 1922, Landry and two others had skinned to the summit of 14,000-foot Mt. Rainier. Charles Perryman, a cameraman for Hollywood cinematographer David O. Selznick, filmed the excursion and produced the oldest known skiing film in that state (available on youtube.com).

3. During World War II, Peyrone had served as District Ranger of the Crowley Lake District (Bishop Creek, Rock Creek, McGee Creek).

4. Redmon, interview by author.

5. Ibid.

6. Ethel Van Degrift, "Ski Slants," *Los Angeles Times*, 2 December 1949. Ski filmmaker John Jay and 1948 Gold Medalist Gretchen Fraser raised enough money to purchase team uniforms for the FIS.

7. Italy's Zeno Colo won two gold medals and Norway's Stein Eriksen took a bronze in slalom.

8. "Charlotte Zumstein Sweeps FWSA Events; Awarded Three Trophies," *Inyo Register*, 6 April 1950.

9. "Ski Group 'Honors' Zumstein," *Inyo Register*, 13 April 1950.

10. "Winners Listed in July 4th Ski Meet," Bridgeport Chronicle-Union, July 1949.

11. "Southlanders Sweep Mammoth Ski Meet," *Inyo Register*, 13 July 1950.

CHAPTER EIGHTEEN: *Not to Worry*

1. Among recipients of these properties were Tom Dempsey, Bob Bumbaugh, and the folks who built the Christiania.

CHAPTER NINETEEN: *Prospectus*

1. Ethel Van Degrift, "Ski Slants," *Los Angeles Times*, 28 November 1950.

2. Ibid. 5 December 1950. The shows were held at the Wilshire Ebell Theatre.

3. Ibid. 12 December 1950.

4. Hans Georg, "How I Became A Ski Instructor", *The Skier*, 1 November 1950, 14.

5. Ethel Van Degrift collection.

6. Pat Weller, "Mammoth," *Inyo Register*, 30 November 1950.

7. Dick Barker, Don Lutz, Howard Cooper, and Jim Wilson drove their trucks.

8. These same trucks were used at Mammoth through the 1980s.

9. Warren Miller, telephone interview by author, 5 May 2002.

10. Ethel Van Degrift, letter to Dave McCoy, 4 December 1950. Only because of a chance conversation with Jerry Tidwell, business manager for *The Skier*, did she know Mammoth had 10 inches of new snow.

11. Through negotiations later on, the road was exchanged back to the County for snow removal purposes. The County then found it couldn't handle the snow removal and a third exchange was made with part of the road once again coming under state jurisdiction, where it remains in 2019.

12. Prospectus For A Proposed Ski Development at Mammoth Mountain:

    • The preferred applicant needs to present evidence to the Forest Supervisor that they can financially complete the minimum requirements in the time allowed at an estimated cost of around $250,000.

    • Applicant must construct, maintain and operate one chair lift approximately 3,500 feet in length and one 1,700 feet in length with lift lines 30-feet wide, water system, sanitation facilities and disposal systems, service building which may contain a warming room, first aid room, ski shop, lunch counter and rest rooms.

    • Construction must begin within three months and be completed within 54 months and the use shall be exercised at least 90 days each year.

    • Prior to November 30, 1953, applicant needs to make all necessary surveys and plans for structures and facilities, construct a service building and construct water and sewage disposal systems.

    • Prior to November 30, 1954, applicant needs to install a chair lift and maintain and operate rope tows during the winter of 1953–54.

    • Prior to November 30, 1957, applicant needs to install a second lift and construct a shelter hut at the upper chair lift terminus.

    • Ski jumps, water supply (from Dry Creek for service building and possible storage), sanitation, first aid caches, ski patrol, parking area, etc. will be the responsibility of the permittee.

    • All plans for design of buildings and chairlifts are to be approved by the Forest Service.

    • A minimum fee of $100 per annum is required plus 1.5 % of net sales and other income, due to the USFS.

    • Ski instructors must be certified by the National Ski Association.

13. "New Mammoth Mt. Ski Club Organized," *Inyo Register,* 15 November 1951.

CHAPTER TWENTY: *Heavy Snows*

1. *The Skier,* February 1952.

2. Ethel Van Degrift, "Ski Slants," *Los Angeles Times,* 23 November 1951.

3. Whear family interview by Chris Lizza, Minden, Nevada, 20 October 1996.

4. E.C. Valens, *The Other Side of the Mountain*, 1966, (Harper and Row, New York, N.Y. p18). Information on Jill Kinmont throughout *For the Love of It* is a combination of citing from Valens's extraordinary work, author interviews with Jill, her teammates and friends, including Dave and Roma, and author's general knowledge from many years of friendship with her, from being coached by Dave, and, although several years after Jill, from racing in the various competitions and locations.

5. Ethel Van Degrift, "Ski Slants," *Los Angeles Times*, 7 December 1951.

6. Valens, p.14 and p.19.

7. Kenny Lloyd, interview by author, Bishop, CA, November 2001 and interview by Demila Jenner, Bishop, CA, 1978.

8. Banta, interview by author, Lee Vining, CA.

9. Members of the Mammoth team each wore a gold and black patch with a small figure skiing down the side of two intertwined "M's", the official Mammoth Mountain logo, drawn by Bobby Cooper.

10. Valens, p. 23.

11. "Area Skiers Win 17 Awards at FWSA Meet," *Inyo Register*, 14 February 1952.

12. Dennis Osborn, telephone interview by author, 2000. Osborn placed seventh in the Junior National downhill, and fourth in the American Legions slalom at Sun Valley. The brother-sister team of Buddy and Skeeter Werner from Steamboat Springs dominated all these races.

13. A.P. article by Ethel Van Degrift about Andrea Lawrence. "Andy has been married to former U.S. racer Dave Lawrence almost a whole year. He looks after Andy and his ideas for the future meet with her wholehearted accord. Right now, the idea is to raise cattle somewhere near mountains and snow, perhaps in Wyoming. Andy is not only a skiing phenomenon—she is also a completely natural individual, cool, levelheaded and sensible. Her relations with people are equally direct and uncomplicated. She is a warm, open-minded person, full of fun and affection. She enjoys winning a race, but it is by no means the most important thing in life to her. Her parents ran a ski resort and she grew up in the snow."

14. Valens, p. 27.

15. Ibid., p. 29.

16. "Osborn Tops FWSA Junior Skiers in National Meet," *Inyo Register*, 6 March 1952.

17. Valens, p. 51.

CHAPTER TWENTY-ONE: *So Much Snow!*

1. Valens, p. 21.

CHAPTER TWENTY-TWO: *Gaining Momentum*

1. The Sno-Go had a Ford chassis, front and rear wheel steering, and two gasoline motors, one to drive the vehicle and the other to drive augurs that blew snow off the road.

2. "Olympic Skier Wins Mammoth Mt. Memorial Race," *Inyo Register*, 5 June 1952. Yves Latreille from Canada won the men's race.

3. Ethel Van Degrift, "Ski Slants," *Los Angeles Times*, 18 November 1952 and 21 November 1952.

4. Ibid. Designed by skier/architect Art Lavagnino, a 3-story lodge with a lounge, restaurant, living quarters for the Elvrums and dormitories for employees and a limited number of overnight skiers, plus a 3,000 sq. ft. sun terrace.

5. Sun Valley's Harriman Cup continued to be one of the most prestigious ski races in the U.S. That year, Olympic medal winners Austria's Christin Pravda and Norway's Stein Eriksen, would be competing.

6. "Dennis Osborn, Young June Lake Skiing Sensation, Places in Harriman Cup Races," *Inyo Register*, 28 March 1953.

7. "Cal. Kids Close To Win In Western States Jr. Team Classic," *The Skier*, April 1953.

8. Valens, pp. 64-65.

9. Valens, pp. 38-44.

10. "Kinmont Wins Sonora Races," *Inyo Register*, 3 July 1952.

CHAPTER TWENTY-THREE: *The Permit*

1. These lines showed exactly where Dave eventually built Chairs One, Two, and Three.

2. Based on revenue projections at the rate of 10 percent of gross receipts, Nick proposed minimum annual payments of $12,500 with a seven-year retirement of the loan. The loan proposal included building a prefabricated Ringer double chairlift, (bid at $60,000 plus installation) with a capacity of 600 persons per hour, a three-story 1,600 square-foot warming hut, bid at $18,000, plus $7,000 for furniture and a water line, improving existing and adding additional trails, building a parking lot for 300 cars, and providing working capital for ski area operations with estimated expenditures of $2,045 per month including:

   • $800 to McCoy as sole proprietor
   • $125 for salaries [unpaid volunteer factored in]
   • $30 for telephone
   • $40 for office expense
   • $75 for legal and accounting
   • $50 for travel to races

- $250 for promotions (including trophies)

3. Todd Watkins, interview by author and Penny McCoy, Bishop, CA, 21 August 1994.

CHAPTER TWENTY-FOUR: *Mammoth's Warming Hut*

1. Ethel Van Degrift, "Ski Slants," *Los Angeles Times*, 29 December 1953.

2. McCoy, interview, 2002. The spring was behind Chair 12. The tank was not replaced until around 1960. People warned Dave he wouldn't find water because of rock barriers and fractures. Eventually he drilled two wells, one under Chair One, another on a hillside near the Inn. At that time, the town was supplied by a 2.5-inch hose from Spring Canyon, and another from below the Tavern in a place called Murphy's Gulch.

3. P-Nut McCoy interview by author, 2002: "The only one who might have seen this was Sheriff Bob, but he was such a cool guy he would have helped them mix the cement. He also drove the elementary school bus. One time someone sped past him, so he ran the culprit down with the bus and gave him a ticket."

4. "Two Storms Put Mammoth Ski Slopes in Top Condition," *Inyo Register*, 19 November 1953.

CHAPTER TWENTY-FIVE: *Living at McGee*

1. T.J. author interview, 2000. T.J. moved to Lee Vining when he got a job teaching school there. On weekends, he taught skiing for Hans Georg on Dave's rope tows. There was no uniform, no certification. At the end of each day, Hans pulled a wad of bills out of his pocket and paid the instructors half of what was collected from the lessons. One weekend, T.J. made $50, enough to pay a full month's rent in Lee Vining.

2. Valens, pps. 66 and 75.

CHAPTER TWENTY-SIX: *Olympic Dreams*

1. Jill Kinmont, interview by author, Bishop, CA, 2002.

2. Ibid.

3. "Jill Kinmont Wins Mammoth Mt. Women's Honors," *Inyo Register*, 17 December 1953.

4. "Inyo-Mono Juniors Win 25 Medals At Dodge Ridge," *Inyo Register*, 21 January 1954.

5. "Juniors Win 14 Medals" and "Osborn, Lloyd Win Honors in Class A Downhill Race," *Inyo Register*, 4 February 1954.

6. Ethel Van Degrift, "Ski Slants," *Los Angeles Times*, 29 January 1954.

7. Valens, pp. 98-99.

8. "Jill, Bob Kinmont Win National Titles, McCoy-Coached Team Takes Six of 18 Medals," *Inyo Register*, 11 March 1954.

9. Valens, p. 93.

10. Valens, p. 98.

11. "Jill Kinmont Wins National Senior Slalom Title, Second in Combined," *Inyo Register*, 18 March 1954.

12. Kinmont, interview by author, 2002.

13. "Osborn Leads Inyo-Mono Skiers In National Giant Slalom Meet," *Inyo Register*, 1 April 1954.

14. Valens, pp 106–107.

15. "Jill Sweeps Three 1ˢᵗ's in Western States Championships," *Inyo Register*, 8 April 1954.

16. Valens, pps. 99-100.

CHAPTER TWENTY-SEVEN: *Summer 1954*

1. "Ringer Chairlifts," http://www.skilifts.org/old/chairlift_manufacturers_ringer.htm. Dave had originally planned to use Ringer Chairlifts, but patent problems and a fatal accident had forced the company out of business.

2. Dave moved the beginners' tow east of the Warming Hut and relocated the top of Number One tow 200 feet to the west where he extended it halfway up the bowl. At full capacity, the 1,700-foot Number One tow with a 100-horsepower Cummins diesel engine could handle 1,600 skiers per hour, and the 2,000-foot Number Two tow with a 165- horsepower Cummins diesel engine could haul about 1,400 skiers per hour. Dave also extended Number Three tow, which went to the very top of the North Knob (also called the shoulder of Mammoth Mountain), another 300 vertical feet.

3. Davison's property was near where Canyon Lodge is in 2019. In the 1960s, he built a short-lived chairlift from Lake Mary Road to just beyond the top of his steep road.

4. Dave didn't think Walter would come out right on that price so he told Walter he would repay the true price even though it would take him longer than the original agreement. Nick explained, "When the chairlift was finished, sure enough, we couldn't quite make the payments, but by then we were able to secure a loan from a bank in San Francisco and pay Walter the actual cost of $125,000."

5. Martignoni proposed that "United Tramway (UT) furnish the engineering design of all mechanical equipment, all structural steel, and, with the exception of concrete work, and will place in working order a UT Double Passenger Chair Lift having a carrying capacity of 750 passengers per hour in each direction."

6. Lester LaVelle, "Mammoth Area Ski Conditions Are Termed Ideal," *Inyo Register*, 18 November 1954.

CHAPTER TWENTY-EIGHT: *Jill*

1. Valens, p. 117.
2. "Inyo-Mono Skiers Dominate Mammoth Mt. Alpine Combined," *Inyo Register,* 16 December 1954.
3. Valens, p. 118.
4. Ibid., p. 124.
5. Ibid, p. 126.
6. Ibid., pp. 137–138.
7. Ibid.
8. Kinmont, interview, 2002.
9. Valens, p. 139.
10. Andrea Lawrence, interview by author, Mammoth Lakes, CA, March 2002.
11. Kinmont, interview, 2002.
12. Charlotte Zumstein, telephone interview by author, Bishop, CA, August 1998.
13. Lawrence, interview, 2005.
14. Ibid.
15. "Jill Kinmont Recovering in Salt Lake Hospital," *Inyo Register,* 2 February 1955.
16. Valens, p. 128.
17. Kinmont, interview, 2002.
18. Valens, p. 148.
19. http://www.whonamedit.com/synd.cfm/2793.html. A frame that holds the patient stable while it turns the patient into various planes.
20. Valens, p. 150.
21. Valens, p. 179.
22. Ibid., pp. 179-180.

CHAPTER TWENTY-NINE: *Resilience*

1. Osborn, interview by author. To pay for his ski racing Dennis had worked as a summer packer at Silver Lake Pack Station. Locals had held box socials and other fundraisers in his name, and Kneissl and Strolz sponsored his equipment. In order to train at the national camps and to race the senior circuit, he had turned down skiing scholarships from Dartmouth and the University of Colorado.
2. Valens, pp. 182-3.
3. Zumstein, interview by author, 2002.

4. Valens, pp. 199-203. In 1957 Dick Buek died in a plane crash over Donner Lake. In 1964, while skiing for a film, Buddy Werner died in an avalanche in Switzerland.

CHAPTER THIRTY: *Those Durn Fools*

1. Batchelder interview by author, 2001. Originally from Laconia, New Hampshire, Batch had helped build one of the early rope tows in the United States and had also spent seven years constructing huts in the White Mountains with the Appalachian Mountain Club. In the 1930s after WWII broke out in Europe, he secured a job at Lockheed Aircraft in Burbank. After the war, Batch and his family explored California skiing. In Long Valley, Batch bargained with Happy Jack Partridge to lower the price of lodging in his motel if his family used their sleeping bags and didn't touch the sheets. The next morning at McGee, Dave sold the Batchelders' rope tow tickets for a price far lower than the posted prices.

2. Chris Buckley, interview by author, July, 2017.

3. "New Mono Ski Lift Awaits First Snow," *Inyo Register*, 1955.

4. Gus Weber interview by author, 1995. The winter before, Gus had been teaching at Timberline, Oregon, until the manager didn't pay the bills. The electricity was turned off, the chairlift stopped running, and the building turned black as midnight. So Gus moved on to Alta, Utah to teach for Alf Engen, the legendary Norwegian ski champion. There, Gus met a California skier who suggested he apply at Mammoth.

5. http://www.skilifts.org/old/glossary.htm. A massive weight at either the top or bottom of a lift, attached to the bullwheel, which keeps correct amount of tension on the haul rope - and therefore, the appropriate amount of friction between the haul rope and the wheel. Many new lifts are tensioned by either pneumatic or hydraulic tensioning systems instead of counterweights.

6. Lester LaVelle, "Dave McCoy Makes Improvements For New Mammoth Mt. Ski Season," *Inyo Register*, 25 October 1956.

CHAPTER THIRTY-ONE: *Jill Comes Home*

CHAPTER THIRTY-TWO: *Opening Day*

1. "Mammoth Mt. Draws Record Crowds Opening Weekend," *Inyo Register*, 1 December 1955.

Every few years there is a wet winter, when the land of even these deserts gets soaked. Then these bushes grow. When it dries, they cease to put forth much fresh foliage or add much new wood, but they do not die—their vitality seems suspended.

William Brewer's 1864 journal entry on the first geological survey of the Eastern Sierra.

Sagebrush in the Rain

In 2017 when I was in the middle of writing For the Love of It,
Roma and Dave McCoy had been married 76 years.
Roma was 97 years old, Dave 102.

Their story was a romance of family, ski racing,
and building Mammoth Mountain Ski Area.
They measured success by how happy the people around them were,
not by how much money they made.

As Dave would say,
"We had a lot of fun, didn't we?" which meant,
"We worked really hard with a great group of people."

Through the years, Roma and Dave's vitality,
like that of high desert sagebrush,
survived drought and flourished in deep snow.

They still laughed, they still inspired.
They were still in love with the Eastern Sierra,
still in love with each other.

They still approached each day eager to celebrate life
as if they were sagebrush in the rain.

Robin Morning
September 2017
Mammoth Lakes, California

The Passing

On February 8, 2020, while taking an afternoon nap in the family home at the Rocking K Ranch with Roma resting by his side, Dave peacefully passed away. He was 104 years old.

When Roma realized Dave was truly gone, sadness overcame her like a heavy veil. Only occasionally did she smile, but in those moments, there were times her eyes lit up and she would say, "Oh, I know where Dave is. He's gone skiing." You could almost hear her thinking, "Now, where are my skis and boots? I want to go with him."

When Dave's passing became public news, the energy of thousands swelled into a heartfelt chant. "Thank you Dave," the people voiced. "Thank you for blessing this world with your generous, joyful, good will. Thank you for sharing your dedication to everything you loved in life. Thank you for teaching us that every day is the best day ever."

When I heard Dave's time had come, I was sitting at the computer, still clinging to the hope I could finish this book during his lifetime. Stoic at first, I stared at the blank screen, searching for something that Dave would want you, the reader, to carry forward. Out of the blue, I remembered what he once said while driving his Rhino up the steep dirt hill behind his house:

"We don't only live this one time, climbing this hill, but many times we'll climb it, then stop and say, my gosh, was that ever a beautiful day!"

ALSO BY ROBIN MORNING

Tracks of Passion:

Eastern Sierra Skiing, Dave McCoy,
and Mammoth Mountain

www.tracksofpassion.com